MN

The Columbia Guide to
Asian American History

THE COLUMBIA GUIDES TO AMERICAN HISTORY AND CULTURES

Columbia Guides to American History and Cultures

Michael Kort, *The Columbia Guide to the Cold War*

Catherine Clinton and Christine Lunardini, *The Columbia Guide to American Women in the Nineteenth Centursy*

David Farber and Beth Bailey,
The Columbia Guide to America in the 1960s

The Columbia Guide to Asian American History

Gary Y. Okihiro

COLUMBIA UNIVERSITY PRESS

NEW YORK

Columbia University Press
Publishers Since 1893
New York   Chichester, West Sussex
Copyright © 2001 Columbia University Press

Library of Congress Cataloging-in-Publication Data

Okihiro, Gary Y., 1945–
    The Columbia guide to Asian American history / Gary Y. Okihiro.
        p.   cm. — (The Columbia guides to American history and cultures)
    Includes bibliographical references and index.
    ISBN 0-231-11510-5 (alk. paper)
    1. Asian Americans—History. I. Title. II. Series.
E184.06 C64 2001
973'.0495073—dc21   2001028952

⊚ Casebound editions of Columbia University Press books are printed on
permanent and durable acid-free paper.
Printed in the United States of America
c 10 9 8 7 6 5 4 3 2 1

To My Colleagues

CONTENTS

INTRODUCTION

Asian American history is an account of America's past. It is America writ large. These United States, after all, had its beginnings in Europe's search for Asia. And it was those Europeans—the seekers—who named America's indigenous peoples "Indians," believing them to be the natives of "the Indies," their fabled land of gold. The Republic's ships headed east around Africa's cape and west around America's horn to Asia, and its wagons and prairie schooners journeyed overland toward the setting sun just beyond the Pacific's rim and the realization of an American and European people's dream. That destiny was made manifest by the nation's vessels that plied the trade of the Pacific and Indian oceans, by its "opening" of Japan, its annexation of Hawai'i and colonization of the Philippines, its "Open Door" policy in China, and its major wars both hot and cold waged periodically throughout the twentieth century.

Asians came to the Americas by way of those currents of commerce and conquest beginning in the mid-sixteenth century with Spain's Manila galleon trade between the Philippines and Mexico. Filipinos and Chinese found passage to Spanish America, and, by the 1760s, Filipinos to the bayous of Louisiana; South Asians settled in port cities along the Eastern seaboard by the 1780s, followed by the Chinese shortly thereafter, and Hawaiians negotiated the coasts and camps of California and the Pacific Northwest by the 1790s. Greater numbers of Asians, initially mainly men, arrived as recruits for the fields and factories of Hawai'i and the American West; eventually, men, women, and children would immigrate as the consequences of U.S. designs in Asia, including economic and cultural hegemony and wars. National independence failed to sever Asia's moorings within the world system and its circuits of capital, goods, labor, and culture, and political and economic refugees and migrant laborers still accompany products from Asia to Europe and North America as they did in the past. Since 1980, the rate of growth among Asian Americans far surpassed that of other groups, including whites, African Americans, and Latinos.

The study of those peoples consorted with and at times promoted those initiatives from at least the mid-nineteenth century. This book documents the evolution of that knowledge production on Asians and Pacific Islanders in the United States and not on America's projects in Asia and the Pacific, despite the numerous parallels and continuities between those two strands of research. Asian American studies is American studies focusing, like all of ethnic studies, on the racialized peoples of the United States, including so-called whites and peoples of color. The center of reference for this book is the United States, then, despite expansive past and present efforts to internationalize American studies and to conceptualize peoples of color, notably African Americans, within global and diasporic frames. Transnationalism's realities in world history, including expansionism, economic and cultural exchanges, and migrations have punctured the myth of exceptionalism, and in the future, I suspect, the boundaries separating ethnic studies, American studies, and area studies will be even less distinct than they appear in the present, judging from the movements within those fields and from cautionary calls for national and local perspectives and politics.[1]

The subject matter, then, is Asians and Pacific Islanders in the United States, including Hawai'i, which was an independent kingdom until its overthrow by white settlers aided by the U.S. minister to the kingdom in 1893 and its annexation by the United States five years later. Although racialized and commonly homogenized culturally as a single group, Asians comprise widely disparate "racial" and cultural entities with divergent and oftentimes conflicting histories, languages, religions, class and caste relations, and national interests. Asian Americans include peoples who derive from an enormous span of the earth's girth and its most populous region from East Asia, Southeast Asia, South Asia, and West Asia. Their classification as Asian was a European invention that named the Orient as spaces east of Europe and assigned natures, Orientalism, to its peoples.[2] Accordingly, from 1850 to World War II, U.S. laws governing immigration, citizenship, and civil and property rights and social convention and practice lumped together Chinese, Japanese, Koreans, Asian Indians, and Filipinos as an undifferentiated group. But that essentializing name was also made in America by Asians during the late 1960s, when they sought a pan-Asian identity premised upon a common past in the United States and upon a racialized politics that they believed would enable and lead to mobilization and empowerment.[3] In this book I include Hawaiians because they are today oftentimes grouped with Asians as "Asians and Pacific Islanders," despite their distinction as indigenous peoples and their affinities with Native Americans on the U.S. mainland.

The systematic analysis of those groups of peoples is now known as Asian American studies. First institutionalized in 1969, the field has, during the past decade, grown rapidly. As shown by the annual directory compiled by Cornell University's Asian American Studies Program for the Association for Asian American Studies, there were twenty-six Asian American studies programs in the United States in 1995 and forty-three programs in 1999.[4] These programs teach thousands of students annually and grant undergraduate minors and majors in Asian American studies; a handful grant graduate degrees in Asian American studies, and many more universities and colleges grant graduate degrees in other fields with specializations in Asian American studies. Encouraged by book series and niches developed by academic and commercial presses, authors find an expanding interest in their manuscripts and a growing readership for their books. My reading list for my graduate Asian American historiography seminar reveals that books published on Asian Americans from 1961 to 1980 about equaled the number of books published on the subject from 1851 to 1960. And in one decade, from 1981 to 1990, the number of books published equaled the number published during the previous two decades, and that number was doubled during the decade 1991 to 2000.

Those humming presses and groaning bookshelves have not been conducive to moments of self-reflection upon the body of work being produced and the field it is creating. Except for occasional bibliographic essays, Asian American scholars have not taken stock of the body of writings on Asian Americans in a systematic way. I am thinking here about definitions and delimitations of the field of study, its purposes and objects, its literature, the methods and theories that inform it, and the interpretations and narratives that constitute it. The anthology *Counterpoint: Perspectives on Asian America* (1976) is pioneering in a number of ways, especially its first part, which contains critical essays on Japanese American history, sociology's treatments of Chinese Americans, book reviews, and theoretical ventures in international politics and the internal colonial model.[5] And an intellectual history of Asian Americans as scholars and subjects in the Chicago school of sociology will provide a much needed foundation for this neglected area in the field's development.[6]

This book builds upon those foundations and attempts several strategic turns. Even as it identifies its subject matters, narrative, chronology, periodization, debates, themes, and literature, the book reminds its readers that those are my constructions and, like history's writings, are subject to criticisms and reworkings. This book offers a definition of a field of study, but also invites contrary renditions. It is a work of reference and a work in progress. And while the national Association for Asian American Studies offers neither a definition of the field nor a formal set of criteria, the field is being defined and redefined constantly by its authors, practitioners, and students and by institutions of higher learning as they write, teach, engage, and establish Asian American studies. Those constituencies debate and struggle over the field's origins and purposes and their meanings for contemporary needs and aspirations.[7] Hierarchies of ethnic groups, especially the dominance of East Asians (particularly the Chinese and Japanese over Koreans and South and Southeast Asians); of geographies in California's centrality over places to its east, north, and west; and of the racial formation that excludes or adds on gender and sexual formations— all invite challenges, because they install and replicate the very system of privileges and poverties that inspired the field's original formulation. As a record, this book reflects those hierarchies but aspires to transcend them through this articulation.

The book is organized into five parts. Part 1 offers a synoptic narrative history and a set of periodizations. Readers should be keenly aware that those constructions are, despite their apparent solid constitutions located in time and place, fluid interpretations. Parts 2 and 3 present a selection of historical debates and emerging themes. Herein I identify historical problems and summarize their relevant literatures. I have included only questions that I consider to be historical as opposed to issues within literary criticism or the social sciences. Accordingly, although I discuss aspects of demography, immigration, and anti-Asianism, I exclude the sociological literature on assimilation, internal colonialism, the split labor market, middleman minority, ethnic enclave, and racial formation.[8] Part 4 is a chronology, in outline form, of important events in Asian American history. Part 5 consists of an historiographical essay and a compilation of book, video, and electronic resources. My determination to include only books was tempered by the underdeveloped state of emerging areas within the field, in which case I have included journal articles and book chapters. But these remain the rare exception.

I have not worked alone on this project, and I regret not having had the luxury and privilege of working with more of my colleagues. In particular, members of the history caucus within the Association for Asian American Studies encouraged my labors on this book and offered to make it a more collaborative effort, as it should have been. But time constraints militated against that otherwise splendid option. My graduate students at Cornell and Columbia have aided me by participating in my historiography seminars and critiquing portions of this book. I acknowledge and thank Pawan H. Dhingra, Tomio Geron, Moon-Ho Jung, Seiko Kihara, Jean Kim, Mary Ting Yi Lui, Susie J. Lee, Minh T. Nguyen, Vu H. Pham, and Sujani Komati Reddy. Funds from Cornell's English department and Asian American Studies Program and from Columbia's

Center for the Study of Ethnicity and Race allowed me to hire my research assistants, Cheryl Higashida, Sue J. Kim, and Elda Tsou, who helped me assemble and annotate the book, video, and electronic resources for which I am extremely grateful. I stand in their debt.

NOTES

1. In Asian American studies, compare Lisa Lowe, "Heterogeneity, Hybridity, Multiplicity: Marking Asian American Differences," *Diaspora* 1(1) (1991): 24–44, with Sau-ling C. Wong, "Denationalization Reconsidered: Asian American Cultural Criticism at a Theoretical Crossroads," *Amerasia Journal* 21(1, 2) (1995): 1–27.

2. See, e.g., Edward W. Said, *Orientalism* (New York: Random House, 1978).

3. See, e.g., Yen Le Espiritu, *Asian American Panethnicity: Bridging Institutions and Identities* (Philadelphia: Temple University Press, 1992); and William Wei, *The Asian American Movement* (Philadelphia: Temple University Press, 1993).

4. Asian American Studies Program (compiler), *Directory of Asian American Studies Programs* (Ithaca, N.Y.: Asian American Studies Program, Cornell University, 1995); and Asian American Studies Program (compiler), *Directory of Asian American Studies Programs* (Ithaca, N.Y.: Asian American Studies Program, Cornell University, 1999).

5. Emma Gee, ed., *Counterpoint: Perspectives on Asian America* (Los Angeles: Asian American Studies Center, University of California, 1976).

6. Henry Yu, *Thinking Orientals: Migration, Contact, and Exoticism in Modern America* (New York: Oxford University Press, 2001). A special issue of *Amerasia Journal* on theory and of the *Journal of Asian American Studies* on power produced some stimulating essays but offered less than a comprehensive or even systematic critique of the field: *Amerasia Journal* 21(1, 2) (1995) and *Journal of Asian American Studies* 1(1) (Feb. 1998). See also Gary Y. Okihiro et al., eds., *Reflections on Shattered Windows: Promises and Prospects of Asian American Studies* (Pullman: Washington State University Press, 1988).

7. See, e.g., Sucheng Chan and Ling-Chi Wang, "Racism and the Model Minority: Asian-Americans in Higher Education," in *The Racial Crisis in Higher Education*, ed. Philip G. Altbach and Kofi Lomotey (New York: State University of New York Press, 1991), 43–68; and Lane Ryo Hirabayashi and Marilyn C. Alquizola, "Asian American Studies: Reevaluating for the 1990s," in *The State of Asian America: Activism and Resistance in the 1990s*, ed. Karin Aguilar-San Juan (Boston: South End Press, 1994), 351–64.

8. For a quick summary of these theories, see Timothy R. Fong and Larry H. Shinagawa, eds., *Asian Americans: Experiences and Perspectives* (Upper Saddle River, N.J.: Prentice-Hall, 2000), 3–8.

The Columbia Guide to
Asian American History

PART 1

Narrative Overview

Chapter 1

NARRATIVE HISTORY

This narrative history provides an amplification of the chronology supplied in this book. Like all histories and chronologies, it is interpretive, based on assumptions and biases. In my chronology and hence narrative history I clearly stress, for example, the interactions of Europeans and Asians, the deeds of men, the articulations of capital and labor, and the events typical of political and legal history. These in my view provide the mere skeleton for the more substantial, fleshy matters of history—the thoughts and actions of a more diverse group of people, raced, gendered, classed, and sexualized, who shape and are molded by social institutions and processes. But heterogeneity has been sacrificed in this account for the more conventional ideas of history. For fuller treatments of the Asian American past, I refer readers to the standard texts: Ronald Takaki, *Strangers from a Different Shore: A History of Asian Americans* (Boston: Little, Brown, 1989), and Sucheng Chan, *Asian Americans: An Interpretive History* (Boston: Twayne, 1991).

As early as the fifth century B.C.E., Europeans formed opinions about Asians. Of course, the notions of "European" and "Asian" were alien constructs at the time and can be attributed to Europeans only in retrospect. The ancient Greeks distanced themselves from peoples to their north—"barbarians"—and referred to peoples to their east as Asians. This distinction between European and Asian was at variance with nineteenth-century U.S. representations of Europeans as northern Europeans and Asians as East and possibly Southeast Asians. Still, the ideas of Asia and Asians appear consistent and longstanding within the European imagination. Insofar as those representations constitute a single genealogy, the notions of Hippocrates, the father of Western medicine, bear relevance to Asian American history.

Hippocrates held an environmental determinist view of human conformation and behavior, and noted the extreme difference between Europeans and Asians. Asia, he speculated, with its mild and uniform climate supported lush vegetation and plentiful harvests. Those conditions engendered a lazy, monotonous, and pleasure-seeking people who were content to be ruled by despots, unlike Europe with its harsh, varied climate and its strong, courageous, and high-spirited people. Uniformity, he argued, yields slackness and cowardice, while heterogeneity fosters endurance and bravery in both body and soul.[1] His representations might in retrospect be seen as racializations of Europeans set in opposition to Asians and as genderings of Europeans with manly virtues against Asians with womanly infirmities.

Alexander, king of Macedon and Greece, in 334 B.C.E. led his army eastward to Persia and then on to India in 327 B.C.E.. Both an expedition of conquest and scientific discovery, Alexander's thrust toward India affirmed European superiority over Asia and promoted an assimilation of cultures through intermarriage with Asian women of the noble class and absorption of Asians into his military, schools, and colonial bureaucracy. Arrian, a Roman historian and assimilated Asian, memorialized Alexander's Asian conquests about four hundred years after his death. He contrasted the conqueror's ingenuity and irrepressible spirit with the cowardice of the barbarians who fled before him. He recorded a speech by Alexander to his troops reminding them that Greeks were a free people and ever conquerors, like men, while Asians, a nation of slaves and always defeated, were like women. According to Arrian, Alexander proclaimed that the Greeks were "inured to warlike toils" while the Asians were "enervated by long ease and effeminacy," and he called them "the wanton, the luxurious, and effeminate Asiatics."[2]

By 375 C.E., Polynesians had settled the islands of Hawai'i. Some believe that Polynesians originated in Asia and became island peoples when they settled on the islands of Indonesia, where they built canoes and learned seafaring technologies that carried them gradually eastward to Micronesia or New Guinea and eventually to the islands of Polynesia. Population growth, warfare, expulsions and flight, and the spirit of adventure might have prompted these migrations. Whatever the cause, the migrants knew the requirements of ocean travel—sturdy vessels, navigational skills, a supply of food and water, and plants and animals for propagation once they found land. The first Polynesians to settle Hawai'i were from eastern Polynesia, likely the Marquesas Islands.

The feat was immense and was undertaken in stages. Making landfall certainly required prodigious knowledge of the sea and sky for direction, and also experience transporting domesticated plants and livestock for breeding. Shoots, tubers, vine cuttings, and slips had to be carefully wrapped to preserve them against voyages of uncertain duration. Chickens, dogs, and pigs had to be selected and fed. And the travelers' provisions had to be carefully chosen with consideration for their weight, bulk, durability, and nutritional and social value. The first settlers probably took only the bare essentials, and might have been surprised to find that Hawai'i had no wild taro, sweet potato, or coconuts, all of which were common to most of the islands of Polynesia. Some of these settlers returned to Polynesia to direct subsequent waves of land-seekers, who would bring additional plant and animal life to Hawai'i.

What familiar plant life the migrants did find in Hawai'i was brought there by ocean currents and birds. The migrants settled along the shore where the fishing was good and planted their crops along streams. They later cleared, terraced, and irrigated fields of wet-taro in the rich valleys. By 1100, Hawaiian culture and language was distinctive from that of other Polynesian peoples. With some variation between individual islands, it embraced the entire island chain. Subsistence farming and fishing made possible the social system of extended families that maintained stewardship over the land and its natural resources. Over the next three hundred years, new waves of migrations from Tahiti introduced to the islands priests and high chiefs, resulting in intermarriage, warfare, and new, elaborate systems of economy, religion, and government. Between 1400 and 1600, the Hawaiian population grew; food production increased with irrigation, terracing, and aquaculture; and the surpluses sustained the stratification of society into the classes of chief, priest, and commoner.

About the time of the migration of high chiefs and priests from Tahiti to Hawai'i, the Mongols, led by their military and leader Chinghis Khan (1155–1227), pressed China and conquered Korea, central Asia, west Asia, and eastern Europe. Their cavalry tactics and weapons maximized their striking force, and with their horses and light baggage they were able to cover long distances quickly. The Mongols devastated the nations they conquered, but they also unified vast areas and brought together diverse groups of people. It was during the Mongol Empire that Marco Polo, a Venetian, traveled in relative safety across Europe and Asia to China, where he served as a minor Mongol official from 1275 to 1292. His account of his travels followed a script familiar to Europeans such that John Masefield, in his introduction to the 1908 edition of *The Travels of Marco Polo the Venetian*, could write: "[H]is picture of the East is the picture which we all make in our minds when we repeat to ourselves those two strange words, 'the East,' and give ourselves up to the image which that symbol evokes."[3] Part of that image involved Polo's generous accounts of prostitutes, sex, and angelic and delicate women who lived in luxury and abandon.[4]

Marco Polo's travels were inspired in large measure by notions of Asia's wealth, and his was simply one of many excursions Europeans made to Asia, especially after the thirteenth century. Portugal and Spain led the way in the fifteenth century, seeking maritime avenues to Asia by which they might avoid the long, perilous, and expensive overland trade routes. Portuguese sailors traveled down Africa's west coast and rounded its southern tip at the Cape of Good Hope, and Vasco da Gama made it to India in 1498. Six years earlier, Christopher Columbus, sailing from Spain, reached the islands off America's shore and, believing he had landed in the East Indies, named the islanders accordingly. Spain pursued an American empire for gold, and its explorers and conquistadors mapped and conquered land that they later settled. In 1513, Vasco de Balboa was the first European to gaze upon the Pacific Ocean; Hernando Cortes began Mexico's conquest in 1518; and Ferdinand Magellan led an expedition that sailed around South America, crossed the Pacific, and claimed the Philippines for Spain in 1521.

Those initiatives by Portugal and Spain laid the foundations for a global network of trade and exchanges that involved European ships and goods, European colonies, and indigenous laborers and products. Europeans, introducing diseases that decimated native peoples who had no immunities to them, suffered vitamin deficiencies and tropical diseases that felled many of them. The nation-state endowed commercial firms like the Dutch East India Company, formed in 1602, with trade monopolies and the power to wage war, make treaties, coin money, and establish colonies in Africa and Asia. Similarly, the British East India Company, created two years before its Dutch rival, held a monopoly over Britain's trade with Asia. The British government granted the company, which was on the brink of bankruptcy in 1773, an exemption from taxes on tea exports and a monopoly on tea exports to the American colonies, thereby undercutting American merchants who already were required to pay taxes on their imports. The act led to widespread resentment, cries against taxation without representation, a tea boycott, and the Boston Tea Party of 1773, which became a theater of the American Revolution.

Portuguese success in the Indian Ocean trade was built in large measure on Asian and African slaves who manned the ships that carried Asia's products to Europe. By the early sixteenth century, enslaved laborers from Bengal, Sri Lanka and southern India, the Indonesian archipelago, the Philippines, and Japan made up the majority of the crews on board Portuguese ships in the Indian Ocean, mainly because so many white sailors had succumbed to disease. By the end of the century the Dutch had eclipsed the overextended Portuguese commercial empire in southeast Asia. The British surpassed the Portuguese in the rest of Asia shortly thereafter. In 1658, the Dutch introduced Asian slaves, along with African slaves, into their refreshment station at the Cape of Good

Hope. By 1834, when slavery was abolished, there were approximately 34,000 slaves there.

In 1565 Spain began its galleon trade, which took Mexican and Peruvian silver from Acapulco amd Callao to Manila. From there, Asia's products reached the Americas and eventually Europe. In this way, America's silver reached China, where it was traded for the silk, porcelain, and lacquer that enriched Spanish society in its American colonies and in Spain. America's crops, notably maize and potatoes, entered Asia via Manila, and helped to sustain increases in China's population. The galleon trade also conveyed Filipino and Chinese sailors from Manila to Acapulco, where some of them remained and traveled to Spain's other colonies in the Americas. Filipino "Manila men" reached Louisiana and established fishing and shrimping villages in the bayous near New Orleans possibly as early as 1765. These were probably the first permanent settlement of Asians in North America.

Asia was still on European minds when in 1776 British Captain James Cook, after two research expeditions to the South Pacific, was directed to find the fabled Northwest Passage, which would open a straighter highway from Europe to Asia's products. Cook's departure from Plymouth, England, was just nine days after the American Declaration of Independence. When he accidentally made landfall on January 19, 1778, on the island of Kaua'i after stops in Polynesia, the process of consolidation begun by the migrations from Tahiti in 1100 was reaching a culmination. Around the mid-fifteenth century, warfare increasingly determined political authority. Warriors replaced hereditary chiefs, and the social divide between chiefs and commoners, whose labor the chiefs taxed, widened. These changes in Hawaiian society would accelerate with the advent of Europeans who placed the islands on their maps and used them as a provisioning station between the Americas and Asia.

On board one of Cook's ships was John Ledyard, an American. Although the voyagers failed to discover the Northwest Passage, they did discover in America's Pacific Northwest furs and skins that Chinese merchants valued. This find led to a trade network among the fur-bearing regions of the Pacific Northwest, Canada, and Alaska, the sandalwood-producing regions of the Hawaiian islands, and the regions of China producing silk, porcelain, and other products. In Robert Morris, a leading businessman and financier, Ledyard found a receptive ear for his schemes for trade between America and China. Even before the end of the Revolutionary War, Morris and others planned the creation of a company, similar to the British East India Company, to lead American trade with Asia. The *Empress of China* was one of the ships designated for the voyage. But instead of taking the risky Ledyard route to the Pacific Northwest and its furs, the investors loaded the ship's cargo bay with American ginseng and pointed it across the Atlantic and the Cape of Good Hope in 1784, about five months after the treaty that recognized America's independence. The young nation's entry into Europe's reach for Asia, the *New York News Dispatch* predicted, "will promote the welfare of the United States in general, by inspiring their citizens with emulation to equal, if not excell their mercantile rivals."[5]

In the same year of the *Empress of China*'s departure from New York's harbor, an American trade ship arrived in Calcutta, and the first American ships entered the Pacific Northwest fur trade in 1787, the year the U.S. Constitution was adopted. That same year, a Hawaiian woman, Winee, was perhaps the first to leave the islands on a European ship when a British ship captain hired her as his wife's personal servant for the voyage to China. During the journey, Winee fell with fever, as would later many of her fellow islanders. She died and was buried at sea. Hawaiians and Asians traveled the globe mainly as laborers on European and American ships. In the year of George Washington's inauguration in 1789, ten ships from Salem, Massachusetts, sailed the waters of the Indian Ocean, and during the 1790s Asian Indians arrived in Salem and worked on the India wharves for some of the biggest shippers and as domestic servants. They might have married African American women and become members of Salem's African American community. Asian Indian indentured servants, including James Dunn, John Ballay, Joseph Green, George Jimor, Thomas Robinson, and others, served whites in Pennsylvania, and, if freed, probably married into African American communities. Chinese men, conveyed like Asian Indians on American ships, appear in New York City's records as early as the 1820s.

America's Asian trade brought increasing numbers of ships into Hawaiian waters, where they initiated exchanges that proved wide-ranging and oftentimes fatal. On the island of Hawai'i, Kiwalao succeeded his father, Kalaniopu'u, in 1782. His ambitious cousin, Kamehameha, contested the succession and defeated and killed Kiwalao. Over the next nine years, Kamehameha battled other contenders to the chieftaincy and finally prevailed. Not content with his domain, Kamehameha gathered a fleet of canoes and a huge army and in 1795 invaded and took the adjacent islands of Maui, Moloka'i, Lana'i, and Kaho'olawe. From Moloka'i he launched the invasion and conquest of O'ahu. Kamehameha succeeded in uniting the entire island chain under his rule in 1810, when Kaua'i's chief, Kaumuali'i agreed to pay him tribute.

Kamehameha's rise to supreme power was accompanied and aided by the arrival of Europeans and the weapons of war they brought with them. Hawaiian chiefs, in their contest for power, eagerly traded their agricultural products for metal, guns, and cannons, and Kamehameha employed Europeans to build his ships and man his cannons. The arms race and the chiefs' drive for land and power had profound consequences for the masses of people. Besides the loss of laborers and resources caused by warfare, enormous efforts had to be expended in building the implements of war and in producing the food required to feed the armies and to exchange for guns. Kamehameha's planned invasion of

Kaua'i, for instance, required the building of a fleet of 800 canoes to transport his army of several thousand men, a task that took five years to complete. The planned invasion entailed the conscription of about 1,000 men to build large taro ponds, each requiring months to years to construct, for food for the expedition. Warfare severely disrupted and dramatically changed the nature of the Hawaiian economy and polity.

With the advent of European traders, Hawaiians were introduced to, indeed swept into, the world economy. During the pre-capitalist period, Hawaiians for the most part produced their own food, shelter, and clothing and maintained a limited system of exchange. Under capitalism, those farmers became laborers employed by chiefs to produce for and become consumers of the global, market economy. In that exchange between Hawaiians and foreigners, the chiefs exercised a monopoly and thereby accumulated wealth and political power. By the late eighteenth century, the convergence of warfare and foreign trade had led to the rise of the chiefs and to the separation of chief from commoner. Like warfare, trade affected Hawaiian agriculture by diverting labor away from subsistence cultivation to the production of goods demanded by the market. The islands' sandalwood, an aromatic tree sold for incense in the China trade as early as 1792, became nearly extinct because of overcutting. Then, because large numbers of laborers were engaged in that activity, the food crops were left untended and a famine resulted.

On board one of those sandalwood traders was Tze-Chun Wong, who settled on the island of Lana'i in 1802. There, with his sugar mill and boiling pans, Wong began the first commercial manufacture of sugar in Hawai'i. He left about a year later when his venture proved unprofitable. Wong was not the first Chinese in Hawai'i, named by the Chinese "Sandalwood Mountains," but was preceded by others possibly as early as 1794. And by 1828 there were 30 to 40 Chinese living among the estimated 400 foreigners in Honolulu.

Following the lead of Winee, two young Hawaiians, Hopu and Opukahaia, joined the crew of an American vessel in 1807 and sailed for the Pacific Northwest, where the ship took on a cargo of seal skins. After returning to Hawai'i, the ship headed west for China, staying there for about six months before sailing for Africa's Cape of Good Hope and landing in New York's harbor two years later. Hopu served in the War of 1812, was captured and imprisoned by the British in the West Indies, and after the war returned to New England, in 1816. There he was reunited with Opukahaia, who had enrolled at Yale, and the two studied for the ministry in preparation for their return to Hawai'i. Opukahaia, however, died of typhus in 1818. Hopu reached his island home in 1819.

Contrary forces were at work in Kamehameha's kingdom. Wars caused great destruction and loss of life but ushered in a period of peace and relative prosperity. Foreign trade disrupted pre-capitalist relations and accelerated the gulf between chiefs and commoners but provided some opportunities for escape

from chiefly prerogatives and controls. Hawaiian men like Hopu and Opukahaia found employment in the new economy. By 1830 they constituted the
majority of the crews on American fur-trading ships in the Pacific Northwest
and were widely employed at trading posts throughout Oregon country. During
the 1840s, 300 to 400 Hawaiians worked for the Hudson's Bay Company, generally for periods of three years at ten dollars per month. Like the Indians,
Hawaiians were at the bottom of the social and economic scale, and were
flogged and imprisoned and treated like slaves. Hawaiian women traded sexual
favors for goods from Europeans and thereby gained some economic standing.
And men and women felt free to violate chiefly kapus, or prohibitions, when
on board European trading vessels anchored offshore.

   In 1819, shortly after the death of Kamehameha and the accession of his
son, Liholiho, the great king's influential wife, Ka'ahumanu, invited the young
Liholiho to a banquet to eat with women—a violation of the *kapu* system.
Ka'ahumanu was a powerful woman even when Kamehameha was alive. In a
society that conferred near absolute power to the king, Ka'ahumanu frequently
argued with her husband and ran away from him several times. He placed a
kapu on her body, but she slept with other chiefs, loved to drink liquor, and
openly ate pork and shark's meat, foods forbidden to women. When the great
king died, Ka'ahumanu created a new post and appointed herself *kuhina nui*,
or executive officer, because, she claimed, she was acting on the will of the
dead king. Liholiho accepted Ka'ahumanu's invitation, and by eating with
women he ended the *kapu* system and the gods and temples that gave it its
authority.

   The *kapu* system was installed essentially to separate chiefs and priests from
commoners, men from women, and to assign power and privilege to the chiefs,
priests, and men. Although of chiefly rank, Ka'ahumanu was separated from
power by her gender. The abolition of the *kapu* system, she knew, would result
in greater freedoms for women. But the *kapu* system was also the preserve of
hereditary chiefs who were often in conflict with the central government. Accordingly, the destruction of the *kapu* system undermined the bases of their
authority and strengthened the powers of the kingdom, which appointed governors who served at the king's discretion. In addition, the abolition of *kapus*
was economically rational under mercantile capitalism. *Kapus* restricted trade
and ocean travel to certain months of the year and disallowed women's labor
in cultivation, fishing, and food cooking. With the end of the *kapu* system,
resources were redirected from ritual to trade, and women labored in subsistence farming, freeing men to pursue capital through wage labor. Of course,
these opportunities were not untrammeled, as they enabled the few to amass
wealth and required the many to engage in exploitative labor.

   The coming of New England missionaries in 1820 accelerated the process
of social change already underway. The end of the *kapu* system and state reli-

gion created a space for Christian missionaries to convert significant numbers of Hawaiians to a new religion and lifestyle. Christianity required, according to the missionaries, an end to the Hawaiian worship of ancestors and gods, the system of ethics and morality particular to Hawai'i, and even subsistence economics. Instead, the missionary effort had the effect of promoting wage labor, production for the capitalist market, and the consumption of Western-manufactured goods. Missionary schools and presses taught literacy and westernization, and missionaries and their families formed permanent communities in the islands and became prominent in transforming Hawaiian society—economically, politically, and ideologically.

About the same time, New England and British whalers anchored in Hawaiian waters. Although seasonal, their presence stimulated the rise of mercantilism and provided the impetus for business houses devoted to services and to the import and export of goods. Some of these companies—C. Brewer, for example, and Theo. H. Davies, American Factors, and Castle and Cook—evolved into leading firms that dominated the Hawaiian economy for more than a hundred years. Ladd and Company, a mercantile trading house, directed William Hooper to the island of Kaua'i to establish the Koloa Plantation in 1835. Like the missionaries, Hooper saw his sugar enterprise as a means by which to transform Hawaiian society through wage labor and capitalist consumption. Besides Hawaiians who worked mainly in the fields, Hooper hired Chinese to extract the sugar in the mill. Throughout the islands Koloa Plantation's success spawned similar operations, which were characterized by its ethnically stratified system of labor.

Hawai'i's sugar industry followed the pattern of its more mature counterpart in the Caribbean, where imported laborers supplanted indigenous peoples in the colonial production of agricultural commodities. Enslaved Africans first arrived in the Spanish colony of Santo Domingo (Haiti and the Dominican Republic) in the early sixteenth century to labor in sugar production. The British, French, and Dutch played leading roles in the commercial and technological development of the sugar industry. That development included the system of African enslavement that made sugar production profitable and that continued through most of the nineteenth century. And when it became clear that British slave ships supplied much of the plantation labor used by Britain's rivals, abolitionism emerged as a way to erode the position of those rivals and thereby strengthen Britain's position in the sugar market. Accordingly, Britain in 1807 made illegal its involvement in the slave trade, and in 1834 declared an end to slavery in its possessions. Shortly thereafter, in 1838, the first Asian laborers arrived in the Americas, on indentures in British Guiana, opening a veritable stream of South Asian and Chinese indentured workers in the Caribbean sugar complex.

In Hawai'i, as the numbers of foreigners increased, the population of Hawaiians decreased precipitously. Although rough and notoriously imprecise, the figures given for Hawai'i's population vary between 200,000 and 800,000 at the time of European contact. By 1878, that number had declined to less than 48,000, suggesting a great devastation that was typical of the encounter between Europeans and native peoples of the Americas and Pacific Islands. Many were the causes of that slaughter. Famine resulting from war, and specifically from the chiefs' displacement of agricultural workers, was surely one factor in the decline. But it was disease more than any other cause that produced the decimation. Indigenous populations had effective immunities against microbes in their homelands, but their bodies lacked defenses against many of the diseases introduced by Europeans. Epidemics of syphilis, influenza, cholera, typhoid, and bubonic plague swept through the islands with devastating effects during the nineteenth century, and thousands of Hawaiians died as a result.

Besides suffering those loses, Hawaiians saw their sovereignty slip away. Beholden to missionary advisors, Kamehameha III in 1840 created a constitutional monarchy with executive, legislative, and judicial branches, and he appointed whites to prominent positions in the new government. In 1845, nearly 6,000 Hawaiians petitioned the king in protest over the influence of foreigners in the kingdom and the rumored plans for land sales to whites. Despite the petition, the king proceeded with the privatization of land, and in 1848 promulgated the Great Mahele, which made land private property and divided the islands into crown lands reserved for the monarchy, chiefs' lands, and government lands. Commoners could file claims against the land allocated to chiefs. Although all adult males were eligible to make land claims, only 29 percent received land, while the rest remained landless. Given the right to lease land in 1848 and the right to purchase land in 1850, foreigners controlled or owned 75 percent of O'ahu's total land by 1862.

Like Hawai'i, Asia felt the influence of foreigners through trade, colonization, and Christian missions. The British East India Company encouraged the cultivation of opium in India to pay for its purchases of Chinese tea and silk. Americans found the trade extremely profitable, but the traffic depleted Chinese specie and bodies, and the imperial government declared opium smoking illegal and sought to end the trade. China confiscated and destroyed British opium stores. Britain declared war on China in 1839, destroyed China's antiquated navy, attacked Canton, and occupied Chinese cities. China capitulated in 1842 with the Treaty of Nanking, by which it agreed to pay a war indemnity, open five ports to foreign commerce, and cede Hong Kong. Similarly, Japan banned European missionaries in 1587 and expelled all Western traders in 1638. But caught without a navy and the modern instruments of war, Japan was forced to open its trade ports after a visit by Matthew Perry, an American, in 1853.

Christian missionaries recruited Hawaiians and Asians to the United States to study and then return to their homelands to convert their people. Between

1818 and 1825, five Chinese students attended a mission school in Cornwall, Connecticut, and in 1847 Wing Yung, Shing Wong, and Foon Wong left China for the Monson Academy in Massachusetts. Shing Wong returned to China because of poor health; Foon Wong left the United States to study in Edinburgh, Scotland, after graduating in 1850; and Wing Yung continued his education at Yale College. After graduating from Yale in 1854, Yung returned to China but came back to the United States in 1872 as head of the Chinese Educational Commission, a government-sponsored program to educate Chinese youth in America.

Asians left for Hawai'i and the United States for certain educational and professional opportunities, but also because whites recruited them for their labor. In 1850, Hawai'i's sugar planters formed the Royal Hawaiian Agricultural Society, and its legislature passed the Masters and Servants Act to regulate labor in the kingdom. The act, probably modeled on labor laws in New York and Massachusetts, provided for apprentices and contract laborers who bound themselves to periods and terms of service. Faced with a declining population and reluctant work force, the kingdom's planters sought cheap, docile labor in China. The Royal Hawaiian Agricultural Society succeeded in bringing to Hawai'i the first group of Chinese contract laborers—195 of them, in 1852, from Amoy in Fujian province. They signed five-year contracts that provided for a wage of three dollars a month and food, housing, and passage. Although the Chinese workers proved industrious, the uncertainty of the sugar market and a general decline in the industry precluded further recruitments until 1865.

California's gold rush attracted more than 20,000 Chinese in the same year that the first Chinese contract workers arrived in Hawai'i. Like Chinese migrants whose labor in the islands was regulated, Chinese migrants to California encountered restrictions on their pursuit of a livelihood. In 1850, California imposed a tax on all foreign miners, especially Mexican and Chileno, but its application fell principally on the Chinese, and its supreme court in 1854 ruled that Chinese could not testify for or against whites in the courts. San Francisco instituted segregated schools for Chinese children in 1857, as it had for American Indian and African American children, and the following year the state passed a law barring entry to Chinese and "Mongolian" migrants. Although most of these restrictions were later rescinded or declared unconstitutional, the provisions showed the prevalence and power of anti-Asian sentiment.

Hawaiians, like the Chinese, were drawn by the lure of California's gold rush. In truth, many were already along the West Coast engaged in the Pacific Northwest's fur and timber industries and on the Pacific coast as seamen. They had fought against and made peace with American Indians, and Hawaiian men had married American Indian women in Washington and Oregon. A traveler in 1842 reported that as sailors and navigators Hawaiians were indispensable to ships in California waters. In 1847 the forty Hawaiians—thirty-nine men and one woman—in San Francisco constituted nearly ten percent of that settlement's total population. Most of the Hawaiians worked as boatmen on San Francisco Bay. John Sutter, before gold was discovered on his property, brought workers from Hawaii for his cattle ranch, and he employed Hawaiian sailors on his ships. Thus, when gold was discovered, Hawaiians already on the West Coast and from Hawai'i flocked to the gold fields, like many other fortune seekers. A camp of Hawaiian miners at Indian Creek in El Dorado County, California, consisted of twenty-four men and women, mostly Hawaiian men but also two Hawaiian women, three Indian women, and four Hawaiian/Indian children. Two of the Indian women spoke Hawaiian fluently, the visitor reported, and their children spoke and read Hawaiian. California's racism and anti-foreignism drove Hawaiians, like the Chinese, from mining and severely restricted their opportunities.

In Hawai'i, California's gold rush led to a brief boom in the demand for livestock, potatoes, onions, squashes, and sugar. The Royal Hawaiian Agricultural Society reported the frenzy: "Our coffee and sugar no longer remain piled in our warehouses. Our fruits and vegetables no longer decay in the spot where they were grown. We are not even compelled to seek for them a market, but clamorous purchasers come to our very doors and carry off our supplies."[6] The U.S. Civil War cut off the North's supply of sugar from the South, and prices climbed from four cents a pound in 1861 to twenty-five cents a pound in 1864. Hawai'i's sugar producers responded and sugar exports increased from 572 to 8,865 tons. Premature in its optimism but ultimately accurate in its prediction was the editorial of June 17, 1865, in the *Hawaiian Gazette*: "But a new era has dawned upon the Islands—the era of sugar—and the cultivation of cane overshadows by far all other agricultural enterprises. A large proportion of the floating capital in the community has been absorbed in new plantation enterprises, and it is considered beyond a doubt that sugar is to be, in the future, as it already is at present, the staple product of our Islands." The Reciprocity Treaty of 1876 allowed Hawaiian sugar to enter the United States duty-free, boosting sugar production in the islands and installing "king sugar" and the corporations that dominated its production, financing, and shipping.

Labor migration enabled Hawai'i's sugar production and the West's development under capitalism. And Hawaiian and Asian workers were key elements in those relations of production. The Central Pacific Railroad relied on Chinese laborers to complete its western link of the transcontinental railroad, and Hawai'i's planters recruited Japanese workers in 1868. The Burlingame-Seward Treaty of that same year secured the rights of migration between the United States and China. Despite its language of reciprocity, the primary effect of the treaty was to allow the recruitment of Chinese laborers for America's growing industries. Illustrating America's continued control over migration undiminished by international agreements was the Page Law of 1875, which barred entry to Asian, principally Chinese, women prostitutes, whom the law grouped with felons and contract workers. Immigration officials interpreted the law generously and thereby excluded Chinese women whether they were prostitutes or not. Although the labor of Chinese men was essential, Chinese women had the capacity to produce children, who under the Fourteenth Amendment of 1868 were citizens if born in the United States. The prospect of permanent Asian American communities along with nonproductive children and seniors was politically fraught and, it was feared, economically draining. California's elite favored the migration of Chinese men, accordingly, but not women.

Employers exploited Asian workers and hired them with a view toward depressing wages and disciplining unruly laborers. Before the Civil War, Southern planters considered following the example of sugar planters in the Caribbean who employed Asian Indians and Chinese. But only after the end of slavery and emancipation did actually they recruit Chinese workers, in an attempt to replace and punish African Americans who left white employment for greater freedoms in farming and business. Drawn from Cuba, China, San Francisco, and New York, Chinese workers arrived in 1867 for the sugar and cotton plantations of Louisiana and the lower South. The end of Reconstruction and the era of segregation restored the power of whites over blacks, and white interest in Chinese labor diminished. In 1870, embroiled in a work action at his shoe factory in North Adams, Massachusetts, Calvin T. Sampson hired seventy-five Chinese workers from California to break the strike. The success of Sampson's experiment encouraged other factory owners in the East to recruit and hire Chinese laborers.

Asian workers, however, were not forever or uniformly docile. In 1867 some 2,000 Chinese struck against the Central Pacific Railroad for higher wages and shorter work hours. Instead of accepting thirty dollars a month, they asked for forty, and enduring dawn-till-sunset workdays, they asked for a ten-hour day on the surface and an eight-hour day inside the tunnels. Additionally, the Chinese demanded the right to seek employment elsewhere and an end to the practice of overseers whipping them. The company cut off their provisions, and after a week the strikers returned to work. Three years later, Chinese railroad workers sued the Houston and Texas Central Railroad for back wages and a refusal to comply with work contracts. Both of those collective acts of resistance failed, revealing the vulnerable position of the workers and the power of their employers, but they also showed that Asian workers opposed exploitation and sought to ensure their slender rights.

The fragility of their freedoms was demonstrated in mob violence directed against them. In Los Angeles in 1871, whites descended on the Chinese quarters and hanged, shot, and burned twenty-one Chinese, and in 1880 a mob destroyed most of the buildings in Denver's Chinatown and kicked and beat to death a laundryman, Sing Lee. In 1885 in Rock Springs, Wyoming, whites hunted, shot, burned, and killed 28 of the 331 Chinese who had been brought in by the Union Pacific Railroad ten years earlier to break a strike in the coal mines. And throughout the 1880s, whites shot, lynched, and expelled Chinese from urban and rural areas in places like Seattle, Tacoma, Portland, Humboldt County in California, Pierce City in Idaho, and the Hell's Canyon gorge in Oregon, where a white gang robbed, murdered, and mutilated the bodies of thirty-one Chinese miners.

The West's forcible entry into Asia prompted debates over national development and military might. The British triumph over China in the Opium War, like Matthew Perry's squadron in Tokyo Bay, demonstrated the West's military superiority over China and Japan. And even as Britain was losing a colony in America it was gaining another in India. The India Act of 1784 established British rule in India, and the following year Lord Cornwallis, the general who had surrendered the British forces at Yorktown, arrived in India as governor-general. Despite Indian rebellions, British power spread over the subcontinent, leading to a new sense of Indian national identity, which would later blossom into an independence movement, but also nurturing Westernization, especially among the Indian elite. Learning from the West, whether under colonial tutelage or study abroad in Europe and the United States, seemed the necessary engine for modernization and national greatness. Governments in China, Japan, and the Philippines sent students to America, among other places, and individuals like Korean diplomats and Korean and Asian Indian political refugees chose to study in the United States.

China, however, also resisted Western encroachment in a second war with the British from 1858 to 1860 and in mass violence against traders and missionaries. Japan, by contrast, embraced Westernization after the Meiji Restoration in 1868, and sought through that means to gain equality with Western nations. Displaced by the change were supporters of the replaced Tokugawa rulers, one of whom sent a contingent to California to establish the Wakamatsu Tea and Silk Colony in 1869. Exercising national sovereignty, Japan's government controlled the recruitment and migration of workers from 1885 to 1894, when private companies, under government regulations, handled the outflow. By the 1890s, Japan's efforts at modernization, with its growing industries and modern navy and army, led it to wars against the Chinese in 1894–95 to gain dominance over China's dependency, Korea, and against the Russians in 1904–05 to reduce Russia's threat to Korea through its extending influence in Manchuria. Victorious, Japan inherited Russia's position in Manchuria, and in 1910 Japan formally declared Korea its colony.

Japan's interest in Korea long predated its formal colonization of the peninsula. It invaded Korea in 1592 and 1597, and in 1876 forced Korea to sign the Treaty of Kanghwa, which was modeled on the unequal treaties forced upon China and Japan by Western powers. To gain trade privileges there, the United

States entered Korea in 1882 with a treaty, and was followed by European countries. Horace N. Allen, an American missionary, gained the confidence of King Kojong, with the result that Christian missionaries were given access to Korea. Allen became secretary of the American legation in Seoul and acted as a broker between the U.S. and Korean governments and between private individuals and enterprises. In 1902, he agreed to work for the Hawaiian Sugar Planters' Association to secure for them Korean laborers, and the following year the first group of Korean migrants arrived in Hawai'i. Missionaries were key figures in promoting the migration of some 7,000 Koreans from 1903 until 1905, when the migration ended because of the maltreatment of Korean laborers in Mexico and the pressure exerted by Japan to stop the flow to Hawai'i.

Like the European imperial powers in Asia and upstart Japan, the United States saw Asia and the Pacific as its domain as early as 1784 with the launching of the ship *Empress of China* and the start of the U.S.-Asian trade. The United States secured use of a Samoan harbor at Pago Pago in 1878. After jockeying with Britain and Germany over dominance in Samoa, it secured in 1899 a treaty that divided Samoa between the United States and Germany. But its arrival as a colonial master in the Pacific began with American settlers in Hawai'i and with a war in the Caribbean against another empire, that of Spain. In Hawai'i, a Hawaiian nationalist movement calling for "Hawai'i for the Hawaiians" grew with the expansion of white influence in government and the economy. It opposed the 1876 Reciprocity Treaty with the United States, and opposed especially the treaty's renewal, which ceded the use of Pearl Harbor, in 1887. But the planter oligarchy prevailed and imposed on King Kalakaua the Bayonet Constitution of 1887, which reduced the king's powers, limited Hawaiian voting rights, and disenfranchised Asians. The planters also organized the secret Hawaiian League, which plotted the overthrow of the monarchy.

King Kalakaua died in 1891 and was succeeded by his sister, Lili'uokalani, who openly opposed the planter elite and sought to nullify the 1887 constitution. In 1893 the queen proposed a new constitution which restored the powers of the monarchy and the vote to all male subjects. The cabinet refused to adopt the new constitution, and the planters and their allies formed the Committee of Safety to carry out the overthrow of the queen. John L. Stevens, appointed U.S. minister to Hawai'i by President Benjamin Harrison four years earlier, requested the landing of American troops from the U.S.S. *Boston,* already anchored in Honolulu harbor, so they might protect American property and lives. In fact, they functioned to bolster the armed members of the Committee of Safety who rounded up the royalists and captured the queen. The revolutionaries declared a provisional government, and Stevens proclaimed Hawai'i a U.S. protectorate.

The act was premature, and President Grover Cleveland relieved Stevens of his post and sought to restore the queen and the monarchy. But the provisional government refused to surrender its authority and continued to pursue American annexation through the U.S. Congress. Sugar production, Hawai'i's planters held, would once again surge if the islands, by becoming part of the United States, enjoyed duty-free access to the American market, a privilege eliminated in 1890 by a tariff. In 1894, a Senate committee exonerated Stevens of wrongdoing, and in 1895, while held as a prisoner, Queen Lili'uokalani was forced to abdicate in favor of the newly constituted Republic of Hawai'i. The final annexation had to await the election of a new president favorable to empire, William McKinley, and a war with Spain.

Although America's "splendid little war" was some years in the making, as "yellow journalism" whipped up popular dislike of the Spanish masters of Cuba, the immediate cause of the war was the sinking of the American battleship *Maine* in Havana harbor in 1898. War hysteria swept the country when a naval court of inquiry mistakenly reported that a mine had caused the disaster, which cost more than 260 lives, and Congress declared war on Spain on April 25, 1898. American troops engaged the Spaniards in Cuba and Puerto Rico, while America's Pacific squadron attacked the archaic Spanish fleet in Manila Bay. The Treaty of Paris, signed in December 1898, ended the conflict. Cuba's independence was recognized and the United States took possession of Puerto Rico, Guam, and the Philippines. The latter was added on for twenty million dollars. Ratification of the treaty was hotly debated, but imperialism won the day. That result was confirmed by the election of 1900, in which McKinley triumphed over fervent anti-imperialist William Jennings Bryan. In the midst of the war with Spain, Congress adopted a joint resolution on Hawai'i's annexation, and McKinley signed the resolution on July 7, 1898.

Acquiring the Philippines from Spain did not mean possession of the colony. It had to be conquered. When the American fleet arrived in Manila Bay, the Spaniards were on the verge of defeat against Filipino nationalists who had been waging an anticolonial war. The Americans simply inherited the colonizers' mantle, and fought a long and bitter guerilla war from 1898 to 1902, when the United States unilaterally declared an end to the conflict. The war, ostensibly waged for the uplift of "our little brown brothers," cost about 4,300 American and at least 50,000 Filipino lives. The "white man's burden," the title of the poem Rudyard Kipling wrote in 1899 to stiffen American resolve in its war in the Philippines, involved the "benevolent assimilation" of untutored Filipinos. Part of America's civilizing mission included the sending of students to the United States, beginning in 1903, and the recruitment of Filipino labor for Hawai'i's sugar plantations in 1906.

Even as U.S. interests promoted labor migration they sought to regulate it by instituting discriminatory controls and exclusionary measures. The U.S. Supreme Court ruled in 1878 that Chinese migrants could not become naturalized citizens. It affirmed the same for Japanese migrants in 1922, and for Asian Indians in 1923. Congress in 1882 prohibited entry to Chinese workers; a 1907 agreement with Japan accomplished the same for Japanese; the Immigration Act of 1917 barred entry to West, South, and Southeast Asians; the 1924 Immigration Act excluded virtually all Asians, and the 1932 Hawes-Cutting Act rendered Filipinos aliens ineligible for citizenship and reduced their immigration to 100 persons a year. In 1896, the Supreme Court validated segregation in *Plessy v. Ferguson*; states and cities discriminated against Asians in marriage, employment, education, and housing; and Western states passed alien land laws that denied Asian migrants the right to own and rent land. In 1922, Congress mandated the loss of citizenship to American women who married Asian men who were aliens ineligible for citizenship, and in 1935 it passed a bill to encourage Filipino repatriation by providing free transportation to the Philippines.

America's institutions were instruments both of control and of resistance. Crucial to Asian Americans and to all Americans was the Fourteenth Amendment, which guaranteed equal protection under the law. In 1884, Chinese parents Joseph and Mary Tape sued the San Francisco school board over the exclusion of their daughter from the public schools. California's supreme court ruled in favor of the Tapes, citing the Fourteenth Amendment, but the state's legislature passed an amendment to an act mandating separate schools for Asian children. Two years later, in a landmark civil rights decision, the U.S. Supreme Court ruled in *Yick Wo v. Hopkins* (1886), a case brought by Chinese laundries, that laws, however neutral their language, that discriminate in their application violate the equal protection clause of the Fourteenth Amendment. By subjecting to scrutiny the intent and application of the law in determining discrimination, *Yick Wo* became one of the most cited decisions in cases involving equal protection under the Constitution. And in 1898, the Supreme Court ruled in *Wong Kim Ark v. U.S.*, the case of a Chinese American, that the birthright of citizenship provided for by the Fourteenth Amerndment could not be taken away.

Besides pursuing their civil rights through the courts, Asian Americans formed voluntary associations dedicated to preserving their civil liberties and freedoms. In 1895, Chinese Americans founded the Native Sons of the Golden State, later renamed the Chinese American Citizens Alliance. Japanese Americans established the Japanese Association of America (1900), the Federation of Japanese Labor (1919), and the American Loyalty League (1923), the precursor of the Japanese American Citizens League. Korean Americans formed mutual aid societies and groups dedicated to the anticolonial struggle for Korean independence. These included the New People's Association (1902), the Friendship Association (1903), later renamed the Mutual Cooperation Federation and Korean National Association, the Korean Women's Association (1908), and the Women's Friendship Association and Korean Women's Patriotic League (1919). Filipino Americans established the Filipino Higher Wages Association (1911), the Filipino Federation of America (1925), and the Filipino Agricultural Workers Union (1939). Asian Indians founded the Hindustani Association and the revolutionary Ghadar Party (1913). These organizations promoted the welfare of their members, and defended their rights against anti-Asian sentiments and groups like the Asiatic Exclusion League, which was formed in 1905.

Yet another strategy employed by Asian Americans was their withholding productive labor by running away from contracts, breaking tools, feigning illness, setting fire to fields and buildings, and striking. Chinese railroad workers struck and sued for unpaid wages, and Japanese organized strikes against Hawai'i's sugar planters. Japanese and Mexicans formed the Japanese Mexican Labor Association in 1903; against sugar beet growers in Oxnard, California, they won a strike that left one Mexican striker dead and two Mexican and two Japanese wounded. Japanese shut down significant numbers of O'ahu's sugar plantations in 1909, and Filipinos and Japanese joined in a massive strike in 1920. Filipino sugar plantation laborers in 1924 organized an eleven-month strike in which sixteen strikers and four police officers died, and Filipino farm workers went on several strikes in California's fields during the 1930s. Mexican berry pickers struck against Japanese growers in El Monte, California, in 1933, and three years later Mexican, Filipino, and Japanese celery workers went on strike against Japanese growers in Venice, California. And in 1938, Chinese women garment workers organized a strike against the National Dollar Stores, which were owned by a Chinese, and in what became known as the "Hilo massacre," or "bloody Monday," a multiracial demonstration of men and women workers in Hilo, Hawai'i, resulted in fifty of the demonstrators being injured by police.

At times, Asians skirted restrictive laws with varying degrees of success. The 1906 San Francisco earthquake devastated the city, including Chinatown, but it also destroyed immigration records that were crucial to enforcing the Exclusion Act of 1882. Without immigration records, Chinese could claim to have been born in the United States. As citizens they would be entitled to bring to America their offspring in China. These were their children, usually sons, but they could also sponsor someone else's child called their "paper son." Similarly, after the Gentlemen's Agreement of 1907, which limited labor migration to the United States, Japanese and Korean men already in America sent for their wives, called "picture brides," because they were often matched by photographs and married in Asia despite the couple's physical separation. Under pressure from the United States, Japan's government ended the practice in 1921.

Despite the discouragement of American consuls in India, Asian Indians ventured to the Untied States throughout the nineteenth century. The 1900 U.S. census counted 2,050 Asian Indians, and the 1904 British Columbia census lists 258 Asian Indians, mostly Sikhs, who worked in mines, farming, and lumber. In 1908, after 2,124 Asian Indians had immigrated during the previous year, Canada adopted a law that restricted entry only to those who held continuous passage from their country of birth to Canada. In 1914, Baba Gurdit Singh chartered the *Komagata Maru* to challenge, with 376 passengers on board, the 1908 Immigration Act. Immigration officials denied it landing rights and kept the passengers on the ship without fresh supplies for six weeks. Armed troops and a warship finally forced the *Komagata Maru* to leave Canadian waters after it was allowed supplies for the return journey. When it arrived in India, police attempted to arrest Gurdit Singh, sparking a riot in which nineteen of the passengers were killed. Others escaped, and some were imprisoned.

Filipinos were a special category because of their U.S. colonial status. Until 1925, when the U.S. Supreme Court ruled that naturalization did not extend to Filipinos, who were classed as "nationals," they were presumably exempt from the laws that applied to other Asians. In 1932, Congress declared Filipinos to be aliens ineligible for citizenship. In 1945, however, the Supreme Court ruled that Filipinos were nationals and not susceptible to the various laws against aliens. In reality Filipinos were only technically immune from the laws that excluded and restricted the opportunities of other Asians, because as Asians they encountered anti-Asian violence in mass expulsions and threats in Dryden and Wenatchee, Washington, in 1928; in Yakima Valley, Washington, in 1937; and in Turlock, California, in 1934. In 1930 they were the victims of a riot that left one dead in Watsonville, California, and of a rooming house bombing that killed one and injured three Filipinos in Imperial Valley, California. And in 1933, Salvador Roldan won his petition to marry a white woman because Filipinos, he argued, were Malays and not Mongolians and were thus unconstrained by California's anti-miscegenation law, but the state's legislature quickly closed the loophole by amending the law to include Malays.

Racial ambiguity prompted the petition by Bhagat Singh Thind for American citizenship. His principal argument was that science classed Asian Indians as Caucasians and therefore he qualified as a free white person. In its 1922 *Ozawa* decision, the U.S. Supreme Court had equated Caucasian with white. In this case, however, the Court reversed itself and ruled that race was not a matter of scientific opinion but the observation of the "average man." "It may be true that the blond Scandinavian and the brown Hindu have a common ancestor in the dim reaches of antiquity," the Court conceded, "but the average man knows perfectly well that there are unmistakable and profound differences between them today."[7] Thus, in 1923, the Supreme Court classed South Asians as nonwhites, as other courts had done in 1909 and 1917, despite other decisions—in 1910, 1913, 1919, and 1920—in which South Asians figured as white. And in the application of the law at the local level, individual officials of the state frequently determined the racial classification, and hence privileges, of applicants. South Asians were classed variously as "brown," "black," or "white" by clerks who made those judgments based on their perception of the petitioner's skin color.

Hawaiians, like Filipinos, were colonial subjects, but they were also U.S. citizens, albeit through force and not consent. Hawaiian dispossession and persistent poverty prompted leaders like Prince Jonah Kuhio to request of Congress land ostensibly for the rebuilding of Hawaiian society. Accordingly, Congress in 1920 approved the Hawaiian Rehabilitation Act, which established the Hawaiian Homes Commission to provide public lands at nominal leases for ninety-nine years to persons with at least one-half Hawaiian blood. Despite the hopes of its sponsors, the act failed because only a small fraction of the acreage set aside for Hawaiian homesteads was suitable for agriculture and they were in dry, isolated areas that promoted rather than countervailed poverty. Large companies eagerly sublet the areas suitable for agriculture, and so, instead of creating small farmers, the act encouraged land concentration under the control of corporations. For the oligarchy, it was business as usual rendered in the name of Hawaiian rehabilitation.

World War II began for most Americans when Japan attacked Pearl Harbor in the Hawaiian Islands. But for many Chinese Americans the war started a decade earlier, when Japan's armies marched into northwestern China in 1931 and into Shanghai the following year. In response, Chinese Americans launched the "save China" movement by organizing parades and rallies and a fund-raising campaign to support China's resistance to Japan's invasion. The Chinese Hand Laundry Association, begun in 1933 when New York City proposed discriminatory taxes against hand laundries, realized that the "save China" campaign was also crucial to the well-being of Chinese in America, because a strong China could defend the rights of its migrant citizens and their children. Among New York City's Chinese, the Association became a leader in the fight for China's independence and for civil rights for Chinese Americans, and it pursued a strategy of enlisting the sympathy of the broader American public.

Japan's attack on Pearl Harbor engaged two imperial powers in conflict over Pacific dominance. Both Japan and the United States had long anticipated the war, and as early as World I the United States had planned to neutralize the alleged threat of internal subversion by Japanese Americans. In Hawai'i, where the Japanese had severely challenged the planter oligarchy in the strikes of 1909 and 1920, and where the Japanese constituted about forty percent of the total population from the beginning of the twentieth century to the 1940s, the military developed a series of plans that included a declaration of martial law and the detention of Japanese American community leaders in the event of war with Japan. On the mainland, military and civilian intelligence anticipated a program of selective detention, including leaders of the community and others deemed potentially dangerous. Without leaders, the planners reasoned, Japanese Americans would be rendered docile and susceptible to control. The plans unfolded on December 7, 1941.

Within two days, teams of military police, agents of the Federal Bureau of Investigation, and local police officers had rounded up, in Hawai'i and on the mainland, 1,291 Japanese aliens and citizens and 865 German and 147 Italian aliens. Unlike the Japanese, the Germans and Italians were aliens who were suspected, wrongly in many cases, by the government to harbor fascist sentiments. On February 19, 1942, President Franklin D. Roosevelt signed Executive Order 9066, which authorized the military to designate areas from which persons could be excluded and to provide for the transportation and shelter of those affected by the order. Shortly thereafter, Congress passed Public Law 503, imposing sanctions for violations of the executive order. The detention of Japanese American leaders, as planned and carried out by military and civilian intelligence, was insufficient in the opinion of several key figures in the government, but the military's plan in Hawai'i prevailed, despite the president's call for stronger action. Thus began the years of mass removal and exile for Japanese Americans along the West Coast and of selective detention for those in Hawai'i, totaling about 120,000 persons.

Japanese Americans challenged their government's infringement of their rights. Gordon Hirabayashi, a senior at the University of Washington at the time of his arrest in 1942, refused to report for evacuation and was cited for curfew violation. Minoru Yasui, an attorney and second lieutenant in the U.S. Army Reserve, intentionally tested the constitutionality of the curfew order and was found guilty and sentenced to a year's imprisonment. Fred Korematsu was arrested for failing to comply with the military's exclusion order. All three cases reached the U.S. Supreme Court, which in 1943 and 1944 upheld the men's convictions and affirmed the constitutionality of the military's curfew and exclusion orders. Whites, mainly educators and religious leaders, formed the National Student Relocation Council in 1942 to assist Japanese American college students in completing their education. The Council appealed to the military to exempt students from the eviction orders and, when that failed, secured student transfers to colleges and universities outside the exclusion zones. And Japanese Americans in the assembly centers to which they were first confined and the concentration camps which became their places of detention for the war's duration organized resistance movements—in Poston, Arizona, and Manzanar and Tule Lake, California—against perceived injustices and collaboration between internees and camp administrators. In 1944, when the government instituted the draft for Japanese Americans whom it had earlier classed as "enemy aliens," young men organized a draft resistance movement because of the mass removals and detentions that violated their civil liberties. Others, as patriotic as the draft resisters, volunteered and were drafted into the army and women's army corps. About 25,000 Japanese American men and women served in the U.S. armed forces during World War II.

While West Coast Japanese Americans were held in concentration camps, other Asian Americans experienced unprecedented housing and employment opportunities. With China as an ally of the United States, the employment picture for Chinese American men brightened considerably. Of all of them who were employed between 1940 and 1950 in San Francisco, the percentage who were employed in domestic service declined from 13 to 4, while the percentage of them employed in the crafts, professional, technical, and managerial categories increased. Chinese American women likewise moved up into clerical and sales positions. Chinese and Filipino Americans eagerly enlisted in the U.S. military, and served with great courage and distinction. Congress repealed the Chinese exclusion laws in 1943, and immigration restrictions against Filipinos and Asian Indians were lifted and Chinese wives of American citizens were allowed into the United States on a non-quota basis in 1946. The following year, Congress amended the 1945 War Brides Act to allow Chinese American veterans to bring their wives to the United States.

Despite those openings, social mobility for racialized minorities and women during the war was tempered by continued and sometimes increased discrimination and by the fleeting nature of the new prosperity. Period employment figures show that Chinese American men and women remained significantly in the service sectors, were locked out of certain crafts, and were seldom promoted to managerial positions. The "lifting" of exclusion laws against Chinese, Filipino, and Asian Indians was followed by a quota system that allowed only about 100 of them into the United States annually, and was more a public relations effort in America's fight for democracy against fascism than an act of antiracism. According to Congressman Emmanuel Celler, one of its sponsors, the Luce-Celler Act, which allowed immigration and naturalization of Filipinos and Asian Indians, was necessary to "dull the edge of Jap propaganda."[8] When Filipino American farm workers in California struck in July 1945, the Economic Council of Santa Maria reminded them: "At best, Filipinos are guests in the United States. . . . Filipinos want America to build up their homeland and protect them, while their people conduct themselves as strikers in the Santa Maria Valley. . . . If the Filipinos act as they have recently, they should be classified with the Japanese; denied renting land and such, as the Japanese were who also did not act properly as guests in America."[9] And at the war's start, the United States classified Korean Americans as "enemy aliens" even though they had long struggled against Japan's colonization of Korea, and whites commonly treated them as the enemy despite their considerable contributions to the war effort.

The atomic bombs on Hiroshima and Nagasaki might have brought the war to an end, but its legacy continued for years after. The last concentration camp,

Tule Lake, closed its doors months after Japan's surrender, and about 8,000 Japanese Americans were "repatriated" to Japan. The Japanese American Evacuation Claims Act of 1948 failed to remedy the financial damage suffered by Japanese Americans in the mass removal and returned only about $37 million on 26,568 claims, a figure far below most estimates of the total personal and property losses. In 1949, Iva Toguri d'Aquino, a Japanese American trapped in Japan during the war, was tried in San Francisco for treason. Along with other English-speaking women, she had served as a host for programs on Radio Tokyo directed, for propaganda purposes, at Allied troops in the Pacific. The seductive siren "Tokyo Rose," as the soldiers dubbed her, was likely a composite of several women broadcasters and the men's imaginations. Still, only d'Aquino was held in Occupation prisons in Japan for a year. She was released and then recharged in 1948. Found guilty, she was sentenced to ten years in prison and fined $10,000.

The war's end propelled the United States and Soviet Union and their conflicting polities, economies, and cultures to positions of global leadership and contention. The Cold War was a consequence of that confrontation. In Asia, the U.S. hope for a strong, independent China faded with the corrupt government of Chiang Kai-shek and the successes of the communist armies of Mao Zedong. Japan's development posed an alternative to China and served as an American ally to contain communism in the aftermath of Mao's swift victory in 1949. At home, the crusade against communism took the form of political hunts that reached levels of near hysteria during the 1950s. In Hawai'i, Governor Ingram M. Stainback promised in 1947, the year the House Un-American Activities Committee held widely publicized hearings on the alleged communist infiltration of Hollywood, to fight communism's plot to seize control of the islands. Among his first victims were John and Aiko Reinecke, who were fired from their teaching positions because, the territory's school superintendent charged, they were members of the Communist Party. Despite overwhelming testimony of their competence as teachers, the Reineckes were dismissed from their posts. Hawai'i's search for communists culminated with the 1953 trial of the Hawai'i Seven, charged with conspiring to overthrow the U.S. government. They were found guilty but had their convictions overturned five years later. On the mainland, Chinese Americans came under close scrutiny from both the Federal Bureau of Investigation and the Immigration and Naturalization Service in their search for communist agents and spies to uproot and expel. At the same time, about 5,000 Chinese college students studying in the United States in 1949 were granted refugee status when communism triumphed in China.

In 1950, Congress passed, over the veto of President Harry S. Truman, the Internal Security Act with its Title II provision which provided for detention camps. The act required all communist organizations to register with the government and to publish their records, and it installed an emergency detention program that authorized the attorney general to apprehend and detain anyone suspected of engaging in espionage or sabotage. Due process was waived, and the basis for detention was mere suspicion. Between 1952 and 1957, six detention facilities were prepared and maintained in accordance with the law. Congress repealed Title II in 1971 after a four-year campaign by Asian Americans who were keenly aware of the World War II concentration camps. The 1952 McCarran-Walter Act, designed to further circumscribe communist activity, contained clauses that allowed Asia an immigration quota of 2,990 and granted the naturalization rights of Japanese.

In June 1950, America fought yet another war, when the communist armies of North Korea swept across the thirty-eighth parallel and occupied much of South Korea and its capital, Seoul. A legacy of World War II, Korea was divided between Soviet and American forces at the thirty-eighth parallel, and the artificial separation hardened as the Cold War deepened. Troops, mainly American, under the banner of the United Nations pushed the North Korean forces across the contrived border, and the new government in China sent its troops to repel the Allies. The war reached a stalemate. In October 1953 the two sides signed a truce that kept the thirty-eighth parallel as the line of separation between North and South. The war brought enormous destruction to cities and countryside fought over by armies three times, leaving about 800,000 Korean, 800,000 Chinese, and 56,000 United Nations troops dead, about 4 million civilians killed or wounded, and more than 3 million refugees. Korean Americans raised monies in support of war victims, and Koreans, including brides of American servicemen and adopted children, found their way to the United States.

Another legacy of World War II and the cold war was Vietnam. Colonized by France since 1859, Vietnam was taken over by the Japanese in 1940. Vietnamese resistance against the colonizers was constant and bloody, and when the war ended in 1945, Ho Chih Minh and his followers, who had formed a united front against the Japanese, were ready to rule an independent Vietnam. But France, with British and American supplies, reoccupied Saigon in 1945 and bombed Hanoi's harbor the following year, killing as many as 10,000 civilians. After 1949, China sent aid to the Vietnamese, who defeated the French at Dien Bien Phu and won a peace accord at the Geneva Conference in 1954. The agreement partitioned Vietnam along the seventeenth parallel temporarily, pending the withdrawal of foreign troops and the holding of nationwide elections scheduled for 1955. Instead, Ngo Dinh Diem, with American support, declared himself president of a Republic of Vietnam, and began a civil war between the north and south. American military involvement escalated over the years, culminating in 1968 with more than 500,000 troops. That same year, peace talks began in Paris, and in 1973 the United States agreed to withdraw its remaining troops from the country it had devastated with bombs and defoliants. As the last Americans left in 1975, northern forces entered the south's capital, Saigon, and in 1976 the country was reunited as the Socialist Republic of Vietnam. From 1945 to its end in 1975, this phase of Vietnam's war of liberation claimed nearly 2 million Vietnamese dead and 4 million wounded or maimed, more than 1 million refugees, and more than 55,000 American dead and 300,000 wounded. Like America's war in Korea, its war in Vietnam produced an exodus to the United States, including Vietnamese wives of Americans, Amerasian children, and political refugees.

The colonial and civil wars in Vietnam were parts of a more global pattern of anti-colonial struggles in Africa and Asia before, during, and after World War II. The British partitioned South Asia, and in 1947 India and Pakistan won their independence. The division led to mass violence and the displacement of more than ten million people as Hindus fled from Pakistan and Muslims from India. In 1971, East Pakistan became Bangladesh after an election and a war. The Soviet and American partition of Korea in 1945 resulted in the two Koreas and a war, and Vietnam's division produced a civil war. Both wars involved the interventions of China and the United States. In most of Southeast Asia, European colonization was followed by Japanese occupation and then by a restoration of European colonial rule. All of those were resisted, and the Philippines gained its independence from the United States in 1946. Burma won its independence from Britain in 1948, Indonesia from the Dutch in 1949, Laos from France in 1953, and Cambodia from France in 1954.

In the same year of Cambodia's independence, a coalition of Asians, workers, and organized labor initiated a revolution at the polls in Hawai'i, where the Democratic Party captured control of the legislature from the Republicans, who had controlled politics in the islands since annexation. The change was far-reaching insofar as the Republicans represented whites and the wealthy and the Democrats represented non-whites and the poor, but it also resulted in little change in that, as in many post-colonial nations, one elite replaced another. Yet there was cause for optimism among those previously denied power. World War II gave an impetus for decolonization in Asia and provided an opening for social mobility among racialized minorities, women, and workers in the United States. In 1948, the U.S. Supreme Court struck down California's alien land and anti-miscegenation laws. Amid the cold war repressions and continued immigration restrictions, Asians gained the rights of naturalization, and the Supreme Court closed the era of legal racial segregation. Dalip Singh Saund, a South Asian, became the first Asian American elected to Congress in 1956, and three years later, despite racist fears, Hawai'i became America's fiftieth state. The Civil Rights Act of 1964 was a triumph for all Americans, and in that same year Patsy Takemoto Mink became the first Asian American woman elected to Congress. In 1965, the Immigration Act and Voting Rights Act ended "national"

and racial discrimination in immigration and voting, and Mexicans and Filipinos began the Delano grape strike, which elevated Chicano labor and civil
rights leader Cesar Chavez to national prominence. And in 1968, at the height
of America's war in Southeast Asia, students at San Francisco State College
formed the Third World Liberation Front and institutionalized the study of
racialized minorities in higher education.

Before the 1965 Immigration Act, most migrants to the United States came
from Europe, but by 1990 more than half the total were from Asia. Under the
act, national quotas that discriminated severely against Asians were replaced by
hemispheric limits and a preference system designed to encourage the immigration of professionals and skilled workers. Like civil rights advocates, proponents of the Immigration Act argued that as the leader of the "free world"
America had to repudiate racial discrimination. They did not, however, anticipate the racial composition of the new immigrant stream. Asian immigration
and resettlement were boosted by other legacies of the war against communism.
These included the 1975 Indochina Migration and Refugee Assistance Act, the
1980 Refugee Act, and the 1987 Amerasian Homecoming Act. The laws provided federal aid to states and local governments for Southeast Asian refugee
assistance, systematized refugee admission and incorporation, and allowed children born of Americans and Vietnamese, and certain of their family members,
to immigrate to the United States. As in the past, immigration controls continued to influence the nature of Asian American communities, and immigration
reform continued to increase their numbers and ethnic diversity dramatically.

Like African and Asian nationalists, Hawai'i's native peoples continually
waged a struggle for self-determination and sovereignty, which they lost in the
1893 overthrow of the Hawaiian monarchy. Hawaiian language and culture
persisted and flourished despite the physical and social decline of the Hawaiian
people. In 1968, the Kaiser Hawaii-Kai Development Company applied for and
received permission to clear land in O'ahu's Kalama Valley where they would
build a tourist complex, golf course, shopping facilities, and expensive apartments and homes. The sixty-seven families of Hawaiians, Portuguese, and Japanese who farmed the valley were given eviction notices, and in July 1970
bulldozers appeared and began razing the people's homes and farms. Kokua
Kalama, a group of valley residents and others opposed to the development,
resisted the bulldozing. Several of its members were charged with trespassing
and were arrested. The issue gained media attention. At a rally of nearly a
thousand people at the state capitol in October 1970, Kokua Kalama demanded
that the Kaiser Company's plan for the valley be brought to a halt and that the
valley be left for the benefit of the evicted families. "There is a lot at stake in
Kalama Valley for the farmers, Hawaiians, local people, and the environment,"
Kokua Kalama declared. "What is happening to Kalama is a symptom of the
disease which is ravaging the islands and its local inhabitants."[10]

The Kalama Valley protesters lost their demands and the Kaiser Company built its luxury resort and houses, but the struggle over land that confronted the power of large corporations galvanized Hawaiians and their supporters to work toward the idea of Hawaiian self-determination. Groups like the Residents of Halawa Housing in 1971, the Waiahole-Waikane Community Association in 1974, and the fishermen on Mokauea Island in 1975 contested evictions by the state and private companies. The Aboriginal Lands of Hawaiian Ancestry (ALOHA) was organized in 1972 to secure from Congress reparations for Hawaiians based on the precedent of the Alaska Native Claims Settlement Act of 1971, whereby the federal government returned land and paid a cash settlement to Alaska's natives. ALOHA asked Stewart Udall, former congressman and secretary of the interior and a sponsor of the Alaska Native Claims Settlement Act, to draft legislation for Hawaiian reparations. Introduced in 1974, the bill failed to elicit interest or action for years. Instead, Congress in 1983 appointed the Native Hawaiians Study Commission to ascertain the validity of the reparations claim, and after only six months of work, in the same year that another commission recommended redress and reparations for Japanese Americans, the Native Hawaiians Study Commission recommended against the claimants.

In 1974, Peggy Ha'o Ross founded 'Ohana O Hawai'i, noting that the Hawaiian people had never surrendered their sovereignty, even if Lili'uokalani did relinquish the throne. The group took their case of the illegal overthrow to the World Court at The Hague and to other international tribunals, and laid the basis for a declaration of Hawaiian sovereignty. The following year, Hawaiian activists landed on the island of Kaho'olawe, which the military had seized and used for bombing practice since World War II. The island was sacred to Hawaiians, the Protect Kaho'olawe 'Ohana declared, and should be restored and returned to the people. An American court agreed and ordered the military to restrict their bombing and to remove explosives and debris from parts of the island, and it allowed Hawaiians access to other areas of Kaho'olawe. In 1990, the United States suspended its bombing of the island. From 1977 through the 1980s, Hawaiians opposed state evictions and sought to reclaim certain beaches as their homes and as places for subsistence fishing. Drilling into the Kilauea volcano for geothermal energy was regarded as a desecration of the home of the goddess Pele, and other Hawaiians fought against that. The struggle for Hawaiian sovereignty has been over land, culture, and rights, and has led its advocates to seek redress as native and indigenous peoples within the United States and the international community.

The demand for self-determination was made by nationalists in Africa and Asia, by native Hawaiians, and by racialized minorities in the United States. But colonialism was an imperfect model for the condition and aspirations of Asian Americans who sought rights within the United States and not, for the most part, political independence or sovereignty. Their pursuit of rights as guaranteed by the U.S. Constitution was longstanding, as was their pursuit of inclusion, as immigrants and citizens, within the nation-state. They made their claims in the courts repeatedly, and as late as 1974 the U.S. Supreme Court ruled in favor of Chinese petitioners in *Lau* v. *Nichols*. The case involved Kinney Kinmon Lau and twelve others who in 1970 filed a class action suit on behalf of nearly 3,000 Chinese-speaking students against the San Francisco Unified School District, for failure to provide them special help in English acquisition. The Court agreed with the plaintiffs that "there is no equality of treatment merely by providing students with the same facilities, textbooks, teachers, and curriculum; for students who do not understand English are effectively foreclosed from any meaningful education."[11]

At other times the pursuit of rights took Asian Americans not only to the courts but also Congress, as in the movement for justice for Japanese Americans held in concentration camps during World War II. The successful campaign in 1971 to repeal Title II of the 1950 Internal Security Act provided the impetus for various redress and reparations efforts during the 1970s and 1980s. In 1976, President Gerald Ford rescinded Executive Order 9066, and he issued a presidential pardon to Iva Toguri, the alleged "Tokyo Rose," the following year. In 1980, Congress and President Jimmy Carter formed the Commission on the Wartime Relocation and Internment of Civilians, and three years later the commission found that the wartime detention was "a grave injustice." It recommended a formal apology from Congress, presidential pardons for those who were convicted of resisting the mass removal orders, and $20,000 to each Japanese American survivor who had been confined. The Civil Rights Act of 1988 adopted those recommendations, and President Ronald Reagan signed the bill into law. Also during the 1980s, attorneys for Gordon Hirabayashi, Fred Korematsu, and Minoru Yasui sought to overturn their wartime convictions based on a writ of *coram nobis* that allowed a reopening of cases because evidence and false statements made in the original trials had been suppressed. A judge dismissed Yasui's petition in 1984 and Yasui died before he could appeal, but another court vacated Korematsu's conviction that same year, and in 1988, after an appeal, the court reversed Hirabayashi's conviction.

Violence against Asians continued as in the past. This included several racially motivated murders. In 1982, two white automobile factory workers murdered Vincent Chin in Detroit. In a striptease bar, his assailants reportedly called the Chinese American a "Jap" and blamed him for the loss of jobs in the automobile industry, and they searched for Chin after he and his friends had left the bar. Finding him, one held Chin as the other beat him with a baseball bat. Chin died of his injuries four days later. Brought to trial, the two defendants pleaded guilty to manslaughter and were each sentenced to three years' probation and fined $3,780. The brutal murder and light sentence shocked and infuriated Asian Americans, and Chin's mother, Lily, appealed for help in securing justice for her dead son. Chinese Americans, joined by Fili-pino, Japanese, and Korean Americans, took the lead in forming American Citizens for Justice. The coalition's object of equality and justice for Vincent Chin drew support from African Americans, Latinos, Arab and Italian Ameri-cans, women, and religious organizations. After meetings, demonstrations, and appeals, a 1983 federal grand jury found the two men guilty of violating Vincent Chin's right to enjoy a public place, and the next year a federal jury found one of the two guilty of having violated Chin's civil rights but acquitted the other. The lone conviction, however, was overturned in a retrial in 1987.

In other racially motivated attacks by whites on Asian Americans, Navroze Mody, an Asian Indian, died in 1987 in Jersey City, New Jersey; Jim (Ming Hai) Loo, a Chinese, died in 1989 in Raleigh, North Carolina; and Hung Truong, a Vietnamese, died in 1990 in Houston, Texas. On January 17, 1989, a gunman dressed in military fatigue and armed with an AK47 assault rifle shot and killed five Asian American children—four Cambodian and one Vietnamese—and wounded twenty in their schoolyard in Stockton, California. At the time nearly sixty percent of the school's enrollment was Southeast Asian children, and the gunman had expressed particular animosity toward Southeast Asians, Califor-nia's attorney general found. The Los Angeles riots of 1992 especially targeted Asian Americans and their property in the aftermath of the trial of white police officers charged in the beating of Rodney King, an African American. The multiracial disturbance, involving Latinos, African Americans, and whites, left 58 dead, 2,383 injured, and more than 17,000 arrested. Total property damage has been estimated at up to $1 billion, and about half of the 4,500 businesses damaged (2,300) belonged to Korean Americans who lost between $350 and $400 million. Rooted in poverty and injustices, the civil unrest was expressed racially, in large part, against Asian and Korean Americans.

Laws and their enforcement defended as well as victimized Asian Americans. That was evident throughout their history. Encouraged by politicians, anti-foreignism found fertile ground in California and across the nation during the 1980s and 1990s. Congress passed the Immigration Reform and Control Act of 1986, creating an amnesty program to legalize undocumented immigrants and establishing employer sanctions for employers who hired undocumented work-ers. As a consequence, employers discriminated against Latina/os and Asians in the hiring process, as shown in a 1990 report by the government's General Accounting Office. California passed Proposition 187 in 1994 and Proposition 209 in 1996. Proposition 187 denied basic rights and services to undocumented immigrants, including access to the public schools and non-emergency health care and social services from government providers. Further, all citizens and non-citizens were required to prove their lawful immigration status to obtain those rights and services. Aimed at undocumented immigrants, Proposition 187, like the Immigration Reform and Control Act of 1986, discriminated especially against Asians and Latina/os, on whom fell the burden of proof of their legal standing in the United States. Race-neutral in language, the law discriminated nonetheless in its impact. Similarly, Proposition 209, advocating a "color-blind" society, aims to eliminate state-sponsored affirmative action programs, even while racial inequality persists. In a federal version of California's Proposition 187, Congress passed the Illegal Immigration Reform and Immigrant Responsibility Act of 1996. The law sought to reduce the number of undocumented immigrants by denying them federal entitlements and augmenting the border patrol, and it established minimum income requirements for sponsors of legal immigrants. The law had adverse effects on Latina/os and Asians as immigrants and as frequent sponsors of immigrants, commonly family members.

After the Soviet Union's collapse in 1991, the cold war mentality found new archenemies in China and North Korea, which rose to the fore as threats to the United States. The 1999 arrest and imprisonment of physicist Wen Ho Lee for allegedly mishandling restricted government information at the Los Alamos National Laboratory appeared to many Asian Americans to be a case of racial profiling and a fear of China. Although an extensive investigation cleared Lee of the charge that he passed classified or restricted information to China, the allegation persisted in the media, encouraged by federal prosecutors who charged Lee with improperly downloading data with intent to harm the United States. According to a report by a Department of Energy task force in January 2000, Asian American and Pacific Islander scientists complained that they were being singled out for investigation because of their race, and the number of Asian applicants for positions at the national weapons laboratories, especially at Los Alamos, declined after Lee's arrest and calls by two Asian American educational organizations to boycott the laboratories. The Lee case and the controversy it has sparked have deep roots in American history, in which the particular stereotype of Asians as a monolithic ethnic group perilous to whites and the nation have been played out along with the more general fears of non-whites, immigrants, and foreigners. The story is both old and new.

NOTES

1. *Hippocrates*, trans. W. H. S. Jones (Cambridge, Mass.: Harvard University Press, 1923), I: 105–33.

2. *Arrian's History of the Expedition of Alexander the Great, and Conquest of Persia*, trans. John Rooke (London: W. McDowall, 1813), 42, 112, 117, 123, 146.

3. *The Travels of Marco Polo the Venetian* (London: J. M. Dent, 1908), xi.

4. Henry H. Hart, *Marco Polo: Venetian Adventurer* (Norman: University of Oklahoma Press, 1967), 117, 135.

5. Quoted in John Kuo Wei Tchen, *New York before Chinatown: Orientalism and*

the Shaping of American Culture, 1776–1882 (Baltimore: Johns Hopkins University Press, 1999), 39.

6. Cited in Ronald Takaki, *Pau Hana: Plantation Life and Labor in Hawaii, 1835–1920* (Honolulu: University of Hawaii Press, 1983), 18.

7. Ian F. Haney López, *White by Law: The Legal Construction of Race* (New York: New York University Press, 1996), 91.

8. Ronald Takaki, *Strangers from a Different Shore: A History of Asian Americans* (Boston: Little, Brown, 1989), 368.

9. Ibid., 363.

10. "Save Kalama Valley—Hawaii," *Black Panther* 6:15 (May 8, 1971), 1.

11. L. Ling-chi Wang, "*Lau* v. *Nichols*: History of a Struggle for Equal and Quality Education," in *Counterpoint: Perspectives on Asian America*, ed. Emma Gee (Los Angeles: UCLA Asian American Studies Center, 1976), 240.

Chapter 2

PERIODIZATION

Chronologies are laden with assumptions. They are not simple timelines agreed upon by everyone. They are creations peculiar to the historian who concocts them. They reflect, of course, a line with a starting and end point as opposed to a cyclical conception of time and history. As linear texts they suggest, especially during our age, evolution, development, progress—a teleology. The past is prologue; the future, destiny. A chronology's starting and end points should alert the reader to the perspective from which the timeline was constructed, and to all of the assumptions on which the timeline is based. Historians write of the past from the present. And the events historians choose to include and exclude from their chronologies reveal the significances they attach to them. Significance, of course, is a matter of judgment.

Periodization builds on the work of chronologies. In that sense, historical periods are discrete blocks of time, with starting and end points that are characterized by certain features distinctive to each period. Periodization is helpful in that it organizes a long, apparently unconnected series of events, and highlights both the disjunctions and continuities of history. To show the assumptions at work in periodizing Asian American history, I will devise several periodizations based on different sets of valuations. At times those assumptions go unstated, as in what I will call the standard periodization.

The standard assumes a U.S. base, where the nation-state exists with its citizens and its institutions. Asians derive from over there, away from the United States, and come here to the United States as immigrants, as strangers to our shores. They interact, natives (citizens) and aliens, and the foreigners become Americans through assimilation or acculturation. In this narrative, the processes of immigration and the means by which the nation-state is constituted are underscored. It is a nationalist narrative. And immigration, both closed and open, structures the nation and its constituent parts—in this case, Asian America.

STANDARD PERIODIZATION

1848–1882. The Period of Immigration. Characterized by open immigration. Chinese men created bachelor societies in California and along the West Coast. These immigrants were "pushed" by necessity (poverty in China) and "pulled" by attractions (opportunities in the United States).

1882–1965. The Period of Exclusion. Characterized by exclusionary laws that barred successively Chinese, Japanese, Koreans, Asian Indians, and Filipinos. These Asians faced racism and discrimination both in institutional and social practice, and within those contexts sought to build communities.

1965–present. The Post-Exclusion Period. Open immigration allowed Asian communities to grow dramatically in numbers and ethnic diversity (involving especially South and Southeast Asians), and the post–civil rights era provided unprecedented opportunities for Asian Americans in housing, business and employment, and education.

World War II sometimes poses a break within the standard periodization in that Japanese Americans continued to live under exclusion in America's concentration camps while Chinese, Asian Indians, and Filipinos experienced some gains during those years. Still, immigration quotas severely limited the mobility of those groups.

The standard periodization relies on the racialization of those classed as "Asians" and on its manifestations in immigration and citizenship. Further, racialization turns on the relations between those named "whites" and those named "Asians." But that racial binary fails to capture the fullness of the U.S. racial formation. How would that periodization change if we conceived of it in terms of the relations between "blacks" and "Asians"?

"BLACKS" AND "ASIANS" PERIODIZATION

5th century–16th century. The Period of Interaction. Asian traders from South Asia, Southeast Asia, and China visited East Africa as far south as Madagascar. Some settled along the East African coast; others introduced cultural objects and food crops. Africans traded commodities and slaves, some of whom rise to become leaders in Asia.

16th century–19th century. The Period of Bonded Labor. Europeans traded with, then colonized and enslaved, Africans and Asians they encountered in Indian and Atlantic Ocean trade and in their colonies in Africa and Asia. Europeans transported Africans to the Americas to labor as slaves in the plantations of the New World. After the end of the African slave trade in the early nineteenth century, they replaced Africans with Asian Indian and Chinese indentured workers called "coolies."

1861–1877. Civil War and Reconstruction. Of great moment to all Americans, the Civil War and Reconstruction engaged economies and systems of labor in the North and South, ideologies and cultures, and white supremacy and African American aspirations for freedom. In 1865, the Thirteenth Amendment abolishing slavery was ratified; in 1868, the Fourteenth Amendment, conferring equal protection and citizenship by birth was ratified.

1896–1954. The Period of Segregation. The U.S. Supreme Court decisions *Plessy* v. *Ferguson* (1896) and *Brown* v. *Board of Education* (1954) defined the limits of the period of segregation. During this time, both Africans and Asians lived and labored under regimes of racial separation, both institutionalized and de facto, and they challenged segregation in various ways, including through the courts. Laws directed at African Americans were applied to Asians, and Asian and African American challenges built on the precedents established by each group. At the same time, there were differences and conflicts between African and Asian Americans.

1954–present. The Civil Rights Period. The struggle for civil rights engages African Americans but also other Americans, including Native Americans, Latina/os, Asian Americans, and whites. At the same time, some whites characterize African Americans as "problem minorities" and Asian Americans as "model minorities." Those perceptions heighten the antagonisms between those racialized groups, despite their wide diversities and their frequently common interests.

Although racialized as a single group, Asian Americans are ethnically diverse and often without unitary pasts or cultures. In fact, many hold racialist notions of one another and have fought wars of conquest and colonization with each other. I will present two periodizations to illustrate how they differ from each other with respect to particular ethnic groups that in the United States are rendered as undifferentiated "Asian Americans."

SOUTH ASIAN PERIODIZATION

1498–1947. Period of European Expansion and Colonialism. Vasco da Gama reached India in 1498 and began the period of European influence over the subcontinent. The Portuguese settled Goa as their principal Asian base, and the British traded with Gujarat in 1612. The British rose in power and by 1800 became the dominant force in India. Some Indian troops rebelled in 1857, but Britain consolidated its hold by dissolving the English East India Company and installing the British government as India's sovereign. Indian resistance and a swelling nationalism ended British rule in 1947.

1780–1908. Period of Migrant Labor. In the context of colonialism and expansion, Europeans used South Asian slaves and indentures on board their ships, and transported them to ports such as Salem, Massachusetts, as early as the 1780s. They also recruited South Asian laborers to fill the void left by the abolition of the African slave trade and of slavery in the Americas. The first contingent of South Asian indentured laborers arrived in British Guiana in 1838, and the British recruited Asian Indians, especially from the Punjab, to work in Africa and the Pacific and to serve in the British Army. Following the circuits drawn by the British empire, South Asians migrated to Canada and the United States as students but mainly as workers. In 1917, the U.S. Congress barred immigration from South Asia.

1908–1965. Period of Exclusion. Canada restricted South Asian immigration by requiring continuous passage from India to Canada in 1908, and it denied entry of the *Komagata Maru* migrants in 1914. The U.S. barred South Asians in 1917. During this period, South Asians attended school, labored, built religious and secular communities, and worked for India's independence. South Asian men formed homosocial relations, called for wives from India, and married African and Mexican American women. Sikh, Muslim, and Hindu temples formed the nuclei of communities, and racism and segregation, although challenged by South Asians, determined much of the opportunities in citizenship, occupation, housing, and marriage.

1965–present. Period of Expansion. Asian Indians increased from about 50,000 before 1965 to 815,500 in 1990. Unlike the migration of Asian Indians from earlier periods, much of this migration involved the professional classes, nearly equal numbers of men and women, and emigrants from Africa, Latin America, and the Caribbean. Burgeoning business clusters appear in major U.S. cities and suburbs, and South Asians make significant impacts in science and technology. Despite these indications of achievement, many South Asians labor in high-risk, low-paid service industries, and are the objects of anti-Asian hatred.

KOREAN PERIODIZATION

1876–1945. Period of Colonization. Korea signed the Treaty of Kanghwa in 1876 with Japan and opened Korean ports to trade. The U.S., Britain, Germany, Russia, Italy, and France signed similar treaties and gained concessions in Korea. Protestant missionaries entered Korea in 1884, and gained great numbers of converts and political influence. Japan defeated China and claimed dominance in Korea from 1895 to 1910 when Japan annexed Korea as its formal colony. Japan drained Korea of its food crops and natural resources including coal, iron, and timber to fuel its industrial development. Japan denied Koreans an education, and restricted their employment to menial labor. Korean resistance was brutally crushed, but laid the basis for a strong Korean independence movement.

1895–1905. Period of Migrant Labor. Japan's colonialism compelled Koreans to migrate to Japan to escape poverty, repression, and forced labor. The Hawaiian Sugar Planters' Association sent a labor recruiter to Korea in 1902, and with the help of American missionaries shipped more than 7,000 Koreans to work on Hawai'i's plantations. About 1,000 left for henequen plantations in Mexico. Korean labor migration ended in 1905, when word of abuse of Koreans in Mexico reached the Korean government and Japan pressured Korea to stop the traffic to Hawai'i.

1907–1965. Period of Exclusion. The United States restricted migration from Korea, a colony of Japan, in a move related to U.S. exclusion of Japanese immigrants beginning with the 1907 Gentlemen's Agreement. Koreans arrived as families, Korean men married through the "picture bride" system, and Koreans established communities and churches in Hawai'i and on the U.S. mainland. Political refugees, students, and Korean Americans formed organizations for the freedom of Korea from Japanese colonialism and were effective in promoting and establishing the independent nation after Japan's defeat in 1945. Cold war politics divided Korea, and the Korean War allowed Korean wives of U.S. servicemen entry into the United States.

1965–present. Period of Expansion. Before 1965, Korean Americans numbered about 45,000, but after the liberating immigration law in 1990 their population stands at almost 800,000. Whereas in the earlier period of Korean immigration to the United States more men than women immigrated, now more women immigrated. Among the new immigrants are substantial numbers of professionals and the highly educated. Korean American business enclaves grow in cities. These formed the major targets of rioters in Los Angeles in 1992. Despite their achievements, Korean Americans face glass ceilings and anti-Asian violence.

Because of its very nature, Asian American studies privileges race and ethnicity above all else. As a consequence, other aspects of the U.S. social formation that conspire with racialization to define and wield privilege and want are slighted. Gender is one of those intimates of race, together with sexuality, class, and citizenship, and yields a periodization configuration different from those of race and ethnicity.

GENDER PERIODIZATION

Beginnings–1819. Period of Patriarchy. Characterized by a predominance of men over women in many Asian societies, along with the separation between domestic and public spheres. Variations, however, abounded. There were differences of ethnicity and class position, and women's resistances moderated and reshaped men's privileges and powers over time. Gender relations were contested and struggled over constantly, and were never unbending and rigid as in "tradition" and "customary law."

1819–present. Period of Greater Freedoms. Women's involvement in the independence movements, the nationalist and Christian rhetoric of freedom, migration to the United States, and women's rise in economic importance contribute to more equality between women and men. Hawaiian women ended the *kapu* system in 1819, and Chinese American women garment workers struck against the National Dollar Stores in 1938. At the same time, Chinese American women were excluded in 1875, women achieved the vote only in 1920, they lost their U.S. citizenship in 1922 if they married "aliens ineligible to citizenship," and they continue to face discrimination and sexual violence.

Periodizations hide as much as they reveal because they are generalizations. They foreground selected aspects of time periods, and obscure other events and processes. They also suggest significances without consideration of the assumptions that underlie them. But periodizations are useful insofar as they help to order history and historical phenomena and to offer explanations for them. Asian American periodizations are complex because their subject matter— "Asian Americans"—are multiply constituted and articulated.

PART 2

Historical Debates

INTRODUCTION

In this section, I summarize debates within the historical literature and present opposing views from historians and scholars on the following subjects:

1. Hawai'i's population before European contact
2. Hawaiians and Captain James Cook
3. Migration
4. The anti-Chinese movement
5. America's concentration camps

These are not all properly "historical" debates engaged by historians, but are problems in Asian American studies across the disciplines, including prominently anthropology and sociology. Still, they bear particular relevance to history and thus their inclusion here.

Readers should recognize that these are my summaries of selected authors. They are not the authors' words, except where indicated by quotations. I encourage readers to consult the works directly to ascertain the full force of the argument. But I have tried to remain faithful to the original texts in the interpretations I offer of their salient arguments. I have thus reproduced the original spellings, even when incorrect, archaic, or inconsistent (e.g., Taiping, Tai Ping, and T'ai-p'ing, and DeWitt and De Witt), and left intact historical inaccuracies made by authors. However, I have chosen to update certain words like "negro" to avoid offensive terms and conform to current usage.

I engage other "historical" debates in Part 3, "Emerging Themes." For various reasons, these debates are less developed than those cited in this section but are of potential significance to the field in the future.

Chapter 1

HAWAI'I'S POPULATION BEFORE
EUROPEAN CONTACT

The question of Hawai'i's population before the arrival of Europeans in 1778 is the subject of this debate. European visitors to the islands provided guesses that formed the bases for subsequent scholarly interpretation on the matter. Lieutenant James King, a member of British Captain James Cook's expedition to the islands, which led to the first encounter between Europeans and Hawaiians, estimated a population of 500,000 Hawaiians but later revised that figure to 400,000. Because his estimate was based on a rich body of detail, which included his method of calculation, his assumptions, and totals for each of the eight inhabited islands, King's enumeration became a standard against which others based their population estimates of Hawaiians before contact with Europeans. Some supported his 400,000 estimate; others criticized it.

Robert C. Schmitt, the state's statistician, in 1971 produced his own figure, which became the new standard. Schmitt cites Captain George Dixon, who visited Hawai'i in 1787. Dixon claimed that King's estimate was greatly exaggerated, and proposed a total of 200,000. Schmitt also notes that William Bligh, another member of Cook's voyage to Hawai'i, estimated the population at 242,200, while Russian Captain V. M. Golovnin in 1778 ventured a figure of 200,000. Schmitt sides with the lower figures because of the common tendency toward overestimation. He concludes that the numbers supplied by Dixon, Bligh, and Golovnin, along with totals for various islands by contemporary

European travelers, suggest a precontact population of less than 250,000, perhaps 200,000.

Inspired by recent developments in pre-Columbian population studies, David E. Stannard, professor of American studies at the University of Hawai'i, applies both internal and external critiques to the historical evidence and its interpretations in his study of Hawaiian demography. He notes that over the last twenty-five years historians and anthropologists have arrived at the conclusion that earlier population estimates grossly underestimated the numbers of America's indigenous peoples, and that their upward revisions have led to the companion view that the population collapse following contact with Europeans was immense. Stannard laments that the lessons from those fields have not intruded on the arrested site of Pacific island studies. He proposes a radical break from that static past, and estimates a population of at least 800,000 on the eve of contact with Europeans. Stannard's analysis relies on a critical reassessment of King's assumptions, the application of a population growth model, a consideration of Hawai'i's resources and the carrying capacity of those resources, a comparison of population declines among native peoples, and anecdotal evidence that point to vastly larger populations before the arrival of Europeans.

Eleanor C. Nordyke, a demographer, objects to Stannard's easy dismissal of earlier studies written by some of the most prominent scholars in Hawaiian studies, and especially the work of Robert C. Schmitt. The latter, she states, is a judicious scholar whose conclusions merit greater regard than Stannard's recent visitation on the subject. She cites population figures from Cook and Abraham Fornander, a nineteenth-century historian, to show how Stannard's numbers are greatly inflated, and also draws from archaeology and anthropology to question some of his assertions about locations of settlements and annual growth rates. Nordyke points out that modern Hawai'i imports about 80 percent of its food supply. How could the ancient Hawaiians, with primitive technologies, support the same number of people as Hawai'i in the 1970s?

Schmitt explains that, when in 1971 he suggested that Hawai'i's precontact population was no more than 250,000, he was attempting to reconcile pre-1832 estimates with the 1831–1832 census counts. Like Nordyke, Schmitt appeals to eminent scholars who agree with the figure of 300,000 or less figure. He notes the counterintuitive nature of Stannard's claim that only in the 1970s did Hawai'i's population reach the total he proposes for 1778. Moreover, Schmitt continues, Stannard relies on generalizations and comparisons that, by neglecting the complexities of the data and the uniqueness of Hawai'i's environment and history, could easily mislead. According to Schmitt's argument, population densities must account for specifics ignored by Stannard; postcontact declines varied greatly from place to place; census figures are frequently unreliable; and mortality rates, life expectancies, and other variables intrude on population projections of the future and past. Without firm facts, an accurate count of Hawai'i's population in 1778 is impossible.

As Stannard reveals, there is more at stake in this debate than mere numbers. An argument deployed by Nordyke and Schmitt, who share the widely accepted view, arises from a defense of their work and that of their intellectual community. They are quick to note that eminent scholars like Romanzo Adams and Andrew Lind share their estimate that the precontact population was 300,000 or less. That estimate, Nordyke adds, was arrived at only after years of careful study and consideration. Folded within this debate, besides the politics of ideas and scholarly traditions, is the politics of race. The higher the population of a native people, the greater the horror that, following contact with Europeans, this population would decline through disease, wars, enslavement, famine, and removals. Some charge that the notion of a pre-European paradise and post-European decline is racist, and affords scant agency to native peoples. Likewise, they add, to blame Europeans for the massive, postcontact population decline is inverted racism and exemplifies liberal guilt. Others respond that ideology should vacate the debate, and that the search for truth should be preeminent and uncompromising.

THE STANDARD VIEW

Schmitt published a research note, "New Estimates of the Pre-censal Population of Hawaii," in 1971. Although modest in size and intention, the population estimates that were presented in the report became widely accepted as the standard figures. It is impossible to know, Schmitt begins, Hawai'i's population in 1778 when Captain Cook first met Hawaiians. The first relatively thorough census, undertaken in 1831–1832, counted 130,000 persons. Early travelers propose figures of 200,000 to 400,000, and later historians, on the flimsiest evidence, surmised totals as low as 100,000. Just as it is difficult to determine the precontact population, it is difficult to determine how much the population declined, and then how much the decline resulted from disease, warfare, famine, sterility, infanticide, human sacrifice, exposure, or social disorganization.

The first population estimates come from Cook and his officers. Drawing on his observations of Kealakekua Bay, James King, Cook's successor, arrived at a persons-per-shoreline-mile figure. He estimated the number of miles of inhabited shoreline and, making allowance for inland settlers, calculated a total population of 400,000. William Bligh, who failed to record his method of calculation, guessed 242,200. Dixon, who landed in Hawai'i in 1787, thought King's estimate too high and offered 200,000. It is obvious that all of these totals are at best crude guesses. Undercounts can easily mar even systematic census efforts, and abandoned villages and fields can lead to conclusions of massive depopulation, and hence to overestimates of previous populations. Because of that danger of overestimation, the "weight of evidence" supports the lower and not higher figures.[1]

Missionaries conducted the first census in 1831–1832, although they discounted the islands of Moloka'i, Lanai, and Kahoolawe. But by accepting this census as the baseline, by modifying the data "in the light of contemporary estimates and known historical developments,"[2] and then by adding numbers from an 1850 census for the missing three islands, one can derive a relative population distribution among the islands and apply it to the lower figures that Dixon and others gave for 1778. The final figures are expressed in a range, underscoring their speculative nature: The population of Hawai'i in 1778 ranged from a low of 200,000 to a high of 250,000.

These new totals indicate that over the fifty-four years from 1778 to 1832 Hawai'i suffered severe depopulation, but not of the magnitude claimed by previous writers. A major factor was declining fertility due to sterility caused by venereal disease, as revealed by statistical data from the 1830s and 1840s. High infant mortality was another important factor. There is disagreement over the extent of infanticide during the first half of the nineteenth century. Emigration depleted the male population; many Hawaiians enlisting as seamen on board whalers and trade vessels. Contrary to traditional belief, epidemics, war, famine, and human sacrifice had negligible effects on depopulation.

A VAST UNDERCOUNT

In his book *Before the Horror* (1989), Stannard proposes that Schmitt and others vastly underestimated the population of Hawai'i's native peoples before 1778. Stannard notes similar underestimates in the Americas, where, scholars less than twenty-five years ago commonly believed, native peoples numbered between 8 and 14 million before the arrival of Christopher Columbus. He reports that, by 1989, the usual figures cited were up to ten times as high. Thus, recent scholarship has revised pre-Columbian population figures upward, and has also multiplied the horror of the population collapse following the arrival of Europeans. Stannard observes that the controversy surrounding these new demographic estimates not only brought intellectual fermentation to the field, but also increased scholarly sophistication.

By contrast, Pacific studies scholars have been content with restatements of old figures and, in fact, have tended to reduce rather than increase the numbers. That those discussions frequently carry political meanings is evident in the writing of New Zealand historian K. R. Howe, who claims that the idea of a post-European collapse of Pacific populations is a "racist" falsehood manufactured to assuage liberal guilt. Howe contends that "inverted racism" assumes

that natives lacked the intelligence to avoid or protect themselves against imported diseases, and also that it betrays a prejudice against the West. "Unfortunately," Stannard concludes, "such muddled logic is now common among
Pacific island scholars writing on this topic." Demographic studies on Hawai'i
have been largely immune to changes over the last fifty years in Amercian
historical demography. "It is time for Pacific island scholars to take another look
at their own long-settled ideas on the subject."[3]

Previous estimates of Hawai'i's population rely on intuitive readings of extremely suspect accounts by European visitors to the islands. A widely cited
figure is 400,000 by King, a member of the 1778 Cook expedition that initiated
European contact with Hawaiians. His estimate was based on several questionable assumptions. He noted that only the coasts were inhabited and not the
interiors, and claimed that there were no towns, only small villages dispersed
along the coasts. He then enumerated the population by taking the number of
houses and multiplying it by six, because he estimated that on average there
were six individuals per house. About nine years later, Dixon, another visitor to
Hawai'i, attacked King's figure as too high, and proposed 200,000 as a more
accurate number. Present-day demographers agree that these early estimates are
mere guesses and are based on questionable assumptions.

Schmitt, the state's leading demographer, ventured a 1778 population of no
more than 250,000 but later revised that to less than 300,000. Although skeptical
of the estimates of contemporary European observers, Schmitt, without sub-
stantiating it, arrives at a figure between that of King and Dixon. He relies, for
example, on the axiom that European travelers generally overestimate indigenous populations and that demographers generally overestimated their postcontact declines. To the contrary, most scholars today believe that both groups
underreported both the true magnitude of native populations and of the disaster
that was visited on them. And in the end, Schmitt's estimates depend on the
very sources he criticizes—contemporary European visitors to Hawai'i.

King's population figure, criticized by Schmitt as too high, is susceptible to
skepticism and should be revised upward, not downward. His house count and
estimate of six individuals per house ignore the "many" poor people living in
caves, and others have given higher house counts than King.[4] In addition, early
travelers report more than six persons living in houses that were not uniform
but varied widely in size.

King visited only the leeward, dry sides of Hawai'i and Kaua'i and not their
windward, wetter sides. Lacking water, the leeward sides would support smaller
populations than their wetter sides. Water sustained people and their livestock,
and it was used to irrigate fields that sustained larger, denser settlements on the
windward side of the islands. In the wetter areas, Hawaiians developed extremely sophisticated agricultural complexes that supported greater numbers of
people. King landed on the arid, more thinly populated parts of the islands of

Hawai'i and Kaua'i and underestimated significantly both their populations, and by extrapolation undercounted the entire island chain.

Cook's ships missed O'ahu, which contains nearly half the island chain's prime agricultural land. He also failed to visit Maui's densely populated eastern coast, which had the largest religious shrine in all of Oceania. King's observations were partial at best. Also, his assumption of peopled coasts and empty interiors was completely incorrect. There is ample archaeological evidence to prove that the fertile valleys and lush uplands were well cultivated and thickly populated.

King's estimate of 400,000 is thus a vast undercount. When his false assumptions about numbers of houses, individuals per house, and the leeward sides of islands and their interiors are corrected, and when in addition the islands he missed entirely are taken into account, Hawai'i's population before contact with Europeans easily jumps from 800,000 to more than one million. Admittedly, those reconsiderations of King's assumptions might have led to exaggerations, and this new population estimate will seem absurd to those who believe the numbers advanced by King or Schmitt. But that was the same reaction that greeted the upward revisions of pre-Columbian populations in the Americas, and this new estimate of Hawai'i's peoples is based on conservative figures reached through a critique of the best contemporary evidence of the 1778 population. This is the same method relied on by Schmitt, and any present estimate must by necessity begin with King.

Another way to test the possibility of the new estimate of 800,000 or more is to ask how an initial, tiny group of Polynesians could have grown to that size by 1778. Hawai'i was one of the last areas settled by Polynesians—around the first century C.E. There might have been another in-migration in the twelfth century, but most of the islands' peoples derived from the original 100 or so. As deliberate settlers who charted their way across the Pacific, they likely arrived with a sex ratio that favored reproduction—i.e., a fairly equal number of women and men. A population model appropriate to Pacific islands assumes 0.9-percent growth each year for the first 300 years, and a subsequent growth rate of 0.52 percent per annum. Those conservative figures would yield a doubling of population at least every six generations. Put into operation, the model projects that Hawai'i's population would be about 6,400 people during the seventh century, and more than 800,000 by the end of the seventeenth century. In 1778, the population would total nearly 1.5 million. This does not account for the in-migration of the twelfth century. Thus, the most conservative population growth models for Pacific islands show that the original group of settlers in Hawai'i could have easily reached the 800,000 figure by 1778.

Crucial to the support of such numbers is the level of available resources or the carrying capacity of the islands. The question is complex and requires detailed analysis of each island and its climate, soil conditions, specific crops grown and their yields under various conditions, other available foods, individual caloric requirements, and so forth. In the absence of that data, it is still safe to state that the islands could amply provide for 800,000 or more people in 1778. That would mean a population density of about 124 persons per square mile and, if 90 percent lived along the coasts, a density there of about 903 per square mile.

Those figures are not unusual for pre-European populations. Vastly different environments such as Peru's coast, the New Guinea highlands, and the Yucatan lowlands supported, respectively, populations of 3,800 per coastal mile, 50 to 750 per square mile, and 600 to 5,000 per square mile. The people in Peru depended almost entirely on the sea for their food, and those in New Guinea and Yucatan, on agriculture. None of those areas had both of the options available to Hawaiians—the resources of both the land and sea. Further, islands can support huge populations like that of Hispaniola, with an estimated 271 per square mile, and of Tapituea in Polynesia, with 500 per square mile.

In addition, estimates by nineteenth-century missionaries would imply that Hawaiian farmers alone could support between 1,300 and 20,000 persons per cultivated square mile, or more than one million people with less than 2 percent of the land under taro cultivation. And that projection disregards the vast support capacity of the sea. Pre-European Hawai'i likely had a population density of about 125 to 150 people per square mile. That range is consistent with the population ranges of Tahiti and the Marquesas, Hawai'i's closest island cousins, and with that of eastern Polynesia, where the population densities spanned from 100 to 1,000 persons per square mile. If Hawaiians possessed the same agricultural and fishing skills of other Polynesians, clearly Hawai'i was capable of supporting a population of at least 800,000.

Just one hundred years after European contact, the Hawaiian population had declined to less than 48,000. This represents a catastrophic loss—whether using for a baseline, pre-European population the figures supplied by King or those by Schmitt. The first credible missionary census found a total native population of about 130,000 in 1832, and 47,508 in 1878. There are ample correspondences in the Americas and Pacific islands. In fact, population disasters of this magnitude were the rule rather than the exception during the years of first contact between Europeans and indigenous peoples. Wars and enslavement led to population declines, but the overwhelming cause was disease introduced to native peoples who had no immunities. Extrapolating from global figures, scholars estimate a depopulation ratio of at least 20 to 1 over the first 100 years of contact. In Hawai'i, that would yield a pre-European population of 800,000 to 950,000. Neither King's nor Schmitt's figures conform to the 20-to-1 ratio of population decline for all indigenous peoples.

Finally, missionaries estimated vastly higher populations in the past than populations in the mid-nineteenth century. An extrapolation from those admittedly unreliable sources would put Hawai'i's precontact population in the range between 750,000 and 800,000. Although merely suggestive and anecdotal, these sources, along with testimonies from Hawaiians, point to pre-European populations exceeding those totals proposed by King and Schmitt.

DEFENDING SCHMITT

Nordyke comments on Stannard's claim of a vast undercount in the traditional literature. She notes the futility of relying on present-day projections of past populations, because they are inconclusive and speculative "in the absence of deliberate anthropologic and archaeologic investigation and without an authentic census or sample survey."[5] Stannard's conclusions, she observes, contradict all estimates of the past two centuries by Pacific voyagers and historians and demographers. In particular, Stannard questions, even denigrates the work of Schmitt, the state statistician, who has conducted meticulous research on Hawai'i for more than forty years; has worked with Romanzo Adams, Andrew Lind, and leading scholars in the field; and has published numerous, well-documented books and articles. Schmitt is cautious in his claims and recognizes his assumptions and limitations in the absence of facts. He admits the softness of his estimates for precontact Hawai'i, but his breadth of knowledge and his company with other scholars gives greater credibility to his work and population figures than to Stannard's study.

Stannard's population figures are inflated "beyond reasonable estimate."[6] For example, he proposes that the tiny island of Ni'ihau had a precontact population between 3,650 and 7,774, whereas Schmitt and others suggest 500 to 1,000 people. Cook in 1778 reported that the island lacked water and fertile soil and that its inhabitants were thinly scattered about. There couldn't be more than 500 people on the island, he claimed. Likewise, Abraham Fornander, a nineteenth-century compiler of Polynesian history, disagrees with King's report of 54,000 inhabitants for Kaua'i and, by implication, with Stannard's 82,000. Cook's estimate of 30,000 inhabitants for Kaua'i, he wrote, was too high.

There is no archaeological evidence to support Stannard's claim that Hawaiians first settled the wetter, windward side of the islands before moving to the drier, leeward side. Instead, Hawaiians settled where they had access to water and shade, where the soil was receptive to cultivation, and where there were fish. And anthropologists agree that the commoners resided primarily along the coast, although the land divisions allowed them use of the upland for agriculture. Also, archaeologists do not believe that many Hawaiians lived inland or settled in dense numbers on the wet, windward side. Most people lived in small villages scattered along the coast. In addition, most of the major sites for chiefs' residences are on the dry, leeward sides of Hawai'i, Maui, Moloka'i, O'ahu, and Kaua'i.

Stannard's initial date of settlement, annual growth rate, and resulting total population are probably overstated. He claims that humans arrived in Hawai'i at least as early as the first century C.E., but archaeologists report that the first settlements can be traced back only as far as the fourth or fifth century C.E., and they are cautious about that estimate because of the paucity of excavated sites. And biometricians describe, instead of an unvarying annual growth as assumed by Stannard, a logistic of population increase that denies an unrestrained multiplication of numbers. Constrained initially by a low proportion of women, Hawaiians increased gradually but encountered changes with the introduction of disease from new immigrants, and with warfare. Other factors included homicide, accidents, abortion and infanticide, diseases, famine and drought, and lack of sanitation.

Hence, if Stannard's estimate of a precontact population is inflated, then his accompanying claim of its drastic decline is overstated. Schmitt's figures for 1778–1888 are probably more accurate. Also, depopulation was not the same for all islands. Both the archaeologist Kenneth Emory and the anthropologist Catherine Summers believe that Moloka'i, which had poor anchorage and therefore less contact with Europeans, did not suffer the same ravages of disease experienced by Hawaiians on the other islands. Instead, the decrease of Moloka'i's population was due largely to out-migration.

Finally, in the 1970s, when Hawai'i had a population approximately what Stannard proposes it was during the precontact period, it imported about 80 percent of its food supply. Could ancient Hawaiians have provided for a population that size using their primitive methods of farming and fishing? What about their water supply? Where is the evidence for water and food storage and distribution systems to accommodate so many people? And what about the burial sites for that enormous number of deceased? Until conclusive scientific data can provide answers to these questions, Stannard's thesis remains mere speculation. And the previous findings of authorities on Hawai'i's history and demography are more credible.

THE UNCERTAINTIES OF PROJECTIONS

Schmitt offers a measured reply to Stannard, whom he praises for his "impressive" work that "demands respect."[7] When Schmitt in 1971 suggested that Hawai'i's precontact population did not exceed 250,000, his primary purpose was to provide for individual islands pre-1832 estimates more consistent with the 1831–1832 census figures than were available from contemporary accounts. A secondary purpose was to move away from the traditional idea of depopulation through famine, war, epidemics, infanticide, and human sacrifice, and instead to stress the impact of low fertility (due to venereal disease, abortion, and other factors), high infant and adult mortality rates, and out-migration. Contemporary witnesses are notoriously unreliable and they commonly exaggerate earlier populations. Abandoned villages and fields, for example, might have been evidence not of overall depopulation but rather of internal migration resulting from people following an itinerant ruler or searching for more fertile land.

Estimates by eminent scholars agree with the figure of 300,000 or less. Romanzo Adams undertook the most thorough study on the subject. In his unpublished manuscript he settles, after careful consideration, on a precontact total of 300,000. Andrew Lind, Bernhard L. Horrmann, Kenneth P. Emory, and others agree with that figure. More recently, the archaeologist Patrick V. Kirch suggests a population of 250,000 in 1778. These scholars all agree that King's original total of 400,000 was too high; Stannard thinks it was too low.

One of the most striking aspects of Stannard's claim is that only around 1970 did Hawai'i's population rise to the level he estimated it was at in 1778. To present-day observers, it seems implausible that ancient Hawai'i, whose economic resources and technology were vastly more limited, could match the high population of modern Hawai'i, which is characterized by declining death rates, prolonged levels of high in-migration, and acres of high rises and other forms of new housing. Much of Stannard's evidence comes from comparative data — relating to population densities, for example — chiefly from the Americas. But gross densities can seriously mislead. Much depends on climate, topography, and soil conditions. Hawai'i's topography is typically rugged, and rainfall patterns result in some areas too wet and others too dry for agriculture. Much of the islands' soil, moreover, is inhospitable to cultivation.

Another comparative claim made by Stannard concerns the depopulation curve following contact between Europeans and native peoples. A much higher precontact population than the standard estimate, he notes, yields a curve more consistent with the data from other parts of the world. Again, Stannard overgeneralizes. Although many societies suffered catastrophic declines following contact, Pacific islands like the Samoan and Tongan groups experienced more modest losses. Hawai'i's early populatoin declines were periodic, not sustained and precipitous, as the global depopulation curve would predict. Similarly, precontact densities and postcontact declines vary widely among Pacific islands and generalizations might not apply.

Census figures are notoriously suspect. Not only are estimates by early travelers frequently inaccurate, but also current census data can reflect substantial undercounts of populations. Population forecasts and retrocasts are both enormously complex and will almost inevitably result in sizable errors.

Not everyone will agree with Stannard's rosy claim that precontact Hawaiians were extraordinarily healthy, and that they had low infant mortality rates and high life expectancies. Instead, scholars believe that, if fertility was high, the islands' precarious ecological balance was maintained by high mortality rates and low life expectancies.

And Stannard's appeal to scholarly trends in other settings is disquieting and has little bearing on the study of Pacific islands in general or of Hawai'i in particular. Conditions in different areas are often very dissimilar. Conclusions relevant to each region should be judged on their own merits and not according to general scholarly fashions. "It is hard enough to estimate the population of a modern community with acceptable accuracy. Estimating the 1778 population . . . without the benefit of either a full-scale, all-island enumeration or modern sampling techniques, is far more difficult. The true number is ultimately unknowable."[8]

NOTES

1. Robert C. Schmitt, "New Estimates of the Pre-censal Population of Hawaii," *Journal of the Polynesian Society* 80:2 (June 1971): 238.

2. Ibid.

3. David E. Stannard, *Before the Horror: The Population of Hawai'i on the Eve of Western Contact* (Honolulu: Social Science Institute, University of Hawaii, 1989), xvi, xvii.

4. Ibid., 14.

5. Eleanor C. Nordyke, "Comment," in Stannard, *Before the Horror*, 105–06.

6. Ibid., 106.

7. Robert C. Schmitt, "Comment," in Stannard, *Before the Horror*, 114.

8. Ibid., 120.

Chapter 2

HAWAIIANS AND CAPTAIN JAMES COOK

First contact between Pacific Islanders and Europeans commonly assumes greater significance than other initial encounters because of its consequences, both real and imagined. Diseases introduced by Europeans and colonization assuredly influenced the lives of indigenous peoples. But interpretations, particularly by the victors, bring their own sense of perspective and proportion. Europeans can constitute the central figures and loom large in European accounts of meetings with non-European others. Histories of Hawai'i often begin with the arrival of British Captain James Cook, like U.S. history's commonplace start with the first European settlers. Those origin stories generally ignore the histories of indigenous peoples, and they constitute narratives from the viewpoint of the invaders rather than the dwellers on the shore. Captain James Cook's arrival in Hawai'i is especially fraught because Hawaiians, many contend, took him to be the god Lono. Others, led by Gananath Obeyesekere, hold that the deification of Cook is a European invention hoisted onto native peoples as part and parcel of the European imperial project. The debate centers on important questions of methodology and interpretation.

Citing contemporary European and Hawaiian accounts, Marshall Sahlins argues that Hawaiians appropriated Captain Cook from and into their social structure. Hawaiian priests of Lono received Cook as Lono during the Makahiki festival, but the king, Kalaniopuu, saw him as a competitor for ascendance and power even as Lono, the god of peace and prosperity, and Ku, the god of war and destruction, were rivals. Cook's death should be seen in that light, and his ritual sacrifice and dismemberment enabled his absorption into the line of Hawaiian kings and ancestors. In this selection, Sahlins tries to reconcile structural anthropology with history and thus proposes that Hawaiians read the historical event, Cook's encounter with them, from their cultural perspective and reformulate the interpretation into material practice. In this way, history is organized by structure and structure, history.

Gananath Obeyesekere questions the "fact" of Cook's deification as a European fabrication, revealing more about Europeans than Hawaiians. The arrogance of omnipotent conquerors and docile natives projects a European fantasy and falsifies the historical reality of violence and resistance. Scholars and anthropologists have been complicit with that myth of conquest and civilization because Cook was one of them, a scientist and man of the Enlightenment who charted unknown (to Europeans) seas and classified exotic plants, animals, and humans. To European colonizers and intellectuals, natives possessed prelogical, childlike minds, mired in mysticism and tradition and unable to grasp the difference between reality and mythology, Cook and Lono. Marshall Sahlins adds theoretical sophistication to the commonplace of the savage mind with his own notion of structural history and the initial encounter and assimilation of Cook as Lono and chiefly ancestor. The historical evidence, however, contradicts and undermines Sahlins's reproduction of a European myth.

What is the basis for Obeyesekere's "pop nativism"? asks Marshall Sahlins in his reply.[1] The underlying thesis is Obeyesekere's assumption that all natives think alike and that being a native of Sri Lanka somehow affords him a special access to Polynesian minds in contrast to Western anthropologists who impose their views on natives. Thus, memories of Sri Lanka, rather than historical and ethnographic evidence, guide Obeyesekere in his attempt to disprove Cook's deification by Hawaiians. But it is Obeyesekere who silences Hawaiians by disregarding their accounts and attributing them to Europeans. And, by assuming a universal, rational, and pragmatic native, Obeyesekere denies the humanism of anthropology that respects cultural difference and human particularities. "The ultimate victims, then, are Hawaiian people. Western empirical good sense replaces their own view of things, leaving them with a fictional history and a pidgin ethnography."[2]

STRUCTURAL HISTORY

Begun as a lecture, Marshall Sahlins's *Historical Metaphors and Mythical Realities: Structure in the Early History of the Sandwich Islands Kingdom* (1981) tries to reconcile structural anthropology with history in the encounter between

Hawaiians and the West. Although founded in opposition to history, structural anthropology can show, in concrete situations, the structures in history and history in structures. Thus, when Captain Cook sailed into Kealakekua Bay on January 17, 1779, Hawaiians received him ritually as the return of their ancestral spirit and not as the famous navigator or visitor from Britain. He became a source of legitimacy for Hawaiian kings through his death and assimilation, and the spirit of Hawaiian kingship and Hawaiian gods became British. Structure, in the form of Hawaiian culture, absorbed history, in the person and agency of Captain Cook. And, conversely, "Culture may set conditions to the historical process, but it is dissolved and reformulated in material practice, so that history becomes the realization, in the form of society, of the actual resources people put into play."[3] In that sense, history is organized by structures of significance.

To Hawaiians, Europeans were chiefs, godlike beings from the invisible land of Kahiki. Although a myth, that belief comprised a truth of Hawaiian history, and Captain Cook's life and death in Hawaii "were in many respects historical metaphors of a mythical reality."[4] Cook arrived in Hawaii during the Makahiki festival that celebrated the arrival of the god Lono and his gifts of peace and prosperity. During that four-month rite, Lono eclipsed Ku, the god of war and destruction and the god of the ruling chiefs. After stepping on shore, Cook was escorted by the priests of Lono to their principal temple, and the people prostrated themselves before him, crying out, "O Lono!" A priest anointed Cook with coconut oil, and a feast was prepared for him. The rite was repeated twice two days later at a Lono temple and a sacred repository of ancestral bones. In detail, the timing of Cook's visit, his movements, and the reception accorded him coincided with rituals of the Makahiki and with the adoration and worship of Cook as Lono.

Cook and Kalaniopuu, the Hawaiian king, represented Lono and Ku respectively, and were power rivals. But Lono would leave for Kahiki, which Cook did, except his ship needed repair, which brought him to return to Kealakekua Bay on February 11. That was a break in the ritual, and relations between the British and Hawaiians broke down quickly thereafter when Hawaiians committed several thefts and the British tried to punish the thieves. Cook resolved to find and keep Kalaniopuu as his hostage for his lost goods, but the chief refused to go with Cook to his ship and a hostile crowd gathered. When Cook fired at a chief who had threatened him with an iron knife, the crowd pressed toward him as he was felled by a dagger blow. The Hawaiians rushed upon the "fallen god to have a part in his death."[5] Like Lono, who was traditionally killed at the end of the Makahiki, Cook was ritually murdered.

The killing of Cook was the Makahiki in historical form and part of the struggle of one god and chief over another. Killing one's predecessor was the legitimate mode of succession among Hawaiians, wherein the victor appropriates the status and spirit of the vanquished in his death and disposition of his body. Usually the flesh is stripped from the bones, the skull reserved for the god and the long bones and mandible for the ruling chief. Cook's body suffered that fate. But his sacrifice as a rival allowed his ideological recuperation later as an ancestor. After Cook's death, Kalaniopuu went into seclusion, following the procedure for both the Makahiki ritual and the death of a king. Through Cook, the spirit of the Hawaiian king became British, "hence the role of the British in Hawaiian politics in the decades that followed, despite their super-cession in Hawaiian economics."[6]

Although Americans dominated Hawaii's economy by 1800, King Kameha-meha "embarked on an explicit and distinctive policy of friendship, royal gen-erosity and honest exchange with British and other foreign visitors" because he had inherited Cook's "murder" and his spirit. Kamehameha also ensured the production required for trade, whereas the chiefs of other islands were less cooperative with foreign visitors because these chiefs "had not had the good fortune to kill the Great Navigator."[7] Kamehameha's special relationship with Europeans gave him the guns, ships, and advisers to enable his conquest of the entire island chain. "This generous reception of foreign merchant and naval vessels on Kamehameha's part was the theory of the Makahiki transposed by the death of Cook into a register of practice."[8]

THE MYTH OF CAPTAIN COOK

Anthropologist Gananath Obeyesekere wrote *The Apotheosis of Captain Cook: European Mythmaking in the Pacific* (1992) not as a biography of the British explorer but as a subversion of the distinction between biography and hagiog-raphy and myth. The "fact" that Cook was taken by Hawaiians to be their god Lono in 1779 tells us more about Europeans than Hawaiians. The historian Ralph S. Kuykendall describes the encounter on January 17, 1779: "To the Ha-waiians, Captain Cook was the god Lono. As soon as he went on shore . . . he was taken in hand by priests and made the central figure of an elaborate cere-mony in the heiau [temple] of Hikiau . . . up to the last day of his life he was treated by the natives with a respect amounting to adoration."[9] "To put it bluntly," Obeyesekere writes in reaction to those representations, "I doubt that the natives created their European god; the Europeans created him for them." And he continued, Europeans as gods to native peoples is familiar as "a myth of conquest, imperialism, and civilization."[10]

Scholars have enhanced Cook's stature because he was one of them, a dis-coverer who sailed not for conquest or plunder but for scientific exploration. His sponsor was the Royal Society, Britain's leading scientific organization, and its patron, King George III, and the Admiralty provided him with the *Endeavour* and its crew. Cook set sail from Plymouth in August 1768 bound for Tahiti. On board his floating laboratory were some of Britain's leading scientists and artists, all intent on collecting, capturing, and naming plant, animal, and human forms. The ship returned in July 1771 to much acclaim from the press. A second expedition, undertaken by the ships *Resolution* and *Adventure*, sailed under the same sponsors for the South Seas to search for a southern continent. Instead, Cook visited and named islands in the Tongan and Melanesian groups and, after three years, returned a famous man. Less than a year after his return, Cook headed his third expedition to find the Northwest Passage, the fabled water link across North America connecting the Atlantic and Pacific Oceans. It was on this journey that Cook bumped into Hawai'i.

On these voyages, Cook is the great civilizer. He not only maps alien lands and renames them with familiar English names, he imparts to them British plants and animals carried aboard his ships for that purpose. He thereby symbolically domesticates savage lands and peoples in a self-conscious and literal act, both for the natives and Europeans who might follow him. And although Lord Morton, president of the Royal Society, instructed Cook to treat the natives with "utmost patience and forebearance," the Admiralty's secret instructions required the claiming of foreign lands for the Crown.[11] Cook's explorations might have been benign as mere scientific expeditions, but they advanced conquest and imperialism as well. Cook himself embodied that paradox of civilization with his home image as "gentle navigator" and his propensity to violence once in the vast Pacific.[12]

A common Western myth model (or a myth and its structure and themes) of the savage mind is that it is prelogical, mystical, and associated with feeling as opposed to thinking. Natives are like children, lacking mature capacities. Contrary to that myth, natives, like all humans, exercise practical rationality or behavior based on pragmatic assessments and choices among options. They are not entirely bound by tradition or culture; they have the capacity to reason and improvise. Following the myth, when James Cook arrived in Hawai'i fortuitously during the Makahiki festival, some anthropologists believed that for Hawaiians he was the god Lono, others, like the historian Kuykendall, thought he was Lono's literal embodiment to Hawaiians. In those scenarios, Hawaiians lack the capacity to discriminate between Cook and Lono because, according to Polynesian ethnography, they are cosmologically determined. Yet it is the native who can discriminate among various shades of meaning, and the anthropologist who fails to make the distinctions.

The reception given Cook by the Hawaiians when he landed in Kealakekua Bay has been unanimously interpreted as that accorded a god. Hawaiians, historians say, believed he was their god Lono, who presided over the Makahiki festival and came from Kahiki. Priests ceremonially welcomed him at the temple and people prostrated themselves before him and brought him offerings.

Even Hawaiian scholars have accepted the identification of Cook with Lono. Such is the power of the myth that it is merely assumed and its bases have not been questioned despite the fact that the earliest account of Cook's deification appeared forty-four years after his death in 1779.

Recently, Marshall Sahlins uses Cook to advance his idea of structural history, thereby imbuing the myth with theoretical sophistication. Sahlins begins with the notion that Hawaiian ritual alternated annually between the dieties Lono, the peaceful and productive god, and Ku, the god of war and destruction. Lono's visit is the occasion for the four-month celebration called the Makahiki. At the end of the festivities, Lono returns to the land of Kahiki from whence he came. The worship of Ku and his representatives, the chiefs, then commences. Cook was a form of Lono, Sahlins surmises, and the chiefs were a form of Ku. Cook's visit to Hawai'i coincided with the Makahiki, and Hawaiians treated him as a god, prostrating themselves and shouting, "O Lono," and associating Cook's name with Lono.[13]

Toward the end of the Makahiki, Lono suffers ritual death and is confined to the temple, not to be seen again until the next year. Lono's canoe is loaded with offerings and set adrift toward Kahiki, and the temples are opened for the Ku rituals. Cook's death enacted this part of the Makahiki too. On February 4, Cook prepared to leave Hawai'i, like Lono, but a theft upset the sequence of the ritual. Cook returned to land to punish the offender but, instead, Hawaiians rushed upon the god to take part in his death, Sahlins recounts. Within the day, priests took pieces of his body to his ship and asked in great sorrow when Lono would return again. The king mourned Lono's death, and by the nineteenth century priests of Lono carried Cook's bones around the island during the annual Makahiki rites.

Although Cook's appearance was unprecedented, Sahlins writes, the Hawaiians interpreted the coming from their tradition and thus wrapped the alien with the familiar. They were simply following a predetermined script, and Cook's arrival, presence, death, and resurrection (through his bones) enacted in the present the Makahiki in historical form. In that way, the people secured their present in the past. In this interpretation, Sahlins's motivation is to assert a structural theory of history, but structuralism fails to easily accommodate history and change except as sets of transformations. He eludes that bind by asserting that Hawaiians absorbed change by fitting a unique event like Cook's arrival into a preexisting structure, the ritual calendar and practice of the Makahiki.

The evidence, however, fails to support Sahlins's historical reconstruction or the structure of the conjuncture. None of the sources mention the ritual death of Lono during the Makahiki. It is impossible to determine if in fact Hawaiians were celebrating the Makahiki when Cook landed in 1779. Not a single journal entry by those in Cook's expedition mentions the Makahiki. In truth, the Makahiki calendar changed from time to time and from island to island, contrary to Sahlins's calculations. In addition, as Sahlins himself observes, Hawaiians had no explicit myth of Lono's annual return from Kahiki until the late eighteenth or early nineteenth century. This was a recent creation and was not part of ancient mythology. Therefore it is possible Cook's arrival predated the myth of Lono's coming. And could Hawaiians have mistaken Lono's mast and canoe for the bulk of Cook's two enormous ships? Cook didn't look Hawaiian nor did he speak Hawaiian. Presumably the Hawaiian god Lono resembled and spoke in the language of the people. Scholars might think that Hawaiians could believe that Cook came from Kahiki, but Hawaiians knew he came from "Brittanee."[14] And Sahlins might depict Cook as an awe-inspiring figure with "white skin and bright flashing eyes," but Hawaiians might have seen him and his crew as half-starved, unwashed foreigners.[15] Finally, no chief prostrated himself to Cook, only commoners did; Cook had to bow to Ku's image and kiss it at the temple, and, instead of visiting the islands with peace and fertility like Lono, his visit spread venereal disease among Hawaiians who accused him of introducing the infection on his first visit to Kaua'i. In truth, the disease and death spread by the affliction, Cook's prostration before Ku, his welcome by a priest of Ku, and Ku's (not Lono's) ritual death during Makahiki points to a correspondence of Cook with Ku rather than Lono.

A Hawaiian perspective offers an alternative to Sahlins's interpretation. Te Rangi Hiroa, an anthropologist, offers a plausible description of Cook's visit and death. Simply calling Cook Lono did not render him a god. It was common for chiefs to assume those names, and, as in the case of Cook, ceremonies installed them to the rank of chieftainship. Instead of a god, a chief was a man who could be, and was, killed by the people when circumstances demanded it. Cook's deification approached when his body was stripped of its flesh because Hawaiians deified selected chiefs after and not before death. Te Rangi Hiroa's account conforms to the records of contemporary journalists among Cook's expedition who distinguished between Cook as Lono and the god Lono who lived in the skies. Further, an account saw the term *Lono* as a title, or rank, given to chiefs.

Cook's greeting by Hawai'i's chief Kalani'opu'u might have been conditioned by his ongoing war with Maui. Kalani'opu'u first invaded in 1759, experienced some successes, but was driven back by Maui's ruler Kahekili around 1775. The next year, Kalani'opu'u counterattacked but was routed by Kahekili, and Kalani'opu'u attacked again in 1777, without much success. Cook's first landing on Kaua'i in 1778 and his second visit in 1779 occurred within the context of this conflict. The pragmatics of common sense dictated that Kalani'opu'u use the occasion of Cook's arrival in his district to advantage in his war on Maui. If so, Cook's installation as chief had practical political implications and symbolic value in a struggle over land and power. Although there is no way to verify this from the available evidence, the scenario is a likely one, based on similar behaviors exhibited by Polynesian chiefs who sought Cook's intervention in their affairs.

Likewise, Cook's death and his body's dismemberment were treated, as suggested by Te Rangi Hiroa, in the manner of chiefs selected for deification. In contrast, Europeans turned Cook into a white god to natives, an apotheosis to European mythmakers. Europeans were impressed by the ceremonies and prostrations, interpreting them as worship, devotion, and adoration in the Christian sense. Hawaiians saw those behaviors as befitting a chief, formalized and moved by abjection and sometimes fear. European sailors frequently believed that natives thought them to be immortal and their leaders a deity. Those assumptions influenced their writings of encounters with native peoples, and the Cook accounts are not exceptional in that regard. But it is also interesting to note the difference between the official and unofficial entries of some contemporary writings. In his official edition, James King described the deference paid Cook as "religious adoration," but the words are absent from his unofficial journal, and the official version holds that presents were given regularly as part of "religious duty" but noted simply as "duty" in his unofficial account.[16]

Soon after news of Cook's death reached Europe, hagiographies idealized Cook as the humane embodiment of the Enlightenment, his mission as the implantation of civilization. These diverse expressions included poems, biographies, paintings, and a theater performance on the famous explorer. Besides mourning the discoverer's death and celebrating his genius, the representations feature grieving natives who hold Cook up as a hero and demigod. In particular, Cook as child of the Enlightenment was especially important in Australia and New Zealand, where he was seen as a founding father to white settlers. But he was also used to advance the idea of a humane imperialism. As noted by art historian Bernard Smith, academics, poets, and artists pushed Cook into the realm where heroes, saints, and martyrs dwell because of the power of his achievement. And intellectuals made Cook into the prototypical hero of imperialism, befitting the notion of *pax Britannica* and the arts of peace and enlightened self-interest.

The notion of Cook as the god Lono is basically a Western myth of the immortal, godlike European to native peoples. Sahlins's anthropological narrative of Cook's life and death is not only a theoretical proposition of structural continuity and conjuncture but also "a continuation, albeit unwitting, of the European myth of the apotheosis of James Cook. Theoretical thought is often enshrined in nontheoretical traditions."[17]

"NATIVES" VERSUS ANTHROPOLOGISTS

Marshall Sahlins responded to Obeyesekere's "flimsy historical case" with *How "Natives" Think: About Captain Cook, For Example* (1995) because, he writes, scholars, instead of taking the work apart, gave his book credence and an award. Obeyesekere, charges Sahlins, turns Hawaiians into bourgeois realists and privileges his insights as those of a fellow native in contrast to anthropologists bound by Western thinking.[18] Some of the theoretical issues involved in a critique of Obeyesekere's book include considerations of the silencing of "natives" by speaking for them, the pidgin anthropology of imputing to them "our" practical rationality, and the futility of casting "their" history from "our" morality. Rather than imposing uniformity, anthropology should be "sensitive to the character and variety of forms of life."[19]

Obeyesekere ignores much of past expositions and debates on the subject of Cook as Lono, and he discounts the fact, based on contemporary documents and Hawaiian ethnographic accounts of the Makahiki, that the rituals Cook was put through precisely matched ceremonies for welcoming the image of Lono. Obeyesekere, like an earlier group of Danish scholars, instead insists that Cook as god is a Western-inspired myth promoted by Christian missionaries and their converts. Beneath the ire of Obeyesekere is his notion that South Asian culture affords special access to Polynesian cosmologies. "The underlying thesis is crudely unhistorical, a not-too-implicit notion that all natives so-called (by Europeans) are alike, most notably in their common cause for resentment."[20]

That assumption of a universal "native" has a moral appeal. Obeyesekere repeatedly invokes his native experience as explanation and authority in defending preliterate Hawaiians against the impositions of the outsider anthropologist. Thus, memories of a Sri Lankan childhood help him to unravel Hawaiian concepts of divinity, and he can speak for Hawaiian natives against the "scholarly purveyors of the imperialist delusion that these people would have groveled before the White Man as before gods." But why is such behavior demeaning? Rather than giving voice to native Hawaiians, Obeyesekere's "dubious anthropology" and "fashionable morality" actually silences them. And when Hawaiians say, or imply, that Cook was Lono, Obeyesekere imputes that operation to whites who would have taught Hawaiians the idea. In this way, Hawaiians "appear on the stage of history as the dummies of Haole [white] ventriloquists."[21]

If Obeyesekere's anthropology assumes a universal native, it adds "a healthy, pragmatic, flexible, rational, and instrumental relation to the empirical realities" over that base. He allows Hawaiians the ability "to know things as they truly are." Hawaiians would thus never mistake a British sea captain for a Polynesian god. Obeyesekere posits a universal native and human disposition of a practical rationality based on common humanity and a shared sense of reality without regard to the possibilities of cultural particulars. The argument fails to account for differences or how Hawaiians, with their empirical good sense, could erect and worship anthropomorphic images quite unlike themselves and made of mere wood. How wide is the gap between the worship of those images and the person of Captain Cook?[22] "Hawaiian thought does not differ from Western empiricism by an inattention to the world but by the ontological premise that divinity, and more generally subjectivity, can be immanent in it."[23]

Besides the explanatory shortfalls of his antiethnocentrisms, in an inverted and symmetrical ethnocentrism Obeyesekere turns against Europeans where they are incapable of freeing themselves from their own myth: that natives take them to be gods. It is as if they hold a prelogical rationalism that simply reproduces the myth of their superiority over two hundred years. Christian missionaries, colonial apologists, historians and anthropologists mindlessly repeat the myth of Cook's divinity for Hawaiians, but also for themselves. In the spell of Cook's apotheosis, Europeans are the myth holders and Hawaiians the rational pragmatists. The inversion is complete.

Moreover, Obeyesekere's ethnocentrism in the name of antiethnocentrism promotes an anti-anthropology that substitutes the particulars of Hawaiian culture for a universal practical rationalism. He thereby undermines the ethnographic respect that is the basis for scholarly anthropology. In a double erasure, Obeyesekere attributes Hawaiian discourse to Western mythical thought and substitutes "our" rationality for Hawaiian culture.[24] He thus maintains that the native's point of view has been assimilated into European folklore and that Hawaiian rituals can be refigured by our a priori assumptions. In these ways, Obeyesekere reinvents Hawaiian culture and practices as "an intellectual version of the Western civilizing mission" and the Enlightenment project of idealizing man by imputing to him empirical reason.[25] Accordingly, Obeyesekere's project has more in common with Cook's scientific expeditions than he would admit.

The documentary evidence is clear. Hawaiians believed Cook was Lono. There might have been differences of perception between chiefs and priests and rulers and commoners. But the priests, as power holders, could orchestrate a worship of Lono that required practical and material tributes from the commoners. Further, Hawaiian authorities presented a normalized, consistent representation of Cook to Hawaiians and Europeans alike. "From 1779 into the 1830s, Hawaiian people testified in direct speech, by their ritual practices, and in their myths that, for them, Captain Cook was an embodied form of their god Lono."[26] Despite the extensive documentation, Obeyesekere claims that Cook's apotheosis is of European provenance. He thereby contradicts and speaks for Hawaiians, denying them agency and culture.

66   HISTORICAL DEBATES

NOTES

1. Marshall Sahlins, *How "Natives" Think: About Captain Cook, For Example* (Chicago: University of Chicago Press, 1995), 60, 61.

2. Ibid., 197.

3. Marshall Sahlins, *Historical Metaphors and Mythical Realities: Structure in the Early History of the Sandwich Islands Kingdom* (Ann Arbor: University of Michigan Press, 1981), 7.

4. Ibid., 11.

5. Ibid., 24.

6. Ibid., 26.

7. Ibid.

8. Ibid., 27.

9. Quoted in Gananath Obeyesekere, *The Apotheosis of Captain Cook: European Mythmaking in the Pacific* (Princeton, N.J.: Princeton University Press, 1997), 3.

10. Ibid.

11. Ibid., 13.

12. Ibid., 14, 15.

13. Ibid., 52.

14. Ibid., 61–62.

15. Ibid., 62.

16. Ibid., 125.

17. Ibid., 177.

18. Sahlins, *How "Natives" Think*, ix.

19. Ibid.

20. Ibid., 5.

21. Ibid.

22. Ibid., 5–6.

23. Ibid., 6–7.

24. Ibid., 9.

25. Ibid., 9–10.

26. Ibid., 114.

Chapter 3

MIGRATION

When historians conceptualize Asian migration to the United States as immigration, they invoke the "push and pull" hypothesis, and when they conceptualize it as migrant labor they deploy the analysis of capital and labor. The conventional notion of immigration examines forces that "push" people from their homes and "pull" them to their destinations. Accordingly, religious persecution, economic hard times, and political turmoil might drive people from their homes, while religious freedom, economic opportunity, and political stability might attract people to their adopted land. This model favors individual immigrants and the free choices they make from among options. The migrant labor hypothesis views migration at its global, macro level, and focuses on the concentrations of capital and its influences over labor. Labor, this thesis holds, moves toward areas of high capital concentration, and the work that is available determines the nature of that labor. Thus, migration involves movements from rural to urban areas, from underdeveloped to developed countries, from Asia to America. Free choice and individualism are less clear in this model of migration. Further, the conventional notion of immigration generally aligns itself with European immigration, while the notion of migrant labor tends to align itself with the literature on conquest and the forced movements of peoples.

IMMIGRATION

I will use as an example of the conventional idea of immigration an account of Chinese immigration as delineated in a pioneering textbook, A *History of the Chinese in California: A Syllabus* (1969), written by Thomas W. Chinn, H. Mark Lai, and Philip P. Choy. The book was written for teachers who expressed the need for a reader for their students, and the work is remarkable for its clarity and precision. In their discussion, the authors examine the "why" and "how" of Chinese immigration to California.

Nineteenth-century China, Chinn et al. note, was ruled by the Ch'ing dynasty, composed of Manchus who imposed their rule, along with their national dress and the queue, on the Chinese in the mid-seventeenth century. Because Chinese rebels fled China and used places like Taiwan as bases for continued resistance, the Manchus forbade the emigration of its subjects. They closed China to the West, and limited trade to certain ports, most notably Amoy and Canton. Cantonese and other Chinese involved in trade gained exposure to ideas and goods from Europe and the Americas and were among the first to entertain notions about travel to the West.

Britain was a leader among European nations in the China trade. From its base in India it sent ships, carrying opium produced in India, to trade for goods in China. In the late 1830s, China sought to terminate the opium traffic because of its detrimental effects on its people. Britain seized on that occasion to wage war against China in the Opium War of 1840, which ended in China's defeat and the Treaty of Nanking, which opened five ports to trade and ceded Hong Kong to the victorious British. In addition, Britain continued to import opium and demanded silver in return, resulting in a rise in the price of silver, in inflation, and in higher taxes and levies because silver was the monetary standard. Finally, Western imports ruined native products, especially the manufacturing of textiles.

Accompanying those foreign influences in China was the decline of the Manchu government through corruption and mismanagement. China's population increase put greater demands on the land and on the state, and more and more land became concentrated in fewer hands. Natural disasters, including periodic floods, droughts, and famines, added to the woes of the peasants. Those pressures, both natural and man-made, fueled popular unrest, and banditry and peasant uprisings became more frequent.

In 1851, the T'ai-p'ings seized control of most of southeastern China before the Manchus could regroup and counterattack. The rebellion lasted thirteen years, and cost millions of lives. The most prosperous area of China, the southeastern provinces, was devastated by the war and famine that followed in its wake. In 1884 the Triad Societies began in the Pearl River Delta region a series of uprisings that lasted nearly a decade. And in 1856, hatred between the Punti (or Cantonese) and the Hakka (or "guest people") flared into a war that lasted about a dozen years. Political instability and the hardships caused by bloody wars led many from this area of China to migrate.

This domestic turmoil caused great economic dislocations and distress and was one of the important factors forcing so many Chinese to decide to migrate from the Pear River Delta region. Since the Cantonese had long had maritime contacts, it was only natural that, when the news came of the discovery of gold in California and good wages to be had, some would consider emigration to America as a solution to their economic difficulties. Thus many took passage to California; others went to Southeast Asia, Australia, South American and the West Indies.[1]

Western nations continued to press China to allow trade and the emigration of its subjects. In 1859, Kwangtung's provincial government allowed foreigners to recruit Chinese laborers, and the following year the Treaty of Peking, signed with Britain and France, formalized that right. And in the 1868 Burlingame Treaty signed with the United States, China recognized the "inherent and inalienable right of man to change his home and allegiance." Those governmental acts simply sanctioned an ongoing coolie trade that had been flourishing since the 1840s. To protect the interests of Chinese indentured laborers in Cuba and Peru and Chinese students in the Untied States, the Manchu government appointed Ch'en Lan-pin to be its first minister to the United States (Ch'en was also minister to Peru and Cuba) in 1878.

The Chinese coolie traffic was a result of the end of the African slave trade and the continued demand for labor in the plantations and mines of the Americas. The first shipment of Chinese indentures left Amoy in 1845, and two years later a Spanish company shipped 800 to Cuba. In 1849, Chinese contract laborers left for Peru; in 1852, for Hawai'i; and later for Trinidad, British Guiana, Sumatra, and Jamaica. In this trade, companies paid recruiters a sum for each worker delivered to the companies' depots, where coolies "signed" contracts for a period of service. Coolies were commonly debtors, kidnap victims, and prisoners taken from wars, and conditions were such that the trade was called "the buying and selling of pigs." Coolie ships resembled African slavers, and onboard riots, murders, and other acts of desperation accompanied the trade. Upon landing, coolie contracts were sold to the highest bidders, and the conditions of labor were typically harsh and unremitting. The United States made illegal the use of American vessels for the trade in 1862; the British in Hong Kong ended the practice in 1873, and the Portuguese in Macao ended it in 1874.

Although some Chinese arrived in California under contract, most came under the credit-ticket system. Contracts were difficult to enforce in the United

States, and Chinese resisted their contracts by running away. Chinese immigrants typically came "voluntarily and not under duress or servile contracts."[2] Many paid their own passage to the United States. Others received from merchant brokers in China credit for their ticket (about forty dollars), and on reaching the United States repaid the debt from their earnings. After the 1882 Exclusion Act, the 1906 San Francisco earthquake and fire provided a means by which to escape this restrictive immigration law. The loss of immigration records allowed many Chinese to claim birth in the United States and, with that, U.S. citizenship, which allowed them to claim citizenship for their children. Those claims represented "slots" that were sold by brokers to those who wanted to enter the United States. These then became "paper sons"—i.e., the children of citizens but their children only on paper.

Hong Kong was the general point of departure for California. The emigrants stayed in dormitories provided by their creditors, and sailed on American and British ships in a business that was profitable for Chinese and whites alike. The trans-Pacific journey took from one to three months, and Chinese passengers spent much of their time below deck in crowded holds. Occasionally, conditions resembled those on coolie traders. The *Libertad*, for example, arrived in San Francisco in 1854 with 100 of its 500 Chinese passengers, along with its captain, dead.

A journalist described the debarkation scene in 1869: "a living stream of the blue coated men of Asia, bearing long bamboo poles across their shoulders, from which depend packages of bedding, matting, clothing, and things of which we know neither the names nor the uses, pours down the plank. . . ." The Chinese appeared to be about twenty-five years old. Although shorter than whites, they seemed "healthy, active and able-bodied to a man." Agents of Chinese companies greeted the newcomers, and marched them off to Chinatown.[3]

Prominent in this account of Chinese emigration by Chinn, Lai, and Choy are the "push" forces that compelled the Chinese to leave China for California. These included natural disasters, such as floods, droughts, and famines; the deeds of men, such as the repressive and corrupt policies of the Manchu government, which enforced dress and hairstyle codes and forbade movements abroad; and civil unrest, such as the devastating T'ai-p'ing rebellion, the Triad uprising, and the Punti and Hakka clan wars. Foreign trade and interventions in China caused inflation and unemployment. The coolie trade, the authors are careful to observe, operated mainly in the Caribbean and South America and not in North America. Chinese migration to the former was a forced traffic; migration to the latter was a free movement. California's attraction or "pull" was news of the discovery of gold and the likelihood of good wages there. Also, Cantonese might have been drawn to the Western Hemisphere, including the

United States, because of their familiarity with and possibly desire for Western products.

MIGRANT LABOR

The clearest and most persuasive case advanced for the migrant labor hypothesis as applied to Asians is found in *Labor Immigration Under Capitalism: Asian Workers in the United States Before World War II* (1984), edited by Lucie Cheng and Edna Bonacich. I will summarize the argument made in their introductory theoretical chapter, which frames the case studies that follow.[4]

The study of immigration, Cheng and Bonacich note, has been dominated by demographers who employ the "push and pull" hypothesis of migration. Sociologists who focus on the processes of immigration, contact, and assimilation complement the demographers. To the extent that they consider the structural aspects of immigration, they take a functionalist or developmental approach that assumes migration benefits both the sending and receiving countries.

A newer way of seeing migration is to contextualize it within broader, global relations and as a part of an interconnected world capitalist system. In that sense, international migration is a product of the logic of capitalism and its development. Specifically, capitalism's rise leads to imperialism, which brings underdevelopment to the Third World. That outcome displaces people and their productive activities, and makes them available for migration. The correlate of Third World underdevelopment is First World development and, with it, requirements for more labor, especially cheap labor. There is a connection and relationship, therefore, between the sending and receiving countries, between the movement of labor from underdeveloped to developed areas, and between the concentrations of capital (and wealth) in the metropole and labor (and poverty) in the colony. The whole forms an interlocking system that advances itself as migrant workers enrich the imperial power and the colony loses its productive members and natural resources.

Employers in the receiving country benefit from and hence welcome migrant workers, but local laborers see them as threats to their jobs and as undercutting their wages. Those competing interests commonly result in anti-immigrant movements among indigenous workers. These movements stress ethnic and racial differences, and employers deploy racism to keep the migrants dependent and exploitable and to retard class-consciousness. As a consequence, migrant laborers are excluded from the mainstream of the working class and are forced into enclaves that resemble "internal colonies." Racism against immigrant workers therefore is a product of the world capitalist system.

The processes Cheng and Bonacich discuss—the origins of imperialism, its consequences for the colonized and labor emigration, and the changing labor needs of advanced capitalist countries—are complexly related and are not linear. Their explanation, however, is linear and is inadequate to model the reality it seeks to capture.

Imperialism arises from the crisis of capitalism, characterized by declining profits, reduced investments, and rising unemployment. That downward spiral, both long-term and cyclical, gives rise to imperialism as an attempt to resolve those crises. For various reasons, the cost of labor rises with capitalism's development. These reasons include an exhaustion of the domestic labor supply and the demands of labor for higher wages and better working conditions. As labor costs increase, rates of profit or surplus value decrease. Employers counter those trends by lengthening the workday, demanding greater productivity, installing mechanization, and using various other strategies. Those measures could be resisted by workers, intensifying the class struggle, and could lead to unemployment and a shrinking consumer demand and market. To resolve that internal crisis, imperialist expansion offers to employers a solution abroad, in the form of cheap labor and new markets.

Labor is cheap in pre-capitalist societies because wage labor often supplements subsistence production. Workers rely on the pre-capitalist sector for their upkeep and see wages as a surplus. Additionally, workers in pre-capitalist societies are unfamiliar with trade unions and have less incentive to advance their interests as a class because they are not dependent on wage labor. A lower standard of living prevails in less developed countries, along with lower expectations and economic needs and desires. Employers can thereby keep wages low.

In other ways too, these discrepancies between developed and underdeveloped countries help answer capitalism's crisis. Trade introduces to the developed nation raw materials and products that are cheaper than those consumed and manufactured domestically. As a consequence, profit margins grow and wages decline. Conversely, certain goods can be produced more cheaply in developed countries and sold for greater profits in less developed countries. The exchange is one-sided, benefiting producers in developed nations at the expense of the underdeveloped nations.

Imperialism is sustained not only by economic motivations but also by state connivance with and intervention in the interests of the capitalist class. The state enables political annexation and provides the military force required for conquest. Imperialism is also advanced by ideology, as in the West's "civilizing" mission, its assuming the burden of the social uplift of benighted races. Imperialism is racialized. And finally, European imperialism carves out new territories for Europe's surplus population and its poor, reducing unemployment (and hence state burdens) at home and transforming those migrants into cheap labor in the colonies.

Imperialism reduces its colonies to states of underdevelopment. Imperial powers tax their wards, profit from exchanges, undermine local crafts and industries, enlarge their markets, impose tariffs, and exploit natural resources and labor. Resistance by subsistence producers to participation in the colonial economy might be broken by taxes that require cash payments and by land tenure policies that institute private property. And the displacements that flow from those initiatives help to facilitate various forms of labor migration, such as the enslavement of Africans, the Asian Indian indenture system, and the Chinese "coolie" trade. In those ways, colonizers coerce subsistence producers to abandon pre-capitalist economies and participate in capitalism and slave or wage labor. But the colonial economy will tend to stagnate because its bound labor lacks the incentive to produce, its employers fail to invest in mechanization, and capitalists at home drain the profits created in the colonies. Also, the system distorts colonial economies by skewing them toward extraction of raw materials rather than production of manufactured goods, and their infrastructures are directed at the export economy rather than at local needs. The end result is underdevelopment.

The foundation for migrant labor is underdevelopment. Peasants are driven off the land and toward the cities, and displaced and unemployed workers are enticed with the prospects of greater wages overseas. Colonial labor migration thus extends itself to international labor migration. Those forces help to determine the migrant's nature. The migrant is typically a young adult man from a subsistence economy, who works for a limited time to supplement the family's earnings. Cash, the family hopes, will enable it to pay off taxes and debts and purchase goods and lost land. The migrant is typically a sojourner with investments in the family and home. In both the colonial and international systems, coercion is a key element in the recruitment of laborers who are driven by the logic of colonialism and bound by contracts and loans. These then resemble more closely debt peons than free wage laborers.

Underdevelopment's counterpart is development. Advanced capitalist societies engage in imperialism, seeking overseas resources, markets, and labor to solve the problems associated with capitalism's cycles and downward spirals. Capitalists profit directly from their overseas engagements, and also indirectly, as international migrant labor tends to depress domestic wages and hence labor costs. Because of the intermediate status of nineteenth-century Hawai'i and California, two places where Asian migrants went, Asian labor migration to the United States fits a model between that of migration from a colony to an advanced capitalist society and migration from a colony to another colony. Still, broadly speaking, Asian migrant workers fit the general pattern of labor migration, and they enlarged the reserve army of labor to the benefit of employers.

Asian migrant workers are susceptible to exploitation because of their political status, which denies them rights and full participation in the host society.

Their lives are regulated. The state can pass immigration laws to allow or deny the entry of certain classes of migrants. It can exclude women, children, the elderly, the sick, and indigents, and thereby limit migrants to those who are efficient and productive, thereby reducing the costs of social upkeep for dependents. Recruiters exercise controls by choosing from among the colonial labor pool workers for the specific tasks required. The state can also keep migrants in legal categories—e.g., the category of permanent aliens—to prevent them from making claims on the state and on employers. And, as aliens, they can be expelled on the slightest provocation. Because of those controls, employers can subject migrant workers to jobs that no one else wants, to long hours and onerous labor conditions, and to lower wages and higher risks. Capitalism's costs decrease, its profits rise, and it can better withstand the worst economic crises.

Cheng and Bonacich stress overarching, global forces that prompt and shape the nature and direction of labor migration. In a sense, their hypothesis can be reduced to the "push and pull" hypothesis underlying the conventional explanation for immigration. Imperialism creates the conditions that "push" migrants from their homes, and capitalism's needs "pull" them to metropolitan countries. But the international labor migration hypothesis goes beyond the discrete happenstances of place and time. Natural disasters and wars, for instance, remain factors in the movements of peoples, but there is a logic at play here, the logic of capitalism, that structures and maintains a global system of concentrations and flows of capital and labor. And those movements are characterized by controls instituted for the benefit of capital and the state. The result is dependent and exploited workers. Classes, however, are divided by race (white and nonwhite) and nation (metropole and colony). Accordingly, workers remain divided, and racism advances the imperial project and capitalism's development. Unlike those who would subscribe to the conventional view of immigration, the authors in their theorizing on Asian migration to the United States underscore coercion as opposed to free choice and social forces as opposed to individualism.

NOTES

1. Thomas W. Chinn, H. Mark Lai, and Philip P. Choy, A History of the Chinese in California: A Syllabus (San Francisco: Chinese Historical Society of America, 1969), 12.

2. Ibid., 15.

3. Ibid., 16.

4. Lucie Cheng and Edna Bonacich, eds., Labor Immigration Under Capitalism: Asian Workers in the United States Before World War II (Berkeley: University of California Press, 1984), 1–56.

Chapter 4

THE ANTI-CHINESE MOVEMENT

Anti-Asianism is the most discussed topic in Asian American history, and because of chronological sequence the anti-Chinese movement sets the pattern for the discussion. Thus historians not only propose that the anti-Chinese movement of the late nineteenth century gave way to the anti-Japanese movement of the early twentieth century; they also maintain that the causes and natures of the anti-Chinese movement were similar to those of the anti-Japanese movement. In addition, those two social movements, historians explain, moved toward certain ends. The anti-Chinese movement, according to that view, culminates with the Chinese Exclusion Act of 1882, and the anti-Japanese movement with the World War II concentration camps. (I discuss America's concentration camps separately.)

All the writers included in this section are concerned with the origins and natures of the anti-Chinese movement, and Mary Roberts Coolidge, Gunther Barth, Stuart Creighton Miller, and Andrew Gyory take aim specifically at the 1882 Exclusion Act and its causes. Elmer Clarence Sandmeyer and Alexander Saxton are more interested in dissecting the anti-Chinese movement, although they track the paths that ultimately lead to exclusion. The authors offer contradictory explanations, but each builds upon the other. For instance, Mary Roberts Coolidge's "California thesis," although much criticized and maligned, remains a crucial ingredient for all subsequent explanations of the anti-Chinese movement.

The special circumstances of California and the times determined the nature of the anti-Chinese movement and the causes for the Exclusion Act, Coolidge contends. Included among the main characters are miners and politicians who played upon American prejudices against foreigners and nonwhites. A wildly fluctuating economy in California and the near equal strength of Democrats and Republicans in both California and the nation at large heightened the tensions between native and alien, white and nonwhite, worker and owner. In the scramble for votes, California's workingmen and its Chinese problem became national political issues that achieved redress in the 1882 Chinese Exclusion Act.

Elmer Clarence Sandmeyer essentially repeats Coolidge's central contentions, but he provides more evidence for her thesis and conceives of the focus by disparate interest groups on the Chinese as a single social movement. Thus named, the anti-Chinese movement became both historical phenomenon and object of study and debate. In addition to developing this refinement of Coolidge, Sandmeyer notes that racism has an economic basis and that the anti-Chinese movement involved, besides the charge of cheap labor, a moral component and, besides legislative actions, judicial decisions that had wide ramifications for Chinese migrants. He was also able to see, because he published his study three decades after Coolidge, that the anti-Chinese movement was just the beginning of a general move to restrict all immigration.

Inverting Coolidge's and Sandmeyer's explanations, Gunther Barth redirected blame for anti-Chinese sentiment from white laborers and politicians to the Chinese. As sojourners, he alleges, the Chinese invited white American hostility because they exported their earnings to China, neglected to invest in America, inhabited segregated enclaves, and refused to assimilate. Their objectives and behaviors clashed with the dream of white Americans who sought to create in California a "true American state." Barth's thesis has largely failed to mobilize either support or opposition in major studies, but his idea that the Chinese question achieved national prominence apart from California and its delegations was taken up by the next extended study.

Stuart Creighton Miller shifts the focus from California to the Northeast, where traders, missionaries, and diplomats left their impressions of China beginning in 1785. Thus, long before California's gold rush, people in the East had already formed opinions of the Chinese. Surveying newspapers and periodicals, Miller shows how in the popular imagination the image of the Chinese was that of heathens and barbarians, immoral and dishonest, and ludicrous in appearance and dress. Denigrating representations of them gained a wide audience through the popularity of the penny press, and they acquired scientific currency with the contemporary projects on racial classification and with concerns over race mixing, public health, and infectious diseases. Those ideas of the Chinese gained currency nationally, and they crossed political-party and class lines, being shared by workers and intellectuals alike. Accordingly, when California presented its case for Chinese exclusion, it found a receptive national audience.

Alexander Saxton begins with a Miller-like intellectual history but returns to the specifics of California and its labor politics and finds the roots of anti-Chinese ideology in both white racism and Jacksonian democracy. The class politics of the Jacksonians pitted America's producers against the capitalists and monopolies, and racial politics cut across class lines to advance white privilege and nonwhite poverty. But the anti-Chinese movement was specific to California, Saxton maintains, hearkening back to Coolidge and Sandmeyer, where politicians and labor leaders deployed the Chinese question to enlist and mobilize their constituencies. Totaling between twenty and twenty-five percent of the state's wage earners, the Chinese were significant in the California of the 1870s and 1880s, and the racial divide was thus drawn between Chinese and non-Chinese.

Andrew Gyory tackles a sacred tenet of U.S. labor history and the historiography of the anti-Chinese movement. Labor, he declares, was uninterested in Chinese exclusion and virtually absent from the forces that pushed for a restrictive national law. In addition, white Americans might have held racist views of the Chinese, as shown by Miller and Saxton, but white workers failed to translate these ideas into actions, despite the efforts of some of their leaders. The white working class, states Gyory, distinguished early on and consistently between Chinese immigration, which they supported, and Chinese cheap contract labor, which they opposed. Their focus was on class alone and and, contrary to Saxton's interpretation, not on race. Gyory agrees with Coolidge and Sandmeyer that politics is at the heart of the anti-Chinese movement, but he parts company with them in seeing the 1882 Exclusion Act not as a culmination of California's efforts from the bottom up but as an initiative by Congress from the top down. Like Coolidge and Sandmeyer, however, Gyory argues that the time was propitious for an airing of the Chinese question because of the close voting between Republicans and Democrats in national elections. Politicians, he maintains, framed the issue as a race and class question, and only in the end with exclusion inevitable did white workers come around to that view.

THE CALIFORNIA THESIS

For obvious reasons, Stuart Creighton Miller has labeled the account of Chinese exclusion by Mary Roberts Coolidge the "California thesis." In her book *Chinese Immigration* (1909), Coolidge sets out to defend Chinese immigration during a time when Congress was considering an extension of the 1882 Chinese Exclusion Act by revisiting and critiquing the allegations made by the anti-Asianists and by explaining the value of China and the Chinese to the United States. I will summarize Coolidge's argument, which centers upon conditions peculiar to California.

China, Coolidge begins, has for decades been "an unknown country," and the Chinese "a strange, weird, incredible people." Missionaries and travelers have since 1850 begun to fill in that void and correct some of the stereotypes of the "Chinaman," "a left-handed, cunning, industrious, stolid, cruel and inhuman creature."[1] In reality, the Chinese are much like other peoples.

In China, there are no castes like in India or feudalism as in Japan. Most of the population engages in agriculture and lives in rural villages with families and kin groups. Merchants have gone all over the world, coolies have labored under contract in Cuba and South America, and the poor have borrowed money from relatives or brokers to travel to California and make a fortune for the family. Chinese farmers are largely free from controls in that they possess land, trade and make goods, participate in self-government, can appeal official abuses, and can rise to any social or political station. Freedom is a hallmark of the Chinese village farmer. "Leaving out of consideration the appointment of higher officials by the Emperor, there is a remarkable similarity between the workings of the governmental system in China and in the United States. The result is a general spirit of democracy among the Chinese."[2]

Although citizenship allows great freedoms, a tangle of rules and customs binds the individual to the family, his relations and village, his society, and his guild. And, despite high morals and great personal integrity, the Chinese appear indifferent to the truth and lie as a matter of course. Opium use is extensive, but many use it only in moderation, and sexual morality is very high, prostitution, divorce, and illegitimacy being rare. Women, especially married women, are restricted and chaste, and prostitution is limited to towns where young men congregate. Still, China's treatment of women is "the darkest blot" upon that nation.[3] Daughters are unwelcome, wives are subordinate to their mothers-in-law, and, among female children, infanticide prevails to a degree.

The Chinese are renowned for their industry; "indeed, the Chinese have almost a passion for labor." Everyone works. "The common laborer combines with this habitual industry patience, docility, accuracy, and temperance. Though he lacks inventiveness and initiative, he has remarkable powers of imitation. He will take low wages and contrive always to live within them; but never any lower than is necessary to keep in work, and at the first opportunity he will demand higher."[4] Chinese workers have shown themselves to be more economically adaptable than European peasants, and in the United States they have become laundrymen, cooks, miners, and merchants.

Because of their variations and complexities, this synopsis hardly suffices as a full description of China and the Chinese. Still, the Chinese are like everyone else. "In short, he would still be democratic and docile, cunning and loyal, deceitful and honorable, superstitious and intelligent, law-abiding and self-governing, clean and dirty, good and bad, all at the same time just as he had always been—and as the rest of the world's inhabitants are."[5]

Except for some in China's southeastern provinces, the Chinese are not prone to migrate, despite fear of them as a menace to Western civilization. The law and family and religious ties hold them to their place of birth. Only the devastations of war and the lure of gold and economic opportunity managed to attract three hundred thousand Chinese to California and the Pacific Coast. Chinese laws forbade emigration, but the 1840 Opium War led to a rise in taxes, the Taiping rebellion of 1850 caused great dislocation, and the terrors of famine and chaos drove many to desperation. News of gold's discovery in California stirred excitement among workers in Canton, and shipping companies exaggerated the enormous profits laborers could reap in the gold fields. Many Chinese, as a consequence, left for the United States.

A majority among that group were young married men. They came from the free agricultural peasantry and were thrifty, industrious, and independent of character—similar in age and class to German and Irish agricultural immigrants of the same period. At first, whites welcomed the Chinese and considered them almost indispensable because "race antipathy was subordinated to industrial necessity" and there appeared to be enough room for them. The Chinese worked in general labor and as carpenters and cooks. They cleared and drained the rich tule lands of the Sacramento delta and took up work scorned by white men. The Chinese learned from whites; "he was a gap-filler, doing what no one else would do, or what remained undone, adapting himself to the white man's tastes, and slipping away, unprotestingly, to other tasks when the white man wanted his job." And, like that gap-filler, the Chinese assumed women's attributes and work. "The cleanliness, unobtrusiveness and industry of the Chinese was often commented upon. As cooks and laundrymen they supplied the places of women domestics."[6]

Even in the mining districts, whites tolerated the Chinese because they were timid and nonaggressive. They did not stake new claims but worked over old ground. "Their rivalry was not feared, for they were said to handle tools like women and to expend a vast deal of labor in their method of working. They were systematic and steady, however, and by degrees learned to use tools and to undertake more extensive works."[7]

Whites tolerated the Chinese because they performed necessary services for the economy and took up manual labor that was undesirable to other workers. And San Francisco was yet innocent of the politicians, labor parties, criminal elements, and hoodlums who would prey upon them. But whites in the mining areas grew jealous of the Chinese and other colored competitors and proclaimed that the state was for them alone. Drawing on the well of anti-Chinese rhetoric, California's governor pandered to his constituents in the mining districts. California for Americans was the rallying cry.

Gold was what brought fortune hunters to California from across the U.S. plains, South America, and the Pacific, including Australia, Hawai'i, and Asia. Americans resented the presence of so many foreigners in the gold fields, especially Mexicans and Chilenos, who, they said, took away the gold from the United States. Both the federal and state governments, however, refused to intervene, and California's first constitution protected the property rights of all legal residents. Nonetheless, competition and contact with foreigners in the mines provoked and intensified conflict between white Americans and darker skinned Mexicans, Indians, South Americans, and Hawaiians as well as between white Americans and the French.

Certain mining camps passed resolutions against foreign miners. They claimed that lawless foreigners threatened American lives and property. In Sonora in 1850, after a riot and attempted lynching, Americans expelled all foreigners. A contemporary writer reported on the accelerating violence, on the gangs that roamed the streets all night and broke into homes. Foreign miners, Coolidge remarked, revealing her prejudice, were sure to retaliate against the robberies and murders of their countrymen because most of them had "Spanish blood."[8]

California's antiforeignism derived from a number of sources and convergences. Greed and jealousy were pervasive among the miners; race antipathy and East Coast ideas of the Know-Nothing Party fanned the flames of hatred. In the mines, whites, including Irish Catholics, joined together against black, brown, and yellow foreigners. Southerners, who made up about a third of the state's population during the first decade, intensified feelings of antiforeignism. Some of these brought their slaves and white supremacist ideas with them to California. Midwesterners, however, formed the white majority; they were ignorant and displayed "extreme race antipathies" toward colored folk, who for them included South Americans, Pacific Islanders, and Asians, but also southern Europeans and the French and Spanish, because of their darker skins and because they were "too high spirited."[9]

The state's 1850 Foreign Miners License law exemplified white American antiforeignism in the gold fields. The law exacted a twenty-dollar monthly tax on all foreign miners, but it was directed at the miners from Latin America. As a result, some mines closed down, and some Mexican miners refused to pay while others armed themselves against the tax collectors; still others became highwaymen or left the state. After having driven the Latino miners from California, white Americans turned against the Chinese. Vast numbers of Chinese slaves, these nativists warned, stood ready to descend upon and pollute the state. Governor John Bigler charged that the Chinese were avaricious coolies, immoral and unassimilable—dangerous to the state's welfare—and a committee of the state's legislature repeated those allegations, recommending the exclusion of Chinese from the mines.

Although the political posturings in Sacramento failed to materialize as laws, they encouraged further hatred against the Chinese in the mining districts, where white miners sought to drive them away. The legislature renewed and annually raised the foreign miners tax, which in 1853 was printed in English, Spanish, French, and, for the first time, in Chinese. Because of antiforeignism and the miners tax, many Chinese left the gold districts and the state. Tax revenues dwindled, especially in the mining areas, and businesses suffered serious losses as a consequence. In 1855, the legislature reduced the foreign miners license tax and urged better treatment for the Chinese. During its lifetime, from 1850 when it was first passed to 1870 when it was declared to be unconstitutional, the foreign miners tax generated about one-half of the state's total income. And from 1855 to 1870 all authorities concede that the Chinese paid practically the whole of the tax. Chinese labor and productivity, whites discovered, were essential elements of the state's economy.

That lesson, however, was lost in California. "The natural human tendency to monopolize any good thing, has had an extreme demonstration in California," concludes Coolidge. "Beginning with the attempt to keep the treasure of the State for the white Americans—that is, white Americans of North European birth or extraction—it developed into a systematic exploitation of the colored immigrants for the purpose of revenue. Anti-foreign prejudice joined hands with race antipathy and was intensified by the lawless greed of a community composed primarily of adventurers rather than settlers."[10] Principal among those nativists were the Irish and Missourians, who held the most extreme prejudices, along with the Latinos, who reciprocated in kind. The Chinese were the inheritors of that legacy of hatred against foreigners and nonwhites between 1860 and 1870, and the race relations in the mining districts, characterized by "greed, jealousy, ignorance and race prejudice, and the primitive spirit of monopoly," were replicated in the state's cities and towns.[11]

In addition to the ideas of racial prejudice, antiforeignism, and material greed, California's politics were instrumental in promoting anti-Chinese sentiment. The state's first governor, John Bigler, campaigned for reelection in 1852 on an anti-Chinese platform to attract the mining district vote. The influential *Daily Alta California* joined Bigler in his attack against the Chinese. In a series of editorials in the spring of 1853, the newspaper charged that the Chinese were debased and servile coolies, inferior to African Americans morally and mentally and immeasurably lower than American Indians, clannish, dangerous, deceitful, and vicious.

California's economy was reeling from periods of boom and bust and suffered from discontent among workers. During the dominance of mining, speculation prevailed in real estate, building, and trade. Profits were enormous and markets were overstocked with merchandise. But, in 1854, when the placers declined and miners pursued gold in Australia, prices, rents, and values fell sharply and investors withdrew their capital, which resulted in widespread business failures and unemployment. Workers struck for higher wages and fastened upon the "cheap" Chinese laborers as the cause of their distress. Shrewd capitalists still made fortunes during this period and benefited from Chinese labor. They too drew the ire of the white working class, who saw them as collaborators with the inferior aliens in the debasement of white labor. The cry against the Chinese thus arose from the conflicts of both race and class.

San Francisco played a particular role in this campaign against the Chinese. The unemployed and discontented flocked to the city. Morality was on the decline and corruption in city government was rampant. With the failure of political leadership, citizens took the law into their own hands. No surprise, then, that during this time the Chinese—indeed, any of the darker-skinned races—became scapegoats for the problems of the time. They were victimized without restraint.

In 1862, Republicans replaced the Democrats in state government, and the Civil War drew most of California's attention. Immigration declined, the Chinese worked on the railroads, and politicians were preoccupied with war and reconstruction. There was thus little incentive for anti-Chinese agitation. But the significant Irish presence in the state focused attention upon labor and race issues in a postbellum electoral politics that repeatedly invoked class conflict and color prejudice. Labor's discontent with the more guarded Republicans helped elect a Democrat as governor in 1867 who had urged the discouragement of Chinese immigration, and the Democratic Party's 1869 platform was violently against railroads, corporations, African Americans, and Chinese.

Because the state was closely divided between Republicans and Democrats, the vote of workingmen was especially crucial, and therefore issues of unemployment, railroad subsidies, and cheap labor dominated the rhetoric of both political parties. And the Chinese, denied the rights of citizenship and suffrage, could mount no opposition to the machinations of unscrupulous politicians, who pledged to advance the interests of whites against the colored races and were intent on simply winning the vote. These circumstances exaggerated the importance of both the workingmen's plight and the Chinese question.

When it became evident that Chinese exclusion was the prerogative of the federal government, Pacific Coast congressmen lobbied for a national exclusion law. Congress was initially indifferent to these efforts. But in the closely contested election of 1876, the interests of the workingman held center stage, and both political parties adopted anti-Chinese pledges in their national platforms. Still, in considerations of Chinese exclusion, party and regional differences prevailed. The Republicans, led by senators from New England, opposed California's exclusion bill. Southern Democrats by and large supported the bill on the basis of race, viewing California's problem with the Chinese as akin to their problem with blacks. Congress eventually passed the bill as amended, but President Chester Arthur had it vetoed as a violation of American treaty obligations with China. A revised version was finally passed and signed by the president in April 1882.

The 1882 Chinese Exclusion Act shows the workings of two conditions—the circumstances of party politics and the rise of the workingmen's movement in California. That convergence led to the success of the anti-Chinese faction in Congress. Particularly because of its constituency of Southerners and the Irish, the Democratic Party was committed to policies against American Indians, African Americans, and the Chinese. Because of Reconstruction, the Republicans lost ground to the Democrats in the national elections of 1876 and 1880, before finally losing the presidency in 1884. California, during this period of tightly contested races, gained in prominence, and the struggle by both parties to carry the state elevated its politics to national significance. Instead of taking on the business monopolies, Congress found it easier to placate California's white workingmen by yielding to their demand for Chinese exclusion. Hence, the law was directed not at all Chinese, as race alone would dictate, but at Chinese laborers, who were presumably the competitors of white workers.

Coolidge's California thesis is foremost a circumstantial argument rooted in the particulars of time and place. California, she argues, was the site of the anti-Chinese movement that began in the gold mining regions of the state. At first, stimulated by greed, competition, and a frontier society of rude men, white Americans clamored against all darker-skinned "aliens," including peoples of color and Latinos, Spaniards, and the French. The state legislature responded by passing the foreign miners tax, which, like the anti-alien agitation, eventually narrowed upon the Chinese as its principal object. Because of tight political contests between Democrats and Republicans both within California and the nation as a whole, California's workingmen and their concerns gained exaggerated prominence. The issues of the state's white working class thus became California's issues, which in turn became the nation's concerns. "The clamor of an alien class in a single State—taken up by politicians for their own ends—was sufficient to change the policy of a nation and to commit the United States to a race discrimination at variance with our professed theories of government, and this so irrevocably that it has become an established tradition," as Coolidge put it.[12]

Elmer Clarence Sandmeyer's *The Anti-Chinese Movement in California* (1939) was begun as a doctoral dissertation in history and completed in 1932. In his study, Sandmeyer builds upon Coolidge's book, which, in his bibliography, he calls the "best work on the subject."[13] Like Coolidge, Sandmeyer provides an argument that begins in California with conditions peculiar to that state, views racial antagonism as reinforced by economic competition, and demonstrates how a regional issue becomes a national one when the two major political parties are evenly matched. And Sandmeyer, like Coolidge, sees the Chinese as victims of California's ills, initially welcomed for their labor and later castigated as the source of the state's many problems. But he offers a closer analysis of California's political and social landscape than had Coolidge, basing it upon readings in laws and treaties, newspapers and magazines, and conventions and speeches.

Sandmeyer begins with the Chinese and the nature of their immigration to California. He outlines the conventional "push" and "pull" of that migration, which include overpopulation and natural disasters like drought, flood, and famine as well as devastations of war like the Tai Ping rebellion. Impoverished Chinese were attracted to California by the discovery of gold, and, in pursuit of fares and labor, shipping and railroad companies promoted and encouraged their migration to the United States. In his description of the migrants, Sandmeyer notes the usual predominance of laborers but is also careful to record the presence of the merchants who became leaders of Chinese American communities and, equally important, women who became the target of many anti-Chinese partisans and were the first to face exclusion with the Page Law of 1875. Similarly, Sandmeyer is attentive to the numbers of Chinese and their distribution in California's counties and throughout the United States, together with their employment, wages, and economic activities, because of their importance to the rise of anti-Chinese sentiment.

A range of motives formed the bases of the anti-Chinese movement, Sandmeyer observes.[14] The designation of various anti-Chinese expressions as a social movement is crucial, for it implies an organized effort directed for specific results. The common goal was Chinese exclusion. The means toward that end were various. The charges against the Chinese fell under three categories: economic, moral and religious, and social and political. Prominent in the economic argument was the notion of coolieism, or servile and cheap labor, which threatened the well-being of America's white working class. That the law barred Chinese coolies or indentured workers from the United States mattered little. What did was the idea that the living and working conditions of the Chinese approximated those of slavery and that Chinese companies and not American courts exercised control over the agreements that brought Chinese workers to the United States. It was the perception and not the reality that concerned "the average Californian."[15]

Behind the condition of California's white workingmen, however, was not the Chinese but the problems of the railroads, land distribution, monopolies, and Eastern capitalists who profited from Chinese labor and the trade with China. And both workers and employers reacted to the Chinese in terms of their own economic self-interest. "With few exceptions employers considered them [the Chinese] beneficial as a flexible supply of labor, cheap, submissive, and efficient; but those whose only capital was their ability to work were almost unanimous in the opinion that the Chinese were highly detrimental to the best interests of the state," observes Sandmeyer. "Each group saw the problem through the spectacles of its own economic interests."[16]

Nearly as important as the charge of coolieism was the allegation of Chinese immorality. The Chinese, their detractors held, lied, smoked opium, gambled, and engaged in prostitution or the enslavement of women. The totality of the argument involved a distinction of culture and the ancient and unbridgeable gulf between Western Christian civilization and Eastern barbarism. As put by a contemporary writer whose prejudices against the Chinese seemed at least equal to his disdain for the Irish: "They [the Chinese] live in close quarters, not coarsely filthy like ignorant and besotted Irish, but bearing a savor of inherent and refined uncleanliness that is almost more disgusting. Their whole civilization impresses me as a low, disciplined, perfected, sensuous sensualism. Everything in their life and their habits seems cut and dried like their food. There is no sign of that abandonment to an emotion, to a passion, good or bad, that marks the western races."[17]

Cultural distinctions were allied with racial or bodily differences. Pollution and disease were prominent markers of the racial divide. Chinatown and Chinese bodies posed threats to the state's moral and physical health. Chinatown was overcrowded, its streets were filled with garbage, the stench was almost unbearable, the sick were everywhere, inadequate cooking facilities posed fire hazards, all the women were prostitutes and all the men gamblers. Chinese prostitutes lured and infected white youth and men with venereal disease, and the Chinese introduced smallpox and leprosy into California. To compound matters, the Chinese refused to assimilate and adopt American ideals and principles and showed no inclination of becoming citizens or making the United States their permanent home.

Race prejudice, however, is not instinctive, Sandmeyer notes. It generally has an economic or social basis. Hence, the charges of coolieism and the degradation of white labor are most important, along with the alleged cultural and racial distinctions that were unchangeable. Through their frequent repetition, white Californians, and eventually Americans, came to believe those ideas, and they sought potent remedies for what they perceived to be the problem.

Although a familiar and recurrent theme in U.S. immigration history broadly, the anti-Chinese movement was, nonetheless, rooted in the particulars of the nineteenth century and the state of California. Like Mary Roberts Coolidge, Sandmeyer's central thesis pivots on the state's workingmen, their organization into labor unions, their focus on the Chinese, and their disproportionate influence over the political parties because of their nearly equal strength. In this relationship there was reciprocity and opportunism. "Organized labor utilized the rivalry between political parties to attain its ends, while the political parties seized upon the Chinese question to capture the labor vote."[18] But that was not the entirety of the causes of the anti-Chinese movement.

One of the most far-reaching actions against the Chinese came not from the state legislature but from its supreme court, which ruled that the Chinese, like blacks, mulattos, and American Indians, could not testify for or against whites in court. The law excluded blacks, mulattos, and American Indians from the white courtroom, but not the Chinese. The court's chief justice who rendered the ruling, Hugh C. Murray, belonged to the Know-Nothing Party, whose central plank was an anti-immigrant nativism. In that sense, politics might have entered into Murray's judicial decision, which read the law in its broadest terms to include the Chinese within its purview but not in the way as explained by workingmen's influence over politicians. The ruling allowed and encouraged assault, robbery, and murder against the Chinese, all of which could be perpetrated by whites with relative impunity. At the same time, condemnation of anti-Chinese violence from especially outside the state prompted calls for justice within it.

By 1876, it was clear that California's politicians needed the workingmen's vote to attain office, and that invariably meant taking an anti-Chinese stand. It was also clear that because of U.S. treaty obligations with China and the Fourteenth Amendment, anti-Chinese statutes in California had become ineffective and were declared unconstitutional by federal courts. Opponents of the Chinese thus concluded that they had to pursue Chinese exclusion with the federal, and not local or state, government. How then to nationalize this heretofore regional issue? The task involved the "education" of the rest of the nation on the Chinese question and bringing pressure to bear upon the national government for relief. These efforts marked a new phase in the anti-Chinese movement.

California's campaign had to overcome mainly Northeastern interests in keeping open the China trade and the field of missions for the uplift of the Chinese. Congress authorized a joint special committee to hold hearings on the matter in 1876, and the following year the committee issued its report. The Pacific Coast benefited from Chinese labor, the report held, but those gains were outweighed by the dangers Chinese migrants posed to white workers and society. Their cheap docile labor and low standard of living depressed wages and caused much unemployment, and their lack of assimilation rendered them unfit for citizenship. The committee recommended that Congress enact legislation to prevent the large influx of Chinese and modify the treaty with China to allow commerce but not the free movement of peoples. Congress, however, failed to act on these recommendations; it merely invited the president's consideration of a treaty renegotiation. However, because of a more favorable national attitude toward California's proposal, it seemed that Chinese exclusion would be only a matter of time.

National support for Chinese exclusion was evident in the reaction to the bill presented in 1882, which suspended the immigration of Chinese laborers, both skilled and unskilled, for a period of twenty years and prohibited U.S. citizenship to Chinese. Those against the bill came mainly from New York and Massachusetts and represented religious groups and men interested in the China trade. Support for the bill came largely from labor groups but was also nationwide: organizers held mass meetings in over sixty cities and towns and drew up resolutions to Congress favoring the bill's passage. President Chester Arthur vetoed the bill but, shortly thereafter, signed a revised version that restricted the entry of Chinese workers for ten years.

The act, Sandmeyer concludes, like Coolidge, was achieved because of "the growing strength of organized labor, and especially the exigencies of national politics, which gave to the Pacific coast states the balance of power between the two great parties. Out of these conditions . . . came the first law on the statute books of the United States restricting the immigration of an entire race."[19]

But restriction failed to achieve California's object of exclusion because Chinese, including laborers, continued to enter the United States under the categories of "merchants," "students," and "teachers." A national outcry demanded that Congress close the law's loopholes. Over the next two decades, Congress grappled with the issue through treaty negotiations and legislative enactments that prohibited the immigration of all Chinese except government officials, merchants, teachers, students, and travelers, allowed the return of registered Chinese laborers with family or property in the United States, extended those restrictions to all U.S. possessions, and authorized the executive branch to enforce the regulations. By that time, concern had shifted from the Chinese to the Japanese and from single groups to the restriction of all immigration.

Sandmeyer's account complements Coolidge's pioneering thesis and forwards evidence in support of their contention that, because of the circumstances of the times, California's politics became that of the nation. In addition to offering greater detail than Coolidge, Sandmeyer proposes that the disparate activities against the Chinese comprised a social movement not of a unified group but of a single object and aim. And, because he wrote his book in the 1930s, he was able to see with hindsight the evolution of the anti-Chinese movement into the anti-Japanese movement and of both those movements into the general drive to restrict all immigration with the passage of the 1924 Immigration Act. In that sense, the anti-Chinese movement helped to locate and define the state's control, in the form of restrictions, over immigration and, therefore, over the constitution of its peoples.

BLAMING THE VICTIM

Gunther Barth's *Bitter Strength: A History of the Chinese in the United States, 1850–1870* (1964) was, like Sandmeyer's book, begun as a doctoral dissertation, under the guidance of the immigration historian Oscar Handlin. Chinese exclusion, Handlin points out in his foreword to Barth's book, flew in the face of the Republic's traditional and up till then inviolate policy of open immigration. Not even the nativist Know-Nothings questioned that principle of free entry. Barth's study undertakes a reassessment of the causes that led to Chinese exclusion and this dramatic turn in the nation's history. The usual view, Handlin reminds us, is that anti-Chinese hostility arose from white racial prejudice that had been conditioned by white relations with American Indians and blacks. The Chinese simply inherited that legacy of hostility. But Barth refocuses attention onto the Chinese themselves and proposes a novel interpretation.

In the mid-nineteenth century, Barth begins, "a tidal wave of Chinese surged into California in pursuit of a dream. The newcomers came with a vision; they would make money to return to China with their savings for a life of ease, surrounded and honored by the families which their toil had sustained."[20] The Chinese, Barth states, came to the United States as sojourners. Unlike the Europeans, they were not immigrants. That distinction was critical. Because they chose not to settle in America, whites excluded them from the privileges and obligations of other immigrants and citizens. And because they were sojourners, they became the docile subjects of Chinese bosses and headmen who dictated their lives and labors in California.

Conditions in Kwangtung and California formed the contexts of the encounter. Political turmoil and economic distress in the Pearl River Delta transformed Cantonese peasants into Chinese sojourners. The news of gold in California fixed the course of their destination. In California, white Americans sought to ensure the "American nature" of the state, perceiving American Indians, Mexicans, Europeans, African Americans, and Chinese as obstacles to the realization of the California dream. "The vision destined the young commonwealth to an elevated position among the states similar to that of the United States among the nations of the world."[21]

As in the global dispersion of the Chinese, a web of economic obligations and familial ties bound the Chinese sojourners in California. Poverty compelled the sojourners to obtain credit for their overseas ticket and with it an agreement to serve indentures that were akin to the notorious coolie trade. The credit ticket system by which Chinese sojourners arrived in California differed from the coolie traffic only in that they were willing participants in their bondage. But the system extended the reach of the "Chinese world" into California, where, in Chinatowns and beyond American influences, Chinese creditors and their district and kinship associations controlled the mass of indentured sojourners. "Regimented labor guaranteed the merchant-creditors a constant return on their investment in indentured emigrants."[22]

Chinatowns were unique places of control and contention. They were the headquarters of the Chinese business elite, who held a tight reign over their affairs. Chinatowns were institutions of social supervision and labor exploitation. But, to Chinese indentured laborers, they offered an illusion of home and outlets for pent-up emotions and repressed desires. Opium, prostitution, and gambling, nonetheless, only ensured the sojourners' submission. To white Americans, Chinatowns with their filth and immorality came to represent the Chinese sojourners and their nature. For some whites, then, Chinatowns embodied the reasons for their conflict with the Chinese. For others, they were the foci for social reform and humanitarian uplift.

The challenge brought on by the "hordes of downtrodden newcomers" stirred Californians "to bring all Chinese into the encompassing realm of American culture. They extended the universal blessings of their institutions and values to the newcomers as a group."[23] But, for most of the sojourners, the blessings of acculturation failed to support their purpose of making money quickly, paying off their indenture, and returning home to their families. The entreaties of the alien world went unheeded, and the sojourners kept their culture and orientation, rejecting the overtures of the new world.

Gradually, however, some Chinese indentures broke out of the close confines of California's Chinatowns and their regimentation by moving to the South and East to find work. They encountered there new ideas and a new perspective on American life, and growing numbers of them changed their outlook. In the process, sojourners became immigrants. But the image of the Chinese as sojourners had already fixed itself in the American imagination, and through political manipulation the Chinese had become a national problem. The initial encounter between white Californians opposed to slavery and Chinese indentures and sojourners dominated the political discussion. Thus the expediencies of politics framed the Chinese question as the inevitable clash of civilizations and national destinies.

In contrast to the studies by Coolidge and Sandmeyer, Barth's novel idea and his contribution to the debate on the origin and nature of the anti-Chinese movement derive from his focus upon the Chinese rather than the anti-Asianists. The pattern of Chinese migration, he argues, as determined by Chinese culture and the political and economic conditions in Kwangtung, created a sojourner whose orientation was directed homeward and not toward the new world. That sojourner mentality was reinforced by the network of ethnic and familial affiliations and the regimentation of creditors and Chinatowns. White Americans arrived in California with the dream of achieving wealth and creating an exemplary American state. They saw foreigners as impediments to that future. The Chinese sojourner, indentured and resistant to assimilation, stood out in that regard and became the object of antagonism by whites opposed to slavery and intent on building a "true American state."[24]

Barth's analysis moves the discussion outside of California to the American South and Northeast where Chinese laborers, he contends, entertained new perspectives and options on their American sojourn. Freed from the clutches of California's Chinatowns and their masters and with the help of white employers, missionaries, and educators, Chinese sojourners became immigrants and settlers. At the same time, their use as cheap labor and strikebreakers in the Northeast paralleled the growing feeling in the West that the Chinese posed an economic threat to white workers. Politicians in both the East and West seized upon the Chinese question and elevated it to national prominence. Although different circumstances molded public opinion in the East and West, these distinctions collapsed in the exigencies of politics.

A NATIONAL PROBLEM

Stuart Creighton Miller's The Unwelcome Immigrant: The American Image of the Chinese, 1785–1882 (1969) builds upon Barth's move to extend the discussion beyond California's borders. Initiated as a study on the idea of the yellow peril at the end of the nineteenth century, the project turned to American notions of the Chinese before 1882 when Miller's sources contradicted conventional historical interpretation that Americans held the Chinese in high esteem at least until the Opium War and those on the East Coast up to 1882. He thus abandoned his original intent for a systematic tracing of the evolution of the image of the Chinese and its role in the national decision to exclude them.

Miller begins with a review of Coolidge's California thesis, noting its influence on subsequent writings on the subject where there is an overwhelming agreement with the explanation. In their California-centered approach, both Coolidge and Sandmeyer, Miller notes, dismiss East Coast anti-Chinese sentiment as exceptional and due to personal ambition or political expediency. But how could a regional issue so fundamentally affect national politics when just a few decades earlier Southern slaveholders failed to move Northern constituencies? Miller asks. The California thesis has the quality of "making the tail seem to wag the dog."[25] In fact, the issue of slavery in California, as observed by both Coolidge and Barth, points to looking east of California, and contemporary East Coast fears over immigration similarly hints at an Eastern parallel to Western anxieties over the Chinese.

American opinions about the Chinese did not originate with Chinese immigration but with American traders and missionaries venturing to China before California's gold rush. Americans had been trading with China since 1785, and Protestant missionaries had been going to China since 1807. Those "inside dopesters" (persons holding an information monopoly and most influential in shaping public opinion) helped to create the Chinese image in the American mind. In addition, massacres of Christian missionaries in China and a bloody Chinese coolie uprising in Peru received wide coverage in the Eastern press. These international events similarly shaped American attitudes toward the Chinese. Images, though, are complexly created and constantly modified. Contradictory notions can exist side by side, and new experiences might resurrect old ideas to prominence. They must accordingly be historicized.

Before 1785, the American mind was generally innocent of notions of China. The China trade triggered American interest in that country, and traders, missionaries, and diplomats who visited China became important opinion makers because of their first-hand inside knowledge of the country and people. Instead of unmitigated praise for Chinese civilization, American traders offered mixed reports of respect and contempt. Their records indicate that few held racist views of the Chinese, and many maintained friendly relations with their Chinese counterparts. At the same time, deep, long-lasting friendships were rare, and traders saw China's government as despotic and its officials as corrupt, cowardly, and deceitful. Traders regularly paid bribes to officials and had to contend with the government's bureaucracy and trade regulations. They observed the Chinese to be a very "peculiar" people, with bizarre rituals and tastes that included an alleged propensity for gambling, smoking opium, and eating dogs, cats, and rats. In fact, most of the traders who went to China before 1840 "regarded the Chinese as ridiculously clad, superstitious ridden, dishonest, crafty, cruel, and marginal members of the human race who lacked the courage, intelligence, skill, and will to do anything about the oppressive despotism under which they lived or the stagnating social conditions that surrounded them."[26]

Diplomats mainly reinforced the negative views of the traders, and missionaries, the most prolific and widely read of the inside dopesters, added the evils of paganism and orgies of idolatry to the list of unfavorable Chinese traits. They railed against Chinese social inequities, treatment of women, infanticide, licentiousness, ignorance, immorality, and filth. They raised the alarm over China's huge population and impugned all aspects of Chinese society. Of course, missionaries had an incentive to highlight China's evils to justify their work of proselytizing. But their message, within the context of religion and the church, acquired greater urgency and currency among a select people.

Besides the dopesters, certain international events helped to introduce China into American parlors. Word of the Opium War (1839–42) benefited from the popularity of the penny press during that period. In its competitions with the established newspapers, the penny press thrived on war and scandal, and the war between China and Britain provided a scoop for the papers. Their coverage did not flatter the Chinese and was in fact highly unfavorable. A Boston newspaper, for instance, reported in 1840 that China was a land of "many letters, many lanterns, and few ideas," and its peoples were "long eared, elliptic-eyed, flat-nosed, olive colored . . . singularly deficient in intellectual physiognomy."[27] And John Quincy Adams praised Britain for extending "her liberating arm to the farthest bound of Asia" against the "churlish and unsocial" and "selfish" Chinese.[28] Even Anglophobes paused in their condemnation of Britain when confronted with the spectacle of the Chinese.

Domestic issues like slavery, racial difference, and health and disease mixed with the Chinese question in volatile ways. Reports linked the coolie trade with the African slave trade, and coolieism with slavery. Conditions onboard coolie ships, mutinies and suicides, and the horrors of the middle passage and plantations reminded readers of the enslavement of Africans and America's peculiar institution. Despite assurances that Chinese coolies never entered the United States, East Coast newspapers commonly associated the coolie with the migrant. And in congressional debates over Chinese immigration and women's prostitution, slavery constituted the leading analogy. The nineteenth century was also a time when American intellectuals wrestled with the notion of race. Deploying various sciences, from cranial measurements to linguistics, Europeans and Americans sought to classify and rank humankind. And having identified superior and inferior races, they warned of the dangers of the "commingling" between races. Thus racialized, the Chinese occupied a level lower than whites, and their exclusion and segregation were means by which to preserve white supremacy. Finally, racial difference intersected with concerns around public health and infectious disease. The Chinese carried diseases, some medical authorities warned, that, because Americans had no natural immunities to them, threatened the nation with debilitating epidemics. All those fears were national rather than regional.

When confronted with the Chinese in California, East Coast readers had already formed opinions of them: the image of the Chinese had long preceded their arrival on the West Coast. Eastern editorials during the 1850s wondered about the economic value of Chinese laborers and praised their sojourning status because it precluded a permanent servile class in America. And editors were quick to note the undesirable qualities of the Chinese as heathens, uncivilized, degraded, and sickly. After the Civil War, editorials condemned the planned introduction of Chinese in the South to replace African American freemen and publicized the arrival of Chinese workers in New York, New Jersey, Massachusetts, and Pennsylvania. As attested by those reports and others as well, Eastern readers were familiar with the Chinese as they were represented by the dopesters and the press.

Coolidge's California thesis is therefore inadequate to explain the national policy of exclusion. "Although the state unquestionably catalyzed and spearheaded the movement for exclusion," concludes Miller, "there were much more potent national and historical forces at work than the mere accident of evenly balanced political parties. Not even a very enthusiastic tail of such small dimensions could have wagged a dog that was less than willing to be wagged."[29] The fear of creating a permanent servile class, racial and cultural anxieties over Chinese commingling and assimilation, and the dread of exotic and contagious diseases were national concerns. And the trickle of Chinese workers on the East Coast forecast for many a downpour from the dark, heavy cloud that was China. Labor might have taken the lead in California, but the national picture involves other players in the anti-Chinese drama. These include the image makers— the traders, diplomats, and missionaries—international events, the press and the merging of slavery, the science of race, and public health and disease with the Chinese question.

RACE AND CLASS

Alexander Saxton's *The Indispensable Enemy: Labor and the Anti-Chinese Movement in California* (1971) returns to California and the question of labor's role in the anti-Chinese movement, but it also recognizes the problem's national contexts of race and class relations. Starting out as a doctoral dissertation in U.S. labor history, *Indispensable Enemy* positions California's and labor's anti-Chinese movement as an extension of the exploitation of American Indian labor, the enslavement and importation of Africans, and the coolie traffic from south China. The movement fits within the pattern of white exploitation of nonwhite labor. Although whites were exploited as workers, especially when thrown into competition with enslaved and "cheap" labor, they benefited from their whiteness. They were both exploited and exploiters. In that sense, "racial identification cut at right angles to class consciousness."[30] So labor's drive against Asians cannot be reduced solely to a matter of free versus cheap labor, and Asian migration was not the same as European immigration. "What happened to Orientals in America, while similar in many ways to what happened to other immigrants, is generally more like what happened to blacks, who were certainly not immigrants in the usual meaning of the term."[31]

To understand the roots of the anti-Chinese movement, Saxton begins, we must explore aspects of Jacksonian democracy in nineteenth-century America. Jacksonians held that the nation's producers, farmers, independent artisans, and workingmen of the South and West, advanced democracy in their battles against the East's capitalists and monopolies. The enslavement of Africans was justified on the basis of racial inferiority, but white workingmen also feared for their wages and jobs when confronted with the specter of African slave or emancipated labor. The Irish, with their high poverty rates, limited resources and skills, and political disempowerment, were the most hard-pressed of whites during this period. Because their whiteness offered them privileges, the Irish were among the leaders in the hatred against blacks in the East and, when reaching California, against the Chinese.

Nativism complemented the racial fears among white workingmen. Even recent immigrants felt the threat of further immigration to their jobs, wages, and privileges. The Know-Nothing Party thrived on these insecurities, and nativist sentiment infused both major political parties. The Democratic Party championed the producer ethic, defended slavery, and, after the Civil War, stressed white racial superiority for the exclusion of blacks and other racial minorities. Republicans were less influential with white labor than the Democrats, with their stand on abolition and human equality, but blacks sometimes fell victim to their pleas for national unity. Embedded within the pervasive uncertainties of workingmen's displacement and deprivation were issues of race and antiforeignism that were carried as ideological baggage across the continent to be unpacked in California.

The gold rush brought diverse groups to California, but the state's labor force was reduced to the divide between Chinese and non-Chinese. The former constituted between 20 and 25 percent of California's wage earners during the 1870s and early 1880s. The latter were united in their opposition to the Chinese, who they saw as tools of the capitalists. Class was thus further divided by race. When white workers vented their sense of frustration and dispossession, they generally struck out against the Chinese. The anti-Chinese movement thus had its origins in economic competition in the West between more or less free and indentured labor. But it was also supported and sustained by the earlier ideologies of Jacksonian politics in the antebellum East.

One of the first breakthroughs for the Democratic Party after the Civil War was in California. Among the state's European immigrants were Democrats from the Midwest and Atlantic regions whose "romantic nationalism and foreshortened egalitarianism" became dominant in California.[32] Here, they encountered few blacks but many Chinese who fitted within their mental boxes reserved for blacks as nonwhites, inferiors, and unfree workers. For Democrats, the Chinese question revitalized the party because it hearkened back to old hatreds without conjuring up the destructive divisions of the Civil War. In 1867, the Democrats swept California and saw thereby the national potential of the Chinese question to split the Republicans. Their defense of the Chinese on the basis of racial equality tied the Republican abolitionists to the capitalist and monopoly class, an indefensible position for the party.

Similarly, union leaders in California used anti-Chinese hatred to galvanize its organizing efforts. Crucial to Democratic success in 1867 were the votes of laborers, and the rise and successes of the Workingmen's Party dramatically demonstrated labor's power and the potential of the Chinese question to mobilize workers. After the exclusion of Chinese laborers, California's unions continued this empowerment strategy in an anti-Japanese crusade. And, despite trade unionist warnings against the dangers of political entanglements, labor leaders forged a symbiotic relationship with politicians that for a time benefited both constituencies. Among workers, the anti-Chinese crusade enabled the dominance of the skilled trades in the labor movement.

Although Saxton's interest in California's anti-Chinese movement was largely piqued by its meanings for the U.S. labor movement, his findings add new details to the historical debate around the causes for and nature of the anti-Chinese movement. He, like Coolidge and Sandmeyer, underscores the economic and political particularities of California and notes the conjoining of interests between politicians and labor leaders around the Chinese question. The Chinese were their indispensable enemy. Moreover, Saxton, like Barth and Miller, shows the national dimensions of the problem in politics and trade unionism and in portable and malleable ideologies that traversed the continent. In addition, he finds the movement's historical antecedents in the rhetoric of Jacksonian democracy, in antiblack racism, and in anti-immigrant sentiment and nativism. The anti-Chinese movement was thus a matter of both race and class and their mutual and clashing interests.

EXONERATING LABOR

Andrew Gyory's *Closing the Gate: Race, Politics, and the Chinese Exclusion Act* (1998) takes up the question of labor's role in the anti-Chinese movement and the 1882 Exclusion Act. Although Coolidge, Sandmeyer, and Saxton were correct about the importance of California and racism in the anti-Chinese movement, Gyory concedes, they were wrong about labor's lead. or even interest, in the anti-Chinese movement. White workers were not involved in the push for Chinese exclusion, and, "contrary to the claims of numerous scholars," Gyory declares, "most workers evinced little interest in Chinese exclusion. Organized labor nationwide played virtually no role in securing the legislation." Instead, he concludes, "the motive force behind the Chinese Exclusion Act was national politicians who seized and manipulated the issue in an effort to gain votes, while arguing that workers had long demanded Chinese exclusion and would benefit from it."[33] White workers might have held racist views against the Chinese and hence their attraction to racist politicians, Gyory points out, but that racism need not have been converted into action, into a concerted movement by labor for Chinese exclusion.

His interpretation, Gyory admits, flies in the face of conventional wisdom. Virtually all U.S. labor historians who have written on the subject agree that the national labor movement consistently supported the exclusion of Chinese workers. But the entire edifice of historical interpretation on Chinese exclusion was built upon an uncritical mutual reliance and repetitions of mainly secondary sources. Instead, primary evidence reveals that Coolidge's California thesis should be turned on its head. Regional politics did not move the national government; rather, "national politicians of both parties . . . seized, transformed, and manipulated the issue of Chinese immigration in the quest for votes." This was the classic case of "top-down politics," and it supplies a unique vantage point from which to view the political system of the Gilded Age.[34] Chinese exclusion comes on the heels of Reconstruction and serves to link antebellum antiblack racism with the era of Jim Crow. It helped fill the racist vacuum of those years and provided a convenient scapegoat for the sputtering economy.

Accordingly, Gyory, like Miller, describes the national stage upon which anti-Chinese hatred was enacted. Nineteenth-century American intellectuals like Ralph Waldo Emerson and Horace Greeley portrayed the Chinese as perverse, uncivilized, and filthy. Even the liberal John Stuart Mill worried over the permanent harm that Chinese immigration might bring to mankind's superior races. During the Civil War, workers attacked the use of European labor migration as a solution in the Northeast to the wartime labor shortage, and after the war they were united in seeking the eight-hour workday. Slavery personified evil — caste, bondage, barbarism, despotism. Contract labor, when associated with slavery, took on its odious, postbellum attributes, and Congress, in 1868, repealed the Contract Labor Law of 1864, leaving its regulation to the states. The issue unified labor, and, seventeen years later, labor convinced Congress to outlaw contract labor completely. Unmentioned in national labor circles, unlike among labor in California, was the question of Chinese migration. Even warnings of a Chinese invasion to the East Coast enabled by the transcontinental railroad's completion and news of schemes in the South to import Chinese labor failed to rouse Eastern workers.

Calvin T. Sampson's vow to break the Knights of St. Crispin strike at his shoe factory in North Adams, Massachusetts by importing Chinese workers in 1870 elicited mass protests by white workingmen. The battle line was drawn on the basis of class for rank-and-file white workers who defended free immigration but not imported labor, which they likened to slavery. They generally resisted the appeals to racism of some of their leaders and were consistent in their distinction between immigration and labor importation. Employers in the North and South watched Sampson's experiment with great interest and inundated Chinese labor recruiters with orders. And they used the threat of Chinese workers to scare white laborers into accepting lower wages. White workers took these erosions of their gains seriously and marched in the streets for their livelihoods in protest against Chinese labor importation and not against Chinese immigration.

Contrary to earlier authors, white workers, many of whom had served as soldiers, claimed credit for having abolished slavery. They grasped the war's meaning and during Reconstruction seized the free labor legacy of the Civil

War. Leading abolitionists like William Lloyd Garrison, by contrast, stood on Sampson's side, defended his right to import foreign workers, and denounced the labor leaders as "political demagogues."[35] Once the nation's conscience on freedom and racial justice, the abolitionists lost that position to the working class with the ratification of the Fifteenth Amendment in the early 1870s. Working-class ideology and demands were couched in the language of freedom versus slavery for which they continued the abolitionists' struggle and risked their lives and livelihoods.

A year after Sampson's actions in North Adams, Representative William Mungen (D-Ohio) introduced a Chinese exclusion measure. Congress failed to act on the measure because there was no national interest in the bill. Even when California served as a hotbed of anti-Chinese agitation, from 1870 to 1875, the Chinese question receded into the background at the national level. President Ulysses S. Grant took up California's cause when in his 1874 annual message he characterized Chinese immigration as bound labor that included the importation of women for shameful purposes. The following year, Congress passed the Page Act, which restated the legality of free Chinese contract labor but prohibited entry to women prostitutes from China, Japan, or any Asian country. The act failed to address California's desire for an end to Chinese immigration or demands by Eastern workers for the abolition of imported contract labor.

In the years leading up to the 1876 presidential elections, California's politicians launched a national campaign to introduce the anti-Chinese issue onto the national agenda by arguing that California's anti-Chinese movement would attract the workingmen's vote, and they proceeded to detail the Chinese menace to white labor. Despite opposition, especially among Republicans, both political parties went on record favoring restrictions on Chinese immigration. Noting that, Congress pledged investigations into the question, but labor seemed singularly unimpressed. Many saw the Chinese as a mere symbol of the problem and not the problem itself—cheap labor, not the Chinese, was the problem. And they generally resisted the barrage of anti-Chinese rhetoric fired by California politicians. "The first wave of anti-Chinese activity crested early in the East without engulfing working people."[36]

Politicians were a different matter. Acutely attuned to public opinion, politicians followed that lead. And both political parties, nearly evenly divided in the 1876 national election, recognized the importance of California's vote, and that of the West overall. Thus, politicians like James G. Blaine (R-Maine), and presidential aspirant in the 1876 and 1880 elections, plotted in his private papers the public's responses to anti-Chinese rhetoric. With his embrace of the anti-Chinese movement, Blaine hoped to capture the votes of California and the Western states and those of workingmen nationwide. Indicative of both party's bow to the political efficacy of anti-Chinese sentiment, the Fifteen Passenger

Bill of 1879 limiting Chinese immigration sailed through Congress and was only vetoed by President Rutherford Hayes on a technicality, its likely unconstitutionality because of the Burlingame Treaty. When American diplomats signed a new treaty with China in 1880 that gave to the United States the power to regulate Chinese immigration, a restrictive law was only a matter of time. The treaty was ratified the next year.

Amidst this activity, white workers were largely silent. Chinese immigration was a side issue to most. With the new treaty, Congress easily passed a Chinese exclusion bill in 1882, and, upon President Chester Arthur's objections, passed a revised bill that the president signed. The Chinese Exclusion Act became law in 1882 because the time was ripe for its passage. Studies that focus on California show how anti-Chinese sentiment developed in the West. Those that detail the national contexts of racist ideology suggest that Americans could largely accept anti-Chinese hatred. But they ignore the political dimension of the movement, and "politics are at the core of the Chinese Exclusion Act."[37] With little demand for and little to gain from Chinese exclusion, politicians made no effort to address the problem. But the political landscape changed. Class conflict rose to the forefront of Gilded Age politics, and politicians seized upon the Chinese question as a convenient rallying point for getting out the vote. White workers, indifferent and at first focused solely on class, came around to the politicians' framing of the issue as a matter of race and class, but only toward the end, when exclusion was inevitable. White workers welcomed the Chinese as immigrants but not as imported contract labor.

NOTES

1. Mary Roberts Coolidge, *Chinese Immigration* (New York: Henry Holt, 1909), 3.

2. Ibid., 7.

3. Ibid., 10.

4. Ibid., 12.

5. Ibid., 14.

6. Ibid., 21, 22, 23.

7. Ibid., 24.

8. Ibid., 28.

9. Ibid., 29.

10. Ibid., 39.

11. Ibid., 40.

12. Ibid., 182.

13. Elmer Clarence Sandmeyer, *The Anti-Chinese Movement in California* (Urbana: University of Illinois Press, 1991), 123.

14. Ibid., 25.

15. Ibid., 29.

16. Ibid., 33.

17. Ibid., 35.

18. Ibid., 41.

19. Ibid., 95.

20. Gunther Barth, *Bitter Strength: A History of the Chinese in the United States, 1850–1870* (Cambridge, Mass.: Harvard University Press, 1964), 1.

21. Ibid., 2.

22. Ibid., 3.

23. Ibid., 5.

24. Ibid., 131.

25. Stuart Creighton Miller, *The Unwelcome Immigrant: The American Image of the Chinese, 1785–1882* (Berkeley: University of California Press, 1969), 6.

26. Ibid., 36.

27. Ibid., 84.

28. Ibid., 95.

29. Ibid., 191.

30. Alexander Saxton, *The Indispensable Enemy: Labor and the Anti-Chinese Movement in California* (Berkeley: University of California Press, 1971), 1.

31. Ibid., 2.

32. Ibid., 261.

33. Andrew Gyory, *Closing the Gate: Race, Politics, and the Chinese Exclusion Act* (Chapel Hill: University of North Carolina Press, 1998), 1.

34. Ibid., 15.

35. Ibid., 57.

36. Ibid., 90.

37. Ibid., 254.

Chapter 5

AMERICA'S CONCENTRATION CAMPS

The mass removal and detention of Japanese Americans during World War II
is a part of the historiography of anti-Asianism. In fact, it is probably the subject
most written about within that literature and perhaps even within Asian American history as a whole. Books on America's concentration camps include those
that emanated from study projects during the wartime period, personal accounts
by those who experienced the forced removals and detentions and those who
administered the program, critical accounts by civil libertarians and others, oral
histories, and creative writings and art from the camps. And within Japanese
American history, America's concentration camps constitute the great temporal
and psychic divide between "before" and "after" the war.

There were three major research undertakings during the war. First, a group
of social scientists, mainly anthropologists, studied the camps for the War Relocation Authority, the camp administrators.[1] Then, under the joint sponsorship
of the Navy, Office of Indian Affairs, and War Relocation Authority, Alexander
H. Leighton directed a research project at the camp in Poston, Arizona.[2] Like
the first project, Leighton's research was used to advise the camp administrators
on governing the confined peoples. Finally, the Japanese American Evacuation
and Resettlement Study (JERS), headed by Dorothy Swaine Thomas of the
University of California, Berkeley, began with social scientists studying the unfolding Japanese evacuation and relocation program in early 1942.[3] They saw

the project as a sociological study of the effects of forced mass migration and dislocation; as a social anthropology study concerning cultural contact and change; as a political science study of camp governance and the interplay of local, state, and national policies; as a social psychology study of collective adjustments to confinement; and as an economic study of the consequences of the program for detainees.

Those purposes have invited reactions from critics of the camps and from those concerned with Japanese Americans as historical subjects. All three war-time research projects saw the camps as social laboratories in which to study the behavior of human beings in confinement. The results of the first two studies were directly translated into camp governance, although Leighton believed that his study bore broad, general application to situations of stress and rehabilitation. The JERS researchers state that they took special care to remain aloof from the camp administrators and to protect the confidentiality of their human subjects, though subsequent accounts have raised doubts about the thoroughness of the researchers' efforts in that regard.[4] And, in the pages of books intent on unraveling the camps' meaning for all Americans, students of Japanese American history find missing the central figures of that story—not those who perpetrated the forced removals and detentions, but their victims, Japanese Americans.

Apart from those concerns of research and emphasis, there have been two major debates within the literature of the camps. I discuss the first debate, which focuses on Japanese American reactions to confinement, under "Japanese American Resistance" in the "Emerging Themes" section, because, on the question of what the causes for the camps were, this first debate is not as developed as the second. In the first debate, newer generations of scholars reject the views of their predecessors who depict Japanese Americans as helpless, even contented victims of the wartime removals and detentions.[5] In the second debate, scholars argue about the theories of responsibility or the causes for the decision to remove and confine Japanese Americans during World War II. Although they do not exhaust the various interpretations, I have chosen to narrow my discussion of this debate to the following topics: regional pressure groups, the Army and government, exonerating General DeWitt, the President, and Hawai'i.[6] It is striking that none of these scholars have accepted the legitimacy of the government's wartime claim that the mass evacuation was justified because of military necessity.[7]

Morton Grodzins' reading of his interviews and field notes, public and private sector records and publications, and especially California newspapers convinced him of the ground swell of support for mass evacuation along the West Coast. Behind the evidence, nonetheless, is his assumption of American democracy—i.e., that policy is enacted by demands made by constituencies to their representatives at the local, state, and national levels. Grodzins argues that regional pressure groups mounted a campaign, based on a long history of anti-Asian agitation and fear of the "yellow peril," for mass exclusion. The war and patriotism provided convenient covers for the economic and political self-interest of agricultural groups and politicians. West Coast demands influenced the War Department, which was given control over the program after the Justice Department washed its hands of the matter. The President, as commander in chief, signed the executive order that enabled the mass evacuation, and Congress and the Supreme Court sanctioned the deed.

Jacobus tenBroek, Edward N. Barnhart, and Floyd W. Matson are critical of Grodzins' pressure-group theory, but share his view that the mass evacuation was unique, unprecedented, and a radical departure from American ideals and principles. And like Grodzins, tenBroek et al. begin with the history of West Coast anti-Asianism, drawing generously from Mary Coolidge's California thesis. They isolate from the anti-Asian movement the Chinese and Japanese stereotype, especially the idea of the "yellow peril" as depicted in popular magazines, fiction, and films. Japan's unprovoked attack on Pearl Harbor activated and reconfirmed the stereotype and fear that stirred popular anger and fostered official acquiescence. Lieutenant General John DeWitt, in charge of the defense of the West Coast, pushed for Army control and a mass evacuation. This plan prevailed when the Justice Department agreed and the president signed Executive Order 9066. The pressure-group and politicians theories fail to explain General DeWitt's central role in this decision because he was immune to public pressure. And the undertaking of mass evacuation by the Army and government was the result of a combination of factors, including the anti-Japanese stereotype, the West Coast public, and the individuals and groups who demanded and supported it.

Military historians Stetson Conn, Rose C. Engelman, and Byron Fairchild find a different General DeWitt and a different Army in their reading of military documents. Unlike tenBroek et al., in whose work the general and Army appear for the most part static, Conn, Engelman, and Fairchild reveal a vacillating DeWitt, who shifted from one position to another, and a war department that was divided. At first DeWitt opposed mass evacuation because many of the evacuees were U.S. citizens and he remained confident that the loyal could be distinguished from the disloyal. Major Karl Bendetsen, sent from office of the provost marshal general in Washington, D.C., convinced DeWitt that he should insist on stronger measures, including the designation of exclusion zones to protect strategic interests. DeWitt was also influenced by politicians like California's Governor Culbert Olson, who reported to him that support for mass evacuation was swelling. But it was Bendetsen who served as DeWitt's spokesman and who added steel to his spine, and it was the office of the provost marshal general within the War Department from which emanated the most enthusiasm for mass evacuation. The president sided with that position, and he signed the executive order on February 19, 1942.

Roger Daniels supplies a synoptic view of the various theories of responsibility building upon the work of previous scholars. Like tenBroek et al., he sees the anti-Japanese movement and "yellow peril" stereotype as antecedents of the wartime evacuation, and like Grodzins he cites the role of economic interest groups and politicians in pressing for the camps. And like the military historians Conn et al., he details the pivotal interventions of Bendetsen and the shifts in the positions of DeWitt and of the War Department. But in the end, Daniels concludes, it was Franklin D. Roosevelt who signed the executive order and he alone bears final responsibility. The president, he suggests, was motivated by expedience and racial prejudice. Victimizing the Japanese was popular especially when the war was not going well for the Allies, and Roosevelt harbored prejudice against the Japanese as a group, viewed them with suspicion, and favored their mass internment in Hawai'i.

Gary Y. Okihiro contends that Hawai'i took the lead in the ideas of removal and confinement. Like tenBroek et al. and Daniels, he sees historical continuities in the anti-Japanese movement before the war and the wartime actions against America's Japanese. But he structures that movement around the social relations involved in the move from migrant labor to dependency, and particularly in the escalating forms both of the oppression that accompanied that move and of the resistance with which Japanese Americans met it. The 1920 strike of sugar workers was a key event in resistance but also in the oppression that followed. Hawai'i's leaders, both the planter plutocracy and military, were united in representing the strike as an attempt by Japan to capture the Territory's sugar industry and thereby its economy. For military and civilian intelligence, the strike accelerated their surveillance of Japanese Americans, and it inspired a series of plans by the military to contain the Japanese peril during the 1920s and 1930s. DeWitt and Roosevelt, among others, were involved in those plans, which mandated a declaration of martial law, the registration of enemy aliens, and internment camps for enemy aliens and eventually for U.S. citizens. As community leaders, the captives would serve as hostages to ensure the good behavior and productivity of Japanese Americans as a whole. Because of its strategic location in the Pacific and its demography—its population was predominantly Japanese American—Hawai'i was of primary concern to those responsible for the nation's internal security. When war came, Hawai'i led the way and the West Coast followed in its wake.

REGIONAL PRESSURE GROUPS

Morton Grodzins began the research for his book *Americans Betrayed: Politics and the Japanese Evacuation* (1949) when he was a member of JERS, and he wrote it to show the causes for the decision to evacuate Japanese Americans from the Pacific Coast during World War II. It is foremost a study of government and of the decision-making process and of policymaking. The evacuation was "a major event in the history of the American democracy, without precedent in the past and with disturbing implications for the future."[8] It was the first time that the United States confined an entire group of people defined solely by their race rather than by their individual guilt. Although the evacuation affected a small minority and was made during a wartime emergency, its impact extends to all Americans, because the Supreme Court has declared it to be constitutional.

In that sense, the evacuation is less important as history than as legal precedent. And "it is less important for what it did to Japanese Americans than for what it might do to all Americans."[9] It is not about Japanese Americans; it is about all Americans. It is not Japanese American history; it is American history. And because it is necessary to understand how this decision was reached in order to prevent it from happening again, the evacuation is less important as government policy than as a process in policymaking. The process of government is continuous, and what it produced for Japanese Americans it can produce for other Americans. And yet, despite their wider significance, the origins of evacuation's origins are remarkably unique.

"The extraordinary mass movements were the product of an extraordinary situation."[10] Of about 127,000 Japanese on the U.S. mainland, more than 112,000 lived in concentrated enclaves along the West Coast. Their race, Old World culture, economic competition, segregated communities, and uncertain allegiance to the United States set them apart from their white neighbors and made them unpopular with many. Pearl Harbor unleashed some of that old hostility and suspicion, and rumors of Japanese treachery and possible sabotage circulated widely. The Army, charged with protecting the nation's western flank, concluded that "military necessity" required the removal of Japanese residents from that area to the interior. But before that policy was adopted and pursued, there was a strong regional demand for that action. "Evacuation was only one event in a long series of related events."[11]

Chinese workers, at first welcomed, became unpopular when they demanded higher wages. Likewise, Japanese laborers were welcomed because they were regarded as more docile than the Chinese. By the start of the new century, however, agitation against the Japanese began. In 1906, San Francisco ordered the segregation of Asian students, and in 1913 that state passed the Alien Land Law, which prohibited immigrant Asians from owning land. Other Western states followed California's lead. And another pattern was set by these anti-Asian activities. Western animus against the Japanese shaped national policy. Thus, the Gentlemen's Agreement of 1907, signed by Japan and the United States, averted war over San Francisco's school segregation order. Similarly, pressure from Pacific Coast groups was instrumental in the passage of the 1924 Oriental Exclusion Act by Congress.

Anti-Japanese hatred was premised on racial and economic grounds. A recurrent theme was that Japanese fecundity threatened to swamp the entire state and make it flow with "Oriental blood." The racial divide was ensured by the impossibility of Japanese assimilation. As the *San Francisco Chronicle* declared in February 1905: "The Asiatic can never be other than an Asiatic, however much he may imitate the dress of the white man, learn his language and spend his wages for him."[12] And in any case, a assimilation of whites and Japanese was not only "unthinkable" and "morally indefensible," it was "biologically impossible," according to the *Los Angeles Times* of July 15, 1920.[13] Labor opposed the Japanese because they represented cheap labor against which whites could and should not have to compete. And as Japanese moved up the economic ladder from laborers to landowners and entrepreneurs, agitation against them grew, manipulated by politicians, including San Francisco mayor, Eugene Schmitz, for their own ends.

Political interest groups knew well the efficacy of the Japanese question for attracting votes, funds, and influence. In 1908, the Oriental Exclusion League claimed a membership of 110,000 and was the most dominant anti-Asian group in California before 1923. The California Joint Immigration Committee, made up of patriotic, nativist, and labor groups, absorbed the Exclusion League in 1924, and worked single-mindedly for the exclusion of Japanese. There were no comparable groups protecting the interests of Japanese. Mainly churchmen, but also educators, formed groups that aimed to defend the rights and interests of Japanese immigrants, but these were largely ineffectual in moving either the public or the government toward their position.

Anti-Japanese polemics revealed deep-seated animosity toward the Japanese, but it was their emotional character that gave them their strength and effectiveness. California assemblyman Grove Johnson in February 1909 asked rhetorically, and thunderingly: "Do you want your daughters—your little daughters—in school with Japanese? They are not boys. They are men—grown men—with all the base passions of men. That is why they ought to be kept out of the schools. They have no more regard for morality than do beasts. They live like beasts. They are beasts. Do you want your daughters in school with such as these?"[14]

After passage of the 1924 Exclusion Act, anti-Japanese agitation declined and some of that animosity was redirected at Filipinos. The course of the movement for immigration exclusion shows a progression from agitation against the Chinese to agitation against the Japanese, and finally against the Filipinos. The *nisei* came of age, and they assimilated into the economic and social life of the majority far better than their parents had done. Consequently, despite the rise in international tensions, relations between whites and Japanese in the United States improved during the period 1924–1941. Still, anti-Japanese feeling ran deep, and powerful groups had a long history of involvement in trumpeting the threat of the "yellow menace."[15] These economic and political regional interests set national agendas and policies on immigration and international relations, and they would reawaken with the sudden blow at Pearl Harbor.

At first, political leaders pleaded for public calm and fair play for the Japanese. But the old anti-Japanese organizations realized that war with Japan gave them a splendid chance to achieve their long-term goals. Concerning the stir of support shown the California Joint Immigration Committee in the month after Pearl Harbor, a member of the committee observed: "This is our time to get things done that we have been trying to get done for a quarter of a century."[16] The unfinished agenda for some was the complete removal of Japanese from the United States. For certain agricultural and business groups, the expulsion of Japanese from California was the objective. The Western Growers Protective Association was active in this regard. Its members were large producers of row crops sent almost exclusively to canneries and eastern U.S. markets. Most Japanese farmers who sold their garden crops to local markets were not in competition with these growers. Still, the Association maintained that the removal of Japanese from the Western states would benefit white farmers and have little impact on agricultural production overall. The Grower-Shipper Vegetable Association of central California was less nuanced. Their managing secretary, Austin Anson, was quoted as saying: "We're charged with wanting to get rid of the Japs for selfish reasons. We might as well be honest. We do. It's a question of whether the white man lives on the Pacific Coast or the brown men."[17]

Other groups joined the call by agricultural interests for Japanese removal. These included the chambers of commerce of various cities, merchants and manufacturers groups, civic organizations like the Pacific League, patriotic groups like the American Legion and Native Sons of the Golden West, and labor unions. These constituted pressure groups that called on the national government for Japanese evacuation. They publicized their positions in newspapers, passed resolutions, and engaged in letter-writing campaigns. Many were unapologetic about the fact that they stood to gain financially from their calls for Japanese removal. Even members of the Western Growers Protective Association realized profits from the evacuation, despite their contrary claims. An economic motive moved some; for others, evacuation was a means to remove an alien culture and stem the tide of Japanese reproduction in California. Patriotism—the war lent new urgency to the exigency of national defense—served as a timely pretext for advancing certain economic, racial, and political interests. In addition, these same organizations active in Japanese evacuation had shown a willingness to violate the rights of free speech and assemblage and the right for labor to organize. To disregard the civil liberties of the Japanese was an easy step for them.

Politicians from the West Coast assumed primary responsibility for the evacuation of the Japanese. Congressman Ed. V. Izac (D-California) stated: "Evacuation would never have taken place if the united Pacific Coast delegations had not applied pressure—not only upon the Attorney-General and the Secretary of War—but also on the President himself."[18] Despite being ad hoc, the bipartisan caucus of Pacific Coast representatives called government officials as witnesses, demanded reports, and made recommendations. It acted as a duly constituted congressional committee, and exerted its political muscle to achieve Japanese evacuation.

Like other government officials, West Coast representatives urged tolerance and caution during the first few weeks of the war. In early January, Congressman Leland Ford of Los Angeles expressed to Secretary of State Cordell Hull his fear that Japanese treachery might imperil California's security. He sent identical letters to other top officials, and later outlined his plan for "all Japanese, whether citizens or not, to be placed in inland concentration camps." Japanese loyalty could thereby be assured.[19] Soon others in the delegation joined Ford's campaign. This effort was reinforced by the Los Angeles Chamber of Commerce, which presented to the California congressional delegation, including Congressman John Costello of Los Angeles, a strong supporter of the effort, its desire for Japanese evacuation. Although members of the delegations from California, Oregon, and Washington voted unanimously to support evacuation, there was no consensus on the issue. Neither the Justice Department nor the Army shared the opinion of those favoring the evacuation of alien and citizen.

Even among their colleagues in Congress, there were only three from the South who showed an interest in Japanese evacuation. At this time, the vast majority were unacquainted with or simply uninterested in the question. Still, the West Coast bloc made their views known in newspaper accounts, and residents of those states pressed their representatives for action. And while it is simplistic to say that congressional activity caused the evacuation, it was one of the determining factors that made the War Department more willing to supervise the evacuation and the Justice Department less willing to oppose that violation of civil rights.

State and local politicians generally expressed faith in the Japanese at first, but, because of a basic distrust of them and an inability to separate the loyal from the disloyal, many came to favor mass evacuation of the Japanese, regardless of citizenship. And although these politicians had no single voice, they made their views known directly to their representatives and to the military officers in their districts, and thereby influenced federal officials to favor evacuation.

Regional pressure groups favoring Japanese evacuation wrote letters to federal officials demanding Japanese removal. At first, their letters to the U.S. attorney general did not constitute sufficient evidence of great public pressure for evacuation, but beginning around mid-January 1942 the demands for evacuation far exceeded calls for tolerance. Political leaders began to interpret as overwhelming popular sentiment the actions of organized pressure groups and the growing preponderance of letters supporting evacuation.

The federal government's disorganized efforts to arrest enemy aliens, declare prohibited zones, and remove enemy aliens from those zones in the days immediately after Pearl Harbor failed to reassure the public that the threat had been contained. Instead, those acts only heightened public suspicions and fears. And the interior states believed that, by pushing the Japanese from the coast to the interior, California was simply dumping their problem onto them. Racial prejudice, sectional distrust, and misinformation about the government's intentions led to the failure of this program of partial evacuation.

Although the Army favored mass evacuation, the Justice Department refused to endorse the plan. It held that the alien control program was sufficient. The Army pressed for larger prohibited zones. The Justice Department declined. Finally, on February 14, 1942, DeWitt, the commander of the Western Defense Command, recommended to the War Department a mass evacuation of all Japanese, aliens and citizens, as soon as possible, in order to protect the Pacific Coast. The War Department agreed with DeWitt's plan, and sought a presidential order to implement it. Although divided, the Justice Department agreed to relinquish control of the program to the military. In effect, the Army's plan for mass evacuation prevailed because the Justice Department relinquished to the War Department its responsibility for internal security. Both departments drew up the evacuation proclamation and presented it to the president, who signed it a few hours after having received it and never having discussed it in a cabinet meeting.

Executive Order 9066, based upon the president's authority as chief executive and commander in chief of the armed forces, was sweeping. It delegated to the appropriate military commander authority to designate areas from which all persons would be excluded. Congress sanctioned the order by passing Public Law 503, which imposed criminal penalties for opposing the order, and the Supreme Court, in test cases brought up by Japanese Americans, affirmed that the evacuation was constitutional. The order and the mass evacuation it enabled followed regional demands for the action. Those regional pressures "markedly influenced" War Department policy. The Army's justifications for mass evacuation "paralleled, and in some cases copied verbatim, falsities and half-truths that characterized the regional demands. Military officers at first denied any necessity for evacuating Japanese from interior areas of California, then insisted upon that action in response to renewed regional pressure."[20] Also, some military officers, including DeWitt, shared the public's racist attitude toward the Japanese. The Justice Department's abdication of responsibility to the War Department allowed the Army's plan to go forward. And Congress and the Supreme Court sanctioned the evacuation.

In sum, "Japanese Americans were the immediate victims of the evacuation.

But larger consequences are carried by the American people as a whole. Their legacy is the lasting one of precedent and constitutional sanctity for a policy of mass incarceration under military auspices. This is the most important result of the process by which the evacuation decision was made. That process betrayed all Americans."[21]

Because of their parallels, studies of the anti-Chinese movement and the Exclusion Act and studies of the anti-Japanese movement and the concentration camps bear comparison. (See my discussion of the anti-Chinese movement in the "Historical Debates" section.) Like Mary Roberts Coolidge and the Chinese Exclusion Act, Morton Grodzins sees the Japanese evacuation as unprecedented in U.S. history and of greater importance to Americans as a whole than to the Japanese Americans who were immediately and directly affected. As Coolidge and Elmer Clarence Sandmeyer see the anti-Chinese movement in terms of a regional issue that pressed itself on the national government, so Grodzins views Japanese evacuation. Like Coolidge, Grodzins assumes that public policy emanates from the ground up and not, as Gunther Barth assumes, from the top down. And Grodzins, like Sandmeyer, perceives the anti-Japanese movement as a descendant of the anti-Chinese movement. Nonetheless, these are separate and distinctive events that share similarities.

THE ARMY AND GOVERNMENT

Prejudice, War and the Constitution (1954) by Jacobus tenBroek, Edward N. Barnhart, and Floyd W. Matson offers a critique of Grodzins' regional pressure-group theory.[22] They ask why DeWitt bowed to various pressures and petitions. Public opinion might sway politicians, but the military? Further, defense of the West Coast depended on military strategy, so why should the Army have followed the opinion of civilians and civilian organizations? The answer is that DeWitt's racism and that of his staff predisposed them to believe that Japanese presence in the United States posed a danger. They did not need to be persuaded of this danger. They already believed it.

The book emanates from the University of California JERS project. It concerns itself with the historical origins of the evacuation, its political characteristics, and its legal implications. "Thus it is less a study of the Japanese Americans in particular than of Americans in general."[23] *Prejudice, War and the Constitution* follows two other books from JERS—Dorothy S. Thomas and Richard S. Nishimoto's *The Spoilage* (1946), which examines Japanese evacuee responses to confinement in the camps, and Dorothy S. Thomas's *The Salvage* (1952), which studies the resettlement of Japanese outside the camps. Thomas, before leaving JERS in 1948, asked tenBroek to write what would become *Prejudice, War and the Constitution*, to serve as the historical base for her studies of the courses of the lives of individuals in and after the camps. The book's title spells out its three sections—pre-war anti-Japanese prejudice and its activation at the war's onset, the wartime evacuation, and its constitutional significance.

Like Grodzins, the authors begin with the observation that the evacuation and detention during World War II were unprecedented. They were "a radical departure from American ideals and principles."[24] To understand that violation of democracy's basic tenets requires an appreciation of the West Coast anti-Asian and anti-Japanese prejudice and suspicion that endured for nearly a century. That history helped to determine white responses to the Japanese following Pearl Harbor. Also, the causes for the "unprecedented racism" of the camps were influenced by the immediate historical contexts of the decision to evacuate the Japanese and by the characters involved in it.[25] The Army claimed that "military necessity," and the possibility of Japanese sabotage and espionage, required the program of mass removal and detention. Others, like the Japanese American Citizens League, countered that evacuation was not a military necessity but was the result of pressure groups, economic interests, and General De Witt's racism.

Anti-Asian agitation began with the anti-foreignism of American gold miners in California. Among this "weirdly assorted" throng, "lawlessness" and "obsessive greed" bred "innate intolerance" for Indians, Mexicans, and the Chinese. A combination of "low-grade southerners," "border ruffians," and rough and crude frontiersmen joined the ranks of whites against nonwhites, especially in the mining districts. "A stereotyped view of the role and character of the dark-skinned minorities had taken root in the consciousness of Californians and was to endure long after the veins had run dry of gold and the mining camps had closed down."[26] Later groups of whites accepted the stereotype and carried on the tradition of social inequality, physical attacks, and exclusion.

As nonwhites, the Chinese suffered from the manifestations of white supremacy. White workers sought their exclusion, politicians manipulated the Chinese question, and local and state governments legislated against them. The Chinese stereotype evolved from that agitation. The Chinese were a moral evil, they were virtual slaves, and they were two-faced and treacherous, incapable of assimilation and unworthy of citizenship. There was an unbridgeable racial difference, a physical and moral gulf between whites and Chinese, between the superior and inferior races. Most importantly for this study, the Chinese were a "yellow peril," a peaceful invasion that threatened America. The Chinese were heirs to anti-foreignism; the apprehensions of white workingmen; the exploitation of politicians, newspapers, and writers; and the "ingrained prejudices" of white Americans against "dark-skinned minorities."[27]

A few years after the 1882 Exclusion Act had retired the Chinese question, "the Chinese stereotype became the Japanese stereotype."[28] The "heathen Chinee" was the psychological foundation upon which the "Jap" stereotype was built. Japanese moved into agriculture and the urban trades as replacements for the Chinese and were thus lumped together with the Chinese as cheap labor. As groups, they were inevitably compared, and were collapsed into a single category. The Japanese acquired the undesirable traits of the Chinese stereotype and none of its virtues. And the menace of the Japanese to America as the "yellow peril" was compounded with the rise of Japan. Its sweeping victory over Russia in 1905 inspired visions of a peaceful and military invasion of California and the Pacific Coast, and the fear of war with Japan was pervasive throughout America. There was a hiatus in anti-Japanese agitation during World War I, when Japan was a U.S. ally, but the agitation resumed after the war, goaded by pseudoscientific racism and the eugenics movement. Japan's aggressions in Asia, Hollywood's filmic representations of sinister and inscrutable Asian villains, and parallel images in mass-circulation magazines and popular fiction kept alive the negative stereotype of the Japanese.

As in the anti-Chinese movement, white workers in the anti-Japanese movement took the lead, campaigning to exclude the Japanese. Labor sought to discourage Japanese immigration by law or treaty, and employed boycotts to drive the Japanese, like the Chinese before them, from urban trades. In their newspapers, unions railed against the Japanese, and they held mass meetings and petitioned the public and politicians to join them in their cause. In 1905, they helped form the Japanese and Korean Exclusion League, later called the Asiatic Exclusion League, which became a leading voice in the anti-Asian movement.

Politicians rode the anti-Japanese wave to elective office, and patriotic groups like the American Legion conducted their private wars against the alien and subversion. The Legion worked for legislative exclusion and expulsion of those they considered seditious or unpatriotic. It contrived propaganda against the Japanese, promoted the alien land laws, and opposed Asian immigration and naturalization. The Native Sons of the Golden West opposed the Japanese on white supremacist grounds, and were second only to the American Legion in their effectiveness in the anti-Japanese campaign. Even after passage of the 1924 Exclusion Act, the Native Sons pressed its work against the Japanese by opposing dual citizenship, any relaxation of immigration restrictions, and, because of Hawai'i's large Japanese population, Hawaiian statehood.

Agricultural groups exerted their muscle in the anti-Japanese campaign especially after the Japanese managed to lease land and begin independent farming. Agricultural interests opposed the upward mobility of Japanese from farm laborers to owners, fearing competition and loss of their labor supply. The California Farm Bureau built up its membership to 20,000 by 1920 largely through its manipulation of the Japanese problem. It sought the exclusion of Japanese and Asian Indians from the rank of producers but not as farm workers, whom its members found useful. California's alien land laws were thus directed against owning and leasing land. And the politics of prejudice appeared to contribute more to the Farm Bureau's organization membership and projects than to any immediate economic benefit the Bureau might have gained from the presence or absence of Japanese farmers. Similarly, with its membership declining to 100,000, the National Grange experienced a revival during the period of its agitation against the Japanese, when its membership soared to nearly 150,000.

By 1941, after about fifty years of anti-Chinese hostility and fifty years of anti-Japanese agitation, whites along the West Coast held "a rigidly stereotyped set of attitudes" toward Asians, which "centered on suspicion and distrust."[29] The stereotype matured during the 1920s with California's alien land law and the immigration Exclusion Act, and then during the 1930s with Japan's aggressions in Asia and the Great Depression in the United States. The Pearl Harbor attack revived the stereotype, and public attitudes toward the Japanese crystallized around the familiar themes of treachery and disloyalty, and the Japanese became the objects of white suspicion, anxiety, and anger. The old stereotype fed rumors of espionage and sabotage, and the attack gave substance to the oft-repeated fears of the "yellow peril" and the peaceful invasion.

The Japanese stereotype circulated in rumor and opinion, in private and public declarations, by unionists and politicians, among farm groups and patriots. Foremost was the idea of the "yellow peril" and its corollary, the identification of Japanese Americans with actual or potential spies and saboteurs. So strong was that belief that the absence of any proof of Japanese American collusion with the enemy only affirmed the likelihood of that prospect. Their geographical concentration in strategic military and industrial areas confirmed their prescience and planning; their adherence to Japanese culture showed that they were held under the sway of their leaders and the emperor; and their Buddhist and Shinto temples, language schools, and newspapers were evidences of their disloyalty. Cheap labor and unfair competition made them undesirable, and race hatred constituted a compelling argument for mass evacuation—to protect them from the threat of riots and acts of violence. Although almost entirely untrue in content, those rumors and beliefs held tragic consequences. They revealed a deep-seated hostility against the Japanese without regard for distinctions of birth or citizenship or for their constitutional rights. The wave of anti-Japanese sentiment swept away all opposition in "a vortex of popular anger and official acquiescence."[30]

The ideas formed the basis for the actions that followed. The Justice Department put into effect its long-prepared plan for alien-enemy control. By the evening of Pearl Harbor day, 736 Japanese nationals on the mainland had been placed under confinement. These were Japanese community leaders, including businessmen, officers of Japanese associations, Buddhist and Shinto priests, and

Japanese-language schoolteachers. By mid-December, DeWitt, commander in charge of the defense of the Pacific Coast, became dissatisfied with the Justice Department's enforcement of the alien-enemy control program and was convinced that military security required the establishment of prohibited zones around strategic sites. As a result, enemy aliens were removed and excluded from prohibited zones designated by the military and approved by the Justice Department. By early February, however, DeWitt had reached an impasse with the Justice Department, and in mid-February he recommended the evacuation of all Japanese, alien and citizen alike. He also recommended that anyone deemed dangerous be excluded from designated areas, and that this program of evacuation and exclusion be controlled by the military. DeWitt's plan envisioned the mass evacuation and internment of enemy aliens; Japanese American citizens would be given the option of voluntary internment or exclusion from all military areas. Mass internment would be a temporary expedient pending resettlement.

DeWitt's "final recommendation" was approved by the War Department, which based its decision on the general's estimate of the situation from a military point of view. At a joint meeting between the departments of War and Justice, the latter agreed to allow the military to head the program, despite its view that mass evacuation was unnecessary and unconstitutional for U.S. citizens. The next morning, on February 18, 1942, the agreement was worked out, and on February 19 the order was presented to the president for his signature. Executive Order 9066 declared that the successful prosecution of the war required the exclusion of all persons from designated military areas, and that the federal government would provide their transportation, food, shelter, and other accommodations necessary for the order to be carried out.

What were the causes of Executive Order 9066? There are two widely held theories. Most historians discount the official government explanation of "military necessity." The first theory is the pressure-group theory, according to which various West Coast groups out of self-interest exerted pressure on the government for the mass evacuation. The second theory is the politician theory, according to which West Coast politicians, for *their* own ends, inflamed an apprehensive public. Morton Grodzins in *Americans Betrayed* offers the most sophisticated argument in support of the pressure-group theory. He notes that agricultural and business groups were among the most active proponents of evacuation and that they were influential in shaping that government decision and policy. But Grodzins fails to show that agricultural interests were uniformly or even substantially for evacuation. In fact, only six of the hundreds of West Coast agricultural associations publicly supported it. Further, before February 14, 1942, that support was trivial, as it consisted of eight letters to congressmen from officials of three associations, a visit by an officer to Washington, the adoption of a single resolution, and a telegram to a governor that was passed on to U.S. Attorney General Francis Biddle. Grodzins exaggerates the extent and efficacy of the "pressure" from agricultural groups.

Similarly, Grodzins cites the Pacific League of Southern California as an organization demanding evacuation, but the League's membership was fewer than 100, and its own officials admitted that their lobbying efforts with local, federal, and Army leaders met with no success. And Grodzins states that at least eighteen union locals and councils passed resolutions calling for evacuation, when in fact only one local and one council actually passed resolutions. Even the American Legion, the most active of the patriotic groups named by Grodzins in the evacuation movement, was not united in this cause. Of the 873 posts and 50 area and district organizations of the Legion before February 14, 1942, only 25 urged the mass evacuation of Japanese. Some favored the removal of only enemy aliens or Japanese nationals, while others urged the evacuation of all the Japanese. In sum, the pressure-group theory rests on shaky ground.

The politician theory holds that West Coast politicians, alert to public anxieties, capitalized on those fears by advocating evacuation. Yet before mid-February 1942 none of the governors of Western states or their state legislatures called for the Japanese evacuation, and only seven county boards in California and one in the non-Western states called for evacuation. Thus, it appears that the politician theory is a generalization without demonstrable support. Several authors, including Grodzins, assume that the congressional delegations from Western states put pressure on the War and Justice departments. Grodzins concedes that the politician theory is an oversimplification, but maintains that pressure from politicians was one among several significant factors that led to the evacuation. But there is no evidence to show that any West Coast politician contacted General De Witt before mid-February, and the earliest record of political pressure are the several letters from California congressman Leland Ford to Attorney General Biddle at the end of January, 1942, urging that the Japanese be confined to concentration camps. Biddle, in his replies to Ford, stated his firm opposition to mass evacuation. A group of West Coast senators and representatives met and recommended mass evacuation on February 12, 1942, but their plan to meet with the president was called off because Executive Order 9066 had already been signed.

When examined closely, the pressure-group and politicians theories fall short of their claims. They fail to demonstrate the magnitude of the support for evacuation and how the pressure generated by those groups effectuated public policy. In the end, it was General De Witt's recommendation that resulted in Executive Order 9066, though his judgment in this matter was military and not political. This does not mean, however, that the invocation of military necessity was legitimate or that De Witt stood apart from the public opinion that surrounded him. "It is a central contention of this book that the claim of 'military necessity' was unjustified—but that the dereliction was one of folly, not of knavery."³¹ The Army and the government bear responsibility for this decision, but it was also shared by all those who demanded and supported it, including politicians, businessmen, farmers, and patriots—indeed, by the Pacific Coast public. And the history of the anti-Japanese stereotype and the familiar specter of the "yellow peril," reactivated during this period of war, stirred anxiety, fear, and anger among Americans generally, and "they struck out blindly at its shadow—not knowing that by this blow they were to damage, not the enemy, but the constitutional safeguards of their own free way of life."³²

EXONERATING DE WITT

In *Guarding the United States and Its Outposts* (1964), military historians Stetson Conn, Rose C. Engelman, and Byron Fairchild examine the U.S. Army's role in its defense of the Western Hemisphere during World War II. A chapter of the book is devoted to the Japanese evacuation from the West Coast. Of particular interest to the historical debate over the causes for the mass evacuation is this reassessment by Army historians of De Witt's place in the decision-making process that led to Executive Order 9066. This detailed study of discussions internal to the War Department and the Army modifies the account by Jacobus tenBroek et al. regarding De Witt.

As commander of the Army's Western Defense Command, General De Witt was of several minds. On December 26, 1941, in response to a report that the Los Angeles Chamber of Commerce had recommended the evacuation of all Japanese from the area, De Witt stated his opposition, arguing that an evacuation that included citizens would include loyal Japanese as well as disloyal ones, and would run the risk of alienating the former. It would be better, he said, for the police and people in the community to monitor their Japanese neighbors rather than interning them. "I don't think it's a sensible thing to do," De Witt said. "An American citizen, after all, is an American citizen. And while they all may not be loyal, I think we can weed the disloyal out of the loyal and lock them up if necessary."³³ Instead, the focus was on the prompt arrest of enemy aliens and confiscation of radio transmitters, cameras, and the like to prevent espionage and sabotage.

The Department of Justice, in charge of the enemy alien detention program, sent representatives of consult with De Witt on January 4–5, 1942. In advance of the meeting, Major Karl R. Bendetsen, head of the aliens division in the office of the provost marshal general, recommended that General De Witt exercise the Army's prerogative to designate strategic areas from which all enemy aliens could be excluded. Bendetsen also insisted on a new and complete registration of enemy aliens and a "pass and permit" system for them. During the meeting, De

Witt expressed his serious concern over the alien problem and his special distrust of the Japanese, both aliens and citizens. But he opposed a mass evacuation
of the Japanese, according to the recollection of a Justice Department official.
The conference ended with an agreement to proceed quickly with an alien
registration program, with FBI searches satisfactory to General De Witt, and
with the designation of strategic zones from which enemy aliens could be
excluded by order of the attorney general but with input from the Army.

De Witt made his recommendations for exclusion zones in California on
January 21, 1942, and for Arizona, Oregon, and Washington State on February
3. By then, however, the alien exclusion program was being eclipsed by a drive
to evacuate all the Japanese from the West Coast. The agitation for mass evacuation reached significant levels about a month after Pearl Harbor, beginning
with Congressman Leland M. Ford's letters of January 16, 1942, to the secretary
of war and other cabinet members urging that all Japanese be placed in concentration camps for the war's duration. Behind that plan lay a profound suspicion of the Japanese—on January 20 and 21, De Witt admitted that he feared
that any enemy raid on the West Coast would probably be joined by "coordi-
nated and controlled sabotage" by resident Japanese. And on January 24,
De Witt expressed one of the main arguments for mass evacuation: "The fact
that nothing has happened so far is more or less . . . ominous" in that "there is
a control being exercised."[34]

The Roberts Commission report on the Pearl Harbor disaster was published
on January 25, and was crucial. The report charged that before the Pearl Harbor
attack there had been widespread espionage in Hawai'i by Japanese consular
agents and resident Japanese. Although proven false after the war, the allegation
inflamed public opinion and prompted government action. On January 27, after
a conversation with Governor Culbert L. Olson of California, De Witt reported
that "there's a tremendous volume of public opinion now developing against
the Japanese of all classes, that is aliens and non-aliens, to get them off the
land. . . . Since the publication of the Roberts Report they feel that they are
living in the midst of a lot of enemies. They don't trust the Japanese, none of
them."[35] Two days later, De Witt stated that he now unqualifiedly supported the
mass evacuation of all Japanese from California, and was willing to take over
the enemy alien program if given that responsibility.

Major Bendetsen played a key role in these events. He reported General
De Witt's sentiments to West Coast congressmen and Justice and War Department representatives in Washington, D.C., and he conveyed to De Witt the
sentiments in Washington as he saw them. Bendetsen also embellished his
accounts. For example, his description of a congressional delegation's sugges-
tion for an evacuation of enemy aliens and dual citizens from critical areas
became a call "for the immediate evacuation of all Japanese from the Pacific
coastal strip including Japanese citizens of the age of 21 and under, and . . . for

an Executive order of the President, imposing full responsibility and authority (with power to requisition the services of other Federal agencies) upon the War Department."

On January 31, De Witt agreed that "the only positive answer to this question is evacuation of all enemy aliens from the West Coast and resettlement or internment under positive control, military or otherwise."[36] He wanted, he told Bendetsen, the removal of German and Italian aliens and all Japanese.

On February 3, De Witt reported his support for a California plan to move all Japanese from urban and coastal areas to agricultural areas in the state's interior. His only concern, he said, was to get them away from aircraft factories and other like places. At the same time, the War Department opposed the mass evacuation of Japanese and cautioned De Witt against taking a stand favoring mass evacuation. Later, De Witt clarified his position. "You see, the situation is this: I have never on my own initiative recommended a mass evacuation, or the removal of any man, any Jap, other than an alien. In other words, I have made no distinction between an alien as to whether he is a Jap, Italian, or German. . . . The agitation to move all the Japanese away from the coast, and some suggestions, out of California entirely—is within the State, the population of the State, which has been espoused by the Governor."[37]

Lieutenant Colonel Bendetsen (he was promoted) on February 4 recommended to the Army's provost marshal that the president issue an executive order authorizing the secretary of war to designate, on De Witt's advice, military areas from which all unauthorized persons would be removed. In endorsing Bendetsen's plan, the provost marshal's office expressed concern over De Witt's "weakening" on the matter of the Japanese, and charged that his support of the California plan was "too much of the spirit of Rotary" and lacked "the necessary cold-bloodedness of war." Lenient treatment of the Japanese, the office warned, was "extremely dangerous."[38] It recommended to the assistant secretary of war the removal of all alien Japanese to the east of the Sierra Nevada mountains, the voluntary evacuation of their family members who were citizens, and the exclusion of all Japanese American citizens from restricted zones.

On February 11, Secretary of War Henry L. Stimson recorded in his journal that the president was very supportive of his plans, which included the immediate evacuation of both citizen and alien Japanese from strategic areas. That same day, Assistant Secretary of War John J. McCloy reported Stimson's conversation with the president to Colonel Bendetsen, who was in San Francisco consulting with De Witt. McCloy stated that the president had given the War Department carte blanche on the matter and that the president specifically authorized the evacuation of citizens if it was dictated by military necessity. With that endorsement and Colonel Bendetsen's assistance, De Witt drafted his recommendations to Stimson on February 13. In addition to his earlier recommendation for the removal of enemy aliens, De Witt proposed the forced evacuation of Japanese American citizens from strategic areas. His memoran-dum had, however, no effect on the president's executive order.

The War Department had begun to plan the mass evacuation of the Japa-nese. On February 17, the provost marshal's office sent a telegram to corps area commanders informing them to expect orders "within 48 hours" for a "very large evacuation of enemy aliens of all nationalities predominantly Japanese" from the Pacific Coast. "Internment facilities will be taxed to utmost. Report at once maximum you can care for, including housing, feeding, medical care, and supply."[39] Later that day, department officials met to plan the mass evac-uation. That evening, representatives from the departments of War and Justice met. After hearing the War Department's draft of the presidential order that authorized the secretary of war to designate areas from which citizens and aliens would be excluded, Attorney General Biddle accepted the draft without further argument, "because the President had already indicated to him that this was a matter for military decision."[40] After more meetings, the executive order was presented to the president, and he signed it on February 19, 1942.

THE PRESIDENT

Writing with the benefit of hindsight, Roger Daniels builds on the work of his predecessors in his *Concentration Camps: North America, Japanese in the United States and Canada During World War II* (1981). Originally published ten years earlier as *Concentration Camps, U.S.A.*, the book is a slender though rich guide to the Japanese American and Japanese Canadian wartime experi-ence. Daniels devotes a chapter to the decision for mass evacuation, and in it he reviews the debate and adds new insights into the question of responsibility. Like Jacobus tenBroek et al., Daniels describes the anti-Japanese movement and "yellow peril" stereotype as preludes to the wartime detention, but he also makes the perceptive observation that the first few weeks after Pearl Harbor was a time of remarkable restraint and tolerance. Anti-Japanese hatred before the war failed to trigger an immediate activation of negative stereotypes and intol-erance at the war's onset, as hypothesized by tenBroek et al. Instead, Daniels notes, a national climate of hatred against America's Japanese had to be "created."[41]

At the end of December, the Justice Department authorized searches of enemy alien homes for contraband. Although these were innocent objects such as cameras, shortwave radios, and binoculars, the well-publicized entries by FBI agents and the loot they collected made for sensational newspaper headlines and fomented suspicion of the Japanese. Major Bendetsen's arrival at General De Witt's West Coast headquarters from the provost marshal's office seemed to add resolve to the Western commander's view of the situation. Bendetsen drafted for DeWitt a memorandum that whose message became the general's policy of comprehensive registration of enemy aliens for the purpose of establishing a pass-and-permit system. Bendetsen became DeWitt's voice in matters concerning aliens. At DeWitt's insistence, the Justice Department agreed to launch a new registration drive, order the FBI to conduct spot raids, and establish restricted zones to which entry would be restricted.

Meanwhile, responding to telegrams and letters from his California constituency, Representative Leland Ford, who had been urging restraint, now advocated the confinement of all Japanese in concentration camps. Many in government and the military agreed with Ford that, because to separate the loyal from the disloyal was impossible, the distinction between alien and citizen was of little importance. That argument received a boost from the Roberts Report on the Pearl Harbor attack. Released to the press on January 25, 194, the report falsely alleged that Japanese espionage in the islands greatly abetted the enemy. This charge fed already prevalent rumors that resident Japanese were involved in fifth-column activities for Japan. Two days later, DeWitt heard from Culbert Olson, California's governor, that public opinion had turned against all Japanese, citizen and alien, and that pressure was building for a mass evacuation.

On January 29, DeWitt indicated his support for the mass evacuation of Japanese from the West Coast, and indicated his willingness to head the enemy aliens program if it was handed over to him by the Justice Department. The next day, the president's cabinet took up the issue of internal subversion especially in Hawai'i, and the congressional delegations from the Pacific Coast states met with Bendetsen and officials from the Justice Department to discuss the West Coast situation. The congressional delegations then met with Secretary of War Stimson and urged the mass evacuation of all enemy aliens and their families. Attorney General Biddle opposed the mass evacuation in early February, despite the mounting pressure for it from both the Congress and military. Biddle hoped that Justice Department action would satisfy the military and forestall the demands for mass evacuation. Similarly at this time, the civilian heads of the War Department—i.e., Stimson and his assistant, John J. McCloy—were against the mass evacuation. DeWitt began to waver, and how supported the California plan whereby all Japanese would be moved into the state's interior to work on farms.

DeWitt's apparent softening disgusted those in the Army who supported mass evacuation, especially because his support for mass evacuation was crucial to their argument of military necessity. West Coast politicians, like Governor Olson and Los Angeles mayor Fletcher Bowron, fanned the flames of anti-Japanese hatred by alleging that California's Japanese were conspiring to aid the enemy. The only solution, they insisted, was mass internment. With that encouragement, the provost marshal's office pressed on with its mass evacuation plan. Bendetsen flew out to the West Coast to strengthen DeWitt's resolve. By

February 10, McCloy, the assistant secretary of war, seemed to have been won over to the side favoring mass evacuation, although Secretary Stimson remained unconvinced. The next day, in a telephone conversation between the president and the Secretary of War, Roosevelt told Stimson to "go ahead and do anything you think necessary," even if it involves citizens, as long as it is dictated by "military necessity." And, he added, "be as reasonable as you can."[42]

McCloy reported the good news to Bendetsen, who was at DeWitt's head-quarters in California. McCloy predicted that he might be able to turn Stimson's opinion around and persuade him to support mass evacuation. On that note, Bendetsen helped DeWitt draft his report that called for mass evacuation on the grounds of military necessity. President Roosevelt signed Executive Order 9066 on February 19, 1942. Therewith, "the myth of military necessity was used as a fig leaf for a particular variant of American racism."[43]

Racism was not peculiar to California and the West, but was prevalent throughout America, at all levels of society. The decision for mass evacuation was popular both along the Pacific Coast and nationwide. But "the leader of the nation, was, in the final analysis, responsible. It was Franklin Roosevelt, who in one short telephone call, passed the decision-making power to two men who had never been elected to any office, saying only, with the politician's charm and equivocation: 'Be as reasonable as you can.'" Why did he agree? Because it was "expedient," and because he harbored "deeply felt anti-Japanese prejudices."[44] It was expedient because in early 1942 the war was going badly for the Allies and there were calls for retribution against Japanese Americans. A mass evacuation was popular. And Roosevelt was convinced that the Japanese, alien and citizen alike, were dangerous to America's security. He had pushed for the mass internment of Hawai'i's Japanese and had been blocked by the military's opposition. His suspicions of Japanese loyalty argued for a mass evacuation of Japanese Americans from straegic locations on the U.S. mainland.

HAWAI'I

Conventional views of Hawai'i set it apart from the U.S. mainland, writes Gary Y. Okihiro in *Cane Fires: The Anti-Japanese Movement in Hawai'i, 1865–1945* (1991). A reexamination of their respective histories, Okihiro proposes, reveal parallels that merit a reconsideration of the standard interpretation. Hawaiians, like American Indians, were dispossessed of their land by white expansion. Whites recruited Asian migrant labor to displace indigenous workers. Asians arrived sequentially—Chinese were followed by Japanese, and then by Korean and Filipino—after the previous group had been excluded. A single gender, men, predominated, and most of them labored in agriculture. Whites imposed a system of economic, political, and cultural dependency to contain Asian settlers who created communities and struggled for better wages and civil rights. Anti-Asianism in Hawai'i and on the U.S. mainland formed distinctive yet comparable and sometimes intersecting movements. Their consequences for Japanese Americans during World War II were martial law and selective detention in Hawai'i and mass removal and confinement on the West Coast. *Cane Fires* structures anti-Asianism around the social relations that proceed from the transition from migrant labor to dependency. In its treatment of the anti-Chinese movement and the anti-Japanese movement, *Cane Fires* offers an alternative to the interpretation of Jacobus tenBroek et al. As for this discussion on the theories of responsibility for the concentration camps, *Cane Fires* points to Hawai'i.

Hawai'i's anti-Japanese movement began with America's thrust toward Asia, where it sought markets and commodities. Among those commodities was Asian labor, so considered by Hawai'i's capitalists who ordered them like implements and farm equipment. The reliance on migrant labor was anti-Japanese in that it was designed to exploit and manage Japanese workers and expel them when their utility had been exhausted. Laborers, however, resisted white control by breaking tools and burning cane fields, running away from binding labor contracts, and engaging in collective work actions and strikes. In the process, they advanced their interests and secured greater freedoms, but also prompted the need for more sophisticated forms of repression. Planter paternalism and dependency was the next stage in Hawai'i's anti-Japanese movement, established to ensure profits for the islands' planters, stifle worker unrest, erase ethnic identity, and hinder the full development of the migrants' children.

Although competitors for land and power, the U.S. military and planter plutocracy made common cause in the "Japanese problem." The military's interest in the Japanese was centered on its strategic mission. Hawai'i was the western gate of America's domain, and its arsenal sheltered American interests in Asia and pointed eastward toward Japan's imperial ambitions in the Pacific. From 1900 to 1940 the Japanese were the Territory's largest single ethnic group and the most prominent pool of labor, especially in the sugar industry, which dominated the economic life of the islands. Strikes by Japanese workers threatened Hawai'i's economy, and, in the racialized eyes of the white planters and military chiefs, implied Japan's ascendancy in this U.S. territory.

During World War I, military intelligence both in Hawai'i and on the mainland concerned itself with the activities of aliens, radicals, and communists, and especially German aliens. By the war's end, however, Army intelligence in Hawai'i shifted the focus of its surveillance to the Japanese. A 1918 report noted with alarm the increasing disparity between the growth rate of the Japanese and that of the white population. It cited the presence of Japanese women and their fecundity as reasons for the difference. Whites, outnumbered four to one, lived among "hostile foreigners" who, through the ballot box, will eventually take political control of Hawai'i.[45] The Japanese government monitored its subjects and actively promoted Japanese nationalism. Japanese-language schools taught children Japanese history, religion, customs, and literature. And Buddhism negated the influences of Christianity and Americanism. The permanent presence of this alien and antagonistic community, the report concluded, posed a danger to the American way of life and to national security. Naval intelligence and postal censors repeated the warnings about the sources and perils of the Japanese problem.

The sugar plantation strike by Filipino, Puerto Rican, and mainly Japanese workers in 1920 injected new energy and urgency into the drive to contain the Japanese. The strike involved 8,300 workers or about 77 percent of the entire plantation work force on the island of Oahu, lasted for nearly six months, and cost the planters an estimated $11.5 million. It began as an effort by laborers to increase their wages and bonuses, secure an eight-week paid maternity leave for women workers, and gain expanded and improved health-care and recreational facilities. Labor leaders framed the strike as an American action for American wages, but Hawai'i's planters portrayed it as an attempt by Japan and its forces to control the islands' industries. An Army intelligence officer saw the strike as "espionage" and lamented the absence of stricter laws and the inability of democracy to prevent industrial disturbances.[46] The Army, prevented by the Territory's acting governor from intervening in the strike, contacted sugar plantation managers to keep its intelligence unit informed of any emergency arising from the strike.

The strike prompted a comprehensive assessment of the problem by the head of military intelligence in Hawai'i. The labor conflict, he observed, pointed to a new crisis in relations between the United States and Japan in light of the latter's strategy for the conquest of America. The plan involved reliance on aliens, radicals, and pacifists to tie America's through discontent among the working class, labor strikes, and peace movements that drain the national vigor. Japan's propaganda had lured the Eastern states with the enticements of trade and has thereby pitted them against the Western states, and through peaceful expansion Japanese immigrants had established a foothold in America and now awaited Japan's every command. Japan maintained a "very complete system of espionage," involving the Japanese consul, Buddhist and Shinto priests, Japanese-language schoolteachers and editors of newspapers, labor leaders, and workers. While America slept, Japan prepared for total war. Enjoying the protections of the U.S. Constitution, Hawai'i's Japanese formed half the population of the islands and were "practically impervious." Their tentacles reached "every phase of American life in this territory, from government bureaus to the homes of very poor people."[47]

Besides attracting the attention of military intelligence, the strike prompted the Bureau of Investigation (forerunner of the FBI) to contact Army intelligence and to send one of its agents to the field in Hawai'i. In 1921, military intelligence, the Bureau of Investigation, and the secret service of the Hawaiian Sugar Plant-ers' Association joined in a surveillance network to monitor the Japanese situ-ation. Among the several reports that emanated from that group was a 1922 Bureau report that listed by name, residential address, and occupation 157 Jap-anese who were deemed subversive or potentially dangerous. The list included 40 businessmen, 31 Buddhist priests, 24 Japanese-language schoolteachers and principals, 19 laborers, 10 Christian ministers, and 4 professionals. Seven years later, an Army intelligence list of leaders in Hawai'i's Japanese community followed closely the earlier list, and by 1933 the decision to intern Japanese American leaders supplanted the search for spies.

For Hawai'i's planters, the 1920 strike reinforced the old lesson of divide-and-rule through by employing a diversified work force. Chinese laborers, they believed, would provide them with cheap, reliable labor and free them from the intractable Japanese. But U.S. law restricted Chinese immigration, so the planters sought relief from the Congress, asking it to suspend the exclusion law because of the emergency caused by the Japanese menace. In response, Presi-dent Warren G. Harding in 1922 dispatched the Hawaiian Labor Commission to study the Territory's labor situation, to determine the danger of Japanese economic and political control, and to recommend a plan for a "balance" of the races to guarantee U.S. control of the islands. Although the commission found no labor shortage and advised against the importation of Chinese work-ers, it raised the alarm over the "menace of alien domination," which was presented as a matter of "national defense." Hawai'i may have its labor prob-lems, the commissioners reported, "but *we believe the question of National Defense and the necessity to curtail the domination of the alien Japanese in every phase of the Hawaiian life is more important than all the other problems com-bined* [emphasis in original]."[48]

Information from intelligence established the parameters for military plan-ners in mapping the defense of Hawai'i. Among the various war scenarios was the prospect of a Pacific conflict with Japan. An officer in the Army's War Plans Division in 1923 was one Colonel John L. DeWitt, who would later play a pivotal role in the mass removal of Japanese Americans from the West Coast. DeWitt worked on a plan for the defense of O'ahu, and his involvement in this effort might have influenced his view of America's Japanese years later, during World War II. The plan, approved in 1921 and revised in 1923, envisioned a proclamation of martial law, registration of all enemy aliens, internment of those deemed to be security risks, and restrictions on labor, movement, and public information. Military necessity, DeWitt argued, required the extraordi-nary measure of martial law. "From a military standpoint and as a measure for adequate defense, . . ." DeWitt wrote, "the establishment of complete military control over the Hawaiian Islands, including its people, supplies, material, etc., is highly desirable."[49] Although it evolved over time, the Army's plan consistently contained the main elements in DeWitt's version: martial law, selective rather than mass detention, and the twin goals of ensuring internal security and maximizing labor productivity.

In the military's thinking, the Japanese problem was global, and likewise its solution. Hawai'i was always integral to that broad defensive scheme that centered on the U.S. mainland and extended outward to its territories and possessions. Because of that, and because the belief of the Washington military establishment that Hawai'i's preparations were deficient, the general staff ordered a revised plan in 1934. The danger involved not only enemy aliens but also Japanese American citizens, and even before actual conflict the danger existed in the form of Japanese espionage and sabotage. The president too sensed the peril. Writing on August 10, 1936, during a time when the military anticipated from sea and air a surprise attack aided by "hostile sympathizers" on the islands, Roosevelt offered this: "One obvious thought occurs to me—that every Japanese citizen or non-citizen on the Island of Oahu who meets these Japanese ships or has any connection with their officers or men should be secretly but definitely identified and his or her name placed on a special list of those who would be the first to be placed in a concentration camp in the event of trouble." And he added, "Please let me have further recommendations after studies have been made."[50]

Harry H. Woodring, acting secretary of war, responded to the president's "obvious thought" and request by noting that the Hawaiian commander had established a "service command" that would serve as the link between military and civilian forces to prevent sabotage, civil disturbances, or local uprisings. And the military's Joint Board added: "It is a routine matter for those responsible for military intelligence to maintain lists of suspects, who will normally be the first to be interned under the operation of the Joint Defense Plan, Hawaiian Theater, in the event of war." Working to further unify what had been independent efforts to anticipate Japanese sedition in Hawai'i, the president in June 1937 designated the secretary of war to head an interagency committee consisting of the attorney general and the secretaries of labor, navy, state, treasury, and war. The committee's purpose was "to work out some practical solution to the problem" of curbing Japanese espionage.[51]

So, on the eve of World War II, America's comprehensive strategy to contain the Japanese problem was both defensive and proactive. In 1919, the Army had enlisted the help of Hawai'i's legislature to control and limit the growth of Japanese-language schools, and during the 1920 strike it had encouraged plantation managers to call on its assistance. And because the Army saw the U.S. Constitution as an impediment to its role in defending the nation against an uncommon enemy, it anticipated a declaration of martial law and the internment of Japanese American leaders, aliens and citizens, in concentration camps. Those confined leaders would serve as "hostages" to guarantee the docile and good behavior of Japanese Americans as a whole and to ensure their productivity in labor, which would sustain the Territory's economy.[52] Meanwhile, military intelligence and the FBI planted Americanizers among Japanese Americans to counter Japanism, to separate the first from the second generation, and to exacerbate white racism in order to coerce public demonstrations of loyalty by Japanese Americans even if it meant repudiating their parents and their ethnic identity.

As fire and smoke was still rising from the wreckage that had been America's Pacific fleet until December 7, 1941, those plans were put into operation both in Hawai'i and on the mainland. But it was Hawai'i that took the lead in this action. Because of its strategic location and its demography, the Territory and its Japanese Americans became the focus of military and civilian intelligence and planning at least as early as World War I. When in 1920 workers struck for higher wages and better working conditions, the Hawaiian Labor Commission magnified the strike into a race war, and the "specter of alien domination" argued for a military solution because of military necessity. By 1922, military and civilian intelligence both in Hawai'i and on the mainland had come to regard the Japanese problem as their leading concern, but it was in the islands, not on the mainland, that detailed preparations for countering the Japanese menace took place. By 1923, the Army in Hawai'i had planned the imposition of martial law, the registration of all aliens, and internment of selected enemy aliens, whereas on the mainland it was not until 1940 that the Navy had sought to expel Japanese fishermen from Terminal Island in Los Angeles harbor and that the FBI had planned the internment of enemy aliens. And when war came to Pearl Harbor, the military put its plan into operation in Hawai'i, while on the West Coast, apart from the Justice Department's roundup of enemy aliens, the government response was defined largely by inaction, as General DeWitt, caught in the push and pull between the War and Justice departments, temporized. Hawai'i, by contrast, stood prepared.

NOTES

1. See Peter T. Suzuki, "Anthropologists in the Wartime Camps for Japanese Americans: A Documentary Study," *Dialectical Anthropology* 6:1 (1981): 23–60.

2. See Alexander H. Leighton, *The Governing of Men: General Principles and Recommendations Based on Experience at a Japanese Relocation Camp* (Princeton, N.J.: Princeton University Press, 1945).

3. See Dorothy Swaine Thomas and Richard S. Nishimoto, *The Spoilage* (Berkeley: University of California Press, 1946); Rosalie H. Wax, *Doing Fieldwork: Warnings and Advice* (Chicago: University of Chicago Press, 1971); and Yuji Ichioka, ed., *Views From Within: The Japanese American Evacuation and Resettlement Study* (Los Angeles: UCLA Asian American Studies Center, 1989).

4. See Suzuki, "Anthropologists in the Wartime Camps"; Ichioka, *Views From Within*; and Richard S. Nishimoto, *Inside an American Concentration Camp: Japanese American Resistance at Poston, Arizona*, edited by Lane Ryo Hirabayashi (Tucson: University of Arizona Press, 1995).

5. See, e.g., Gary Y. Okihiro, "Resistance in America's Concentration Camps: A Re-evaluation," *Amerasia Journal* 2 (Fall 1973): 20–34; Arthur A. Hansen and David A. Hacker, "The Manzanar Riot: An Ethnic Perspective," *Amerasia Journal* 2:2 (Fall 1974): 112–57; and Nishimoto, *Inside an American Concentration Camp*.

6. On the argument for racist ideology as the basic cause for the camps, see Lane Ryo Hirabayashi and James A. Hirabayashi, "A Reconsideration of the United States Military's Role in the Violation of Japanese-American Citizenship Rights," in *Ethnicity and War*, edited by Winston A. Van Horne (Milwaukee: University of Wisconsin System American Ethnic Studies Coordinating Committee, 1984), 87–110.

7. On the falsity of this claim known even to the government, see Peter Irons, *Justice At War* (New York: Oxford University Press, 1983).

8. Morton Grodzins, *Americans Betrayed: Politics and the Japanese Evacuation* (Chicago: University of Chicago Press, 1949), vii.

9. Ibid., 1.

10. Ibid., 2.

11. Ibid., 3.

12. Ibid., 7.

13. Ibid., 8.

14. Ibid., 14.

15. Ibid., 15.

16. Ibid., 20.

17. Ibid., 27.

18. Ibid., 62.

19. Ibid., 65.

20. Ibid., 362.

21. Ibid., 374.

22. For a background on this debate, see Peter T. Suzuki, "For the Sake of Inter-university Comity: The Attempted Suppression by the University of California of Morton Grodzins' *Americans Betrayed*," in Ichioka, *Views From Within*, 95–123.

23. Jacobus tenBroek, Edward N. Barnhart, and Floyd W. Matson, *Prejudice, War and the Constitution* (Berkeley: University of California Press, 1954), x.

24. Ibid., 2.

25. Ibid., 3.

26. Ibid., 14, 15.

27. Ibid., 21.

28. Ibid., 22.

29. Ibid., 68.

30. Ibid., 96.

31. Ibid., 207–08.

32. Ibid., 208.

33. Stetson Conn, Rose C. Engelman, and Byron Fairchild, *Guarding the United States and Its Outposts* (Washington, D.C.: Center of Military History, United States Army, 1964), 117–18.

34. Ibid., 121.

35. Ibid., 122.

36. Ibid., 123.

37. Ibid., 126.

38. Ibid., 128.

39. Ibid., 134.

40. Ibid., 135.

41. Roger Daniels, *Concentration Camps, North America: Japanese in the United States and Canada During World War II* (Malabar, Fla.: Robert E. Krieger, 1981), 42.

42. Ibid., 65.

43. Ibid., 71.

44. Ibid., 72.

45. Gary Y. Okihiro, *Cane Fires: The Anti-Japanese Movement in Hawai'i, 1865–1945* (Philadelphia: Temple University Press, 1991), 104.

46. Ibid., 77.

47. Ibid., 111.

48. Ibid., 94, 95.

49. Ibid., 124.

50. Ibid., 173–74.

51. Ibid., 175.

52. Ibid., 175–77.

PART 3

Emerging Themes

INTRODUCTION

In this section, I summarize the following emerging themes within Asian American studies:

1. Space
2. Women and gender
3. The law
4. Japanese American resistance

Although all of these topics in Asian American studies are longstanding, the assumptions behind them have only recently been critically reexamined. In addition, no substantial, book-length studies exist that debate the topic, and define the subfield, of space and Japanese American resistance. And while significant bodies of work have been devoted to the topic of women and gender and the law, they have yet to transform the canon of Asian American history. Despite their fundamental importance, these themes are emerging—rather than established—in this field of study. (For more developed arguments on selected historical problems, see the "Historical Debates" section.)

Readers should recognize that here, as in the "Historical Debates" section, they are reading my summaries of certain authors' ideas and their work. These are only glosses and not the authors' own words, except where indicated by quotation marks. I thus encourage readers to consult the works directly for another reading of the argument. I have tried to remain faithful to the original texts and their intentions but, in the end, the summaries do reflect my own interpretations. Further, I limit my discussion to summaries of the texts and have steered away from commentary as much as possible. I am accordingly constrained by the texts.

Emerging within the idea of space, for instance, is a criticism of regionalism as displayed in the California-centrism found in Asian American studies. In this model, California—seen as the original location of Asian America, with its community of Chinese American men, mainly workers, and its anti-Chinese movement—serves as a paradigm for Asian American history. In that way, the pattern was cut, to paraphrase a prominent Asian American historian, and was simply replicated with the successive waves of Japanese, Koreans, Asian Indians, and Filipinos who came to these shores. Although fairly commonplace in the field today, criticism of California's centrality has not yet become systematic or been elaborated in book-length studies. I have no doubt that such studies will eventuate, but their absence restricts my present discussion of this important historical theme. Existing scholarship does mention different historical config-urations in the Filipino communities near New Orleans; the South Asian slaves, indentures, and freedmen of Salem, Massachusetts, and Philadelphia; and the Chinese and Irish families of New York City. All of these groups preceded the arrival of gold-seeking Chinese men in California,[1] but references to them remain, by and large, as marginal and exotic footnotes to California's narrative.

I have left similar emerging themes out of my discussion. Most prominent is the ethnic hierarchy within the literature and its valuation of the Chinese and Japanese experiences as central and paradigmatic. This judgment is usually defended on the basis of time and size—the Chinese and the Japanese were the first Asian groups in the United States and the largest until the 1970s. On similar grounds, women have been excluded from narratives of the nineteenth century. Of course, a consideration of origins can lead to stories at variance with the California claim. Filipinos, South Asians, and New York's Chinese constitute older claimants, and one might argue that Asian American history began not with Asian migrations to the United States but with Europe's imag-ining of and voyaging to Asia.[2] And numbers alone need not suggest signifi-cance. Women and gender, for instance, are central to Asian American history at large, despite their near absence throughout Asian American history of the nineteenth century. And although the case has yet to be made, I have no doubt that Cambodians, Filipinos, Indonesians, Koreans, Laotians, South Asians, Thai, Vietnamese, and West Asians have histories that will transform Asian American narratives of the period before the 1970s, and that their small numbers in the United States during that period will have no relevance to their impor-tance to that past.[3]

Cultural history and critical studies of representations are emerging and thriving but have not yet made the same impact upon historical writing as the other themes I discuss in this section. I refer readers to the list of books under the "Cultural Studies and Cultural Criticism" heading in the "Resources" section of this book. These studies show the ubiquity and power of representations in films, books, television, and the theater, and how they concoct and assign racialized, gendered, and sexualized natures to Asian bodies. Although some of the studies are conceived historically, the extant literature reveals that there is a great need for systematic textual analyses of particular cultural forms, their production and audiences, contexts, and continuities and changes over time.

Other important subjects not discussed in this section on emerging themes include multiracialism, sexuality, religious history, generations, and transnationalism. I list books in these areas in the "Resources" section. Most of these topics have been approached as questions for social science, not history. For instance, studies on multiracialism and sexuality have been mainly concerned with the identities of those groups and with their constitutions and significances for Asian American subjectivities and politics. As an analytic category, generations, a concern mainly for Japanese American studies, has found new life among post-1965 immigrants, including Koreans, South Asians, and Southeast Asians in the United States. In many of these works, generations comprise groupings of identities and show the processes of assimilation and acculturation from immigrant to subsequent generations, and the distances and conflicts that result from those social adaptations. Religious studies had a similar beginning, with scholars studying Asian religions and their assimilation into American life. Asian religions took on new forms in the United States, and their development paralleled and thereby revealed the changes undergone by their adherents, Asian migrants. Of course, the underdevelopment of studies in these areas is at odds with the centrality of race, sexuality, and religion in Asian American studies and history.

Transnationalism or movements beyond the nation-state have taken on several incarnations reflective of political, intellectual, and historical trends. During the 1960s and 1970s, Asian American studies was of two minds. It was emphatically nationalist in its insistence that Asians were Americans and that it was distinctive from Asian studies. At the same time, Asian Americans saw themselves as denizens of the Third World in the United States and claimed solidarity with the revolutions in Algeria, Cuba, and China and with the struggles of Vietnam's peoples against colonial rule. Their identities were thus national and transnational. In the 1980s and 1990s, Asian American studies, like other fields, was moved by the increasingly massive and rapid flows of capital, labor, and culture across national boundaries. The nation state failed to contain products, peoples, and ideas, and the global became the canvas for mapping the subject along with the destabilized borders of nation-states. The Pacific Rim acquired economic, political, and intellectual currency, and American studies (including Asian American studies) and area studies (including Asian studies) found a widening common ground. Those changes, however, are only now being explored and debated in Asian American studies, through diasporic and comparative approaches and projects, and they constitute important areas of inquiry in this rapidly expanding field.[4]

NOTES

1. See, e.g., Marina E. Espina, *Filipinos in Louisiana* (New Orleans: A. F. Laborde & Sons, 1988); Joan M. Jensen, *Passage from India: Asian Indian Immigrants in North America* (New Haven, Conn.: Yale University Press, 1988); and John Kuo Wei Tchen, *New York before Chinatown: Orientalism and the Shaping of American Culture, 1776–1882* (Baltimore: Johns Hopkins University Press, 1999).

2. See, e.g., Gary Y. Okihiro, *Margins and Mainstreams: Asians in American History and Culture* (Seattle: University of Washington Press, 1994), 3–30.

3. See, e.g., the critical commentary on South Asian and Asian American studies in Lavina Dhingra Shankar and Rajini Srikanth, eds., *A Part, Yet Apart: South Asians in Asian America* (Philadelphia: Temple University Press, 1998).

4. Shirley Hune et al., eds., *Asian American Studies: Comparative and Global Perspectives* (Pullman: Washington State University Press, 1991) is pioneering in this regard.

Chapter 1

SPACE

Asian American scholars constructed space, albeit without acknowledgment, even as they naturalized and universalized their social geographies. As Michel Foucault reminds us, space is treated as fixed, unchanging, and monotonous whereas time appears as moving, transforming, and various.[1] The main spatial binary in the extant literature is between the urban and rural. Urban Asian America is assumed to be typical of the Asian American experience. Studies on Japantowns, Chinatowns, and Koreatowns naturalize those social formations that are often built on the foundation of East Asian culture and its supposed stress and dependence on collectivity and hierarchy. Those urban spaces have been classed as self-contained, isolated communities, ethnic enclaves that are both insular and connected to American society, and as transnational ports for the flow of goods, capital, and labor. Discursive analyses reveal Chinatown to be a constructed space initiated by whites and abetted by certain classes of Chinese, a place of racialization for whites and Chinese alike. Asian suburbia and new urban aggregations cast a different light on the nature of Asian American communities, and the contrasts point to the static and situational character of the urban model. But rural studies have been more effective in critiquing the urban paradigm and underscoring that space is both social and historical. Finally, emerging from within this evolving consideration of the spatial dimension of Asian American studies are regional considerations brought to the fore by scholars east of California who seek to unsettle the California-centrism that dominates the field.[2]

Shotaro Frank Miyamoto's *Social Solidarity Among the Japanese in Seattle* (1939) is an influential study of an Asian American community in an urban setting. Miyamoto sees the Japanese community in Seattle as a paradigm for other Japanese American communities along the West Coast. All of them, he writes, share a common bond of ethnic solidarity as a "predisposition" that stressed the group over the individual. In fact, Japanese culture with its ethical system of collective obligations gives the Japanese family "a type of solidarity hardly to be conceived in the Western mind."[3] For Miyamoto, culture, social homogeneity, and collectivism draw Japanese Americans into spatial concentrations like Seattle's Japanese community. He recognizes racism as a factor in mandating that grouping but sees Japanese culture as more influential in shaping Japanese ethnic solidarity and geographical clustering. He advances Seattle's urban community as representative of all Japanese American communities.

More than Japantowns, Chinatowns have come to be regarded as exemplary Asian American communities. Studies abound. Examples include Victor G. and Brett De Bary Nee, *Longtime Califomʼ: A Documentary Study of an American Chinatown* (1972); Peter Kwong, *Chinatown, New York: Labor and Politics, 1930–1950* (1979); Peter Kwong, *The New Chinatown* (1987); Chalsa M. Loo, *Chinatown: Most Time, Hard Time* (1991); and Min Zhou, *Chinatown: The Socioeconomic Potential of an Urban Enclave* (1992).[4] As a spatial and social entity, Chinatown has been stereotyped as rigidly insular and separate from American society.[5] Sociologists like Min Zhou see Chinatown as an ethnic enclave that both shields its members from and enables their assimilation into America because of its intrinsic ties to the larger society. Peter Kwong and others have extended the compass of Chinatown's circle to include the global arena of politics and economy, especially in its ties to Taiwan and China. Chinatown's transnational spaces are examined in Renqiu Yu, *To Save China, To Save Ourselves: The Chinese Hand Laundry Alliance of New York* (1992); Jan Lin, *Reconstructing Chinatown: Ethnic Enclave, Global Change* (1998); John Kuo Wei Tchen, *New York before Chinatown: Orientalism and the Shaping of American Culture, 1776–1882* (1999); and Yong Chen, *Chinese San Francisco, 1850–1943: A Trans-Pacific Community* (2000).[6]

Studies of Korean migrants, similar to those of Japanese and Chinese, feature urban locations. Examples include Illsoo Kim, *New Urban Immigrants: The Korean Community in New York* (1981); Eui-Young Yu, Earl H. Phillips, and Eun Sik Yang (eds.), *Koreans in Los Angeles: Prospects and Promises* (1982); Ivan Light and Edna Bonacich, *Immigrant Entrepreneurs: Koreans in Los Angeles, 1965–1982* (1988); Nancy Abelmann and John Lie, *Blue Dreams: Korean Americans and the Los Angeles Riots* (1995); Pyong Gap Min, *Caught in the Middle: Korean Communities in New York and Los Angeles* (1996); Kyeyoung Park, *The*

Korean American Dream: Immigrants and Small Business in New York City (1997); In-Jin Yoon, *On My Own: Korean Businesses and Race Relations in America* (1997); Edward T. Chang and Jeannette Diaz-Veizades, *Ethnic Peace in the American City: Building Community in Los Angeles and Beyond* (1999); and Kwang Chung Kim (ed.), *Koreans in the Hood: Conflict with African Americans* (1999).[7]

Although largely unmarked, urban spaces such as Japantowns, Koreatowns, and Chinatowns achieve within the literature on Asian American communities the status of representative and typical. Even studies on rural settlements of Chinese Americans center around the concentrations that bear the name "Chinatown," as in Rose Hum Lee, "The Chinese Communities in the Rocky Mountain Region" (1947) and Melford S. Weiss, *Valley City: A Chinese Community in America* (1974).[8]

New communities of Chinese and other Asian Americans, especially in suburbia, present different configurations of space and social relations. The notions of Chinatowns as concentrations, ghettoes, and hierarchies of kin-based organizations no longer apply to these dispersed communities of businesses, residences, and cultural centers that interact not only with whites but also with Latinos, African Americans, and other Asians. Studies that expand on those themes include Hsiang-shui Chen, *Chinatown No More: Taiwan Immigrants in Contemporary New York* (1992); Timothy P. Fong, *The First Suburban Chinatown: The Remaking of Monterey Park, California* (1994); John Horton, *The Politics of Diversity: Immigration, Resistance, and Change in Monterey Park, California* (1995); and Leland T. Saito, *Race and Politics: Asian Americans, Latinos, and Whites in a Los Angeles Suburb* (1998).[9]

Kay J. Anderson's *Vancouver's Chinatown: Racial Discourse in Canada, 1875–1980* (1991) opens a new avenue into Chinatown's location.[10] Rather than seeing it as an exotic creation of Chinese immigrants, Anderson views Chinatown and "Chineseness" from the eyes of Europeans, those who named, circumscribed, and represented it. The study of Chinatown is an examination of the process of racialization. From its inception in the late 1880s, Vancouver's Chinese settlement was an important site through which white Canadians constituted and reproduced their concepts of race. While the state was restrained from racist excesses by constitutional arrangements that created autonomous levels of jurisdiction and allowed for Chinatown residents to challenge for protection of their rights, it also manufactured and managed "Chinatown" through representations and acts that policed morals and sanitation, strengthening the stigma and isolation of place and race. Chinatown's social construction, however, depended not only on whites but also on the assent and complicity of some of Chinatown's residents, notably its merchants who profited from the notion of Chinatown's exotic and deviant nature. Its emergence as an "ethnic neighborhood" by the late 1960s, coupled with the multiculturalism of the

1970s, completed Chinatown's reversal from a place to avoid to a space to embrace. Crucial to both representations of Chinatown is the constant racialization of the Chinese as other and nonwhites.

Like the insights introduced by transnationalism, suburban communities, new "Chinatowns," and discourse analyses, studies of Asian Americans in rural settings point to the particular and not paradigmatic nature of urban communities and add perspective to their formations. At the same time, a rural community is a social construction, like its urban counterpart. Neither is isolated from the other, but instead both are linked by social relations and geography. Many studies of rural Asian American communities began as local history projects and sometimes the result of collaborative work among interested researchers.[11] Individual scholars added to the list.[12] Sandy Lydon's *Chinese Gold: The Chinese in the Monterey Bay Region* (1985) describes Chinese American communities and economies based upon families with children, quite unlike the bachelor society of men in urban Chinatowns, and Timothy J. Lukes and Gary Y. Okihiro's *Japanese Legacy: Farming and Community Life in California's Santa Clara Valley* (1985) reveals a spatial and social arrangement at odds with Shotaro Frank Miyamoto's Japantown.[13] Japanese Americans spread farms widely throughout the Santa Clara valley; they grouped them into clusters that showed the effects of anti-Japanese laws and practices rather than a cultural proclivity to aggregations. Amidst cooperation, there was also individualism and competition nurtured by capitalism and its exigencies and allure.

Sucheng Chan's *This Bittersweet Soil: The Chinese in California Agriculture, 1860–1910* (1986) examines California's agricultural history to illuminate the collective histories of Chinese, Japanese, Koreans, Filipinos, and Asian Indians and show its effects in structuring the state's race relations.[14] Moreover, Chan's study documents the spatial and social contrasts between the urban and rural experiences of Asian Americans and the error of scholars who maintain that the urban was representative of all of Asian America. Before the turn of the century, the majority of Chinese Americans lived in rural areas and labored mainly in agriculture as vegetable peddlers, merchants, farm workers, and cooks, tenant farmers, and farm owners and operators. Their class structure differed; in urban areas during this period more Chinese belonged to the merchant and professional classes, but in the rural regions more than 80 percent of the Chinese were members of the working class. Furthermore, the power of the Chinese urban elite resided in their intermediary roles between China and the United States, whereas those in the rural areas derived their power from their intermediary roles between Chinese workers and white farmers and markets. Finally, despite their contributions to California agriculture, Chinese were driven from rural to urban areas. Laws excluded the entrance of Chinese laborers and rendered Chinese farmers less competitive and economically vulnerable.

NOTES

1. Michel Foucault, "Questions of Geography," in *Power/Knowledge: Selected Interviews and Other Writings*, edited by Colin Gordon (New York: Pantheon, 1980).

2. See Stephen H. Sumida, "East of California: Points of Origin in Asian American Studies," *Journal of Asian American Studies* 1:1 (February 1998): 83–100.

3. Shotaro Frank Miyamoto, *Social Solidarity Among the Japanese in Seattle*, University of Washington Publications in the Social Sciences, vol. 11, no. 2 (Seattle, 1939), 57, 60.

4. Victor G. and Brett De Bary Nee, *Longtime Californ': A Documentary Study of an American Chinatown* (Boston: Houghton Mifflin, 1974); Peter Kwong, *Chinatown, New York: Labor and Politics, 1930–1950* (New York: Monthly Review Press, 1979); Peter Kwong, *The New Chinatown* (New York: Hill and Wang, 1987); Chalsa M. Loo, *Chinatown: Most Time, Hard Time* (New York: Praeger, 1991); and Min Zhou, *Chinatown: The Socioeconomic Potential of an Urban Enclave* (Philadelphia: Temple University Press, 1992).

5. See, e.g., Gwen Kinkead, *Chinatown: A Portrait of a Closed Society* (New York: HarperCollins, 1992).

6. Renqiu Yu, *To Save China, To Save Ourselves: The Chinese Hand Laundry Alliance of New York* (Philadelphia: Temple University Press, 1992); Jan Lin, *Reconstructing Chinatown: Ethnic Enclave, Global Change* (Minneapolis: University of Minnesota Press, 1998); John Kuo Wei Tchen, *New York before Chinatown: Orientalism and the Shaping of American Culture, 1776–1882* (Baltimore: Johns Hopkins University Press, 1999); and Yong Chen, *Chinese San Francisco, 1850–1943: A Trans-Pacific Community* (Stanford, Calif.: Stanford University Press, 2000).

7. Illsoo Kim, *New Urban Immigrants: The Korean Community in New York* (Princeton, N.J.: Princeton University Press, 1981); Eui-Young Yu, Earl H. Phillips, and Eun Sik Yang, eds., *Koreans in Los Angeles: Prospects and Promises* (Los Angeles: Center for Korean-American and Korean Studies, California State University, Los Angeles, 1982); Ivan Light and Edna Bonacich, *Immigrant Entrepreneurs: Koreans in Los Angeles, 1965–1982* (Berkeley: University of California Press, 1988); Nancy Abelmann and John Lie, *Blue Dreams: Korean Americans and the Los Angeles Riots* (Cambridge, Mass.: Harvard University Press, 1995); Pyong Gap Min, *Caught in the Middle: Korean Communities in New York and Los Angeles* (Berkeley: University of California Press, 1996); Kyeyoung Park, *The Korean American Dream: Immigrants and Small Business in New York City* (Ithaca, N.Y.: Cornell University Press, 1997); In-Jin Yoon, *On My Own: Korean Businesses and Race Relations in America* (Chicago: University of Chicago Press, 1997); Edward T. Chang and Jeannette Diaz-Veizades, *Ethnic Peace in the American City: Building Community in Los Angeles and Beyond* (New York: New York University Press, 1999); and Kwang Chung Kim, ed., *Koreans in the Hood: Conflict with African Americans* (Baltimore: Johns Hopkins University Press, 1999).

8. Rose Hum Lee, "The Chinese Communities in the Rocky Mountain Region," Ph.D. diss., University of Chicago, 1947; and Melford S. Weiss, *Valley City: A Chinese Community in America* (Cambridge, Mass.: Schenkman, 1974).

9. Hsiang-shui Chen, *Chinatown No More: Taiwan Immigrants in Contemporary New York* (Ithaca, N.Y.: Cornell University Press, 1992); Timothy P. Fong, *The First Suburban Chinatown: The Remaking of Monterey Park, California* (Philadelphia: Temple University Press, 1994); John Horton, *The Politics of Diversity: Immigration, Resistance, and Change in Monterey Park, California* (Philadelphia: Temple University Press, 1995); and Leland T. Saito, *Race and Politics: Asian Americans, Latinos, and Whites in a Los Angeles Suburb* (Urbana: University of Illinois Press, 1998). See also Wei Li, "Building Ethnoburbia: The Emergence and Manifestation of the Chinese Ethnoburb in Los Angeles' San Gabriel Valley," *Journal of Asian American Studies* 2:1 (February 1999): 1–28.

10. Kay J. Anderson, *Vancouver's Chinatown: Racial Discourse in Canada, 1875–1980* (Montreal: McGill-Queen's University Press, 1991).

11. See, e.g., Gloria Sun Hom, ed.,, *Chinese Argonauts: An Anthology of the Chinese Contributions to the Historical Development of Santa Clara County* (Santa Clara, Calif.: Foothill Community College, 1971); Diane Mei Lin Mark, *The Chinese in Kula: Recollections of a Farming Community in Old Hawaii* (Honolulu: Hawaii Chinese History Center, 1975); Kesa Noda, *Yamato Colony: 1906–1960* (Livingston, Calif.: Livingston-Merced Japanese American Citizens League Chapter, 1981); Robert N. Anderson, *Filipinos in Rural Hawaii* (Honolulu: University of Hawaii Press, 1984); Kazuko Nakane, *Nothing Left in My Hands: An Early Japanese American Community in California's Pajaro Valley* (Seattle: Young Pine Press, 1985); Jeff Gillenkirk and James Motlow, *Bitter Melon: Stories from the Last Rural Chinese Town in America* (Seattle: University of Washington Press, 1987); David Mas Masumoto, *Country Voices: The Oral History of a Japanese American Family Farm Community* (Del Rey, Calif.: Inaka Countryside Publications, 1987); Thomas K. Walls, *The Japanese Texans* (San Antonio: University of Texas Institute of Texan Cultures, 1987); Sylvia Sun Minnick, *Samfow: The San Joaquin Chinese Legacy* (Fresno, Calif.: Panorama West Publishing, 1988); Linda Tamura, *The Hood River Issei: An Oral History of Japanese Settlers in Oregon's Hood River Valley* (Urbana: University of Illinois Press, 1993); Thomas H. Heuterman, *The Burning Horse: Japanese-American Experience in the Yakima Valley, 1920–1942* (Cheney: Eastern Washington University Press, 1995); and David T. Yamada and Oral History Committee, MP/JACL, *The Japanese of the Monterey Peninsula: Their History & Legacy, 1895–1995* (Monterey Peninsula Japanese American Citizens League, 1995).

12. See, e.g., Robert Seto Quan, *Lotus Among the Magnolias: The Mississippi Chinese* (Jackson: University Press of Mississippi, 1982); Lucy M. Cohen, *Chinese in the Post-Civil War South: A People Without a History* (Baton Rouge: Louisiana State University Press, 1984); and Valerie J. Matsumoto, *Farming the Home Place: A Japanese American Community in California, 1919–1982* (Ithaca, N.Y.: Cornell University Press, 1993).

13. Sandy Lydon, *Chinese Gold: The Chinese in the Monterey Bay Region* (Capitola, Calif.: Capitola Book Company, 1985); and Timothy J. Lukes and Gary Y. Okihiro, *Japanese Legacy: Farming and Community Life in California's Santa Clara Valley* (Cupertino: California History Center, 1985).

14. Sucheng Chan, *This Bittersweet Soil: The Chinese in California Agriculture, 1860–1910* (Berkeley: University of California Press, 1986).

Chapter 2

WOMEN AND GENDER

Gender has always been a category in the writing of Asian American history, but it was commonly normalized as the experiences of men. Women were generally ignored, especially during the nineteenth century, ostensibly because of their relatively small numbers. Throughout the nineteenth century, for example, women totaled a mere 5 percent of all Chinese Americans.[2] Accordingly, women are largely invisible during this period of decades characterized by the "bachelor society." Men constituted the immigrants (as adventurers, fortune-seekers, and sojourners), laborers doing the work (as in gold prospecting, railroads, and laundries), and took part in the community (as in voluntary affiliations, religion, and gambling, prostitution, and opium smoking). The anti-Chinese movement culminates with the 1882 Exclusion Act, which prohibited the entry of Chinese laborers, mainly men, but the historiography on that movement tends to ignore or devalue the impact of the earlier 1875 Page Law, which in its application excluded most Chinese women. And when they are considered in the histories of Asian Americans, Asian women appear as consorts to men or as prostitutes or wives, undifferentiated and without agency.

The entry of women within the pages of Asian American history is both recent and long overdue. It is, distressingly, an emerging theme. Women's histories compel a fundamental rethinking of a past that has been generalized as that of men, and clarifies the social category of gender and its relations to other formations such as race, sexuality, class, and nation. As Shirley Hune observes, "Asian American women's history changes what we know and how we know. Infusing them in history, placing them at the center of power relations, and seeing the world through their experiences challenge the many historical paradigms that currently govern our understanding of American history. . . . The history of Asian American women serves as a crossroads to a new synthesis and in so doing redefines and enlarges traditional notions of historical significance."[2]

Hune's *Teaching Asian American Women's History* (1997) is a helpful guide to the subject. She shows how women's history helps to transform understandings of family formations, work and labor, and social affiliations. Instead of summarizing her insights here, I refer readers to Hune's work, especially to her bibliographic essay that organizes studies on Asian American women into general works, biographies, and memoirs, and by individual ethnic groups.[3] I simply update some of the books that have been published since 1997. These include: Shamita Das Dasgupta (ed.), *A Patchwork Shawl: Chronicles of South Asian Women in America* (New Brunswick, N.J.: Rutgers University Press, 1998); Elaine H. Kim and Chungmoo Choi (eds.), *Dangerous Women: Gender and Korean Nationalism* (New York: Routledge, 1998); Huping Ling, *Surviving on the Gold Mountain: A History of Chinese American Women and their Lives* (Albany: State University of New York Press, 1998); Eileen Sunada Sarasohn, *Issei Women: Echoes from Another Frontier* (Palo Alto, Calif.: Pacific Books, 1998); Soo-Young Chin, *Doing What Had to Be Done: The Life Narrative of Dora Yum Kim* (Philadelphia: Temple University Press, 1999); Wendy Ho, *In Her Mother's House: The Politics of Asian American Mother-Daughter Writing* (Walnut Creek, Calif.: AltaMira Press, 1999); George Anthony Peffer, *If They Don't Bring Their Women Here: Chinese Female Immigration before Exclusion* (Urbana: University of Illinois Press, 1999); Traise Yamamoto, *Masking Selves, Making Subjects: Japanese American Women, Identity, and the Body* (Berkeley: University of California Press, 1999); Judy Yung, *Unbound Voices: A Documentary History of Chinese Women in San Francisco* (Berkeley: University of California Press, 1999); Margaret Abraham, *Speaking the Unspeakable: Marital Violence among South Asian Immigrants in the United States* (New Brunswick, N.J.: Rutgers University Press, 2000); and Patricia P. Chu, *Assimilating Asians: Gendered Strategies of Authorship in Asian America* (Durham, N.C.: Duke University Press, 2000).

TEXTBOOKS

The most influential texts in Asian American women's history have been interdisciplinary readers. *Asian Women* (1971) is a classic in the field. The "journal" emanated from a discussion group at Berkeley, California, that met "to critically examine and discuss our roles as Asian women."[4] Upon discovering that other women's groups met for a similar purpose, the collective decided to publish the journal in order to share thoughts, ideas, and experiences. Most of the editors met in a class on Asian women at the University of California. There they quickly saw that stereotypes were commonplace, while accurate information was rare. "We were not satisfied with the traditional Asian roles, the white middle-class standards, nor the typical Asian women stereotypes in America. We wanted our own identity."[5] The editors put out a general call for submissions but found that women were reluctant to put their thoughts to paper. Asian men had their own stereotypes of Asian women, and they assumed privileged knowledge of Asian women. Their sexism inhibited the project and strained personal relationships. Other problems prevailed but in the end the journal was finished. "If there is anything that we have learned in the last year," the editors write, "it is that personal experiences are not private but common to all women. Out of common experiences political struggle is created."[6]

Academic and creative writing, personal accounts and interviews are organized into sections on history (herstory), reflections, Third World women, and the politics of womanhood. Chinese and Japanese immigrant women, representations of women in Japanese literature, and the Japanese American family during World War II are the topics of herstory. Reflections center upon Asian American women's identities and bodies as bound by racism and patriarchy, but also as liberated through martial arts, exercise, and sex.

The section on Third World women includes essays on women's liberation in North Korea, Saudi Arabia, and Iran, but revolves primarily around the Indochinese Women's Conference held in April 1971 in Vancouver, Canada, for attendees from western North America. America's war in Vietnam was raging when 150 women from North America met with six women from Vietnam to forge a common struggle of Third World women and promote the cause of peace. It is notable that this section moves beyond the borders of the United States, intellectually and physically, and includes Asian ethnicities other than Chinese and Japanese—Koreans, Vietnamese, and west Asians. The final section on the politics of womanhood covers subjects such as work, family, birth control, leadership, politics, and solidarities.

This pioneering text closes with an essay, presumably written by the editorial collective, titled "Politics of the Interior." In this summary, the authors conclude that it is capitalism, not men, that is the enemy, insofar as the social system oppresses both women *and* men. Moreover, the authors conclude, birth control is a right and one that should be shared by men; gays and lesbians should have the right to self-definition; Asian American women face the double bind of racism and sexism; the "woman question" must not be ignored; and Asian American women feel a common bond with all Third World women both within and outside the United States. "All people who are oppressed must not only recognize the causes of their oppression but also recognize the validity of other struggles," the authors declare. "We cannot underestimate the realities of factors which contribute to and re-enforce oppression. We must always be prepared for the struggle, to strengthen ourselves both in character and in the rightness of our position, and to realize that sisterhood *is* powerful."[7]

Like *Asian Women*, the anthology *Making Waves* (1989) was also assembled by an editorial collective. Published eighteen years later, this collection of scholarly and creative writings exhibits a very different orientation. Perhaps most striking is that the earlier search for solidarities through commonalities as Asian American and Third World women now gives way to a celebration of diversity and difference. "This anthology is the first major compilation of primarily unpublished works by and about Asian American women since the early 1970s," the editors observe. "During the past decade and a half, many people have been recording the experiences and history of those women in America who can trace their roots to Asia—China, Japan, Korea, the Philippines, South Asia, and Southeast Asia. The works collected here reflect our heterogeneity."[8] But unlike the first journal, this one put out a call for submissions that met with an overwhelming response, drawing more than three times the number finally published. But a red thread runs through both texts—the shattering of the stereotype of the passive, submissive Asian American woman. The readings show that "we are not afraid to rock the boat," the editors write. "Making waves. This is what Asian American women have done and will continue to do."[9]

The contents of this textbook are organized poetically around water images, an idea suggested by the poet and writer Janice Mirikitani. Topics covered include immigration, war, work, generations, identity, injustice, and activism. A woman-centered history provides the background to the themes and diverse ethnic groups held together by the book's pan-Asian perspective. That collective identity was made in the United States. The author of the introduction writes that "Asian women in America have emerged not as individuals but as nameless and faceless members of an alien community. Their identity has been formed by the lore of the majority community, not by their own history, their own stories."[10] A common past thus asserted, the editors proceed with the diversity of women's lives in Asia and the United States.

Poverty, war, and oppression drive women from Asia to America, but so does the search for adventure (it should be noted that family ties and culture are cut, but never completely severed). In the United States, Asian women face a hostile reception that alienates them from mainstream America, and their ingenuity and pluck enable them to survive and adapt. Poems, essays, and oral histories express those immigration themes of Asian Indians, Chinese, Filipinos, Japanese, Koreans, and Vietnamese. World War II leads to the confining of Japanese American women in concentration camps, the Korean war exiles and separates Korean women, and the aftermath of the U.S. war in Southeast Asia leaves refugees and survivors struggling to contend with the war's horror. America's wars in Asia drove women from their homes, imprisoned them, and brought them to these shores as brides of U.S. military men and as refugees.

The labor of Asian women was prodigious and unrelenting, and often oppressive to them—to Chinese prostitutes of the nineteenth century, Japanese sugar plantation workers, low-paid Asian seamstresses, Filipina electronics assemblers, South Asian fruit and vegetable cannery laborers, and even Asian professionals in broadcasting. Racism, sexism, and economic necessity are the daily companions of Asian women working in the home as well as outside it. Generations clash even as they converge in behaviors and conversations; ancestors root women's pasts while children reach for the future. Identities, including those shaped by gender and race, by sexuality and physical disabilities, are multiply conceived and determined. Similarly, discrimination has several faces conformed by stereotypes and popular images, racism and sexism, and economic necessity and physical violence. But unlike the docile, passive victims of the popular imagination and media, Asian American women have struggled for their communities, families, and selves. Activism—making waves—involved feminist and civil rights causes, redressing past and present injustices, and engagements in mainstream politics. Like their predecessors in *Asian Women*, the editors of *Making Waves* conclude with activism and self-agency: "In the end, though, no one else can speak for them [Asian American women]. They, like all of us, must speak for themselves. We can expect no one else to fight our battles; we must fight them ourselves. We must make our own waves."[11]

Making More Waves (1997) followed on the commercial success of its original, and features the works of a new generation of Asian American women writing for a growing readership.[12] That same year, the sociologist Yen Le Espiritu published her *Asian American Women and Men* (1997), marking the emergence of gender formation as an explicit social category of analysis in Asian American studies. As a central organizing principle, gender helps to explain race, class, sexuality, and nation, as well as the relations between Asian American women and men in the home, community, and workplace. The dynamic is the tension between women and men. The theory ascribes agency to women and men, and accounts for social change. But Espiritu, moving beyond the sole privileging of gender and the binaries of race and gender, shows that Asians are multiply oppressed on the bases of both gender and race, that they are neither black nor white, neither woman nor man as represented by America's white middle class, and thus present a challenge to those norms.[13]

METHODOLOGY

Those intent on recovering women's lives and voices have had to rely on oral and life histories because they left few written records. Of course, the same could be said of Asian American men, especially working-class men, but the deeds of Asian American men can frequently be deduced from the records, whereas typically Asian American women are absent altogether from those pages. Accordingly, although not self-consciously or critically, oral accounts constitute a primary source of information for the history of Asian American women. Examples include: *Linking Our Lives: Chinese American Women of Los Angeles* (Los Angeles: Chinese Historical Society of Southern California, 1984); Joyce Chapman Lebra, *Women's Voices in Hawaii* (Niwot: University Press of Colorado, 1991); Eileen Tamura, *The Hood River Issei: An Oral History of Japanese Settlers in Oregon's Hood River Valley* (Urbana: University of Illinois Press, 1993); Sucheng Chan (ed.), *Hmong Means Free: Life in Laos and America* (Philadelphia: Temple University Press, 1994); Pepi Nieva (ed.), *Filipina: Hawaii's Filipino Women* (Honolulu: Filipino Association of University Women, 1994); Steven DeBonis, *Children of the Enemy: Oral Histories of Vietnamese Amerasians and Their Mothers* (Jefferson, N.C.: McFarland, 1995); Yen Le Espiritu, *Filipino American Lives* (Philadelphia: Temple University Press, 1995); Lillian Faderman with Ghia Xiong, *I Begin My Life All Over: The Hmong and the American Immigrant Experience* (Boston: Beacon Press, 1998); and Eileen Sunada Sarasohn, *Issei Women: Echoes From Another Frontier* (Palo Alto, Calif.: Pacific Books, 1998).

Biographies, autobiographies, and memoirs are another important source of information on women's lives. These include: Helena Kuo, *I've Come a Long Way* (New York: D. Appleton-Century, 1942); Jade Snow Wong, *Fifth Chinese Daughter* (1945; reprint, Seattle: University of Washington Press, 1989); Monica Sone, *Nisei Daughter* (1953; reprint, Seattle: University of Washington Press, 1987); Li Ling Ai, *Life Is for a Long Time: A Chinese Hawaiian Memoir* (New York: Hastings House, 1972); Jeanne Wakatsuki Houston and James D. Houston, *Farewell to Manzanar* (Boston: Houghton Mifflin, 1973); Akemi Kikumura, *Through Harsh Winters: The Life of a Japanese Immigrant Woman* (Novato, Calif.: Chandler & Sharp, 1981); Yoshiko Uchida, *Desert Exile: The Uprooting of a Japanese-American Family* (Seattle: University of Washington Press, 1982); Kiyo Hirano, *Enemy Alien* (San Francisco: JAM Publications, 1983); Elaine H. Kim with Janice Otani, *With Silk Wings: Asian American Women at Work* (San Francisco: Asian Women United of California, 1983); Tomoko Yamazaki, *The Story of Yamada Waka: From Prostitute to Feminist Pioneer*, translated by Wakako Hironaka and Ann Konstant (Tokyo: Kodansha International, 1985); Le Ly Hayslip with Jay Wurts, *When Heaven and Earth Changed Places: A Vietnamese Woman's Journey from War to Peace* (New York: Doubleday, 1989); Mary Paik Lee, *Quiet Odyssey: A Pioneer Korean Woman in America* (Seattle: University of Washington Press, 1990); Mari J. Matsuda (ed.), *Called from Within: Early Women Lawyers of Hawai'i* (Honolulu: University of Hawai'i Press, 1992); Meena Alexander, *Fault Lines: A Memoir* (New York: Feminist Press, 1993); Claire Gorfinkel (ed.), *The Evacuation Diary of Hatsuye Egami* (Pasadena,

Calif.: Intentional Productions, 1995); Annette White-Parks, *Sui Sin Far/Edith Maude Eaton: A Literary Biography* (Urbana: University of Illinois Press, 1995); Shirley Geok-Lin Lim, *Among the White Moon Faces: A Memoir of Homelands* (New York: Feminist Press, 1996); Daisy Chun Rhodes, *Passages to Paradise: Early Korean Immigrant Narratives from Hawai'i* (Los Angeles: Academia Koreana, 1998); and Soo-Young Chin, *Doing What Had to Be Done: The Life Narrative of Dora Yum Kim* (Philadelphia: Temple University Press, 1999).

Prompted by necessity and a privileging of experience, oral histories, biographies, and memoirs, like all documents, can inform as well as misinform if they elude critical review.[14] Writings on Asian American women, besides giving voice those women, have added to the theoretical sophistication of the field.

THEORY

Evelyn Nakano Glenn's *Issei, Nisei, War Bride: Three Generations of Japanese American Women in Domestic Service* (1986) began as an oral history project because, she reasoned, women's own words about themselves and their work "seemed the best vehicle for illustrating how gender, race and class intersect to shape the lives of racial-ethnic women."[15] But as the research progressed, she realized that the study had to be broadened to encompass the larger historical and social forces that affected Japanese American women's experience as domestic workers during the first half of the twentieth century. Women's accounts of their lives revealed more complicated interiors than the stereotypical exteriors of passive victims and servants to husbands and children. That revelation pointed out the inadequacies of "static models of class, race, and sex" that could not account for the contestations that formed the core of women's lives. "To capture the contradictions and dynamism of Japanese American women's situations, I would have to take a dialectical approach to class, race and gender, an approach that captures the struggle inherent in all relations of dominance and hierarchy and thereby takes into account not only the efforts of dominant groups to maintain their privileged position, but also the active resistance of subordinate groups striving to carve out ares of autonomy and power."[16]

Nakano Glenn sees capitalist labor systems as segmented according to immigrants and natives, nonwhites and whites, women and men, and as influential in structuring the family life and culture of workers. In the past, state policies militated against the formation of families, and women's low wages perpetuated their subordination to men within the home. Never static, oppression sets off resistance through legal and extralegal means because "subordinate groups do not passively acquiesce."[17] Cohorts of Japanese American women—*issei*, *nisei*, and war brides—confronted the evolving labor market and its constraints, and they responded to shifting conditions in the workplace and family. Oppression

and resistance were historical, and they were structural and never wholly idio-
syncratic. Further, Japanese American women's labor comprised unique but,
more significantly, shared aspects of "the labor systems of capitalist economies,
the role of immigrant and racial-ethnic women in those systems, and the consequences of race- and gender-stratified labor systems for the family and cultural
systems of minority groups."[18]

Nazli Kibria argues that immigration poses sharp social and cultural challenges because of "the novelty of the new society and the pressures associated
with beginning a new life."[19] It is at this point that the disjuncture is at its
greatest and that immigrants reflect on their prior realities and respond to their
new circumstances. Kibria finds, contrary to popular depictions of Vietnamese
success in America, that Vietnamese American families are changing and unbound by tradition. Instead of being defined by the Confucian values that the
media represents these families as strongly adhering to, family life was "an arena
of considerable conflict and flux. I saw and heard women, men, and children
struggling to reconstruct and redefine the structure and meaning of family
life."[20]

Migration disrupted Vietnamese families and their networks. Children arrived in the United States without their parents, and husbands without their
wives. The rebuilding of families thus involved unconventional arrangements
in which distant relatives and even friends were drawn together into a tight
family circle in the United States. Those who were middle-class in Vietnam
became working-class in America, and Vietnamese men confronted racial discrimination in seeking employment. Men's losses led to greater economic, social, gender, and generational equality, resulting in increased opportunities for
women to assert their independence from the claims of men, and youth from
the claims of adults. Despite the change and its accompanying tensions, women
did not try to restructure family life along more egalitarian lines but were deeply
ambivalent about departures from the values of collectivism and cooperation.
Thus, they walked an ideological tightrope, "struggling to use their new resources to their advantage but not in ways that significantly altered or threatened
the traditional family system."[21]

Like Kibria, the anthropologist Kyeyoung Park studied Asian immigration
and its impact on family life and culture in the United States.[22] Her research
on Korean Americans in New York City focuses on small businesses and their
structuring of gender, family, and community relations. Like Nakano Glenn,
Park sees the labor market and relations of production as influential in the
shaping of individual lives and culture, and she assigns movement and change
to the dialectical engagements between oppression and resistance. Like Kibria's
Vietnamese Americans, Park's Korean migrants experience downward class mobility in the United States. Drawn into small business out of necessity and
opportunity, Korean Americans discover that in order to succeed they need

unpaid family labor. Accordingly, single men seek marriage, and married women and their children work in the family business. In that way, economic forces reshape domestic life.

Korean American women have played a central role in immigration. As a result of the Korean War, when women entered the United States as war brides, and then of the immigration reform act of 1965, when women migrated under occupational preferences and family reunification provisions, Korean women often preceded and exceeded men. Further, Korean American women often sponsored the immigration of their kin and thereby obtained the familial support that their husbands often lacked. Typically, the husband runs a business that employs these family members, who thereby exert even more influence over him. Accordingly, in the United States, kin relations are tighter and more encompassing than in Korea, with kinship ties tending toward the bilateral. In contrast to the male dominance that is the rule in Korea, sisters in Korean American families direct their brothers, wives supervise families, and husbands live and work with his wife's parents and siblings.

Still, most Korean American businesses are male-initiated and male-registered. Men buy and transport produce from the wholesale market to the store, while women and children generally provide the labor at the retail end. About the same number of women work in family businesses as in the manufacturing and service industries. Although many families adhere to the notion of patriarchy, increasing numbers of women are developing improved self-esteem, self-confidence, and autonomy. Men commonly see those changes as more "American" and less "Korean," although some have taken on more household responsibilities to share in domestic chores. And wage earning, although frequently tedious and strenuous, affords Korean American women greater freedom and a sense of dignity as more equal members of the household and society.

Literary criticism has posed a busy intersection for feminist interventions. Using literary texts by Asian Americans, Patricia P. Chu shows how they claim "Americanness" for Asian American subjects and simultaneously construct Asian ethnicities.[23] She proposes that the gendering of Asian American history explains why Asian American men and women position themselves differently as racialized and gendered subjects in the work of assimilation and as authors in an American literary tradition. Traise Yamamoto writes of Japanese American women, long perceived by dominant culture as perpetual foreigners or exotic others, as deploying "the very surface whose opacity has denied them particularity and humanity in order to claim and preserve both."[24] Japanese American women enacted selves apart from society's definitions, as well as masked selves from its dehumanizing gaze. In rescuing the self from the dustbin of postmodern subjectivity, Yamamoto proposes a critical humanism that disrupts and is not determined by social and discursive structures.

Rachel C. Lee reveals that gender and sexuality mediate and complicate the view of "America" as conceived by Asian American writers. She points to the limits of racial critiques, couched in the language of cultural nationalism, that reinstate and naturalize women's dependency, and instead assumes that "gender opposition, gender difference, and gender hierarchy become convenient ways for understanding, enacting, and reinforcing opposition, difference, and hierarchy more generally and in an array of social relationships criss-crossed by racial, class-based, regional, and national differences."[25] But to link feminist interventions with the fate of cultural nationalism is limiting and elides the power of feminism to address transnational and post-national realities. "America" exceeds the bounds of geopolitical space, and its domestic realm is indistinct from its cultural exports, its history of empire, and its participation in the flows of international capital and labor. A gendered reading of Asian American history makes that clear. Lee thus posits an intellectual frame that accounts for the multiple and shifting terrains of gender in national and transnational spaces and Asian-Pacific and postcolonial identity formations.

HISTORY

Historical accounts of Asian American women appear as memoirs, biographies, and autobiographies, and are scattered in journals, anthologies, and collections of oral histories. I limit this discussion to book-length, interpretive histories of Asian American women.

Mei T. Nakano's *Japanese American Women: Three Generations, 1890–1990* (1990) is a pioneering work inspired by the absence of women in the extant histories and by the need for a more inclusive history that records the lives of both elites and the masses, men and women alike. "The history of women, told by women," Nakano writes, "is a recent phenomenon. It has called for a fundamental reevaluation of assumptions and principles that govern traditional history. . . . We are challenged to push the former boundaries of history and record not only the lives of the heroic, but that of the undervalued, of women as well as men. Above all, we need to think of history as primarily about people, not events, as an account of their states of mind as well as their actions."[26] The book is organized around generations—first, second, and third. Each part is divided by subjects that are pertinent to that generation and period, and is supported by individual stories and recollections.

Barbara F. Kawakami's has likened her *Japanese Immigrant Clothing in Hawaii, 1885–1941* (1993) to a spiritual journey.[27] A dressmaker by profession, Kawakami reentered school to earn her high school diploma and enrolled in college at the age of fifty-three. A senior class project, Kawakami's research into clothing worn by Japanese migrants took her on a journey to her plantation past and to Japan, where return migrants remembered their years of labor in Hawaii's sugar plantations. Kawakami also reconstructed a copy of a woman's work outfit. Her book shows that Japanese men were less fussy than women about clothing and readily adopted the plantation outfits of their fellow workers. But Japanese women were more selective and inventive, assimilating ideas from other ethnic groups with their own traditions. This new style of clothing was also functional and protected them from the tropical sun, dust, mud, sharp pineapple and cane leaves, and the sting of centipedes, scorpions, bees, and wasps. Using American blue denim material for their arm guards and leggings, Japanese women fashioned jackets patterned after those worn by Chinese women, skirts after those worn by Hawaiian, Spanish, and Portuguese women, and head coverings after those worn by Spanish, Portuguese, and Puerto Rican women. They tied their clothing together with a wide sash, a typically Japanese item that provided comfort, security, and strength for women accustomed to hard labor and pangs of hunger. Clothing, Kawakami shows, reveals much about culture, its continuities and adaptations, and about history.

Valerie J. Matsumoto's *Farming the Home Place: A Japanese American Community in California, 1919–1982* (1993) is not an account of Japanese American women but of an entire community. Matsumoto is especially attentive to the lives of women and to the gender relations that constitute the community of Cortez, California. She was motivated by the challenges of reconstituting a community through history, inserting Asians within America's black-and-white racial binary, and articulating a rural dimension to the social and cultural questions raised by urban researchers. Relying on published and unpublished sources and on a large number of oral interviews, Matsumoto weaves an intricate story about the making of a rural ethnic community over three generations and about the interplay of work, race, and gender and the opportunities and constraints they posed. Discrete lives are as complex and contradictory as aggregates, she concludes, and they inform the wider arenas of history and society. "The men and women of Cortez shared with me a richly textured past woven from the sturdy threads of their lives. Major themes in Japanese American studies took on greater dimension when examined through the range of their experiences."[28]

Benson Tong's *Unsubmissive Women: Chinese Prostitutes in Nineteenth-Century San Francisco* (1994) revisits the history of perhaps the most written about group of Asian American women. He reads against the grain of accounts—mainly in polemics against vice and immorality, barbarism, and an inferior people—that depict Chinese prostitutes as slaves and hapless victims. In truth, Chinese prostitutes were valued only for their labor, were relegated to the lowest level of Chinese and white society, and were strictly controlled by Chinese tongs and the state. "Yet a significant number of these ethnic women refused to succumb to the socioeconomic forces that threatened to overwhelm them. They retained a grip on the choices available to them and attempted to remedy the misfortune of having been forced into prostitution. Though many failed to resist the pressures exerted on them by society, they retained the will to survive. Some even adapted to their new environment; others made use of available resources to change their lives for the better. A number of them eventually left the trade for the comforts and security of family life."[29]

Judy Yung's *Unbound Feet: A Social History of Chinese Women in San Francisco* (1995) follows her pictorial history and precedes her documentary history of Chinese American women.[30] In the course of trying to understand women's work, family, and political lives through an interpretation of how gender perceptions, roles, and relationships changed over time, Yung discovered race theories that overlooked gender, feminist theories that failed to account for race, and scholarship about women of color that was limited to the black-and-white binary. For the purposes of her study of Chinese American women, all were unsatisfactory on their own. She therefore had to draw from all three approaches and create a synthesis of race, gender, and class as equally important historical categories. In addition, her study of Chinese American women shows that their lives were influenced by developments in the United States and China, stressing the transnational natures of women's pasts. "Faced with discriminatory exclusion from American life throughout most of their history," Yung writes, "Chinese Americans remained attached to homeland politics and highly influenced by developments there—including women's emancipation—until the 1940s, when Chinese exclusion ended and diplomatic relations between the United States and China broke off."[31]

Huping Ling's *Surviving on the Gold Mountain: A History of Chinese American Women and their Lives* (1998) offers a comprehensive history of Chinese American women from the mid-nineteenth century to the close of the twentieth century.[32] It also compares the life histories of Chinese American women, both rural and urban, with the lives of other immigrant women. Family structures changed in the new environment, wage earning elevated women's place within the family, immigrant women experienced cultural alienation from American society and their American-born children, and daughters of immigrants found themselves marginal to immigrant and American culture. Many immigrant women shared those changes. Chinese American women differed from Jewish and Irish women in that they were less visible in trade unionism and political activities until the 1960s. And Chinese American women's history points to the limits of the male-centered periodization of 1848–1882 as the period of free immigration, 1882–1943 as the period of exclusion, and 1943–present as the postwar period. In fact, the Page Act of 1875 restricted Chinese women's immigration and hence the period of free migration ends in 1875 and not 1882, and the War Brides Act of 1945 and the G.I. Fiancees Act of 1946 were more important to Chinese women than the 1943 repeal of the 1882 Exclusion Act.

George Anthony Peffer's *If They Don't Bring Their Women Here: Chinese Female Immigration Before Exclusion* (1999) documents the importance of the 1875 Page Act for Chinese women and for the Exclusion Act seven years later.[33] Peffer shows that the labor of Chinese men was welcomed by California's elite but that Chinese women were undesirable because their children, if born in the United States, were U.S. citizens and as permanent residents could make claims on the state. A comparison of Chinese women's migration to Hawaii, Australia, Singapore, Penang, and Malacca shows the force that U.S. institutions and practices had on their migration to America. But Chinese women were more than victims of state control and, as such, led complex and full lives. Despite the limitations of his sources—government documents, census records, treaty negotiations and law digests, court records, and newspapers—that privilege the opinions of white men, Peffer uses the scraps of evidence to give voice to Chinese women. In this way he demonstrates, while building on and adding to Judy Yung's work, continuities between Chinese American women before and after general exclusion in 1882. In fact, a more accurate periodization of Chinese American history, Peffer notes, looks like this: 1852–1868, the period of male sojourning; 1869–1874, the period of unrestricted family immigration; 1875–1882, the period of female exclusion; and post-1882, the period of general exclusion.

Feminist interventions within Asian American studies have centered on women and have made gender and its relations explicit, fundamentally transforming the field's theoretical underpinnings. Race was and still is the primary category of analysis. But feminist writings reveal the analytical power of gender and its intimacies with race, sexuality, class, and nation. And a focus on women's pasts shows clearly the transnational nature of Asian America and the inaccuracies of periodizations built around men only. Not yet an established theme, women and gender is, however, an emerging theme, one that can no longer be ignored or slighted in future works of consequence.

NOTES

1. Judy Yung, *Unbound Feet: A Social History of Chinese Women in San Francisco* (Berkeley: University of California Press, 1995), 24.

2. Shirley Hune, *Teaching Asian American Women's History* (Washington, D.C.: American Historical Association, 1997), 4–5.

3. Hune, *Teaching*. In her bibliographic essay, Hune refers her readers to Brian Niiya's compilation of works on Asian American women in *Unequal Sisters: A Multi-Cultural Reader in U.S. Women's History*, edited by Vicki L. Ruiz and Ellen Carol DuBois (New York: Routledge, 1994), 590–93.

4. *Asian Women* (Berkeley: University of California, 1971), 4.

5. Ibid.

6. Ibid., 6.

7. Ibid., 130.

8. Asian Women United of California, ed., *Making Waves: An Anthology of Writings By and About Asian American Women* (Boston: Beacon Press, 1989), ix.

9. Ibid., xi.

10. Sucheta Mazumdar, "General Introduction: A Woman-Centered Perspective on Asian American History," Asian Women, *Making Waves*, 1.

11. Asian Women United, *Making Waves*, 348.

12. Elaine H. Kim, Lilia V. Villanueva, and Asian Women United of California, eds., *Making More Waves: New Writing by Asian American Women* (Boston: Beacon Press, 1997).

13. Yen Le Espiritu, *Asian American Women and Men: Labor, Laws, and Love* (Thousand Oaks, Calif.: Sage Publications, 1997). For a collection of Asian American women's political writings, see Sonia Shah, ed., *Dragon Ladies: Asian American Feminists Breathe Fire* (Boston: South End Press, 1997).

14. See e.g., Joan W. Scott, "Experience," in *Feminists Theorize the Political*, edited by Judith Butler and Joan W. Scott (New York: Routledge, 1992), 22–40.

15. Evelyn Nakano Glenn, *Issei, Nisei, War Bride: Three Generations of Japanese American Women in Domestic Service* (Philadelphia: Temple University Press, 1986), ix.

16. Ibid., xii.

17. Ibid., xiii.

18. Ibid., xiv–xv.

19. Nazli Kibria, *Family Tightrope: The Changing Lives of Vietnamese Americans* (Princeton, N.J.: Princeton University Press, 1993), 10.

20. Ibid., 7.

21. Ibid., 9.

22. Kyeyoung Park, *The Korean American Dream: Immigrants and Small Business in New York City* (Ithaca, N.Y.: Cornell University Press, 1997).

23. Patricia P. Chu, *Assimilating Asians: Gendered Strategies of Authorship in Asian America* (Durham, N.C.: Duke University Press, 2000).

24. Traise Yamamoto, *Masking Selves, Making Subjects: Japanese American Women, Identity, and the Body* (Berkeley: University of California Press, 1999), 3.

25. Rachel C. Lee, *The Americas of Asian American Literature: Gendered Fictions of Nation and Transnation* (Princeton, N.J.: Princeton University Press, 1999), 4.

26. Mei T. Nakano, *Japanese American Women: Three Generations, 1890–1990* (Berkeley, Calif.: Mina Press, 1990), xiii.

27. Barbara F. Kawakami, *Japanese Immigrant Clothing in Hawaii, 1885–1941* (Honolulu: University of Hawaii Press, 1993).

28. Valerie J. Matsumoto, *Farming the Home Place: A Japanese American Community in California, 1919–1982* (Ithaca, N.Y.: Cornell University Press, 1993), 16.

29. Benson Tong, *Unsubmissive Women: Chinese Prostitutes in Nineteenth-Century San Francisco* (Norman: University of Oklahoma Press, 1994), xviii–xix.

30. Judy Yung, *Chinese Women of America: A Pictorial History* (Seattle: University of Washington Press, 1986); and Judy Yung, *Unbound Voices: A Documentary History of Chinese Women in San Francisco* (Berkeley: University of California Press, 1999).

31. Judy Yung, *Unbound Feet: A Social History of Chinese Women in San Francisco* (Berkeley: University of California Press, 1995), 5.

32. Huping Ling, *Surviving on the Gold Mountain: A History of Chinese American Women and their Lives* (Albany: State University of New York Press, 1998).

33. George Anthony Peffer, *If They Don't Bring Their Women Here: Chinese Female Immigration before Exclusion* (Urbana: University of Illinois Press, 1999).

Chapter 3

THE LAW

Asian American legal history arose because the law constrained and protected Asian American lives and rights, and Asian Americans actively contested and reshaped those laws and their application. Asian Americans and the law is a longstanding issue but, in Asian American studies, an emerging theme. As these selections show, scholarship on this theme has evolved from merely documenting the history of law to participating in current theoretical debates. Japan's consulate general and the Japanese American Citizens League collected and published law cases involving Japanese Americans, and Milton R. Konvitz advocated for liberal courts to protect the slender freedoms of aliens and Asians as disenfranchised groups. Moritoshi Fukuda showed how both domestic and international law affected the legal condition of Japanese in the United States, and Bill Ong Hing revealed how U.S. immigration law sculpted the demographic profile of Asian America. Charles J. McClain exhibited an Asian Americanist perspective in arguing for Chinese American centrality and agency; Hyung-chan Kim located Asian Americans within U.S. anxieties over race, nativity, class, and culture from the colonial period to 1990; and Lucy E. Salyer framed Chinese American challenges to immigration law within her interest in administrative structure and law. Asian Americanist perspectives contributed to theoretical debates in legal scholarship in the writings of critical race theorists and in the books by Angelo N. Ancheta and Robert S. Chang.[1]

Japan's government maintained a keen interest in its national sovereignty, and consequently in its treaties with other governments and in the legal standing of their subjects in the countries to which they migrated. Accordingly, the Japanese consulate in San Francisco compiled and published a two-volume set, *Documental History of Law Cases Affecting Japanese in the United States, 1916–1924* (vol. 1, *Naturalization Cases and Cases Affecting Constitutional and Treaty Rights* [1925]; vol. 2, *Japanese Land Cases* [1925]). The collection reproduces transcripts of cases without commentary or explanation of the criteria by which they were selected.[2]

The first legal history of Asian Americans is Milton R. Konvitz's *The Alien and the Asiatic in American Law* (1946). Prompted by the race and alien "problems," Konvitz's study examines the U.S. Supreme Court's responses to challenges posed by aliens and Asians and assesses the evolving legal status of those groups. Although their number is relatively small and diminishing, aliens and Asians will remain a contentious issue, Konvitz predicts, because "many elements in our society will continue to demand uncompromising conformity, will seek to eliminate all traces of unlikeness, will express a passion for homogeneity, and will compel races, nationalities, and religious groups to play the role of antagonistic classes in the American social and economic structure."[3] Premised on the desire for unity and the fear of disintegration, the drive for assimilation ignores America's unifying memories and sense of integration and social identity molded by a common history and common ideals.

The book focuses on the rights of exclusion and expulsion, citizenship, land ownership, work, access to natural resources, language, schools, and marriage. Konvitz devotes chapters to World War II and to alien registration with respect to Japanese Americans. The Chinese exclusion acts asserted the rights of the U.S. government to exclude aliens generally and certain classes in particular because of their race. In addition, quota laws limited immigration by nationality and discriminated against southern and eastern Europeans. The Supreme Court upheld repeatedly in the broadest possible terms the power of Congress over immigration, and the law thereby permitted discrimination on the basis of race, national origin, and religious affiliation. Expulsion followed exclusion as a consequence of immigration controls. Although laws permitting it were first passed in 1798, alien expulsion was never carried out until 1882, when the policy of Chinese exclusion made deportation a necessary part of immigration restriction. As exclusion broadened, the practice of expulsion likewise widened to include illegal immigrants and other aliens.

Naturalization was restricted to free white persons by Congress in 1790. Blacks became eligible for naturalization by an act in 1870. Asians were excluded from those racial categories and thus rendered ineligible for naturalized citizenship. Naturalization, like immigration, was not considered a right but a legislative privilege, and the law discriminated on the basis of race. Congress conferred naturalization on selected Asian groups during the 1940s. Aliens ineligible for citizenship were denied the fundamental economic right of land ownership. And, deprived of land, they were restricted in employment. Further, states required citizenship of anyone engaged in certain businesses and professions, barring aliens and especially those aliens ineligible for citizenship. States maintained the right to restrict the access of aliens to natural resources, segregate schools by race, and prohibit racial intermarriages, but they could not interfere in the rights of parents to control their children's education in foreign language acquisition. Finally, in the case of Japanese Americans during World War II, a majority of the Supreme Court ruled that curfew and exclusion were necessary as war measures, but the government had no power to detain citizens without judicial review.

Konvitz's book is both a study of selected Supreme Court decisions and a polemic against the suppression of freedoms. Employing the language of advocacy, Konvitz reasons: "The alien, since he does not enjoy the franchise, and suffers under other handicaps as well, has no remedy in the legislature; his only remedy is in the courts. The courts should, therefore, zealously seek to give him the protection that will be commensurate with his need."[4]

The Japanese American Citizens League commissioned Frank F. Chuman's *The Bamboo People: The Law and Japanese-Americans* (1976) as a part of its attempt to document the entire history of Japanese in the United States through its Japanese-American Research Project at the University of California, Los Angeles. Arranged chronologically, the book begins with immigration laws in the late nineteenth century and moves to immigration agreements and alien land laws through the 1920s, World War II, and the postwar liberalization of restrictions. Instead of an interpretation of the legal past, the book is a collection of laws and court decisions discussed in time sequence. Few connecting strands link events and social forces. *Bamboo People*, however, is useful as a reference work on many of the most important legal decisions affecting Japanese and other Asian Americans. It concludes that the struggle for equal opportunity waged by Japanese Americans benefited other racialized minorities and all Americans.[5]

Moritoshi Fukuda's *Legal Problems of Japanese-Americans: Their History and Development in the United States* (1980) began as a dissertation for a law degree at the University of Michigan and was motivated by the hope that it would lead Japanese Americans to a "better understanding of their past and contribute to the foundation of a stronger union of friendship between the two nations [Japan and the United States]."[6] It examines the legal problems encountered by Japanese in the United States from the late nineteenth to the mid-twentieth century, problems involving international law, aliens and the law, and constitutional law. Japanese Americans contested and were constrained by restrictions against their immigration, naturalization, ownership and use of land, and occupational mobility. They faced exclusion as aliens and as racialized minorities who were neither black nor white. But the legal condition of Japanese in the United States was not simply a matter of domestic policy but also one of international relations. Because of its inexperience, Japan failed to ensure that the treaties it negotiated had explicit language to protect the rights of its citizens in the United States. It thus allowed openings against them by the U.S. federal and state governments. Still, the rise of the civil rights movement and new interpretations of the equal protection clause of the U.S. Constitution were ultimately more effective in dismantling legal discrimination than were treaty negotiations.

Bill Ong Hing in *Making and Remaking Asian America Through Immigration Policy, 1850–1990* (1993) shows how immigration legislation shaped the six largest Asian American communities—Chinese, Filipinos, Indians, Japanese, Koreans, and Vietnamese. Exclusion laws reduced dramatically the numbers of immigrants from the excluded groups, and they manipulated gender ratios that influenced population growth among the affected groups. Liberalization of the immigration laws enabled rapid growth in Asian American communities, especially among Filipinos, Indians, and Koreans. Current immigration policies favor Asian settlements in the West, population concentrations if ethnic enclaves like Chinatowns, and the employment patterns and economic profiles of immigrants. Because of the far-reaching influence their decisions have, policymakers should appreciate and understand the bases for and consequences of them. But scholars, the popular media, and community organizers and activists are equally culpable of purveying myths about Asian Americans with little foundation in evidence. "It is plainly naïve to think that immigration laws have shaped every facet of Asian American experience. Yet it is equally misguided to discount the effects of such laws on the decision to immigrate and on what happened to people once they arrived. Careful attention must be paid to demographics, to the influence of law and policy on demographics, and the connection between demographics and how these groups live."[7] That describes the book's central thesis and purpose.

Charles J. McClain wrote *In Search of Equality: The Chinese Struggle Against Discrimination in Nineteenth-Century America* (1994) from his interest in constitutional history. A key case on the equal protection clause of the Fourteenth Amendment is the 1886 Supreme Court decision of *Yick Wo v. Hopkins*, in which the court agreed with San Francisco Chinese laundrymen that city ordinances that discriminated against them in their intent and application violated their constitutional rights. The ruling, McClain held, was important historically but also flew in the face of conventional stereotypes of the Chinese as docile, unassimilable aliens. And *Yick Wo* was not exceptional. Chinese Americans were politically astute and engaged, and appeared as litigants before the U.S. Supreme Court some twenty times between 1880 and 1900. "Indeed during the second half of the nineteenth century, the Chinese mounted court challenges to virtually every governmentally imposed disability under which they labored. . . . The Chinese readiness to resort to the courts to remedy perceived wrongs is an aspect of their experience in the United States barely touched on in the published literature. Yet it is surely one of the most salient and defining features of that experience."[8] The book reveals that the Chinese, in their legal challenges, shaped American constitutional jurisprudence, and it situates itself in the Asian Americanist historiographical tradition by positioning Chinese Americans as central to the shaping of history.

Hyung-chan Kim in A *Legal History of Asian Americans, 1790–1990* (1994) follows *Asian Americans and the Supreme Court* (1992),[9] which he edited, offers an overview of the legislative and political purposes of various immigration laws and their applications by the Supreme Court.[10] In its attempts to control immigration, Congress employed the criteria of quantity and quality to include people it considered desirable and exclude people it considered undesirable. Those judgments of members of the community as suitable or unsuitable were shaped by the perceptions and attitudes of English colonists toward American Indians, black slaves, and non-English Europeans. During the colonial period, English colonists developed strong sentiments against people of color, non-English lower classes, and adherents of religions other than their own. The founding fathers, during the period of the Revolutionary War, harbored strong resentments against foreigners, restricting naturalization by law and, in the Constitution, requiring residency for candidates for public office. Those prejudices against people of color, foreigners, religious minorities, and working classes came to a head in anti-Chinese legislation during the second half of the nineteenth century, and during the early twentieth century led to the restriction of, and a halt to, trans-Pacific immigration from Asia. Asians were deprived of citizenship and freedoms until 1952, when they gained naturalization rights; in 1965, they were allowed into the United States in unprecedented numbers. The U.S. Supreme Court restored the rights of language, education, and employment to Asian Americans, although immigration reform resulted in renewed discrimination against them.

Lucy E. Salyer's *Laws Harsh as Tigers: Chinese Immigrants and the Shaping of Modern Immigration Law* (1995) arose from her discovery that Chinese litigants deluged the courts with challenges to enforcements of the Chinese exclusion acts, and from her realization that they contributed "in significant and unexpected ways to the growth of administrative power."[11] Although the federal government assumed sole control over immigration in 1891, the application of exclusion laws rested in the hands of contending groups who argued about the social and economic goals of immigration policy, the proper role of government, power structures in American society, and individual rights in an evolving administrative state. As was shown by Charles McClain and others, Chinese litigants were familiar with their rights as guaranteed by treaty and the U.S.

Constitution. Their successes in the federal courts suggest, contrary to prevailing views, activist judges and a less than omnipotent Bureau of Immigration. Also, the judges in these immigration cases, although they might have held anti-Chinese attitudes, felt constrained by the rules and norms of the court and rendered judgments that contradicted the idea of political intervention in judicial decisions. An institutional approach, wherein judges are inheritors of traditions, helps to explain contradictions in their opinions and actions, and adds to the extant explanations. Exclusionists were frustrated by the courts and sought to curtail their jurisdiction in immigration cases. By 1905, they largely succeeded in replacing the courts with the Bureau of Immigration. Chinese resistance to exclusion thus had radiating effects. It established precedents for the courts and influenced immigration jurisdiction and administrative law.

Angelo N. Ancheta in *Race, Rights, and the Asian American Experience* (1998) examines racial discrimination as experienced by Asian Americans, the responses to racial discrimination in constitutional law and civil rights legislation, and the relations between Asian Americans and selected civil rights laws. A lawyer, an advocate, and a teacher of law, Ancheta employs doctrinal analysis (a blend of history, linguistics, and logic) and critical race theory (the application of postmodern theory, personal accounts, and literature to race relations) in his consideration of race, discrimination, war, immigration, citizenship, language, and identity. Unlike Lucy E. Salyer, who sees the courts as beacons of liberalism because of their activist tradition dating back about a hundred years, Ancheta views the courts as bastions of conservatism because of their adherence to legal tradition and precedent. And unlike Hyung-chan Kim, who groups Asian Americans within an undifferentiated category of peoples of color and aliens, Ancheta criticizes U.S. civil rights laws for following a black-and-white racial paradigm that fails to recognize the varieties of discrimination among diverse racial and ethnic groups and leaves Asian Americans outside the full protection of the law. Racism applies equally to blacks and Asians, but anti-Asianism also involves nativism, cultural and linguistic differences, perceptions of economic competition and the model minority, international relations, and U.S. wars in Asia. Remedies, accordingly, should account for those different manifestations of racial discrimination. "In the area of interethnic relations, as in other areas," Ancheta proposes, "the antidiscrimination laws do not go far enough in recognizing and addressing the problems of Asian Americans."[12]

Robert S. Chang in *Disoriented: Asian Americans, Law, and the Nation-State* (1999) theorizes and enacts a critical Asian American legal studies through his use of narrative and subject position and his insistence on the inclusion of Asian Americans within political and legal processes. He stresses commonalities and differences alike, for the purpose of dismantling racial borders and hierarchies.[13] Like Angelo N. Ancheta, Chang criticizes the black-and-white paradigm for its exclusion of Asians, American Indians, and Latinos, and for its inadequacies in redressing the various forms of oppression these groups experience. And he proposes the development of a critical Asian American legal studies that would correct the failure of critical race theory to show how races, beyond the black-and-white binary, matter differently, and to introduce Asian American perspectives to civil rights and critical race conversations. Like bookends that support and delimit the interior of critical Asian American legal studies are Chang's "meditations" on race's construction, racial borders and their transgressions, the interventions of multiracialism, and an appeal for a move away from identity politics to political identities based on shared political commitments.

NOTES

1. For a sampling of works by Asian Americans in critical race theory, see Kimberlé Crenshaw, Neil Gotanda, Gary Peller, and Kendall Thomas, eds., *Critical Race Theory: The Key Writings That Formed the Movement* (New York: New Press, 1995); Mari J. Matsuda, Charles R. Lawrence III, Richard Delgado, and Kimberle Williams Crenshaw, eds., *Words That Wound: Critical Race Theory, Assaultive Speech, and the First Amendment* (Boulder, Colo.: Westview Press, 1993); and Mari J. Matsuda, *Where Is Your Body? And Other Essays on Race Gender and the Law* (Boston: Beacon Press, 1996).

2. *Documental History of Law Cases Affecting Japanese in the United States, 1916–1924*, vol. 1, *Naturalization Cases and Cases Affecting Constitutional and Treaty Rights* (San Francisco: Consulate-General of Japan, 1925); and *Documental History of Law Cases Affecting Japanese in the United States, 1916–1924*, vol. 2, *Japanese Land Cases* (San Francisco: Consulate-General of Japan, 1925).

3. Milton R. Konvitz, *The Alien and the Asiatic in American Law* (Ithaca, N.Y.: Cornell University Press, 1946), viii.

4. Ibid., 218.

5. Frank F. Chuman, *The Bamboo People: The Law and Japanese-Americans* (Del Mar, Calif.: Publisher's Inc., 1976).

6. Moritoshi Fukuda, *Legal Problems of Japanese-Americans: Their History and Development in the United States* (Tokyo: Keio Tsushin, 1980), 213.

7. Bill Ong Hing, *Making and Remaking Asian America Through Immigration Policy, 1850–1990* (Stanford, Calif.: Stanford University Press, 1993), 13.

8. Charles J. McClain, *In Search of Equality: The Chinese Struggle against Discrimination in Nineteenth-Century America* (Berkeley: University of California Press, 1994), 3.

9. Hyung-chan Kim, ed., *Asian Americans and the Supreme Court* (Westport, Conn.: Greenwood Press, 1992).

10. Hyung-chan Kim, *A Legal History of Asian Americans, 1790–1990* (Westport, Conn.: Greenwood Press, 1994).

11. Lucy E. Salyer, *Laws Harsh as Tigers: Chinese Immigrants and the Shaping of Modern Immigration Law* (Chapel Hill: University of North Carolina Press, 1995), xiii.

12. Angelo N. Ancheta, *Race, Rights, and the Asian American Experience* (New Brunswick, N.J.: Rutgers University Press, 1998), 15.

13. Robert S. Chang, *Disoriented: Asian Americans, Law, and the Nation-State* (New York: New York University Press, 1999).

Chapter 4

JAPANESE AMERICAN RESISTANCE

Although underdeveloped and hence "emerging" as an interpretive paradigm, the idea of resistance has implications for Asian American history as a whole. In her survey history, the historian Sucheng Chan organizes pre–World War II Asian American history as the oppositions of "hostility and conflict" on the one hand the one hand and, on the other, of "resistance to oppression."[1] Ronald Takaki, in his study of sugar plantation life in Hawai'i, surveys the system of labor that regimented the lives of workers and examines the contested terrain of field and factory where workers resisted their exploitation and dehumanization.[2] Gary Y. Okihiro, in his rendition of an anti-Japanese movement in Hawai'i, structures his account as a spiraling dialectic between evolving forms of oppression and patterns of resistance to it, the oppression being sponsored by planters and the state and evolving from the exploitation of migrant labor to the exploitation resulting in the dependency of workers and ethnic minorities, who resisted those social formations.[3] Legal scholar Charles J. McClain, in his study of Chinese responses to discrimination, documents the familiarity of Chinese immigrants with the American legal system and their challenges to virtually every governmentally imposed restriction of their rights.[4] And Benson Tong, in his history of Chinese women prostitutes in nineteenth-century California, restores agency to their lives of bondage by chronicling their efforts to mitigate and alter the conditions of their oppression.[5]

Before the publication of those books, historians explored the theme of re-sistance within the World War II concentration camps for Japanese Americans.[6] Social scientists, however, set the frame. In their analysis of dislocation and adjustment, Dorothy Swaine Thomas and Richard S. Nishimoto posit the stan-dard view of Japanese reaction to their removal and confinement. "The evac-uees had, in the main," they report, "entered the relocation projects with atti-tudes either of optimism or of dogged determination to make the best possible adjustment in building up communities in which they would have to live for the duration of the war." That optimism, Thomas and Nishimoto propose, flowed from the administration's belief that they could summon the "good life" for evacuees in the projects.[7] The dream ended when the administration's prom-ises failed to materialize and when the pressures of confinement and of regional and generational differences and different political loyalties surfaced. The con-flicts eventually resolved themselves through administrative intervention and accommodation as exemplified in the initial settling in at Tule Lake, California, and in the divergent resolutions of the incidents at Poston, Arizona, and Man-zanar, California.

Revisionist historians with their version of camp life brought to the discussion another perspective. Roger Daniels proposes that resistance was more prevalent than orthodox accounts would have us believe, but he also allows that resig-nation rather than resistance typified internee behavior. And in terms similar to the conventional view, he sees resistance as a split between *kibei* and *nisei* and between the "right opposition," who were pro-Japan, and the "left opposi-tion," who adhered to the promise of America.[8] Gary Y. Okihiro, in a series of articles, argues that resistance was directed and purposeful and was the usual response to oppression both before and during the war. Further, resistance was not the result of conflict between generations or of politics expressed as a pro-Japan or a pro-American position but constituted the basic struggle for civil liberties and human dignity. Arthur A. Hansen and David A. Hacker add his-torical details to the resistance paradigm—they call it "ethnic perspective"— especially with respect to the cultural meanings of Japanese reactions to con-finement. Hansen, searching for alternative readings of a New Year's banquet held at Gila River concentration camp, treats it as a representative paradigm drama or a cultural situation fraught with possibilities for change. Cultural politics, he observes, can be strategically enacted.

THE CONVENTIONAL INTERPRETATION

As noted in my introduction to the chapter "America's Concentration Camps" in the "Historical Debates" section, the three major research groups that studied the camps during World War II—community analysts of the War Relocation

Authority; Alexander Leighton's project at Poston, Arizona; and the University of California's Japanese American Evacuation and Resettlement Study—understood the removals and detentions as an experiment in democracy, and the camps as controlled social laboratories to study captive populations. Both approaches conceived of research as bearing on practical, policymaking ends. Those concerned with the camps' meaning for democracy pursued the causal question of theories of responsibility. Those studying human behavior focused on the camps' interiors and their social interactions. And although the University of California study claimed distance from the camp administrators, all three projects served to varying degrees as the data-gathering and analyzing arm for the keepers of the camps. The researchers' network of informants, their observations, and their reports aided in the control and "rehabilitation" of America's Japanese.[9]

The first book to result from the University of California study was *The Spoilage* (1946), written by Dorothy Swaine Thomas, the project's director, and her assistant, Richard S. Nishimoto.[10] The book is important because it provides the interpretative frame for understanding the interactions between the project administrators and Japanese and the splits that the strains of detention created among the Japanese. Of principal concern to Thomas and Nishimoto is the making of "the spoilage," Japanese who were so impaired by the experience that they relinquished their U.S. citizenship or returned to Japan after the war. The focus is on the "disloyals," so designated by the government that confined them to the "segregation" project at Tule Lake, California. There, successive protest movements provoked increasingly repressive measures, including martial law, threats, arbitrary searches and seizures, and incarceration.

Life in the project began quite differently, however. The War Relocation Authority saw as its basic responsibility the provision of shelter and upkeep for its wards and their eventual reintegration into American life. First to arrive at Tule Lake were evacuees mainly from Washington and Oregon in June 1942. They devoted themselves to making their apartments livable by building partitions, tables, and benches and finding suitable employment in the offices, dining halls, and farms. Some *issei* (first generation) found adjustment difficult because of their lack of proficiency in English, but other *issei*, notably the women, "found pleasure in the new leisure, freedom from the burdens of cooking and the worries of providing for a family, and they spent much time at knitting, sewing, handicraft, and English classes," while *issei* men engaged in typical Japanese forms of recreation and games. The younger *nisei* (second generation) found the chance of "unlimited social activities" attractive, especially dances and baseball. Food was "abundant" and meals sometimes approached "lavishness."[11]

So at first, despite the physical hardships of life in a desolate place, conditions were favorable and adjustments smooth. But as more people filled the project,

intergroup antagonisms flared up and relations with the administration declined. Wage payments fell in arrears, promised clothing and clothing allow-
ances failed to materialize, and housing for white administrators took prece-
dence over schools for evacuees. The initial optimism and enthusiasm gave way
to resentment against the administrators. The transfer of 4,000 evacuees from
Sacramento to Tule Lake accelerated the process through competition between
these newcomers and those already at the project. The Californians found that
those from the Pacific Northwest had already taken all the good jobs and scrap
lumber, and conflicts over scarce resources broke out between those regional
factions. The military police suddenly instituted mail censorship, resulting in
increased discontent, and the quality and quantity of food began to deteriorate,
leading to a mess-hall strike on July 6, 1942. Rumors of shortages provoked a
run on the canteens, and people began hoarding rice and canned goods. *Issei*
and *nisei* fought over which forms of recreation to engage in, and evacuees
suspected among their ranks the presence of informers for the administration.

The growing discontent manifested itself in strikes by the farm and construction crews in August 1942. Wages went unpaid, experienced Japanese farmers
resented the supervision of inexperienced whites, and meals were inadequate
for the labor required. On the morning of August 15, some men refused to
board the trucks because of the meager breakfast, and they prevailed on the
others to honor a work stoppage until the entire camp community could discuss
the matter. Delegates met, formulated grievances, presented them to the administration, and received assurances that the food situation would improve.
The mess halls served a substantial breakfast on Monday, August 17, and the
crews returned to work. But other grievances remained, and on September 3
the construction workers called a strike because their crews were subjected to
layoffs and to plans for further layoffs, while whites remained fully employed.
Negotiations settled the matter of work clothing and overdue wage payments.
Although the problem of layoffs was not resolved, the administration persuaded
the construction crews to resume their work on September 5. A month later,
the administration settled a mess hall slowdown strike by agreeing to dismiss
an unpopular white supervisor.

Those interactions between evacuees and administrators formed a clear pattern of adjustment to detention that was typical of all the relocation projects.
"The pattern shows an initial cooperative and surprisingly unprotesting acceptance of a new situation by the evacuees followed by unrest and distrust directed
toward both the administration and fellow evacuees, with periods of protest and
manifestations of revolt against the administration and cleavages among the
residents." In Poston and Manzanar, the period of unrest assumed major pro-
portions. At Poston, a negotiated agreement produced "a superior adjustment"
after the revolt. At Manzanar, administrative repression ended the revolt but
had lasting effects on the project population and administrators.[12]

The incident at Poston began when suspicion over FBI informants led to two beatings on October 17 and November 14, 1942. The administration jailed two *kibei* (*nisei* who had been educated in Japan) for complicity in the beatings, despite delegations composed predominately of *issei* who attested to the innocence of the *kibei* and requested their release. On November 18, rumors that the FBI was coming to Poston drew several hundred protestors in front of the police station to prevent agents from taking the prisoners. By noon, the crowd had swelled to several thousand, and their leaders demanded the release of the men. Disregarding the administration's assurance that the men would receive fair hearings, the evacuees called for a general strike on November 19. That afternoon, the FBI withdrew from the case and the administration decided to release one of the men but turn the other over to the county police. The one selected for release, however, refused to leave without his fellow prisoner.

The mass protest was orchestrated by the *issei*, and *nisei* were simply curious onlookers or pressured into joining the strike. Some of the leaders got increasingly pro-Japanese in their demonstration, praising Japan's empire and warning against informants. Those extreme sentiments prompted some *issei* to seek a more moderate approach to end the stalemate as quickly as possible. They proposed a compromise plan to try the lone accused man by a jury of evacuees, and they promised the project director a more cooperative community in the future. On November 24, the project director exonerated the Japanese from blame for the unfortunate incident and expressed his desire to see Poston become the best community in the United States. After warmly applauding the director for his remarks, the crowd dispersed and the strike was over.

By contrast, the Manzanar riot was bitter, violent, and resulted in numerous injuries and two deaths. Like the Poston incident, the incident in Manzanar began with a beating of a suspected informer on December 5, 1942. The next day, the administration ordered the arrest of a *kibei* who had organized mess hall workers and had publicly accused two administrators of stealing sugar and meat from evacuee warehouses. He was taken to the county jail while other suspects were confined to the project jail. Word spread quickly and a crowd gathered to listen to demands for the immediate release of the popular *kibei* mess hall worker and for an investigation into project conditions. Evacuees spoke of "death lists" and "blacklists" of administrative collaborators in the project, and many believed that the jailed *kibei* was framed and wrongly accused by informants called *inu* (dogs) and that he was being victimized for his stand against the administration.[13] They called for a strike the next day if the jailed *kibei* was not released that night.

The project director met with evacuee representatives on December 6 and agreed to bring the *kibei* back but to confine him in the project jail. Meanwhile, the project director had called on the military police to prepare to intervene. Unhappy with the response of the project director, some evacuees headed for the hospital to "get" the alleged collaborator and others assembled at the project jail. Unsuccessful in finding the hospitalized *nisei*, the evacuees joined the others in front of the police station. The project director called on the military police to declare martial law, and the assistant director requested that the FBI investigate the situation. A detachment of soldiers, having arrived and pushed the crowd away from the police station, formed a line armed with submachine guns, rifles, and shotguns. The evacuees jeered and made obscene gestures. The soldiers fired tear gas into the crowd, and the evacuees fled in panic. The crowd formed again and, without orders, the soldiers fired. One evacuee died almost instantly, another died of his wounds on December 11, and ten evacuees were treated for gunshot wounds. Several others, it seems, also suffered gunshot wounds but did not seek treatment for fear of being implicated in the incident.

Throughout the night of December 6, bells tolled and evacuees gathered. Military police and state guardsmen patrolled the camp's interior. The administration, fearing for the safety of suspected collaborators and their families, removed them from the project. For several days, two-thirds to three-fourths of the project's evacuees wore black armbands as a symbol of mourning for the dead youth. The administration put in the county jail the *kibei* suspected in the original beating and the evacuees allegedly responsible for the "riot," and they were later taken to a Department of Justice internment camp or to a War Relocation Authority isolation camp. Normality returned to Manzanar after about a month.

Evacuee opposition to the Japanese American Citizens League (JACL) and its *nisei* members, including those targeted as *inu*, was at the base of the Manzanar riot. The JACL urged cooperation with the administration. That in turn encouraged and gave privileges to JACL leaders. Even before the war, evacuees suspected that the JACL was collaborating with American intelligence agencies to gather information on the community. Those beliefs simmered in the project, and resentment built against the JACL and their leaders.

RESISTANCE

A new view of Japanese reaction to confinement first appeared in the writings of historian Roger Daniels and Douglas W. Nelson, his graduate student at the time. Nelson wrote a master's thesis, "Heart Mountain: The History of an American Concentration Camp," that influenced Daniels's views on Japanese resistance and was later published.[14] "Most of the existing literature about the camps stresses the cooperation and compliance of the inmates," writes Daniels, "thus perpetuating the basic line of both the WRA [War Relocation Authority] and the JACL [Japanese American Citizens League]. Like most successful myths, this one contains elements of truth. There was little spectacular, violent resistance; no desperate attempts to escape; even sustained mass civil disobedience rarely occurred. But from the very beginning of their confinement, the evacuated people were in conflict, both with their keepers and with each other. These conflicts started even before the evacuation began, grew in the Assembly Centers, and were intensified in the concentration camps."[15]

Unlike proponents of the conventional view that initial period of cooperation was followed by a difficult time of adjustment and finally an amiable and sometimes uncertain resolution for the duration of the camps, Daniels suggests that internee resistance, both active and passive, occurred, and that it was more significant than is generally realized. Still, he concedes, "resignation rather than resistance was the more common response of the internees."[16] In Santa Anita Assembly Center on August 4, 1942, internee resentment built over searches and confiscations of Japanese reading matter and phonograph records. Rumors spread about informants, the *inu*. A crowd of men and women set on a suspected informer and beat him, and they harassed the camp's security police. The military police quickly put down the disturbance, but it was typical for those under the stress of confinement to displace their anger onto their fellow internees, of whom most were *nisei* and many were JACL leaders.

The *kibei*, rather than the *issei*, were the leaders of this "right-wing" opposition.[17] By contrast, the *issei* felt powerless because of their status as enemy aliens. The *kibei* were American citizens, like their *nisei* counterparts, and partly Americanized. Some of them, and many *issei* as well, held pro-Japan sympathies. The *nisei* blamed the *kibei* for everything that went wrong, and the *kibei* attacked the *nisei*, especially JACLers, for allegedly collaborating with the administration. That was evidenced in the Manzanar riot of December 6, 1942, when a *kibei* was accused of beating a prominent *nisei* leader of the JACL.

The Heart Mountain camp witnessed another kind of resistance. Classified as a "happy camp," Heart Mountain from its very start was characterized by conflict and organized resistance. In October and November 1942 there were protests and demonstrations over the barbed wire fence surrounding the camp. In a petition signed by half the adult population, it was denounced as "devoid of all humanitarian principles" and "an insult to any free human being."[18] In November, coal work crews walked off the job in protest over wages and work clothes; hospital staff members staged a strike over wages and their supervision by whites less qualified than they, and the evacuee internal security police struck to force the resignation of their white chief. In December, when thirty-two children, none of whom was more than eleven years old, were arrested for security violation because they went sledding on a hill outside the camp, anger boiled over and the evacuees staged a general protest against "the whole theory and practice of the evacuation." This was the "left opposition," in that they demanded the immediate restoration of their rights as Americans, as distinguished from the "right opposition" of those who "rejected American and professed Japanese ideals."[19]

In a series of articles, Gary Y. Okihiro criticizes the extant camp literature for depicting the Japanese as powerless victims and characterizes that interpretation as essentially a species of liberalism. Japanese resistance is portrayed as sporadic and generally minor in scope and attributed to frustration-aggression and to a small group of "pro-Fascist troublemakers." Further, the divide that leads to conflict in those portrayals was between those who were "pro-American" and those who were "pro-Japan," and between *issei* and *kibei* on the one hand against the *nisei* on the other. Instead, Okihiro draws from revisionist histories of African reaction to European colonialism in Africa and enslavement in the United States. Those works recognize the oppressive natures of colonialism and slavery but they also emphasize "the continuity of African and slave societies, their resiliency and vitality. . . . Behind these histories of slave revolts and African resistance lie the basic notions that societies tend to resist externally imposed change of their institutions, that these acts of resistance are continuous and that they are effective."[20]

After reviewing the incidents at Poston and Manzanar, as undertaken in Thomas and Nishimoto's *The Spoilage*, Okihiro proposes two models of resistance. At Poston an acceptable solution is reached, while at Manzanar administrative intransigence redirects resistance away from direct confrontation to "para-administrative" forms. He speculates that Japanese resistance was primarily of the Manzanar variety and was illustrated in Japanese resistance to "Americanization" and in the persistence of Japanese culture. If so, life in the camps would not follow the trajectory, advanced by Thomas and Nishimoto, of cooperation followed by conflict and then adjustment. Rather, resistance in the Poston model will decline, but in the Manzanar model it will only increase. Okihiro concludes that, although Manzanar forms of resistance are largely invisible, the true history of Japanese reaction to confinement resides in the quiet struggle for "possession of the children's minds and habits."[21]

In another article, Okihiro expands on the nature of cultural resistance and proposes that Japanese religious belief formed the basis of a wider network of cultural resistance. He notes that cultural resistance was directed against the attempt of the War Relocation Authority to "Americanize" the Japanese and in some instances was effective in preserving the ethnic community from total disintegration. Resistance historians, he states, "regard the internment as the culmination of nearly a century of anti-Asian agitation and racial discrimination in America, the essential thrust of which was physical expulsion and cultural hegemony. Resistance for the pre-war Japanese, according to that interpretation, was a means of survival to maintain their physical presence and culture in the face of white supremacy."[22] That struggle continued in the camps where the

Japanese resisted manipulation of their lives and the erasure of their ethnic identity.

Religious belief constituted the core of Meiji culture and ethics, especially in filial piety and ancestor worship, and in aesthetic expressions such as landscape gardening, flower arrangement, *sumo*, music, drama, and poetry. The efflorescence of those cultural forms, the resurgence of Buddhism and folk beliefs, and the ascendance of the Japanese language all developed in the context of the administration's effort to promote Americanization and constituted acts of resistance after the Manzanar model. More basic was ethnic solidarity, which emphasized a common "Japanese spirit," and the preservation of the family unit, an *issei*-dominated authority structure. It was through them that "resistance was rechanneled away from open rebellion into folk beliefs and practices. Religion and culture, therefore, were both a vehicle for and an expression of the people's resistance."[23]

Finally, in a reconsideration of Thomas and Nishimoto, Okihiro asserts that Japanese resistance at Tule Lake was at base a struggle for human dignity. The protest movement that led to the declaration of martial law at that camp espoused genuine democratic principles in seeking to secure elemental civil liberties such as freedom of speech and of assembly and freedom from arbitrary search, arrest, and detention. But more fundamental was the people's struggle for a simple recognition of their basic humanity by the white administrators. Resistance historians confront formidable obstacles in the historical records that were primarily written and preserved by the War Relocation Authority and its allied research projects. Their biases filter Japanese voices and as a consequence resistance historians are unable to determine "the number of people who actually resisted, the degree of mobilization, the exact role of coercion, and even the forms and nature of resistance. . . . What is needed are a number of microstudies which demonstrate the historical validity of their claim."[24]

Arthur A. Hansen has provided some of those "micro-studies" in resistance. In a coauthored article written about the same time as Okihiro's first article on resistance, Hansen and David A. Hacker are critical of the orthodox interpretation of the Manzanar riot. It trivializes the mass protest movement by reducing it to an "incident," views the event episodically and as devoid of historical contexts and precedents, fails to see that the riot was part of a wider pattern of camp resistance, and conceptualizes the riot as a conflict between pro-American and pro-Japanese factions. It confuses the American patriotism of a small group—the JACLers—with the *nisei* as a whole, and misconstrues ethnic identity to be subversive and anti-American.

Instead, they propose an "ethnic perspective" and contrast the two approaches: "Whereas the WRA-JACL perspective . . . has interpreted the riot in terms of its *ideological* meaning within American society, the Ethnic one focuses upon the riot's *cultural* meaning within the Japanese American community." They proceed to depict the riot as a "revolt," an "intense expression of a continuing resistance movement," crediting the historical actors with purposeful behavior directed toward meaningful social change.[25] They find historical explanation for the revolt in the pre-war Japanese American community, and identify the cultural significance and consistency of various aspects of the revolt. Hansen and Hacker conclude that the revolt manifested the community's struggle for self-determination and ethnic identity and against the Americanization program of the War Relocation Authority.

In another article, Hansen expands on his idea of cultural resistance in a critical reading of a New Year's banquet at the Gila River concentration camp.[26] The presence of camp administrators—along with the menu that included mock turtle soup, fried chicken, and apple pie—at this Japanese-hosted occasion might have been interpreted by conventional historians as an indication of harmony and goodwill. But an alternative interpretation, one consonant with resistance histories, sees the gathering as a representative paradigm drama wherein possibilities abound in the engagement among actors and between the actors and audience. In truth, Hansen shows, the banquet revealed a profound shift in the relations of power among the inmates and between the administrators and Japanese.

NOTES

1. Sucheng Chan, *Asian Americans: An Interpretive History* (Boston: Twayne, 1991).

2. Ronald Takaki, *Pau Hana: Plantation Life and Labor in Hawaii, 1835–1920* (Honolulu: University of Hawaii Press, 1983). See also, Edward D. Beechert, *Working in Hawaii: A Labor History* (Honolulu: University of Hawaii Press, 1985).

3. Gary Y. Okihiro, *Cane Fires: The Anti-Japanese Movement in Hawaii, 1865–1945* (Philadelphia: Temple University Press, 1991).

4. Charles J. McClain, *In Search of Equality: The Chinese Struggle against Discrimination in Nineteenth-Century America* (Berkeley: University of California Press, 1994). See also, Lucy E. Salyer, *Laws Harsh as Tigers: Chinese Immigrants and the Shaping of Modern Immigration Law* (Chapel Hill: University of North Carolina Press, 1995).

5. Benson Tong, *Unsubmissive Women: Chinese Prostitutes in Nineteenth-Century San Francisco* (Norman: University of Oklahoma Press, 1994).

6. For a review of this literature, see Alice Yang Murray, *What Did the Internment of Japanese Americans Mean?* (Boston: Bedford/St. Martin's, 2000).

7. Dorothy Swaine Thomas and Richard S. Nishimoto, *The Spoilage* (Berkeley: University of California Press, 1946), 38.

8. Roger Daniels, *Concentration Camps: North America, Japanese in the United States and Canada During World War II* (Malabar, Fla.: Robert E. Krieger Publishing, 1981), 106, 107, 118.

9. Alexander H. Leighton, *The Governing of Men: General Principles and Recommendations Based on Experience of a Japanese Relocation Camp* (Princeton, N.J.: Princeton University Press, 1945), vii.

10. See Richard S. Nishimoto, *Inside an American Concentration Camp: Japanese American Resistance at Poston, Arizona*, edited by Lane Ryo Hirabayashi (Tucson: University of Arizona Press, 1995).

11. Thomas and Nishimoto, *The Spoilage*, 39.

12. Ibid., 45.

13. Ibid., 50.

14. Douglas W. Nelson, "Heart Mountain: The History of an American Concentration Camp," M.A. thesis (University of Wyoming, 1970); and Douglas W. Nelson, *Heart Mountain: The History of an American Concentration Camp* (Madison: Wisconsin State Historical Society, 1976).

15. Daniels, *Concentration Camps*, 105.

16. Ibid., 106.

17. Ibid., 107.

18. Ibid., 117.

19. Ibid., 118.

20. Gary Y. Okihiro, "Japanese Resistance in America's Concentration Camps: A Re-evaluation," *Amerasia Journal* 2 (Fall 1973): 21.

21. Ibid., 26, 31, 32.

22. Gary Y. Okihiro, "Religion and Resistance in America's Concentration Camps," *Phylon* 45:3 (1984): 221.

23. Ibid., 233.

24. Gary Y. Okihiro, "Tule Lake Under Martial Law: A Study in Japanese Resistance," *Journal of Ethnic Studies* 5:3 (Fall 1977): 72–73.

25. Arthur A. Hansen and David A. Hacker, "The Manzanar Riot: An Ethnic Perspective," *Amerasia Journal* 2 (Fall 1974): 120, 121.

26. Arthur A. Hansen, "Cultural Politics in the Gila River Relocation Center, 1942–1943," *Arizona and the West* 27:4 (Winter 1985): 327–62.

PART 4

Chronology

CHRONOLOGY

This chronology builds on Sucheng Chan's chronology found in her *Asian Americans: An Interpretive History* (Boston: Twayne, 1991), 192–99. See also chronologies in Masako Herman, *The Japanese in America, 1843–1973: A Chronology & Fact Book* (Dobbs Ferry, N.Y.: Oceana Publications, 1974); Hyung-chan Kim and Wayne Patterson, *The Koreans in America, 1882–1974: A Chronology & Fact Book* (Dobbs Ferry, N.Y.: Oceana Publications, 1974); William L. Tung, *The Chinese in America, 1820–1973: A Chronology & Fact Book* (Dobbs Ferry, N.Y.: Oceana Publications, 1974); Hyung-chan Kim and Cynthia C. Mejia, *The Filipinos in America, 1898–1974: A Chronology & Fact Book* (Dobbs Ferry, N.Y.: Oceana Publications, 1976); and *He Alo Ā He Alo, Face to Face: Hawaiian Voices on Sovereignty* (Honolulu: Hawai'i Area Office of the American Friends Service Committee, 1993).

BCE

5th cent.   Hippocrates represents Asia and Asians.
4th cent.   Alexander ventures into India.

CE

375   Polynesians settle Hawai'i.

12th cent.	Hawaiian society embraces all of the islands; high chiefs and priests from Tahiti migrate to Hawai'i.

12th cent.   Hawaiian society embraces all of the islands; high chiefs and priests from Tahiti migrate to Hawai'i.

13th cent.   Mongols invade Europe; Marco Polo travels to India and China.

1400   Hawaiian society becomes increasingly stratified.

1492   Christopher Columbus "discovers" "the Indies."

1498   Vasco da Gama reaches India by sailing around Africa.

16th cent.   Asian and African slaves serve on European vessels in Indian Ocean.

1513   Vasco de Balboa crosses Panama's isthmus and gazes at the Pacific.

1518   Hernando Cortes leads an expedition into Mexico.

1521   Ferdinand Magellan claims the Philippines for Spain.

1565   Manila galleon trade with Mexico begins

1600   British East India Company formed.

1602   Dutch East India Company formed.

1607   Jamestown.

1658   Asian slaves taken to Africa's Cape of Good Hope.

1760s   Filipino "Manilamen" establish communities near New Orleans.

1773   Boston Tea Party.

1776   American Declaration of Independence.

1778   British Captain James Cook places Hawai'i on European maps.

1783   Treaty of Paris; Great Britain recognizes American independence.

1784   *Empress of China* leaves New York harbor for China.

1787   U.S. Constitution adopted; Winee, a Hawaiian woman, travels on a British ship to China.

1789   George Washington becomes U.S. President; Bill of Rights adopted by Congress.

1790   Nationality Act limits naturalization to "free white persons."

1790s   Asian Indians settle on the East Coast.

1794   First Chinese arrive in Hawai'i.

1795   Kamehameha I conquers all of Hawai'i except Kau'ai.

1802   Tze-Chun Wong, a Chinese, begins producing sugar in Hawai'i.

1809   Hawaiians Opukahaia and Hopu arrive in New England via an American ship; Opukahaia enrolls at Yale.

1810   Kau'ai comes under Kamehameha's kingdom, uniting all the Hawaiian islands.

1819   Kamehameha dies; Ka'ahumanu, one of Kamehameha's wives and the kingdom's *kuhina nui* (executive officer), breaks and ends the *kapu* (taboo) system.

1820   New England missionaries arrive in Hawai'i.

1820s   Chinese settle in New York City and on the East Coast.

1835   American William Hooper establishes Koloa sugar plantation on Kau'ai.

1839	Opium War begins.
1838	South Asian indentures arrive in British Guiana.
1840	Hawaiian constitution establishes a constitutional monarchy and institutes property rights.
1842	Treaty of Nanking ends Opium War.
1844	United States and China sign first treaty.
1845	Hawaiians petition Kamehameha III against foreign political and economic dominance.
1847	Chinese students, including Yung Wing, arrive in the United States.
1848	Gold discovered in California, prompting Gold Rush; Treaty of Guadalupe Hidalgo; Great Mahele in Hawai'i privatizes land and disburses it; aliens allowed to lease property.
1850	California imposes Foreign Miners' Tax; Hawai'i passes Masters and Servants Act; Royal Hawaiian Agricultural Society established to recruit plantation workers; aliens allowed to purchase property.
1852	Chinese contract laborers arrive in Hawai'i.
1853	U.S. Commodore Matthew C. Perry "opens" Japan to the West.
1854	In *People* v. *Hall*, California's supreme court rules that Chinese cannot testify for or against whites in court; United States and Japan sign the Treaty of Kanagawa, formalizing relations.
1857	San Francisco opens a school for Chinese children.
1858	California passes a law barring entry to Chinese and "Mongolians."
1861	Civil War begins.
1865	Central Pacific Railroad recruits Chinese workers for the transcontinental railroad; Hawaiian Board of Immigration sends a labor agent to recruit Chinese laborers for the kingdom's sugar plantations; Civil War ends; Thirteenth Amendment abolishing slavery ratified.
1866	Japanese students, sent by their government, study at Rutgers University.
1867	2,000 Chinese workers employed by Central Pacific Railroad strike for a week; Congress passes Reconstruction plan for the South; Chinese, some from Cuba, work the sugar fields of Louisiana to supplement African American labor.
1868	United States and China sign Burlingame-Seward Treaty recognizing the right of free migration to citizens of both countries; 149 Japanese, the *gannenmono*, are recruited for Hawai'i's plantations; Fourteenth Amendment ratified, conferring citizenship on the basis of birth and equal protection.

1869	Completion of the transcontinental railroad; Japanese establish the Wakamatsu Tea and Silk Colony in California.
1870	California passes a law against the importation of Chinese, Japanese, and "Mongolian" women for prostitution; Chinese railroad workers in Texas sue company for failure to pay wages; Chinese brought from California to North Adams, Massachusetts, to break a strike of white shoe workers; Fifteenth Amendment ratified, guaranteeing the rights of citizens to vote regardless of race, color, or previous condition of servitude.
1871	Los Angeles riot against Chinese, leaving 21 dead.
1872	Chinese allowed to testify in California's courts for or against whites.
1875	Page Law bars entry to Chinese, Japanese, and "Mongolian" prostitutes, felons, and contract laborers.
1876	Reciprocity Treaty signed by the United States and Hawaiian kingdom, providing for duty-free sugar imports from the islands; Korea and Japan sign the Treaty of Kanghwa, opening Korea to trade.
1877	Reconstruction ends.
1878	*In re Ah Yup*, issued by the U.S. Supreme Court, declares the Chinese ineligible for naturalized citizenship; United States gains treaty rights for a base at Pago Pago, Samoa.
1879	California adopts its second constitution—later declared unconstitutional by a U.S. circuit court—that discriminates against Chinese in employment and housing.
1880	United States and China sign treaty allowing the United States to limit but not prohibit Chinese immigration; California passes Section 69 of its Civil Code, thereby prohibiting marriage between whites and "Mongolians, Negroes, mulattoes and persons of mixed blood"; anti-Chinese riot in Denver destroys homes and businesses.
1882	Chinese Exclusion Act prohibits Chinese laborers entry for ten years; United States and Korea sign first treaty allowing for Korean immigration.
1883	Yu Kil-jun, a member of a Korean diplomatic mission to the United States, remains in America to study in Massachusetts.
1884	Joseph and Mary Tape sue the San Francisco school board over segregated schools; Korean political refugees, including Suh Jae-p'il (Philip Jaisohn), arrive in the United States after the reform movement's failure in Korea.
1885	Anti-Chinese riot in Rock Springs, Wyoming, leaves 28 dead; Japanese government-sponsored contract workers arrive in Hawai'i.

1886   In *Yick Wo* v. *Hopkins,* U.S. Supreme Court rules that laws with unequal impacts on different groups is discriminatory; Chinese expulsions from Tacoma, Seattle, Alaska and other places in the West; Hawai'i ends Chinese immigration.

1887   Chinese gold miners attacked by whites in Hell's Canyon on the Idaho-Oregon border, leaving 31 dead; United States and Hawai'i renew the Reciprocity Treaty and the kingdom cedes the use of Pearl Harbor to the U.S. Navy; Hawaiian constitution forced on Kalakaua curtails power of monarchy.

1888   Scott Act renders 20,000 Chinese reentry certificates null and void.

1890   United States ends Hawai'i's favored status in sugar trade.

1892   Geary Act renews the 1882 Chinese Exclusion Act for another ten years and requires all Chinese to register.

1893   San Francisco school board orders, and then rescinds the order, that Japanese children attend the segregated Chinese school; American-led coup topples the Hawaiian kingdom and deposes the queen, Lili'uokalani; its leaders declare a provisional government and seek U.S. annexation.

1894   Republic of Hawai'i declared; *In re Saito,* issued by a U.S. circuit court in Massachusetts, declares Japanese ineligible for naturalized citizenship.

1895   Hawaiian Sugar Planters' Association (HSPA) formed; Native Sons of the Golden State (later the Chinese American Citizens Alliance), a civil rights organization, founded in San Francisco.

1896   In *Plessy* v. *Ferguson,* the U.S. Supreme Court establishes the "separate but equal doctrine" and thereby upholds segregation.

1898   In *Wong Kim Ark* v. *U.S.,* the U.S. Supreme Court rules that Chinese cannot be stripped of their citizenship; United States annexes Hawai'i, the Philippines, and Guam; Korean merchants arrive in Honolulu.

1899   United States declares an "Open Door Policy" toward China; American-Filipino war begins; United States establishes a protectorate over American Samoa.

1900   Organic Act makes all U.S. laws applicable to Hawai'i, ending contract labor and prompting a series of strikes by Japanese plantation workers; health officials burn Honolulu's Chinatown and quarantine about 7,000 Chinese, Japanese, and Hawaiians to camps for several months; bubonic plague scare in San Francisco leads to Chinatown quarantine and the mass inoculation of the city's Chinese and Japanese; Japanese Association of America founded in San Francisco as a civil rights organization.

1901   Five Korean laborers arrive in Hawai'i; United States appoints a civilian government in the Philippines.

1902   Chinese labor exclusion renewed for another ten years; Hawaiian Sugar Planters' Association sends to Korea a recruiter who sends groups of workers to Hawai'i; New People's Association formed to unify Korean Americans for Korea's independence; American-Filipino war declared at an end, resulting in 4,300 American and more than 50,000 Filipino deaths.

1903   1,500 Japanese and Mexican sugar beet workers strike in Oxnard, California, and form the Japanese Mexican Labor Association; 102 Korean migrants arrive in Hawai'i; Friendship Association founded in San Francisco for the promotion of mutual aid among Korean Americans (in 1905, changed its name to the Mutual Cooperation Federation); Filipino students, the *pensionados*, arrive in the United States.

1904   Chinese labor exclusion made indefinite; Punjabi Sikhs arrive in British Columbia; 250 Korean workers hired on Waialua sugar plantation on the island of O'ahu, Hawai'i, to break a strike of Japanese laborers.

1905   Chinese Americans support boycott of U.S. goods in China; San Francisco school board resolves to segregate Japanese children; Korean emigration ends; Korean Episcopal and Methodist churches in Honolulu dedicated; Asiatic Exclusion League formed in San Francisco.

1906   Anti-Asian riot in Vancouver; San Francisco earthquake and fire destroys U.S. immigration records; San Francisco school board orders the segregation of Japanese children; Korean government and businesses send money to Koreans in San Francisco who suffered losses from the earthquake and fire; Presbyterian mission and, later, church established in Los Angeles for Korean Americans; 15 Filipino workers, recruited by the Hawaiian Sugar Planters' Association, arrive in Hawai'i.

1907   United States and Japan sign "Gentlemen's Agreement," whereby Japan agrees to restrict labor migration to the United States; President Theodore Roosevelt issues an executive order prohibiting Japanese remigration to the United States from Hawai'i, Mexico, and Canada; San Francisco school board rescinds its segregation of Japanese children; San Francisco riot against Japanese; Filipino laborers—188 men, 20 women, and 2 children— arrive in Hawai'i; Asian Indians expelled from Bellingham, Washington.

1908	Canada restricts Asian Indian immigration by requiring continuous passage from nation of birth to Canada; Asian Indians expelled from Live Oak, California; an American employee of Japan's foreign office is shot and killed by a Korean American in San Francisco; Korean Women's Association established in San Francisco.
1909	7,000 Japanese sugar plantation workers on O'ahu, Hawai'i, strike for four months; Korean National Association formed from a merger of the Mutual Cooperation Federation and the United Federation.
1910	California restricts Asian Indian immigration by administrative procedures; Japanese "picture brides" arrive; Korean "picture brides" arrive; Japan formally annexes Korea.
1911	Pablo Manlapit forms the Filipino Higher Wages Association in Hawai'i.
1912	Sikhs in California establish the Khalsa Diwan.
1913	California passes the Alien Land Law, which prohibits "aliens ineligible to citizenship" from buying land or leasing it for more than three years; Sikhs in Oregon and Washington establish the Hindustani Association, and Asian Indians in California found the revolutionary Ghadar Party; Korean farm workers are expelled from Hemet, California; Korean Women's Association organized in Honolulu.
1914	*Komagata Maru*, a ship chartered by Gurdit Singh to test Canada's restrictive immigration law, is denied landing in Vancouver; Korean National Association sends money to Koreans suffering from famine in China.
1915	Chinese American Citizens Alliance founded from the Native Sons of the Golden State.
1917	Arizona passes an alien land law; Immigration Act passed by the U.S. Congress declares a "barred zone" from which no immigrants can come; the Act adds West, South, and Southeast Asians to the list of excluded Asians.
1918	Asians who served in the U.S. military during World War I are allowed the right of naturalization.
1919	Japanese in Hawai'i form the Federation of Japanese Labor; Women's Friendship Association formed by Korean women in Los Angeles to promote friendship among Korean Americans, to boycott Japanese goods, and to send funds to the Korean independence movement; Korean Women's Patriotic League founded in California to unite all Korean women's organizations in North America.

1920	8,300 Japanese and Filipino sugar plantation workers on O'ahu, Hawai'i, strike for six months; Hawaiian Rehabilitation Act creates the Hawaiian Homes Commission; California amends its 1913 Alien Land Law to restrict rents; Nineteenth Amendment ratified, guaranteeing the right to vote regardless of sex.
1921	Japanese farm workers expelled from Turlock, California; Washington and Louisiana pass alien land laws; Japan halts passports to "picture brides."
1922	In *Takao Ozawa v. U.S.*, the U.S. Supreme Court affirms that Japanese are ineligible for naturalization; New Mexico passes an alien land law; Cable Act by the U.S. Congress takes away U.S. citizenship from women who marry "aliens ineligible to citizenship."
1923	In *U.S. v. Bhagat Singh Thind*, the U.S. Supreme Court rules that Asian Indians are ineligible for naturalization; Idaho, Montana, and Oregon pass alien land laws; American Loyalty League of Fresno, California, founded (later became the Japanese American Citizens League); California denies Japanese sharecropping rights; in *Terrace v. Thompson*, the U.S. Supreme Court upholds alien land laws.
1924	Immigration Act by the U.S. Congress excludes virtually all Asians; About 9,000 Filipino sugar plantation workers strike in Hawai'i over an eleven-month period.
1925	Filipino Federation of America formed; *In re Toyota*, issues by the U.S. Supreme Court declares Filipinos, except those who served in the U.S. military for three years, ineligible for citizenship; Kansas passes an alien land law; Korean Americans send money to Korea for flood and famine relief.
1927	In *Gong Lum v. Rice*, the U.S. Supreme Court upholds racial segregation in schools and reaffirms the "separate but equal" doctrine; U.S. Supreme Court, on a challenge filed by the schools rules that government control of Japanese-language schools in Hawai'i is unconstitutional.
1928	Filipino farm workers are expelled from Dryden, Washington, and warned to leave town at Wenatchee.
1929	Japanese American Citizens League formed; stock market crash and the onset of the Great Depression.
1930	Anti-Filipino riot in Watsonville, California; a Filipino rooming house in California's Imperial Valley and the office of the Filipino Federation of America in Stockton are bombed.
1931	U.S. Congress amends the Cable Act to allow naturalization to women who were citizens by birth; Japan invades Manchuria.

1932   Congress passes the Hawes-Cutting Act, which declares Filipinos to be aliens ineligible for citizenship and establishes an immigration quota of 100 Filipinos per year.

1933   Filipino field workers in Salinas, California, refuse to work, in protest against growers who failed to deliver on their promised wages; Filipino Labor Union organizes; California's Court of Appeals rules in favor of Salvador Roldan's petition to marry a white woman because Filipinos are Malays and not Mongolians; this prompts the state legislature to amend its anti-miscegenation law to include Malays; Mexican berry pickers strike against Japanese growers in El Monte, California; Chinese Hand Laundry Alliance formed in New York City.

1934   Tydings-McDuffie Act by the U.S. Congress establishes a timeline for Philippine independence and reduces Filipino immigration to fifty persons per year; Filipino farm workers strike in Salinas Valley and walk out in Santa Maria and Lompoc valleys, California; whites expel Filipino workers from Turlock, California.

1935   Filipino Repatriation Act provides free transportation for indigent Filipino Americans to the Philippines; an act of Congress grants naturalization to U.S. veterans of World War I who were before the war aliens ineligible for citizenship (under this act, several Chinese, Filipino, and Japanese American veterans of World War I became U.S. citizens).

1936   American Federation of Labor grants charter to a Filipino-Mexican farm workers union; Mexican, Japanese, and Filipino celery workers strike against Japanese growers in Venice, California; Cable Act is repealed.

1937   White vigilantes expel striking Filipino workers in Yakima Valley, Washington; Filipino Repatriation Act extended to December 31, 1938.

1938   150 Chinese women garment workers strike for three months against the National Dollar Stores, owned by Chinese Americans; dockworkers strike in Hilo, Hawai'i, and in a union march in support of the strikers fifty are wounded by the police.

1939   Filipino asparagus workers strike against growers in Stockton and Sacramento, California, and form the Filipino Agricultural Workers Union; the second Filipino Repatriation Act signed into law.

1940   American Federation of Labor charters the Filipino Federated Agricultural Laborers Association; Filipino American repatriation ends.

1941   Japan attacks Pearl Harbor; United States declares war; military in
Hawai'i declares martial law; Japanese Americans interned in
camps mandated by the Department of Justice; Public Law 360
allows Filipinos to serve in the U.S. Army.

1942   President Franklin D. Roosevelt signs Executive Order 9066, which
begins the mass removal and detention of Japanese Americans
on the West Coast; U.S. Congress passes Public Law 503, which
imposes sanctions for violations of Executive Order 9066; National Student Relocation Council formed to assist nisei students
who want to continue their college education; resistance movements at concentration camps in Poston, Arizona, and Manzanar, California; Chinese, Filipino, Japanese, and Korean
Americans support the American war effort as soldiers and
through national defense bond drives.

1943   U.S. Congress repeals all Chinese exclusion laws, establishes for
Chinese immigration a quota of 105 persons per year, and allows
Chinese naturalization.

1944   Resistance movements at concentration camp in Tule Lake, California; martial law imposed there; draft resistance at other
camps.

1945   U.S. drops atomic bombs on Hiroshima and Nagasaki; World
War II ends; Korea is divided temporarily at the 38th parallel;
U.S. Supreme Court rules Filipinos are not aliens but nationals
and are thus not susceptible to the various laws against aliens.

1946   Luce-Celler Act confers naturalization rights and small immigration quotas to Asian Indians and Filipinos; Philippine Rehabilitation Act allows Filipino students to study in the United States;
the Philippines wins its independence; U.S. Congress allows
Chinese wives of American citizens to immigrate on a non-
quota basis; concentration camp in Tule Lake, California,
closes; the last shipment of "disloyals" sent to Japan as "repat-
riates."

1947   U.S. Congress amends the 1945 War Brides Act to allow Chinese
American veterans to bring their brides to the United States;
Aiko and John Reinecke, alleged Communists, lose their jobs
in Hawai'i; India gains its independence.

1948   In *Oyama v. California*, the U.S. Supreme Court declares California's alien land laws unconstitutional; Japanese American Evacuation Claims Act enables federal restitutions for financial losses
suffered in the mass removal and detention; Republic of Korea
declared with Syngman Rhee, American-educated and based,

becomes its first president; Burma gains its independence; U.S. Supreme Court rules that California's anti-miscegenation law is unconstitutional.

1949   Mao Zedong announces the People's Republic of China; Chiang Kai-shek flees to Taiwan and declares the Republic of China. 5,000 highly educated Chinese from Communist China are granted refugee status in the United States; Indonesia wins its independence; Iva Toguri d'Aquino, allegedly "Tokyo Rose," sentenced to ten years in prison for treason.

1950   Internal Security Act allows for detention camps for those suspected of posing national security threats; Korean War begins; United States recognizes the French puppet government in Vietnam and sends it military and economic aid; Organic Act confers U.S. citizenship on the inhabitants of Guam.

1952   McCarran-Walter Act, repressive of those classed as Communists, grants to Japanese naturalization and an annual immigration quota of 185.

1953   Armistice ends Korean War; Laos becomes independent; Hawai'i Seven, charged with conspiring to overthrow the U.S. government by force, are convicted (this conviction was overturned on appeal in 1958).

1954   Viet Minh forces defeat the French at Dien Bien Phu; Geneva Accords divides Vietnam along the 17th parallel, promises elections in 1955 to reunite the country, and grants independence to Cambodia; in *Brown v. Board of Education*, the U.S. Supreme Court ends "separate but equal" and educational segregation; Democrats gain control of Hawai'i's legislature.

1955   Rosa Parks and the bus boycott in Montgomery, Alabama, inspire a civil rights movement.

1956   Dalip Singh Saund wins in California to become the first Asian American elected to Congress; United States supports the refusal of the South Vietnamese regime to hold free elections as specified by the Geneva Accords and sends military and economic aid.

1959   Hawai'i becomes the fiftieth state.

1964   Civil Rights Act prohibits racial discrimination in public accommodations, federally funded programs, and public and private employment; U.S. Congress passes the Gulf of Tonkin Resolution, allowing the president to escalate American military involvement in Vietnam; Patsy Takemoto Mink wins in Hawai'i and is the first Asian American woman elected to Congress.

1965	Immigration Act abandons "national origins" as the basis for establishing quotas for a hemispheric formula; it also abandons preferences for certain classes of immigrants; Voting Rights Act forbids racial discrimination in voting; strike by Mexican and Filipino grape pickers in Delano, California; riot in the Watts section of Los Angeles leave thirty-four dead; Malcolm X assassinated.
1967	Riot in Detroit leaves forty-three dead.
1968	Tet offensive begins, yielding little military advantage to the Communists but great political and psychological gains for the antiwar movement; students at San Francisco State College form the Third World Liberation Front and strike for ethnic studies; Martin Luther King Jr. assassinated.
1969	Students at the University of California, Berkeley, form the Third World Liberation Front and strike for ethnic studies; United States pursues "Vietnamization" of its war and reduces its military presence.
1970	United States expands its war into Cambodia; Kokua Kalama formed.
1971	Title II, the detention camp measure, of the 1950 Internal Security Act repealed.
1972	Aboriginal Lands of Hawaiian Ancestry formed; U.S. Congress passes the Equal Rights Amendment, which would provide equal rights to women (it would fail to receive ratification from the requisite three-fourths of state legislatures).
1973	United States and North Vietnam sign the cease-fire Paris Accords; Organization of Chinese Americans established in Washington, D.C.; American Indian Movement members occupy Wounded Knee, South Dakota, to press for reforms; in *Roe* v. *Wade*, the U.S. Supreme Court legalizes abortion based on the "right to privacy."
1974	In *Lau* v. *Nichols*, the U.S. Supreme court rules for bilingual education; 'Ohana O Hawai'i is formed.
1975	North Vietnamese troops enter Saigon and end the civil war; more than 130,000 refugees from Vietnam, Cambodia, and Laos enter the United States, fleeing Communist governments; Congress passes the Indochina Migration and Refugee Assistance Act; Voting Rights Act of 1965 amended to include language minorities within the act's purview.
1976	Health Professionals Education Assistance Act reduces the immigration of foreign physicians and health professionals; President

Chronology 189

Gerald Ford rescinds Executive Order 9066; Protect Kaho'olawe 'Ohana formed.

1977 President Gerald Ford pardons Iva Toguri, the so-called "Tokyo Rose."

1978 "Boat people" flee Vietnam; Office of Hawaiian Affairs established by the state to promote the interests of native Hawaiians.

1979 United States and People's Republic of China reestablish diplomatic relations.

1980 Refugee Act systematizes the admission of refugees to the United States; Commission on Wartime Relocation and Internment of Civilians formed.

1982 Vincent Chin murdered in Detroit; Equal Rights Amendment dies for lack of ratification by the states.

1983 Commission on the Wartime Relocation and Internment of Civilians issues its report and recommends redress and reparations to Japanese Americans; Native Hawaiians Study Commission appointed by Congress, and recommends against Hawaiian reparations.

1984 *Korematsu v. United States*, the 1944 U.S. Supreme Court ruling, is vacated and Fred Korematsu's conviction reversed.

1986 Immigration Reform and Control Act creates an amnesty program for undocumented immigrants and installs employer sanctions; John Waihee becomes Hawai'i's governor and is the first Hawaiian to be elected to that office.

1987 Navroze Mody killed in Jersey City, New Jersey; Constitutional Convention for a Hawaiian Nation meets and drafts a constitution.

1988 Civil Rights Act, offering redress and reparations to Japanese Americans, passed by Congress and signed by President Ronald Reagan; *Hirabayashi v. United States*, the 1943 U.S. Supreme Court ruling, is vacated and Gordon Hirabayashi's conviction reversed; Amerasian Homecoming Act allows Vietnamese children of American fathers the right to immigrate to the United States.

1989 Jim (Ming Hai) Loo killed in Raleigh, North Carolina; massacre of Asian American schoolchildren in Stockton, California, by a gunman who killed five and wounded twenty; China's government suppresses student uprising at Tiananmen Square; Communist governments collapse throughout Eastern Europe.

1990 Murder of Hung Truong in Houston, Texas; bombing of Kaho'olawe suspended.

1992   Los Angeles riots in which Korean American businesses in partic-
        ular were targeted results in losses of exceeding $350 million.

1993   U.S. Congress passes a joint resolution, signed by President Bill
        Clinton, apologizing for America's role in the 1893 overthrow of
        Queen Lili'uokalani.

1994   California passes Proposition 187, which denies rights and govern-
        ment services to undocumented immigrants.

1996   Illegal Immigration Reform and Immigrant Responsibility Act cur-
        tails the rights of undocumented immigrants to receive federal
        entitlements, limits due process for political asylum applicants,
        and increases enforcement of immigration laws; California
        passes Proposition 209, which eliminates governmental affir-
        mative action programs.

1999   FBI arrests Chinese American scientist Wen Ho Lee and charges
        him with mishandling restricted nuclear data at the Los Alamos
        National Laboratory.

2000   U.S. Justice and Interior departments release a draft report recom-
        mending sovereignty for Hawaiians; President Bill Clinton signs
        Executive Order 13125 establishing the President's Commission
        on Asian Americans and Pacific Islanders to improve the quality
        of life for those groups; Federal government drops fifty-eight of
        fifty-nine charges against We Ho Lee, who pleads guilty to a
        single charge of mishandling nuclear secrets, and Judge James
        A. Parker apologizes to Lee for "the unfair manner" in which
        he was held.

PART 5

Historiography and Resources

Chapter 1

HISTORIOGRAPHY

The major contours of Asian American historiography were shaped during the second half of the nineteenth century, when America's economic, political, and religious ambitions in the Pacific and its domestic debates over Asian migration were at their hottest.[1] The themes include U.S. trans-Pacific relations of trade and Christian missions, expansionism and colonialism, competition and conflict (including wars), and Americans' attitudes toward Asian immigration and, in particular, discrimination and assimilation. Typically, both their international and national variants were framed as "problems," the enigma and threat posed by Asians for white Americans—the "yellow peril" from abroad and the "Oriental problem" at home—and as refutations of those alleged problems. Therefore, writing on Asian American pasts commonly fell under the rubric of either diplomatic or immigration history, as relations with foreigners abroad or foreigners within, and rarely as central to the main currents of American history.

I suggest there are three main interpretive strands in the scholarly literature on Asian Americans—crafted by those to whom I refer as anti-Asianists, liberals, and Asian Americanists. Although separate and distinct, these interpretations of the Asian American experience have edges that overlap, and although they can typify certain times and historical periods, they can reappear in other times and periods, albeit with different meanings and resonances. I will discuss each of the three interpretive strands in turn. Readers should note that I do not limit this discussion of historiography to works of history and instead extend my review to books in other disciplines in the humanities and social sciences because Asian American studies is a multidisciplinary field. Further, and perhaps on shakier ground, I include in my historiography a few works that fall outside the circle of "scholarship" because of their claims to and influences upon it.

ANTI-ASIANISTS

The anti-Asianists defined the field's central problematic and established the terms of its debate—what is the place of Asia in the international arena vis-à-vis the United States and of Asians within the United States? Anti-Asianists, as suggested by my undiscriminating label, are those who maintain that Asia and Asian migrants pose threats to the interests of the United States and therefore advocate separation, exclusion, and expulsion. Anti-Asianists direct their writings to white Americans and commonly position themselves as defenders of the American self in opposition to the Asian other.

Typically, anti-Asianists of the nineteenth century ridiculed Asian culture while raising the alarm against the alleged dangers Asians posed to sanitation and wellness, the dignity of labor, morality, the family, and the pursuit of happiness. On March 30, 1876, California's *Marin Journal* outlined the basic argument: "That he is a slave, reduced to the lowest terms of beggarly economy, and is not a fit competitor for an American freeman. That he herds in scores, in small dens, where a white man and wife could hardly breathe, and has none of the wants of a civilized white man. That he has neither wife nor child, nor expects to have any. That his sister is a prostitute from instinct, religion, education, and interest, and degrading to all around her. . . . That the health, wealth, prosperity and happiness of our State demand their expulsion from our shores."[2]

The Chinese figured prominently among the defects of the golden state that are cited in Hinton R. Helper's polemic against California, published in 1855 as *The Land of Gold*. "The national habits and traits of Chinese character," he wrote, "are strikingly distinct from those of all other nations." While markedly different, the Chinese were all the same. "In short," Helper summed up the conundrum for whites, "one Chinaman looks almost exactly like another, but very unlike any body else." Mocking the appearance of Chinese men as "a tadpole walking on stilts," Helper scored Chinese women for having no morals and "no regard whatever for chastity or virtue." Watching a Chinese eat was "an amusing spectacle," he observed. "He seems to cram the food down his throat rather than let it undergo the usual process of mastication." And happening upon a Chinese camp, he reported seeing the men huddled around a fire, cooking rats. The Chinese, Helper alleged, were "so full of duplicity, prevarication and pagan prejudices, and so enervated and lazy that it is impossible for them to make true or estimable citizens."[3]

Pierton W. Dooner's *Last Days of the Republic* (1879) is exemplary of a genre of anti-Asian writing that dressed itself in the vestment of science to claim objective, ordered, useful, and predictive knowledge. Although fictional, Dooner called his account "deductive history" because "the data of thirty years of observation and experiment" led inevitably to the conclusions of his book, like "the product of the multiplication of two given numbers." Chinese immigration, warned Dooner, wasn't what it appeared to be. Cheap Chinese labor, upon which the West's industries grew to depend, became the engine of Chinese economic, and eventually political, might, which spread eastward from California to engulf the entire nation. The United States, complacent and beset with internal divisions, was eventually overrun by China's "swarming horde."[4]

While Dooner worried over the domestic consequences of Asian immigration, English historian Charles H. Pearson concerned himself over the international dimensions of empire and migration. Pearson published his *National Life and Character* (1893) at the noonday of European imperialism and in the same year that U.S. historian Frederick Jackson Turner delivered his seminal paper, "The Significance of the Frontier in American History." In his influential book, Pearson declared an end to the European frontier in the temperate zone and noted that only the tropical band, densely populated by peoples of color and unsuitable for permanent white settlement, remained for European expansion. Whites, he observed, sought the products of the tropics and hence colonized those areas, bringing not only technology, medicine, government, and commerce but also longer life spans, a population explosion, and a desire for Western products among nonwhites. Inevitably, predicted Pearson, in the vein of deductive history, nonwhites, led by Asians, would challenge white colonial rule and spread into the more desirable temperate zones, thereby threatening the white heartland.[5]

Two years after Pearson's *National Life* appeared, Brooks Adams, descendant of two U.S. presidents, published his widely read book *The Law of Civilization and Decay* (1895). The work conjured up an American version of Europe's specter of the "yellow peril" and provided a rationale for U.S. imperialism. Adams agreed with Pearson that European colonialism had animated a passive Asia, but he went on to point to a paradox of the colonial project. The unequal relationship whereby colonial economies extracted raw materials and marshaled masses of cheap labor might at first favor the metropole, which gained products and markets, at the expense of the colonies, which lost goods and labor that benefited the core. But, predicted Adams, cheap labor will draw industries to its source and, as a consequence, the centers of production and exchange would shift from Europe to Asia. Unimpeded, the "progressive law of civilization," according to Adams's "science," dictated that a bloated, soft European civilization would be challenged and eventually supplanted by the exploited but vigorous and tenacious peoples upon whose labor the empire depended. Westward expansion—imperialism, offered Adams, would reverse the process by toughening a flabby America, and colonialism would harness and contain the Asiatic economic beast.[6] Adams's organic analogy of the birth, rise, decline, and revival of civilizations and his foregrounding of Asia and the Pacific affirmed the expansionist sentiments of contemporaries like Theodore Roosevelt and Alfred T. Mahan who were key figures in the creation of America's "new empire" of the late nineteenth century.[7]

With the effective end to the migration of Chinese women in 1875 and of Chinese labor migration in 1882 and the defeat of China and Russia by Japan in 1895 and 1905, Japan replaced China as the principal enemy in the yellow peril scenarios of the anti-Asianists. Homer Lea's *The Valor of Ignorance* (1909) was the counterpart of Pierton W. Dooner's deductive history. Lea, who fancied himself a military strategist and Chinese Republican Army insider, argued, like Brooks Adams, that "the birth, growth and decay of nations is made analogous to the life history of individuals, wherein they pass from the cradle to manhood, expanding in intellect, accumulating vigor and strength, until, in due time, they grow old, die and are forgotten." Decadence, he maintained, leads to the decline of the "militant spirit" that reveals the accompanying "national decay." To arrest its deterioration, warned Lea, America must prepare for "the inevitable struggle for the dominion of the Pacific." In *The Valor of Ignorance*, Lea detailed Japan's rise and national ambitions, the causes (including the indignities of anti-Japanese actions against migrants on the U.S. West Coast) and probable course of the conflict (complete with maps and battles), and the final outcome (if his warnings went unheeded): the disintegration of "this heterogeneous Republic."[8] The book was popular in Europe, where it became required reading in German and Russian military academies, and it underwent multiple printings in Japan, where it was published as *The War Between Japan and America*. It was reissued in 1942 in the United States as a demonstration of Lea's "prophetic" vision and as a popular reference work for charting the course of the Pacific war.

Although in the United States Lea's mass appeal was greatest decades after the initial publication of his book, Madison Grant's 1916 work *The Passing of the Great Race* was greeted with immediate acclaim. Grant employed the "science" of eugenics to establish the primacy of inheritance over environment, the genetic pools of races, and the superiority of one race over another. Perhaps most important, Grant Americanized eugenics, first advanced in England, by arguing its relevance to American democracy and institutions. His contention, thus, that the idea of the melting pot was sheer "folly" and that immigrants (primarily eastern and southern Europeans and Asians, whom he called "undesirable races and peoples") threatened to dilute and reduce the Republic's white genetic pool resonated with wider discussions of Progressive social reform and order. "The danger is from within and not from without," he wrote in the introduction to his fourth edition, after the battle for restrictive immigration had been largely won. "Neither the black, nor the brown, nor the yellow, nor the red will conquer the white in battle. But if the valuable elements in the Nordic race mix with inferior strains or die out through race suicide, then the citadel of civilization will fall for mere lack of defenders."[9] As demonstrated by the influence of eugenics on social policy and the restrictive 1924 Immigration Act, Grant's ideas were not at the fringes of intellectual discourse but at its very center.[10]

Besides the apocalyptic visions of anti-Asianists whose books were sold under the category of nonfiction, writers like Wallace Irwin and Sax Rohmer (Arthur Henry Sarsfield Ward) fed the public's apparent hunger for buffoons and villains against whom they could measure themselves.[11] Irwin invented and assumed the persona of Hashimura Togo, a Japanese "schoolboy," in his satirical *Letters of a Japanese Schoolboy* (1907). Representing Japanese migrants in the United States, Irwin's Togo is a caricature, a social critic and commentator who is himself an object of ridicule. While criticizing the Chinese, Koreans, Asian Indians, African Americans, suffragettes, and robber barons, Togo fails to realize that he is the social problem, the yellow peril. And like his African and Chinese American forebears in song and literature, Togo speaks with a broken tongue — a kind of oriental- and woman-speak — that elicits laughter and deals sharp lessons on the consequences of deviant speech. During the 1870s, the yellowface minstrel Luke Schoolcraft sang "The Heathen Chinee" to the refrain:

> Hi! Hi! Hi! Ching! Ching! Ching!
> Chow, chow, wellie good, me likie him.
> Makie plenty sing song, savie by and bye.
> China man a willie man, laugh hi! hi![12]

Similarly, Irwin's Togo declares, "I have given some brain-study to this Yellow Peril to make sure it is a bad blessing for these Uniteds State. It is. But should we Americans of all-colour enjoy fear of such? Answer is, No!"[13]

Sax Rohmer evoked the quintessential oriental villain with his extremely popular Fu Manchu series.[14] "Imagine a person, tall, lean and feline, high-shouldered, with a brow like Shakespeare and a face like Satan," Rohmer's hero Nayland Smith describes his nemesis, Fu Manchu, "a close-shaven skull, and long, magnetic eyes of the true cat-green. Invest him with all the cruel cunning of an entire Eastern race, accumulated in one giant intellect, with all the resources of science past and present, with all the resources, if you will, of a wealthy government. . . . Imagine that awful being, and you have a mental picture of Dr. Fu-Manchu, the yellow peril incarnate in one man."[15] A companion of that "monster" was his "girl slave," described salaciously by Rohmer's protagonist as "a figure from an opium vision, with her clinging silk draperies and garish jewelry, with her feet encased in little red slippers." That "seductive vision, her piquant loveliness," the narrator mused, stood in marked contrast to "its black setting of murder and devilry."[16] These anti-Asianist works of fiction engaged images in non-fiction and helped to fix within the American imaginary enduring orientalist conventions of race, gender, and sexuality that represented Asian women as objects of desire and Asian men as objects of fear.[17]

Regional politics were revealed in the anti-Asianist claim that California's best interests were being sacrificed on the altar of East Coast capitalism and liberalism. According to the well-worn contention put forward by Montaville Flowers, a Virginian who had moved to California and given anti-Japanese lectures on the East Coast Chautauqua circuit, it was Eastern bankers and missionaries who opposed and obstructed Western attempts at Asian exclusion. His book *The Japanese Conquest of American Opinion* (1917) was written to counter missionaries like Sidney L. Gulick, whose book, Flowers decried, was "ultra in its arguments against us, justifying the mixture of the races, etc." The liberal forces of the Eastern establishment were well-organized and potent, Flowers wrote, and their supporters included "large numbers of prominent Americans ecstatically visualizing America as the Utopia of Universal Brotherhood . . . all organized, active, powerful, using vast institutions especially adapted to spread and vitalize their propaganda." These forces maligned California, charged Flowers, and were effective in their appeal to church congregations, the wealthy, and American sentiments for peace and internationalism. Rather, Flowers alleged, they served the interests of Japan in its pursuit to conquer American public opinion and therewith America itself.[18] Although the book was largely ignored, according to historian Roger Daniels, it started "an entirely new phase of the anti-Japanese movement," in which Californians portrayed themselves as fighting against powerful and entrenched Eastern interests in seeking a solution to the "Oriental problem,"[19] and it reintroduced the idea that Asians deployed the very tenets of American democracy against itself.

Although set in London's Chinatown, British author Thomas Burke's *Limehouse Nights* (1917) achieved notoriety because it played upon the same fears of the Asian in the West but ventured beyond into the forbidden territories of child pornography and miscegenation. A collection of short stories, *Limehouse* established Burke's reputation as a writer and was hailed by London's critics as a "work of genius" comprised of "masterpieces."[20] The most famous of these "masterpieces" was Burke's first story, "The Chink and the Child," made even more popular by American film director D. W. Griffith, whose *Broken Blossoms* (1919) was based upon that work. Burke's Limehouse, a district in London, is a site of both perversity and pleasure and the home of outcasts and immigrants — the residues of empire and industrialization. It is a low-lit, brooding place that "slinks" to and from "the dark waste of waters beyond." Inhabitants of Lime-house, the story's protagonists are the white, working-class boxer, Battling Bur-rows, his illegitimate daughter, Lucy, "a little girl of twelve," and Cheng Huan, the chink, the yellow man. Battling is manly, a boxer and fond of wine, women, and song, while Cheng is womanly, a loafer and a poet, who "felt things more passionately." Pinned between the abusive Battling and loving Cheng is Lucy, "a lurking beauty" and the sexual object of Battling's blows and Cheng's kisses. Cheng, Battling, and Lucy, as natives of Limehouse, are squatters on the fron-tiers of race, gender, sexuality, class, and nation, and they underscore the per-ceived contrasts between light and darkness, civilization and barbarism, middle-class sensibility and working-class vulgarity, hygiene and filth, normality and deviancy.

Anti-Asianist tracts during the 1920s failed to match the frequency and stri-dency of those of earlier decades. As noted by Montaville Flowers, the American public seemed unconcerned about the "Oriental problem"—and with good reason. The tide of Asian labor migration had been largely turned back, Japan was a U.S. ally during World War I, and the postwar economic boom of the 1920s beckoned laborers to the northern industrial cities and the West's factories in the field. To be sure, anti-Asianism reared its head with the continuing pop-ularity of eugenics, exemplified in the alarmist and racist book by Lothrop Stoddard, *The Rising Tide of Color Against White World-Supremacy* (1920), in the writings of V. S. McClatchy, publisher of the *Sacramento Bee*, and in anti-Filipino riots in Washington and California. Endorsed by Madison Grant and armed with a Harvard Ph.D., Stoddard warned that "the question of Asiatic immigration is incomparably the greatest external problem which faces the white world," because it threatened race mixing and hence "our very race-existence, the well-springs of being, the sacred heritage of our children."[21] McClatchy, in his brief to the State Department on behalf of the Japanese Exclusion League of California titled "Japanese Immigration and Coloniza-tion" (1921), charged that the Japanese posed "a grave and imminent danger, not only to the Pacific Coast States, but to the Nation itself."[22] That belief was clearly shared by civilian and military intelligence, especially in regard to the situation in Hawaii.[23] And novels like Wallace Irwin's *Seed of the Sun* (1921) and Peter B. Kyne's *Pride of Palomar* (1921) revisited Montaville Flowers's theme, California's victimization by Eastern capitalists, missionaries, and liberal de-fenders of the Japanese, and reconfirmed the whiteness of the Irish (as "Anglo-Saxons") in the face of the yellow peril.[24] But those rumblings largely failed to disturb the surface tranquility and good times of the "new era" of the 1920s, and after passage of the restrictive Immigration Act of 1924, the Japanese Exclusion League dissolved itself.

It is difficult, in truth, to trace the lineage of anti-Asianist books published from the second half of the 1920s through the 1970s, so dominant during that period is the literature I've labeled liberal.[25] Fu Manchu novels, nonetheless, continued in popularity through the 1950s, and, in 1936, Universal Studios released the first in its extremely popular futuristic *Flash Gordon* serial, which introduced Emperor Ming, the Merciless, who, like Fu Manchu, was the personification of Oriental evil. Wars in Asia and the Pacific from 1941 to 1975 occasioned a harvest of villains and heroes alike in American films, depending upon whether they were the enemies or friends of the United States. But books seemed less concerned with the yellow peril, even in the aftermath of Pearl Harbor, and more interested in the possibilities and consequences of the adaptation and absorption of Asian migrants and their children. Exceptional in this regard is Alan Hynd's sensationalist *Betrayal from the East: The Inside Story of Japanese Spies in America* (1943). Coming on the heels of a similar book on Nazi sabotage plans, *Betrayal* alleges an omnipresent army of Japanese spies, disguised as trusted employees, religious leaders, innocent young women, students, and businessmen, who were critical to Japan's success at Pearl Harbor. And, writing in the midst of the war and mass detention of Japanese Americans, Hynd warns against their release from the camps, calling it "the Japanese sabotage menace of 1943." Many Japanese were dangerous still, Hynd declares, and represented "a terrible potential evil" and a source of "active treachery at work against us."[26]

Coming amidst the cold war, the African American demand for civil rights, and the noonday of liberalism in Asian American studies, Gunther Barth's *Bitter Strength: A History of the Chinese in the United States, 1850–1870* (1964) presents a mixture of both anti-Asianist and liberal sentiments. The book's central concern, as posed by Barth's mentor, the immigration historian Oscar Handlin, is why, in the case of the Chinese, the nation strayed from its tradition of open immigration. The question presupposes a liberal faith in American democracy, and Barth writes sympathetically of the Chinese, victimized by whites and Chinese alike. But like the anti-Asianists, Barth singles out the Chinese as the source of the problem and the cause of Chinese exclusion. White Californians, he stresses, abhorred the taint of slavery and saw the state as a land of opportunity and a place for the realization of the American dream. Ignoring the racist aspects of that California dream, Barth blames American Indians, Mexicans, European immigrants, African Americans, and the Chinese for being obstacles to the realization of that white vision for the golden state. All of these were sojourners, Barth contends, who were easily exploited as foreigners and failed to invest their labors and resources in the Americanization of the state and of themselves. White humanitarians and American institutions tutored and uplifted the sojourners, and anti-Asianism subsided when the Chinese shed their foreignness and became American.[27]

The Japanese and Asian "menace" reappeared in the United States with the economic downturn of the mid-1970s and the "downsizing" and "de-industrialization" of the 1980s. In contrast, Japan's continued economic growth, its lopsided trade balance with the United States, and Japanese investments in prime, high-profile U.S. property reanimated anti-Asianists, who, as in the past, depicted those developments as an economic "invasion" that threatened domestic tranquillity. A rush of books with Japan as enemy topped the charts, and enterprising novelists like Michael Crichton were quick to pick up the scent.[28] In Crichton's *Rising Sun* (1992), America is symbolized as a "small-town girl," a blond "American beauty long-stemmed rose," who prostitutes herself to "little guys" with cash from Japan. Her aberrant tastes and inexplicable naivete, like Pierton Dooner's unsuspecting America, result in her demise, on the forty-sixth floor of the Japanese-built Nakamoto Tower in Japantown, Los Angeles. Crichton chose three aphorisms for his book: "We are entering a world where the old rules no longer apply," "Business is war," allegedly a Japanese motto, and "If you don't want Japan to buy it, don't sell it," attributed to Sony's head, Akio Morita. And like many of its anti-Asianist predecessors, *Rising Sun* counters the charge of bigotry by claiming the vestment of objectivity and science. "Although this book is fiction," Crichton explains in his un-novel-like bibliography, "my approach to Japan's economic behavior, and America's inadequate response to it, follows a well-established body of expert opinion, much of it listed in the bibliography. Indeed, in preparing this novel, I have drawn heavily from a number of the sources below."[29]

Listed within Crichton's bibliography are the works of scholars and journalists who, apparently, verify his warnings of an impending crisis. To political economist Pat Choate, Japan exerted political and economic control over America by buying the government and swaying public opinion. In his *Agents of Influence* (1990), Choate details a network of lobbyists and well-connected insiders, who work for Japan and move in Washington government and business circles, distributing money to legislators and policy makers, scholars, political parties, and schools. Through legal though unethical means, Choate charges, Japan has purchased unprecedented political power and threatens America's national sovereignty.[30] Among books that reaffirm Crichton's call to arms are two sober studies, "future histories" in the tradition of Pierton Dooner and Homer Lea, that predict conflicts with Japan and China. In *The Coming War with Japan* (1991), George Friedman and Meredith Lebard disclaim the title of "Japan-bashing," a prominent exercise in their day, and instead argue that the circumstances in which the United States and Japan find themselves make their collision inevitable. Among these are the end of the cold war, and hence the need of the United States for Japan to serve as its buffer against Soviet expansions in Asia and the Pacific. Japan's depends upon imports of minerals that are controlled by the United States and crucial for its economy. Freed from the Soviet threat, Friedman and Lebard predict, the United States will deal more harshly with Japan in an economic competition that will spiral into a war.[31]

Journalists Richard Bernstein and Ross H. Munro present another scenario in their book, *The Coming Conflict with China* (1997). China, with its vast population, its economic resurgence, its rising nationalism, its absorption of Hong Kong and Macau, and its ambitions for predominance in Asia, Bernstein and Munro foresee, will inevitably come into conflict with the United States.[32] A basic assumption on the part of both of these future histories is that Japan and China maintain deep-seated and persistent views of the United States as their rival and enemy, grounded in economic and political competition but also in a clash of civilizations.

That long-standing suspicion of the unbridgeable distance between West and East lurks in the books by Thurston Clarke and Joel Kotkin. In his *Pearl Harbor Ghosts* (1991), a reflection on the fiftieth anniversary of Japan's attack on Pearl Harbor, Clarke chronicles the sacrifices of the American defenders that Sunday morning and the sacrilege of Japanese tourists and investors, who, fifty years later, made Hawai'i "an economic colony of Japan." And although he takes pains to distinguish between Japanese and Japanese American and praises the heroism of the *nisei* soldier, Clarke confuses them as an undifferentiated race. Recalling a conversation he had with a Japanese American, Clarke remarked candidly, "If I shut my eyes and listened, I heard an American; if I opened them, I saw a Japanese."[33] Similarly, Kotkin identifies the primal bonds of blood and culture and their geographic dispersion as major factors for the collective success of groups—"tribes"—like the Jews, British, Chinese, Japanese, and Asian Indians in the past in international commerce and in the new global economy. Those views, although modern and cast in positive light, reflect the darker essentialisms and yellow perilisms of the past.

Samuel P. Huntington's *The Clash of Civilizations and the Remaking of World Order* (1996) brings those writings I have classed as anti-Asianist full circle. It follows in the line of books from the nineteenth century to the present that posit global conflicts between European and non-European peoples, all premised upon the ancient irreconcilable differences of culture, race, or civilization. Huntington dresses his argument for his present, not as a work of social science, he demurs, but as an "interpretation" of world politics meaningful to scholars and useful to policymakers. He argues against the attempt to Westernize non-Western civilizations (defined on the basis of religion but also geography—Latin America, African, Islamic, Sinic, Hindu, Orthodox, Buddhist, and Japanese—and observes a shifting of the balance of power from the West to the East, including Islamic civilization. In this post-cold-war world, societies with similar cultures are banding together, Huntington notes, and the West's survival is predicated upon its ability to unite under the banner of identity against the assertions of other civilizations.[34]

As astutely observed by the then Harvard lecturer and later secretary of labor Robert B. Reich, those books on the Asian challenge followed in the aftermath of the Soviet Union's collapse and the increasing diversity of America's peoples due to the dramatic rise in nonwhite immigration. Thus the need for a common enemy "to give us a reason to join together . . . as a means of defining ourselves, our interests, our obligations to one another" was "the real logic—the deep hidden message of these books."[35] Ostensibly a "menace" from abroad, yellow perilism had domestic causes and consequences for immigration policies, multiculturalism in education, and nationalism. As proposed by Samuel Huntington, domestic fractures within the West, particularly within the United States, must vanish into a single identity if Western civilization is to halt its decline and overcome the foreign aggressions of Asian economies, a "greater China," and the Islamic revolution.

LIBERALS

Like the anti-Asianists, liberals constitute a broad field of interpretation. Nonetheless, they are in general defenders of Asians and conceptualize their writings in opposition to the contentions forwarded by anti-Asianists. In that sense, the liberal interpretation is a reactive one, and is thus mainly limited to the borders first marked by their predecessors, the anti-Asianists, who establish the terms of the debate. Liberals, for the most part, hold that the United States is a nation of immigrants, that its political and economic institutions allow for boundless opportunities and freedoms among its citizens, and that U.S. history, like the careers of individual immigrants, moves progressively from repression to liberation and from poverty to plenty. That immigration paradigm, applied without distinction to Europeans and Asians alike, responds to the central problematic of Asian American studies, first defined by the anti-Asianists—the processes whereby Asians became or were prevented from becoming Americans, processes of inclusion and exclusion. Liberals frequently speak for Asians, whom they portray as helpless or voiceless victims of anti-Asianists; they translate Asian culture, oftentimes as cultural insiders, to their fellow white Americans and situate themselves, in contrast to the anti-Asianists, as the true defenders of America and of democracy itself.

William Speer, Presbyterian missionary to China, in 1870 published *The Oldest and the Newest Empire: China and the United States*. Chinese immigration to the United States and the consequent awakening of "universal and anxious inquiry as to their character, their capacities and their probable influence upon the future of our country and continent," explained Speer, prompted the writing of his book. As a cultural insider who was "the first to preach the gospel in their own language," Speer gained authority to translate the "Chinese character" to the West and serve as a cultural bridge between China and the United States. Although "a heathen people," the Chinese were no different than other peoples, having their own faults and virtues, explained the missionary. To demonstrate this claim, Speer takes an extensive excursion into Chinese history and culture, beginning with European and European American fascination with China, Marco Polo's late-thirteenth-century account, and America's "discovery" by Europeans intent upon finding a passage to India. But the other part of Speer's argument, which really is an aspect of his principal contention, is that, besides the essentially harmless nature of Chinese immigration, Chinese labor has proven itself economically profitable and trade with China will lead to the fulfillment of America's divine destiny. Like Secretary of State William H. Seward's Pacific vision, Speer foresees "a peculiar glory" in the meeting of the "two great streams of civilization," one in decline, the other ascendant, prompted by U.S. westward expansion.[36]

Having served as U.S. minister to China, George F. Seward, like Speer, saw himself as a cultural broker, but he added to Speer's argument in favor of Chinese immigration by portraying migration as a "natural" process and pointing to the antidemocratic aspect of Chinese exclusion. In his *Chinese Immigration* (1881), Seward explained, as a general rule, that "the United States ought not to interfere unnecessarily with immigration, because in doing so we would depart from principles well established in our national life, and because arbitrary interferences with natural processes prove, as a rule, unavailing and injurious."[37] The book is a point-by-point refutation of charges leveled by anti-Asianists, including exaggerations on the numbers of Chinese immigrants, and claims that Chinese labor was cheap or unfree, that the Chinese displaced white workers, that they exported American resources, that they were an immoral people, that they disregarded the law, and that they refused to assimilate. There is no danger from a flood of Chinese immigrants, Seward counters, and the economic benefits of their labor are manifest in the building of railroads, reclamation of swamp lands, in mining, agriculture, manufacturing, and domestic service.

The question of Asian labor took a particular turn in Hawai'i. As an independent kingdom, Hawai'i, under the influence of whites who dominated the government and economy by around the mid-nineteenth century, instituted a system of contract labor for its burgeoning sugar industry. Under the system, primarily Asians were recruited to work on sugar plantations for set periods of time with fixed wages and benefits. The bound aspects of migrant labor carried the odium of indenture and slavery, and when the United States annexed Hawai'i in 1898, the practice came to an end, based on U.S. laws against slavery and the importation of contract laborers. In the aftermath of that change, the American Economic Association published Katharine Coman's study *The History of Contract Labor in the Hawaiian Islands* (1903), a work that examines the benefits and failures of contract labor and the prospects for wage labor and Hawai'i's economic well-being and growth. The book is replete with prejudices against Hawaiian society and Asian workers even as it is optimistic about the processes of civilization and industry to transform "a primitive agricultural community" into "a highly specialized industrial system." And, argues Coman, Asian, Pacific Islander, and European workers under contract, guided by rational white planners, benefited from the system and advanced the islands' economy.[38]

Joining the debate on the liberal side were a few Asian voices that sought to interpret Asian culture to European Americans and critique the ideals, on the one hand, and the realities, on the other, of life in the United States. Clearly contrary to a liberal contention, Asians were neither passive in their victimization nor without voice. And Asian views, like those of their white American counterparts, were varied and sometimes contradictory. Wong Chin Foo, a publisher and activist, scorned the hypocrisy of Christian missions for preaching equality and goodwill and practicing discrimination and exclusion, while the Christian Yan Phou Lee published a rebuttal to Wong and argued that anti-Asianists were not true Christians.[39] Perhaps exemplary of books by Asians in the liberal tradition is Yung Wing's autobiography, *My Life in China and America* (1909).[40] Born near Macao in 1828, Yung was educated by missionaries in China, Macao, and Hong Kong before being taken to the United States in 1847 to further his education. He became a U.S. naturalized citizen in 1852, and after graduating from Yale in 1854 Yung returned to China where he eventually succeeded in convincing the Chinese government to establish the Chinese Educational Mission to the United States in 1870. From 1872 to 1881, Yung supervised the American education of 120 Chinese students from his headquarters first in Springfield, Massachusetts and then in Hartford, Connecticut. Yung's autobiography expressed his belief in the ideals of American democracy and helped to support the missionaries' claim about the power of Christianity to transform Chinese culture (Yung reported that studying in America had wrought "a metamorphosis in his inward nature") and the potential of education for the "reformation and regeneration" of China (despite his cultural metamorphosis, Yung declared his "undying love for China").[41]

Foundational to the liberal interpretation and the first book in Asian American studies written by a professional academic is Mary Roberts Coolidge's *Chinese Immigration* (1909). The book's immediate context was the debate around the renewal of the 1882 Chinese Exclusion Act, and its text presented the case against exclusion. It was more than a matter of a domestic problem over immigration, explained Coolidge; it was simultaneously an international question of America's political and economic relations with Asia and of America's standing in the world. California's anti-Chinese movement prompted the 1905 boycott of U.S. goods in China, Coolidge pointed out, and in that way anti-Asianism at home has led to strained relations detrimental to U.S. interests abroad. A Stanford University sociology professor, Coolidge tested her ideas for the book in a course she offered on "race problems." Foremost, *Chinese Im-migration* lays out what has since come to be known as the "California thesis," which explains the rise of the anti-Chinese movement.[42] Coolidge's explanation has become the standard interpretation, despite subsequent attempts to revise or diminish it.

When the Chinese first arrived, recounted Coolidge, they were welcomed because of the need for their labor. During this "period of favor," race prejudice took a back seat to economic motives. But after a few years, racial antipathy against the Chinese grew among whites because of a set of particular circum-stances that coalesced in California. The gold rush brought Southerners, former slaveholders, with their racial prejudices against darker-skinned peoples, fron-tiersmen "whose ignorance and extreme race antipathies" grouped all non-whites as inferior, and northern European immigrants, especially the Irish, who resented competition with the Chinese. In addition, Know-Nothing nativism and xenophobia "rolled in a wave across the country from East to West," and a "lawless greed" pervaded California's frontier society, comprised of "adven-turers," not settlers, and dominated by an avaricious, get-rich-quick mentality. Finally, economic decline during the 1850s following the exhaustion of surface mining resulted in unemployment, strikes, and idleness, and these fires of dis-content were fanned by unscrupulous politicians and the press, who narrowed upon the Chinese as "the scape-goats for the evils of the time." California's petition to end Chinese immigration found a receptive ear in Congress because both political parties needed and actively courted California's voters, who were pivotal to their national agendas. Coolidge summed up the process of national exclusion: "The clamor of an alien class [Irish workers] in a single state [Cali-fornia]—taken up by politicians for their own ends—was sufficient to change the policy of a nation and to commit the United States to a race discrimination at variance with our professed theories of government, and this so irrevocably that it has become an established tradition."[43]

Revealed within Coolidge's California thesis are several assumptions and prejudices. The "professed theories of government" presumes a democracy open to all peoples, and therefore the anti-Chinese movement instances an aberration from that ideal because of the circumstances peculiar to California and the nation at the time. It is thus a blot against the Republic's mainstream values of equality under the law. Coolidge therewith upholds liberalism's faith in American institutions and its upward historical trajectory. She assumes that American democracy operates from the bottom up, in that the masses influence politicians and public policy, and believes that capitalism is rational, employing Chinese for profit despite racial prejudice, while racism is irrational, arising from ignorance, bigotry, and greed. In that, Coolidge shows her class bias, blaming ill-mannered workers for acting from "the arrogant and narrow-minded temper bred by pioneer conditions, the monopolistic spirit and the lack of sanity and justice," and reveals her belief in the power of Americanization to domesticate the "alien class" of Irish workers, who, in vilifying the Chinese, acted in an un-American way.[44] Finally, Coolidge exhibits her Yankee prejudice against Southerners, all of whom she assumes to have been white supremacists.

America's involvement in World War I bred an internationalism and peace movement as well as isolationism and a retreat from idealism. Sidney L. Gulick, a missionary to Japan and the object of anti-Asianist Montaville Flowers's ire, championed the Wilsonian search for a new world order from his position with the Federal Council of the Churches of Christ in America. As a representative of twenty-four million American Protestants, the council was a powerful voice in lobbying Washington to advance its social gospel. According to his biographer, Gulick sought "a harmonious world order maintained by reasonable men and reinforced by the Christian spirit" and believed that U.S. domestic social relations were intimately linked with the nation's foreign policies.[45] Discrimination against Japanese in America, he held, soured relations between the United States and Japan and thereby imperiled world peace. Thus, through their publications, lectures, and lobbying efforts, he and the council advocated cross-cultural understanding and nondiscriminatory immigration legislation, as in Gulick's *The American Japanese Problem* (1914) and the council's memorial to the president and Congress urging "an Oriental policy based upon a just and equitable regard for the interests of all the nations concerned."[46]

Although charges of a Japanese conspiracy were much exaggerated by anti-Asianists and U.S. intelligence agencies, Japan's government was indeed concerned about American public opinion toward Japan and Japanese migrants. Accordingly, the government funded, through various means, Japanese publicists in America like Kiyoshi K. Kawakami and Yamato Ichihashi to refute the anti-Asianists and help shape a more favorable attitude toward the Japanese.[47] During the height of the anti-Japanese movement in California, in books like *Asia at the Door* (1914) and *The Real Japanese Question* (1921), Kawakami sought to counter the "campaign of slander and fabrication" that had been directed against the Japanese by "self-seeking politicians and agitators." The books are organized around the allegations made by the anti-Asianists, such as the issue of Japanese assimilation, Japanese contributions to the American West and Hawai'i, and the sources of and solutions to the alleged problem of Japanese migration and settlement.[48]

During the 1920s and 1930s, as anti-Asianist tracts were diminishing, sociologists at the University of Chicago were mapping out a distinctively American social scientific terrain, one that applied the theories of Europe to the realities of America. With his idea of a "race relations cycle," Robert E. Park, a key figure in the Chicago school of sociology, fastened upon "natural" processes like ecological succession to explain U.S. social relations, thereby applying scientific "universal" laws to the American environment. The "Negro" and

"Oriental" problems, however, appeared to deviate from his generalizations of a one-way, linear process of contact (immigration), competition, accommodation, and assimilation, chiefly because of the "physical mark" of Africans and Asians. Race, although a social construct, impeded the full inclusion of Asians and Africans, observed Park. Thus, accounting for the "Negro" and "Oriental" problems became a central feature of the Chicago school's overall attempt to transform U.S. social science. Ernest Burgess, one of Park's colleagues at Chicago, explained that Chinese Americans attracted sociological research attention because "as one of the cultural groups most deviant from the typical native American culture it provided sharp contrasts which clarified theoretical issues which otherwise might be vague."[49]

Seven years before the launching of his Survey of Race Relations (1924–26), which interviewed hundreds of Asians and non-Asians along the West Coast, Park outlined his views on "the general situation" of U.S. race relations in his introduction to the published version of Jesse Frederick Steiner's doctoral dissertation, which had been written under his direction. Modernity, wrote Park, has been characterized by international commerce, a global migration, an uprooting of peoples from the soil and the concentration of them in cities, and the "interpenetration of peoples" caused by "the great cosmic forces which have broken down the barriers which formerly separated the races and nationalities of the world, and forced them into new intimacies and new forms of competition, rivalry, and conflict." In the United States, immigrants—both Europeans and Asians—face prejudice that arises from competition between the old and new inhabitants of the land, but the "Japanese, Chinese, and Negroes cannot move among us with the same freedom as the members of other races because they bear marks which identify them as members of their race." And although racial antipathies are "deep-seated, vital, and instinctive impulses" that help to defend a group from their competitive others, declared Park, they isolate Asians and Africans from America's majority and thereby institute "a vicious circle" of isolation and prejudice, prejudice and isolation. That circumstance, Park maintained, distinguishes Africans and Asians from Europeans in America and presents social science with a "special problem" that "demands a national policy based on an unflinching examination of the facts."[50]

A measure of the impact of Park's ideas on Asian American historiography is not only evidenced in the importance of his research and writings in establishing the liberal tradition but also in the continued influence of the work of his students and colleagues who helped to identify and shape many of the major themes in the literature of Asian and European American relations in the American West and in Hawai'i. They include authors like Romanzo Adams, Emory Bogardus, William Caudill, Clarence Glick, Yamato Ichihashi, Forest LaViolette, Rose Hum Lee, Andrew Lind, Eliot Grinnell Mears, Frank Miyamoto, Tamotsu Shibutani, Paul C. P. Siu, and William Carlson Smith, among others,

struggles and Asian and Asian American identities as well as their transnational nature.[73]

An influential book of the 1950s is Richard Mason's semiautobiographical *The World of Suzie Wong* (1957). Set during the Korean War, the novel retraces a familiar path, the rescue of a victimized Asian woman by a white man, but there are other old tropes and stereotypes embraced in this cold war narrative as well. The world of Suzie Wong is described not by the Asian woman but by her rescuer, the protagonist, British painter Richard Lomax. Wong, like Fu Manchu's "girl slave," is highly sexualized as a Hong Kong prostitute and infantilized as Asian and woman in Lomax's representation of her body, her abuse, and her illiteracy. "Her small Chinese breasts were very white and smooth," observes the artist, "like an immature girl's, but the nipples were mature and wrinkled and proud."[74] The white protagonist's masculinity and art are set and measured against the Asian prostitute's femininity and body. All these ideas had wide currency. But there are also notions particular to this book's immediate contexts. Wong's rescue from prostitution and Asian culture was read in light of the ongoing cold war battles against the evils of Chinese communism. And her surrender to Lomax and domestic bliss (they married, traveled to England, and lived happily ever after), along with Lomax's special contempt for white women, held specific meaning for the stirrings of post–World War II feminist and civil rights awareness in the United States. The book and film versions helped to fix old ideas of Asian women (the Suzie Wong stereotype) and white men (knights in shining armor) as the period experienced fears of communism abroad and calls for greater freedoms and equality at home.

Liberalism dominated Asian American studies from the 1920s through the 1960s. Lawrence H. Fuchs's *Hawaii Pono* (1961), Betty Lee Sung's *Mountain of Gold* (1967), and Bill Hosokawa's *Nisei: The Quiet Americans* (1969) exemplify the liberal tradition at its terminus. Hawai'i, wrote Fuchs, is an exemplar to the nation. Racial politics is central to Hawai'i's past and present, he contended, ever since the arrival of whites, who, in a short span of time, controlled the islands' economy and government. But implanted within that antidemocratic oligarchic order were the seeds of Americanism in the public schools and in universal suffrage. These took root, grew, and blossomed in the post–World War II resurgence of unionism and Democratic Party politics that overthrew the oligarchy and installed democracy. "Hawaii illustrates the nation's revolutionary message of equality of opportunity for all," Fuchs concludes, "regardless of background, color, or religion. This is the promise of Hawaii, a promise for the entire nation and, indeed, the world, that peoples of different races and creeds can live together, enriching each other, in harmony *and* democracy."[75] The book celebrated Hawai'i's statehood, which was granted in 1959, and moreover affirmed the American creed of equality for all to a nation divided by race and a cold war world of competing ideologies and practices.

Betty Lee Sung's *Mountain of Gold* (1967) was written to disprove the prevailing stereotypes of Chinese Americans that arose from "a fixation about the Chinese that demands the sensational, the lurid, the peculiarities, and the mysteries of this national group to the exclusion of fact." In addition, proposed Sung, the book's currency and its particular value rest in America's war in Vietnam and the domestic civil rights struggle. Chinese Americans, she suggested, could serve "as interpreters of the Oriental mind," and their experiences as racial minorities could elucidate upon the black and white racial divide. Against the abundant anti-Asianist images, Sung assembles a portrait of Chinese America and a list of Chinese American contributions to American society to attest to their commonplace humanity, their rapid assimilation, and their extraordinary success.[76] Bill Hosokawa's *Nisei* is similarly inspired and organized. It is an account of the second-generation Japanese American—the *nisei*—who, in the author's words, "approached manhood with an American heart and mind and a Japanese face" and confronted racial discrimination during World War II but survived that "trial by fire, and like fine steel, he emerged from the ordeal tempered, tough, resilient." In the process, Hosokawa contends, the *nisei* demonstrated their mettle and discovered, in the polarized racial formation of black and white, that "it was not particularly difficult to be accepted into the white man's world."[77]

Although in decline, the liberal interpretation continued into the 1970s and 1980s, drawing from the social and political liberalism of the Kennedy and Johnson years of the previous decade and the evolving notion of multiculturalism. These include influential studies on the anti-Chinese and anti-Japanese movements,[78] writings that defend Asian Americans against anti-Asianist claims by citing their contributions and achievements through autobiographical success stories,[79] and general studies that celebrate the Asian American experience.[80] Another aspect of liberalism in its more contemporary guise is to test the assumptions and hypotheses of U.S. race relations and immigration history.[81] Perhaps a fitting representative of the liberal interpretation in the 1980s is Roger Daniels's unfortunately titled *Asian America: Chinese and Japanese in the United States Since 1850* (1988). The book is an impressive summation of over twenty-five years of sustained and productive labor in Chinese and Japanese history, but its title appears anachronistic in light of the demographic and historiographical changes in the field, which recognizes the diversity of Asian ethnicities and experiences and rejects the equation of Chinese and Japanese American history with Asian American history. As he did years before, Daniels argues against "negative history," or the focus on anti-Asianists, and locates his work firmly within U.S. immigration history, seeing the generalizations that apply to most immigrants as fitting most Asians. And he explains that the book and his life's work is to place the Asian American experience within American history, as "a minor motif that is essential to an understanding of the whole."[82]

ASIAN AMERICANISTS

Liberals inhabit a broad spectrum of intentions, including a desire to defend Asians from negative stereotypes and charges leveled by anti-Asianists, to shape a pro-Asian public and foreign relations policy, to advocate internationalism and world peace, to promote a Christian social gospel, to create a uniquely American social science, and to affirm the triumphalist narrative of American history. Although some boldly assumed to speak for Asians, liberals rarely concerned themselves with the perspectives and voices of their ostensible unit of study: Asian Americans, who were, at base, largely incidental to the wider purposes of the authors. In addition, liberals mainly addressed themselves to white America where they continued their contest for influence with the anti-Asianists.

Asian Americanists are concerned with the experiences of Asians in America as a legitimate subject matter quite apart from the problems Asians presumably posed for white Americans. Of course, writers in the Asian Americanist tradition saw their subjects within the more expansive field of U.S. social relations and history, and, clearly, many of them held more complex motives than a singular drive to understand the Asian American experience for its own sake. But what distinguishes them from the anti-Asianists and liberals is the centrality of Asian Americans as their subject matter, authors, and principal readers. Their originating desire was to record and document a people's history: for remembrance as well as the building of a collective sense of community. Asian Americanist writings emerged during the rise of liberalism in the 1920s and supplanted it, eventually, in the 1970s.

Takashi Tsutsumi, secretary of the Federation of Japanese Labor, in 1921 published *Hawaii Undo Shi,* which was translated as "History of Hawaii Laborers' Movement" by an undercover agent of the Hawaiian Sugar Planters' Association; the association exercised a monopoly over sugar production in the islands. Tsutsumi's history was subversive literature to the sugar planters because it chronicled the abuse of the plantation system, the resistance to those injustices, and the union's version of the 1920 strike that involved 8,300 Filipino and Japanese sugar workers, or about 77 percent of the entire plantation workforce on the island of Oahu. Besides raising the class consciousness of first-generation Japanese workers, Tsutsumi hoped to refute some of the planters' claims that the strike was a conspiracy by Japan to take over Hawai'i's economy. Capitalist exploitation and plantation maltreatment, he wrote, and not Japanese nationalism prompted the great strike. And worker resistance is universal, springing from "capitalistic tyranny" and the "heart of men oppressed for ages by the capitalists."[83]

The need to preserve the past became more urgent with the demise of the first generation, who lived and made Japanese American history, and the rise of the second and third generations, who held few memories of that past. Unlike Tsutsumi's book, which was written in Japanese for the first generation, Ernest K. Wakukawa's A *History of the Japanese People in Hawaii* (1938) was written in English because, the writer explains, "today [1938] the second and third generation Americans of Japanese ancestry already outnumber the first generation Japanese by approximately three to one, and English and not Japanese is the medium of expression for the former." Memories are fragile, Wakukawa warns, and there are few accounts to instill in succeeding generations an "appreciation of the achievements and accomplishments of the pioneers and their forebears" and help them understand "their own status and problems in the light of history." Although, like liberal works that are formulated around the charges of the anti-Asianists (such as Japan's alleged designs on Hawai'i and the ostensibly un-American nature of Japanese language schools, the Japanese press, dual citizenship, and picture brides), Wakukawa's book also shows how Japanese migrants became Americans by challenging discrimination and striking for a "living wage," most notably in the Oahu strikes of 1909 and 1920.[84] Problematic were the inequities of the plantation system, not the workers, the institutions and not their victims.

Toshio Mori, like his contemporary Hisaye Yamamoto, wrote short stories that recorded and elucidated Japanese American social history. Their principal interest was the first generation, and, like Ernest Wakukawa, they chronicled their everyday lives for those who followed. Both writers offer sensitive and moving portrayals of women, especially, as well as the passions and conflicts that accompany poverty and racism and the universal human condition. Mori was particularly motivated to write against the prevailing caricatures of Japanese in American fiction, and although his first book, *Yokohama California* (1949), was well-received by white critics, some found his use of language awkward. While praising Mori as "probably one of the most important new writers in the country at the moment," William Saroyan writes, in his introduction to *Yokohama California*, "any high school teacher of English would flunk him in grammar and punctuation."[85] Mori, however, wrote in a language and cadence true to his subjects, unlike the fictive taunts of anti-Asianist Wallace Irwin's Hashimura Togo, and he was a predecessor of Asian American writers like Milton Murayama, who wrote in and thereby helped to codify Hawaiian Creole, commonly called pidgin English.[86]

The production of books on Asian Americans during the 1960s and 1970s nearly equaled the total number published from the nineteenth century to 1959. That veritable effusion of works sprang from the well of ethnic and racial consciousness in the United States and the post–World War II decolonization struggles of "Third World" peoples that inspired the domestic American drive for civil rights, social transformation, and educational reform.[87] Like their forebears, Asian Americanists tried to recover vanishing and buried pasts and construct a collective identity in the struggle for equality and the promise of American democracy, but they also used the contemporary rhetoric of "decolonizing" the academy and its research and curriculum. That self-conscious effort to produce a body of writings that gave "voice" and "agency" to hitherto "silenced" peoples and points of view and the institutionalization of Asian American studies courses and programs resulted in the publication of readers for classroom use,[88] reference works, including bibliographies, dictionaries, and chronologies,[89] and community studies written by and for members of various ethnic communities.[90] This democratization of history—the idea that ordinary lives were historical objects and that history belonged to everyone—continued through the next decades.[91]

The most important of the Asian Americanist textbooks is *Roots: An Asian American Reader* (1971), assembled by a group of editors at UCLA's Asian American Studies Center. Not only was *Roots* the first; its subject matters defined the major questions of the field. The reader was hastily assembled, one of its editors note, because of "the lack of appropriate materials in readily accessible form" and because of "the need for a convenient anthology focusing on the lives of our people. . . . These are critical times for Asian Americans and it is imperative that their voices be heard in all their anger, anguish, resolve and inspiration." Combining both the experiential with the analytical through creative writing, interviews, and academic studies, the editors delineated the core topics of any introductory course in Asian American studies—identity, history, and community. Asian Americans, the editors agree, must define their own identities and must not succumb to stereotypes created by the media. In the process, "they will regain a sense of ego identity and unity that will allow them to act for changing the oppressed positions of Asians and other Americans." Asian Americanist history, *Roots* states, "is *essentially* devoted to analyzing historical events in terms of their significance for Asian Americans rather than a concept that is *primarily* concerned with lavishing praise upon the mechanisms of American democracy." And the search for community, the anthology reminds its readers, is prompted by a pan-Asian and transnational quest for identity and history. "As Asian Americans are recovering their identity and rediscovering their history in America," an editor explains in the midst of the American war in Vietnam, "there is a greater identification with their communities and its problems and people. What is emerging perhaps is a true community, entailing a recognition of responsibility among Asian people toward one another that supercedes the geographical boundaries of the community. For what is truly being considered is the collective fate of Asian people in a society wracked by a racist war in Asia and by racial and economic inequities at home."[92]

During the 1980s and 1990s, publications on Asian Americans more than doubled the output of the previous two decades. Temple University Press began the first book series in Asian Americans studies in 1991, and other university presses launched their Asian American studies series shortly thereafter. The Association for Asian American Studies, the field's professional organization, produced the second academic journal in Asian American studies,[93] the *Journal of Asian American Studies*, in 1998, published by the nation's oldest university press, Johns Hopkins University Press. And many creative writers garnered critical acclaim and commercial success with Asian American topics. A breakthrough book was Maxine Hong Kingston's *Woman Warrior* (1975), which won the National Book Critics Circle nonfiction book award in 1976 and has become the most studied and read work in the Asian American literary canon.[94] Cultural producers have, in turn, enabled cultural critics, who have been at the forefront of defining, organizing, and criticizing Asian American literatures and their disciplinary contexts.[95]

Community studies by Asian Americanists draw from the tradition of the Chicago school of sociology in that they favor urban settings over rural ones and sought to influence public policy and promote social change. But, unlike liberals, who conceive of their studies as tests of theories and social processes external to those communities and as social problems, Asian Americanists frame their labors as a means toward community identity formation and empowerment. Further, Asian Americanists are moved by the ideal of connecting their research and teaching in Asian American studies to the lives of their subjects, Asian Americans and their communities. And, increasingly, Asian Americanists have expanded their range of community studies to rural areas, to groups other than Chinese and Japanese, to specific community issues, especially economic and social organization and stratification, and to conceptions of spatial configurations and global contexts and alignments. Asian Americanists, like anti-Asianists and liberals, are not an undifferentiated group, and they address diverse audiences and hold conflicting motivations and points of view.[96]

Asian Americanists responded to anti-Asianists in different ways. Some sought to refute anti-Asianist charges that Asians were unassimilable by stressing the *American* part of the *Asian American* label. Asians are very American, contribute to American life and letters, and are not to be confused with Asians in Asia. Asian American studies is American studies pure and simple. Another response stressed the connections in the United States between peoples of color and their links with Third World peoples across national borders. The Asian American struggle, in this version, is an offspring of the civil rights movements of African Americans, Latina/os, and Native Americans and with the post–World War II decolonization efforts of Third World nations. In that way, anti-Asianists prompted both national and transnational responses among Asian Americanists. Even the racialized category "Asian American" is in part a reaction to anti-Asianist and white racial politics that collapse distinctive Asian ethnic groups into an undifferentiated whole, prompting similar and connected experiences in the United States, which form the bases for pan-Asian coalitions. The Asian American identity is thus constituted by anti-Asianism.

Even as anti-Asianists circumscribed liberals by their audiences, subject matters, and interpretations, liberals constrained Asian Americanists. In truth, Asian Americanists are more a continuation than a break from the past, despite their criticisms of their anti-Asianist and liberal predecessors. They react to and build upon these foundations and adopt, sometimes uncritically, some of the major liberal topics and interpretations, chiefly because they fail to provide alternative theories and explanations. Asian Americanist historical narratives generally begin with immigration, looking from this shore outward, and its "push" and "pull" hypothesis, and the processes of assimilation and acculturation, of cultural contact, conflict, and resolution comprise the story's core. Social relations pivot on the white-Asian axis, and although they are sometimes and increasingly differentiated by ethnicity, gender, and class, both racializations of white and Asian remain largely unproblematized. Asians are still victimized by and resistant to whites. Moreover, Asian Americanists have had little impact upon the writing of U.S. history as seen in the standard textbooks wherein Asians, when included, continue to appear in familiar roles as immigrants, as the objects of U.S. expansion, as enemies and allies in America's wars in Asia, as domestic victims of anti-Asianism, as contributors, and as model minorities.

Liberalism infuses Asian Americanist writings in some of their choice of subject matter, such as Japanese Americans during World War II. The topic's appeal is both a product of a liberal concern for constitutional rights and an Asian Americanist yearning for a sense of community rooted in a past shared by all Asian ethnicities.[97] The liberal interpretation states that anti-Asianism directed its venom successively at the Chinese, Japanese, Koreans, Asian Indians, and Filipinos. The World War II concentration camps were a culmination of that West Coast movement of politicians, labor unions, and business groups.[98] Insofar as Asian Americanists subscribe to that formulation, they owe an intellectual debt to Mary Roberts Coolidge's California thesis and the social science research projects of World War II that posited the links between the anti-Chinese and anti-Japanese movements and the concentration camps.

Ronald Takaki's *Pau Hana: Plantation Life and Labor in Hawaii, 1835–1920* (1983) and *Strangers from a Different Shore: A History of Asian Americans* (1989) illustrate the persistence of liberalism in Asian Americanist writings. *Pau Hana* is important because it intervenes in the liberal and Asian Americanist tendency to portray Hawai'i's race relations as exceptional and at variance with the West Coast experience of Asian exclusion and segregation. Takaki draws from his training in African American history to depict Hawai'i's sugar plantations and its social relations as parallel institutions and practices with the plantation and slave systems of the U.S. South. Also, *Pau Hana* was inspired by Takaki's personal search for identity and community. He recalls how his uncle's question of writing a book about "us" began his search into Hawai'i's plantation past. At the same time, the book's organizing theme is a liberal one—the multiethnic workforce and its responses to the planters in shaping of Hawai'i's diverse cultures and ethnic groups. Takaki transports that narrative to his next book, *Strangers from a Different Shore*, the first comprehensive history of Asian Americans. He begins the book with multicultural Hawai'i, where "an array of nationalities from different shores were living together and sharing their cultures and a common language," and carries that forward with the diversity of experiences in America among Chinese, Japanese, Koreans, Asian Indians, Filipinos, and Southeast Asian refugees. A culmination of that trajectory, both in terms of his subject matters and audiences, is in Takaki's *A Different Mirror: A History of Multicultural America* (1993), which expands his canvas to include Europeans, Africans, Latina/os, Asians, and American Indians.[99]

Although liberalism informs much of their writings, Asian Americanists have expanded the field of study in significant ways. Although their bias is still with Chinese and Japanese Americans such that these commonly pose as the template for other Asian groups, Asian Americanists have studied Asian Indians, Filipinos, Hmong, Koreans, Okinawans, Vietnamese, and biracials and pan-ethnicities.[100] They have published memoirs, autobiographies, and letters and deployed oral history as a method to recover obscured pasts as well as to valorize the lives of individual "ordinary" people.[101] Gender remains normalized as men's experiences, especially in the historical treatment of various Asian "bachelor societies," but women's histories have begun to emerge as central along with gender's articulations through racial formations.[102] Underdeveloped are class analyses, despite their great promise for explaining Asian American labor and economic history, community social stratification, and transnationalisms.[103] Exemplary of class analyses' power to refigure Asian American history is Lucie Cheng and Edna Bonacich's edited *Labor Immigration Under Capitalism* (1984). Migration is placed within the context of European and U.S. capitalism, imperialism, and the mutual processes of development at the core and underdevelopment at the periphery. Migrants were both displaced in Asia and attracted to the United States by capitalism's career, and that in turn structured community and class formation in Asian America.[104]

In studies on community, Asian American studies is pervaded by regionalism in the form of California centrism and urbanism, although unrecognized and generalized as not merely primary but also pattern setting. These assumptions are being questioned increasingly, however, by works set in rural areas and places outside of California. These have shown that agricultural spaces offer variations on anti-Asianisms, resistances, and social formations from those in urban centers, even as they reveal the arbitrary distinctions of city from farm.[105] Asian Americanists have also expanded the literatures of critical race theory and legal history and literary and cultural criticism.[106] And they have examined the nature of ethnic identity and its articulations with gender and sexuality.[107] Students can choose from several different synthetic texts and anthologies, teachers can reflect on their pedagogies, and scholars have the luxury to comment on the position of Asians in American society based upon a reliable and fairly substantial body of secondary work.[108] Some of the most promising Asian Americanist work engages feminist and queer theory, cultural and postcolonial studies, and notions of diaspora and transnationalism. Asian Americanists have advanced beyond liberalism.

In truth, the three interpretive strands I have proposed for Asian American studies are neither completely distinctive one from the other nor confined to particular historical periods. Anti-Asianists held liberal ideas about American democracy, liberals sought to recover Asian American voices, and Asian Americanists claimed to speak for their subjects as much as the anti-Asianists and liberals. Pierton Dooner's *Last Days of the Republic* (1879), published amidst industrialization, urbanization, and U.S. expansionism, has resemblances to Michael Crichton's "revisionist" novel *Rising Sun* (1992), which appeared in the throes of U.S. capitalism's crisis, urban decay, and reactive white nationalism. Despite their opposing contexts, they both warn against the peril of Asian takeovers of white America in the name of "deductive history" and science. Those continuities and changes can be traced in anti-Asianist writings on race and genetics from the early to late twentieth century. Stanley D. Porteus, a psychologist at the University of Hawai'i, proposed an instrument for intelligence measurement in 1914 called the Porteus maze test. Although he argues that there is no justification for claims of racial superiority because "racial group differences indicated by mental tests may be and frequently are counterbalanced by superiority of equipment in other directions," Porteus contends that geographical isolation has created physical differences of skin color, brain size, and their "mental and temperamental correlates." His maze test, Porteus reports, shows that the Chinese are more literary, with visual memories, and the Japanese more mechanical, with rote memories.[109] During the 1920s and 1930s, Lothrop Stoddard and Madison Grant advanced a similar argument in their claim of racial difference and their mental and behavioral correlates, while parting company with Porteus in their valuations of superior and inferior races. And, in the 1990s, psychologist J. Philippe Rushton proposed that gene-based evolutionary theory proved racial differences that were both physical and behavioral, with Asians as the most intelligent but least sexual, Africans the least intelligent and most sexual, and Europeans between Asians and Africans.[110] Social scientists Richard J. Herrnstein and Charles Murray reached a similar conclusion about race and intelligence in their book *The Bell Curve* (1994).[111]

Anti-Asianists figure prominently in Asian American historiography because they asked the questions and addressed the audiences that established the terms of the debate. Asians, they charged, were a problem for American society as aliens both abroad and at home. In answer, liberals framed their rebuttals similarly, as problems but also as affirmations of American democracy. Asian Americanists took up in a rejection of the liberal paradigm with its inward turn by, for, and from the perspective of Asian Americans and its lack of faith in the liberating capacities of American institutions. Along with the changing demography and times, Asian Americanists face new challenges addressing and speaking for more diverse populations of ethnicities, sexualities, classes, generations, citizenships, religious beliefs, and political agendas in a variety of places across the United States. Most Asian Americanists have, perhaps in part because of these demographic transformations, parted company with the original idea of a single pan-Asian community formation and instead propose multiple and shifting identities and communities. And many have begun to engage in conversations beyond the racialized group in recognition of the complicities of race with gender, sexuality, class, and nation and of the need to transform the disciplines even as Asian American historiography attempts to establish itself as a coherent field of study. Some of the most significant works, in my view, are those that complicate, with an eye toward eradicating, the dualisms and hierarchies of the U.S. social formation.

ACKNOWLEDGMENT

I must thank my Cornell University graduate student assistants, Sue J. Kim and Cheryl Higashida, whose research work in the summer and fall of 1998 greatly facilitated the writing of this essay, which is an updated and revised version of a chapter in my *Teaching Asian American History* (Washington, D.C.: American Historical Association, 1997), 31–45, 50–57.

NOTES

1. For a dated but still useful bibliographic review of writings on Asian Americans, see Shirley Hune, *Pacific Migration to the United States: Trends and Themes in Historical and Sociological Literature*, Research Institute on Immigration and Ethnic Studies Bibliographic Studies No. 2 (Washington, D.C.: Smithsonian Institution, 1977). For more recent reviews, see Sucheng Chan, "Asian American Historiography," *Pacific Historical Review* 65:3 (Aug. 1996): 363–99; and Eileen H. Tamura, "Using the Past to Inform the Future: An Historiography of Hawai'i's Asian and Pacific Islander Americans," *Amerasia Journal* 26:1 (2000): 55–85.

2. Elmer Clarence Sandmeyer, *The Anti-Chinese Movement in California* (Urbana: University of Illinois Press, 1991), 25.

3. Hinton Helper, *Dreadful California*, ed. Lucius Beebe and Charles M. Clegg (Indianapolis: Bobbs-Merrill, 1948), 70, 71, 72, 74, 146, originally published as *The Land of Gold*.

4. P. W. Dooner, *Last Days of the Republic* (San Francisco: Alta California, 1879), 3, 96, 145, 209, 257. Other works in this genre of "deductive history" include Robert

Woltor, *A Short and Truthful History of the Taking of California and Oregon by the Chinese in the Year A.D. 1899* (San Francisco: A. L Bancroft, 1882); and Marsden Manson, *The Yellow Peril in Action: A Possible Chapter in History* (San Francisco: Britton and Rey, 1907).

5. Richard Austin Thompson, *The Yellow Peril, 1890–1924* (New York: Arno, 1978), 18–21.

6. Brooks Adams, *The Law of Civilization and Decay: An Essay on History* (New York: Macmillan, 1895), 286–93.

7. See Alfred T. Mahan, *The Interest of America in Sea Power* (Boston: Little, Brown, 1897), in which he forecasts a clash between Asian and European civilizations, and hence the necessity for the United States to maintain economic power and a strong military to pacify an awakening Asia and protect the citadel of Christian civilization.

8. Homer Lea, *The Valor of Ignorance* (New York: Harper and Brothers, 1909), 8, 24, 115, 307.

9. Madison Grant, *The Passing of the Great Race Or the Racial Basis of European History* (New York: Charles Scribner's Sons, 1916), xxviii, xxxi.

10. See, e.g., Kenneth M. Ludmerer, *Genetics and American Society: A Historical Appraisal* (Baltimore: Johns Hopkins University Press, 1972); Daniel J. Kevles, *In the Name of Eugenics: Genetics and the Uses of Human Heredity* (New York: Alfred A. Knopf, 1985); and Philip R. Reilly, *The Surgical Solution: A History of Involuntary Sterilization in the United States* (Baltimore: Johns Hopkins University Press, 1991).

11. For a review of anti-Asianist renditions in literature, see Elaine H. Kim, *Asian American Literature: An Introduction to the Writings and Their Social Contexts* (Philadelphia: Temple University Press, 1982), 3–14.

12. Quoted in Robert G. Lee, *Orientals: Asians in Popular Culture* (Philadelphia: Temple University Press, 1999), 37.

13. Wallace Irwin, *Letters of a Japanese Schoolboy* (New York: Doubleday, Page, 1909), 21.

14. See, e.g., Sax Rohmer, *The Insidious Dr. Fu-Manchu* (New York: A. L. Burt, 1913).

15. Ibid., 25–26.

16. Ibid., 176, 178–79.

17. Asian women could also be objects of fear as in the trope of "dragon lady." Both images of Asian women—as "lotus blossom" and "dragon lady"—were perhaps best epitomized during this period by actress Anna May Wong. See Judy Chu, "Anna May Wong," in *Counterpoint: Perspectives on Asian America*, ed. Emma Gee (Los Angeles: UCLA Asian American Studies Center, 1976), 284–88. Like Asian women, Asian men's gender and sexuality were ambivalent. Even the "hyper-masculine" Fu Manchu had feminine, "lean and feline" traits. See Rohmer, *Insidious Dr. Fu-Manchu*, 25. See also Gary Y. Okihiro, *Margins and Mainstreams: Asians in American History and Culture* (Seattle: University of Washington Press, 1994), 142–45.

18. Montaville Flowers, *The Japanese Conquest of American Opinion* (New York: George H. Doran, 1917). See Peter B. Kyne, *The Pride of Palomar* (New York: Cosmopolitan Book, 1921), a novel based on Flowers' arguments.

19. Roger Daniels, *The Politics of Prejudice: The Anti-Japanese Movement in California and the Struggle for Japanese Exclusion* (New York: Atheneum, 1970), 81. See also Sandra C. Taylor, *Advocate of Understanding: Sidney Gulick and the Search for Peace With Japan* (Kent, Ohio: Kent State University Press, 1984), 117.

20. Thomas Burke, *Limehouse Nights* (London: Grosset and Dunlap, 1917); and John Gawsworth comp., *The Best Stories of Thomas Burke* (London: Phoenix House, 1950), 8.

21. Lothrop Stoddard, *The Rising Tide of Color Against White World-Supremacy* (New York: Charles Scribner's Sons, 1920), 251.

22. Valentine Stuart McClatchy ed., *Four Anti-Japanese Pamphlets* (New York: Arno, 1978), 2.

23. See Gary Y. Okihiro, *Cane Fires: The Anti-Japanese Movement in Hawaii, 1865–1945* (Philadelphia: Temple University Press, 1991); and Masayo Umezawa Duus, *The Japanese Conspiracy: The Oahu Sugar Strike of 1920* (Berkeley: University of California Press, 1999).

24. Wallace Irwin, *Seed of the Sun* (New York: George H. Doran, 1921); and Kyne, *Pride of Palomar*.

25. See Madison Grant, *The Conquest of a Continent* (New York: Charles Scribner's Sons, 1933), as an example of the persistence of eugenics and anti-Asianist claims during those decades.

26. Alan Hynd, *Betrayal from the East: The Inside Story of Japanese Spies in America* (New York: Stratford, 1943), 286. On the falsity of Hynd's claims, see *Personal Justice Denied*, Report of the Commission on Wartime Relocation and Internment of Civilians (Washington, D.C.: Government Printing Office, 1982), 47–92. In a series of books, John P. Marquand introduces Japanese spy, Mr. Moto. See his *Your Turn, Mr. Moto* (New York: Popular Library, 1935).

27. Gunther Barth, *Bitter Strength: A History of the Chinese in the United States, 1850–1870* (Cambridge: Harvard University Press, 1964). On white philanthropy, see Carol Green Wilson, *Chinatown Quest: The Life Adventures of Donaldina Cameron* (Stanford, Calif.: Stanford University Press, 1931); and Mildred Crowl Martin, *Chinatown's Angry Angel: The Story of Donaldina Cameron* (Palo Alto, Calif.: Pacific Books, 1977).

28. See, e.g., Simon Winchester, *Pacific Nightmare: How Japan Starts World War III, A Future History* (New York: Ivy Books, 1992); Joe Weber, *Honorable Enemies* (New York: Jove Books, 1994); and Tom Clancy, *Debt of Honor* (New York: G. P. Putnam's Sons, 1994).

29. Michael Crichton, *Rising Sun* (New York: Ballantine Books, 1992), 397.

30. Pat Choate, *Agents of Influence* (New York: Alfred A. Knopf, 1990). See also Clyde V. Prestowitz, Jr., *Trading Places: How We Are Giving Our Future to Japan and How to Reclaim It* (New York: Basic Books, 1989); Karel van Wolferen, *The Enigma of Japanese Power* (New York: Alfred A. Knopf, 1989); and James Fallows, *More Like Us: Putting America's Native Strengths and Traditional Values to Work to Overcome the Asian Challenge* (Boston: Houghton Mifflin, 1989).

31. George Friedman and Meredith Lebard, *The Coming War with Japan* (New York: St. Martin's Press, 1991).

32. Richard Bernstein and Ross H. Munro, *The Coming Conflict with China* (New York: Alfred A. Knopf, 1997).

33. Thurston Clarke, *Pearl Harbor Ghosts: A Journey to Hawaii Then and Now* (New York: William Morrow, 1991), 309, 337; and Joel Kotkin, *Tribes: How Race, Religion and Identity Determine Success in the New Global Economy* (New York: Random House 1993).

34. Samuel P. Huntington, *The Clash of Civilizations and the Remaking of World Order* (New York: Simon and Schuster, 1996).

35. Robert B. Reich, "Is Japan Really out to Get Us?" *New York Times Book Review*, February 9, 1992.

36. William Speer, *The Oldest and the Newest Empire: China and the United States* (Cincinnati: National Publishing, 1870), 3–4. Examples of other books written in this tradition include Otis Gibson, *The Chinese in America* (Cincinnati: Hitchcock and Walden, 1877); and Ira M. Condit, *The Chinaman As We See Him and Fifty Years of Work For Him* (Chicago: Fleming H. Revell, 1900).

37. George F. Seward, *Chinese Immigration, In Its Social and Economical Aspects* (New York: Charles Scribner's Sons, 1881), v.

38. Katharine Coman, *The History of Contract Labor in the Hawaiian Islands* (New York: Macmillan, 1903), 2.

39. Wong Chin Foo, "Why I Am a Heathen?" *North American Review* 145 (Aug. 1887): 171; and Yan Phou Lee, "Why I Am Not a Heathen: A Rejoinder to Wong Chin Foo," *North American Review* 145 (Sept. 1887): 308.

40. See also Wu Tingfang, *America Through the Spectacles of an Oriental Diplomat* (New York: Frederick A. Stokes, 1914); and No-Yong Park, *An Oriental View of American Civilization* (Boston: Hale, Cushman and Flint, 1934).

41. Yung Wing, *My Life in China and America* (New York: Henry Holt, 1909), iii, iv. See also No-Yong Park's autobiography, *Chinaman's Chance* (Boston: Meador, 1940); and K. Scott Wong, "Cultural Defenders and Brokers: Chinese Responses of the Anti-Chinese Movement," in *Claiming America: Constructing Chinese American Identities During the Exclusion Era*, ed. K. Scott Wong and Sucheng Chan (Philadelphia: Temple University Press, 1998), 3–40.

42. Stuart Creighton Miller, *The Unwelcome Immigrant: The American Image of the Chinese, 1785–1882* (Berkeley: University of California Press, 1969), 3–5.

43. Mary Roberts Coolidge, *Chinese Immigration* (New York: Henry Holt, 1909), 21, 29, 39, 40, 53, 57–58, 59, 61, 182.

44. Ibid., 495.

45. Taylor, *Advocate of Understanding*, xiii.

46. Sidney L. Gulick, *The American Japanese Problem: A Study of the Racial Relations of the East and West* (New York: Charles Scribner's Sons, 1914). The Council's petition is quoted in H. A. Millis, *The Japanese Problem in the United States* (New York: Macmillan, 1915), vii–viii, a book commissioned by the Council.

47. Taylor, *Advocate of Understanding*, 138–41; and Yuji Ichioka, "Attorney for the Defense: Yamato Ichihashi and Japanese Immigration," *Pacific Historical Review* 55:2 (May 1986): 192–225.

48. Kiyoshi K. Kawakami, *Asia At the Door: A Study of the Japanese Question in*

Continental United States, Hawaii and Canada (New York: Fleming H. Revell, 1914); and K. K. Kawakami, *The Real Japanese Question* (New York: Macmillan, 1921).

49. Ernest Burgess and Donald Bogue, eds., *Contributions to Urban Sociology* (Chicago: University of Chicago Press, 1964), 326.

50. Robert E. Park, introduction to *The Japanese Invasion: A Study in the Psychology of Inter-Racial Contacts*, by Jesse Frederick Steiner (Chicago: A. C. McClurg, 1917), vii–xvii. See also Park's posthumous collection of essays, *Race and Culture* (Glencoe, Ill.: Free Press, 1950).

51. Selected books include the following: Romanzo Adams, *Interracial Marriage in Hawaii* (New York: Macmillan, 1938); Yamato Ichihashi, *Japanese in the United States: A Critical Study of the Problems of the Japanese Immigrants and Their Children* (Stanford, Calif.: Stanford University Press, 1932); Rose Hum Lee, *The Growth and Decline of Chinese Communities in the Rocky Mountain Region* (New York: Arno, 1978); Eliot Grinnell Mears, *Resident Orientals on the American Pacific Coast: Their Legal and Economic Status* (Chicago: University of Chicago Press, 1928); Shotaro Frank Miyamoto, *Social Solidarity Among the Japanese of Seattle* (Seattle: University of Washington, 1939); and Paul C. P. Siu, *The Chinese Laundryman: A Study of Social Isolation* (New York: New York University Press, 1987). From the 1930s at the University of Southern California, Emory Bogardus directed a significant number of graduate students, many Filipino Americans, who wrote theses and dissertations on Filipino American topics.

52. For a study of Park's influence in Asian American studies, see Henry Yu, "The 'Oriental Problem' in America, 1920–1960: Linking the Identities of Chinese American and Japanese American Intellectuals," in Wong and Chan, *Claiming America*, 191–214.

53. Miyamoto, *Social Solidarity*.

54. Rajani Kanta Das, *Hindustani Workers on the Pacific Coast* (Berlin: Walter de Gruyter, 1923).

55. Dhan Gopal Mukerji, *Caste and Outcast* (New York: E. P. Dutton, 1923), 153, 155, 160–62, 166–74, 188–206, 252–82, 301, 302–03.

56. Sudhindra Bose, *Mother America: Realities of American Life as Seen by an Indian* (Raopura, India: M. S. Bhatt, 1934), 65, 67, 72, 243, 285. See also Krishnalal Shridharani, *My India, My America* (New York: Duell, Sloan and Pearce, 1941).

57. Kim, *Asian American Literature*, 32–43.

58. Bruno Lasker, *Filipino Immigration to Continental United States and to Hawaii* (Chicago: University of Chicago Press, 1931).

59. Paul G. Cressey, *The Taxi-Dance Hall: A Sociological Study in Commercialized Recreation and City Life* (Chicago: University of Chicago Press, 1932), 109–10, 145, 153, 161, 167.

60. Ralph S. Kuykendall, *The Hawaiian Kingdom: Foundation and Transformation*, 1778–1854 (Honolulu: University Press of Hawaii, 1938), vii, xi, 3. See also Kuykendall, *The Hawaiian Kingdom: Twenty Critical Years, 1854–1874* (Honolulu: University of Hawaii Press, 1953); and *The Hawaiian Kingdom: The Kalakaua Dynasty, 1874–1893* (Honolulu: University of Hawaii Press, 1967).

61. William Carlson Smith, *The Second Generation Oriental in America* (Honolulu: Institute of Pacific Relations, 1927); and William Carlson Smith, *Americans in Process: A Study of Our Citizens of Oriental Ancestry* (Ann Arbor: Edwards Brothers, 1937). See also Edward K. Strong, *The Second Generation Japanese Problem* (Stanford, Calif.: Stanford University Press, 1934); and Reginald Bell, *Public School Education of Second-Generation Japanese in California* (Stanford, Calif.: Stanford University Press, 1935).

62. Smith, *Second Generation*, 8, 11.

63. For a review of these works, see Kim, *Asian American Literature*, 14–22.

64. Earl Derr Biggers, *The House Without a Key* (New York: Grosset and Dunlap, 1925), 76, 84.

65. Carlos Bulosan, *America Is in the Heart* (New York: Harcourt, Brace, 1943), 326, 327. Cf. Marilyn Alquizola, "The Fictive Narrator of America Is in the Heart," in *Frontiers of Asian American Studies: Writing, Research, and Commentary*, ed. Gail M. Nomura et al. (Pullman: Washington State University Press, 1989), 211–17; and Marilyn Alquizola, "Subversion or Affirmation: The Text and Subtext of *America Is in the Heart*," in Asian Americans: Comparative and Global Perspectives, ed. Shirley Hune et al. (Pullman: Washington State University Press, 1991), 199–209.

66. Pardee Lowe, *Father and Glorious Descendant* (Boston: Little, Brown, 1943).

67. Jade Snow Wong, *Fifth Chinese Daughter* (New York: Harper and Row, 1950).

68. Alexander H. Leighton, *The Governing of Men: General Principles and Recommendations Based on Experience at a Japanese Relocation Camp* (Princeton, N.J.: Princeton University Press, 1945).

69. Dorothy Swaine Thomas and Richard S. Nishimoto, *The Spoilage* (Berkeley: University of California Press, 1946); and Dorothy Swaine Thomas, *The Salvage* (Berkeley: University of California Press, 1952).

70. Jacobus tenBroek, Edward N. Barnhart, and Floyd W. Matson, *Prejudice, War, and the Constitution* (Berkeley: University of California Press, 1954); Morton Grodzins, *Americans Betrayed: Politics and the Japanese Evacuation* (Chicago: University of Chicago Press, 1949); and Rosalie H. Wax, *Doing Fieldwork: Warnings and Advice* (Chicago: University of Chicago Press, 1971).

71. See, e.g., Consulate-General of Japan, comp., *Documental History of Law Cases Affecting Japanese Americans in the United States, 1916–1924*, 2 vols. (San Francisco: Consulate-General of Japan, 1925).

72. Milton R. Konvitz, *The Alien and the Asiatic in American Law* (Ithaca, N.Y.: Cornell University Press, 1946), viii, ix. Other legal histories include Frank F. Chuman, *The Bamboo People: The Law and Japanese-Americans* (Del Mar, Calif.: Publisher's Inc., 1976); Moritoshi Fukuda, *Legal Problems of Japanese-Americans: Their History and Development in the United States* (Tokyo: Keio Tsushin, 1980); Charles J. McClain, *In Search of Equality: The Chinese Struggle against Discrimination in Nineteenth-Century America* (Berkeley: University of California Press, 1994); and Lucy E. Salyer, *Laws Harsh as Tigers: Chinese Immigrants and the Shaping of Modern Immigration Law* (Chapel Hill: University of North Carolina Press, 1995).

73. Louise Yim, *My Forty Year Fight for Korea* (New York: A. A. Wyn, 1951).

74. Richard Mason, *The World of Suzie Wong* (London: Collins, 1957), 300. For a critical reading of the film version, see Gina Marchetti *Romance and the "Yellow Peril"*:

Race, Sex, and Discursive Strategies in Hollywood Fiction (Berkeley: University of California Press, 1993), 109–24.

75. Lawrence H. Fuchs, *Hawaii Pono: A Social History* (New York: Harcourt, Brace and World, 1961), 449.

76. Betty Lee Sung, *Mountain of Gold: The Story of the Chinese in America* (New York: Macmillan, 1967), 2. See also Rose Hum Lee, *The Chinese in the United States of America* (Hong Kong: Hong Kong University Press, 1960); and S. W. Kung, *Chinese in American Life: Some Aspects of Their History, Status, Problems, and Contributions* (Seattle: University of Washington Press, 1962).

77. Bill Hosokawa, *Nisei: The Quiet Americans* (New York: William Morrow, 1969), xvi, 473.

78. Daniels, *Politics of Prejudice*; Barth, *Bitter Strength*; Stuart Creighton Miller, *The Unwelcome Immigrant: The American Image of the Chinese, 1785–1882* (Berkeley: University of California Press, 1969); and Alexander Saxton, *The Indispensable Enemy: Labor and the Anti-Chinese Movement in California* (Berkeley: University of California Press, 1971).

79. Ved Mehta, *Face to Face: An Autobiography* (Boston: Little, Brown, 1957); D. S. Saund, *Congressman from India* (New York: E. P. Dutton, 1960); Easurk Emsen Charr, *The Golden Mountain* (Boston: Forum Publishing, 1961); Daniel K. Inouye, *Journey to Washington* (Englewood Cliffs, N.J.: Prentice Hall, 1967); and Li Ling Ai, *Life is for a Long Time: A Chinese Hawaiian Memoir* (New York: Hastings House, 1972).

80. H. Brett Melendy, *Asians in America: Filipinos, Koreans, and East Indians* (Boston: G. K. Hall, 1977); Bong-young Choy, *Koreans in America* (Chicago: Nelson-Hall, 1979); Tricia Knoll, *Becoming Americans: Asian Sojourners, Immigrants, and Refugees in the Western United States* (Portland, Ore.: Coast to Coast Books, 1982); and Harry H. L. Kitano and Roger Daniels, *Asian Americans: Emerging Minorities* (Englewood Cliffs, N.J.: Prentice Hall, 1988).

81. See, e.g., James W. Loewen, *The Mississippi Chinese: Between Black and White* (Cambridge: Harvard University Press, 1971); Roger Daniels and Harry H. L. Kitano, *American Racism: Exploration of the Nature of Prejudice* (Englewood Cliffs, N.J.: Prentice Hall, 1970); Hyung-chan Kim, ed., *The Korean Diaspora: Historical and Sociological Studies of Korean Immigration and Assimilation in North America* (Santa Barbara, Calif.: ABC-Clio, 1977); and Gail Paradise Kelly, *From Vietnam to America: A Chronicle of the Vietnamese Immigration to the United States* (Boulder, Colo.: Westview Press, 1977).

82. Roger Daniels, *Asian America: Chinese and Japanese in the United States since 1850* (Seattle: University of Washington Press, 1988), 4, 8. See also Kitano and Daniels, *Asian Americans*.

83. Takashi Tsutsumi, *History of Hawaii Laborers' Movement*, trans. Umetaro Okamura (Honolulu: Hawaiian Sugar Planters' Association, 1922) (University of Hawaii at Manoa, Hamilton Library).

84. Ernest K. Wakukawa, *A History of the Japanese People in Hawaii* (Honolulu: Toyo Shoin, 1938), xvii, xix.

85. William Saroyan, introduction to *Yokohama California*, by Toshio Mori (Cald-

well, Idaho: Caxton Printers, 1949), 1. On Hisaye Yamamoto, see her *Seventeen Syllables and Other Stories* (Latham, N.Y.: Kitchen Table: Women of Color Press, 1988).

86. Milton Murayama, *All I Asking For Is My Body* (San Francisco: Supa Press, 1959); *Five Years on a Rock* (Honolulu: University of Hawaii Press, 1994); and *Plantation Boy* (Honolulu: University of Hawai'i Press, 1998).

87. For review essays on works published from the 1960s to the 1990s, see Sucheng Chan, "Asians in the United States: A Selected Bibliography of Writings Published since the 1960s," in *Reflections on Shattered Windows: Promises and Prospects for Asian American Studies*, ed. Gary Y. Okihiro et al. (Pullman: Washington State University Press, 1988), 214–37; Sucheng Chan, "A Selected Bibliography and List of Films on the Vietnamese, Cambodian, and Laotian Experience in Southeast Asia and the United States," in *New Visions in Asian American Studies: Diversity, Community, Power*, ed. Franklin Ng et al. (Pullman: Washington State University Press, 1994), 63–110; and the last number of each volume of *Amerasia Journal*, which, since 1977, has assembled a list of works published on Asian Americans during that year.

88. Thomas W. Chinn, ed., *A History of the Chinese in California: A Syllabus* (San Francisco: Chinese Historical Society of America, 1969); Stanford M. Lyman, *The Asian in the West*, Social Science and Humanities Publication No. 4 (Reno: Western Studies Center, University of Nevada System, 1970); University of California, *Asian Women* (Berkeley: University of California, 1971); Amy Tachiki et al., eds., *Roots: An Asian American Reader* (Los Angeles: UCLA Asian American Studies Center, 1971); Frank Chin et al., eds., *Aiiieeeee! An Anthology of Asian-American Writers* (Garden City, N.Y.: Anchor, 1974); Gee, *Counterpoint*; and Jesse Quinsaat, ed., *Letters in Exile: An Introductory Reader on the History of Pilipinos in America* (Los Angeles: UCLA Asian American Studies Center, 1976).

89. See Chan, "Asians in the United States," 214–17.

90. James H. Okahata, ed., *A History of Japanese in Hawaii* (Honolulu: United Japanese Society of Hawaii, 1971); Kazuo Ito, *Issei: A History of Japanese Immigrants in North America*, trans. Shinichiro Nakamura and Jean S. Gerard (Seattle: Japanese Community Service, 1973); and Tin-Yuke Char, ed., *The Sandalwood Mountains: Readings and Stories of the Early Chinese in Hawaii* (Honolulu: University Press of Hawaii, 1975).

91. See, e.g., Kesa Noda, *Yamato Colony: 1906–1960* (Livingston, Calif.: Livingston-Merced Japanese American Citizens League, 1981); Eui-Young Yu et al., eds., *Koreans in Los Angeles: Prospects and Promises* (Los Angeles: California State University Center for Korean-American and Korean Studies, 1982); Filipino Oral History Project, *Voices: A Filipino American Oral History* (Stockton, Calif.: Filipino Oral History Project, 1984); Editorial Committee, *Linking Our Lives: Chinese American Women of Los Angeles* (Los Angeles: Chinese Historical Society of Southern California, 1984); Women of South Asian Descent Collective, eds., *Our Feet Walk the Sky: Women of the South Asian Diaspora* (San Francisco: Aunt Lute Books, 1993); and Hawai'i Area Office of the American Friends Service Committee, *He Alo A He Alo, Face to Face: Hawaiian Voices on Sovereignty* (Honolulu: Hawai'i Area Office of the American Friends Service Committee, 1993).

92. Tachiki, *Roots*, vii, 4, 131, 247.

93. The first was *Amerasia Journal*, initially published by students at Yale University in 1971, and then by the Asian American Studies Center at UCLA.

94. Maxine Hong Kingston, *Woman Warrior: Memoirs of a Girlhood Among Ghosts* (New York: Random House, 1975). Anthologies have shaped the literary formation beginning with Chin, *Aiiieeeee!* See also Eric Chock et al., eds., *Talk Story: An Anthology of Hawaii's Local Writers* (Petronium Press, 1978); Joseph Bruchac, ed., *Breaking Silence, An Anthology of Contemporary Asian American Poets* (Greenfield Center, N.Y.: Greenfield Review Press, 1983); Shirley Geok-lin Lim and Mayumi Tsutakawa, eds., *The Forbidden Stitch: An Asian American Women's Anthology* (Corvallis, Ore.: Calyx Books, 1989); Juliet S. Kono and Cathy Song, eds., *Sister Stew: Fiction and Poetry by Women* (Honolulu: Bamboo Ridge Press, 1991); Garrett Hongo, ed., *The Open Boat: Poems from Asian America* (New York: Doubleday, 1993); Velina Hasu Houston, ed., *The Politics of Life: Four Plays by Asian American Women* (Philadelphia: Temple University Press, 1993); Roberta Uno, ed., *Unbroken Thread: An Anthology of Plays by Asian American Women* (Amherst: University of Massachusetts Press, 1993); Jessica Hagedorn, ed., *Charlie Chan Is Dead: An Anthology of Contemporary Asian American Fiction* (New York: Penguin Books, 1993); Sharon Lim-Hing, ed., *The Very Inside: An Anthology of Writing by Asian and Pacific Islander Lesbian and Bisexual Women* (Toronto, Canada: Sister Vision Press, 1994); Geraldine Kudaka, ed., *On A Bed of Rice: An Asian American Erotic Feast* (New York: Doubleday, 1995); Walter K. Lew, ed., *Premonitions: The Kaya Anthology of New Asian North American Poetry* (New York: Kaya, 1995); Juliana Chang, ed., *Quiet Fire: A Historical Anthology of Asian American Poetry, 1892–1970* (New York: Asian American Writers' Workshop, 1996); Sunaina Maira and Rajini Srikanth, eds., *Contours of the Heart: South Asians Map North America* (New York: Asian American Writers' Workshop, 1996); Barbara Tran et al., eds., *Watermark: Vietnamese American Poetry and Prose* (New York: Asian American Writers' Workshop, 1998); and Bino A. Realuyo, ed., *The NuyorAsian Anthology: Asian American Writings About New York City* (New York: Asian American Writers' Workshop, 1999).

95. See, e.g., Chin, *Aiiieeeee!*; Kim, *Asian American Literature*; Houston A. Baker, Jr., ed., *Three American Literatures: Essays in Chicano, Native American, and Asian-American Literature for Teachers of American Literature* (New York: Modern Language Association of America, 1982); King-Kok Cheung and Stan Yogi, *Asian American Literature: An Annotated Bibliography* (New York: Modern Language Association of America, 1988); A. LaVonne Brown Ruoff and Jerry W. Ward, eds., *Redefining American Literary History* (New York: Modern Language Association of America, 1990); Amy Ling, *Between Worlds: Women Writers of Chinese Ancestry* (New York: Pergamon Press, 1990); Stephen H. Sumida, *And the View from the Shore: Literary Traditions of Hawai'i* (Seattle: University of Washington Press, 1991); Shirley Geok-lin Lim and Amy Ling, eds., *Reading the Literatures of Asian America* (Philadelphia: Temple University Press, 1992); Sau-ling Cynthia Wong, *Reading Asian American Literature: From Necessity to Extravagance* (Princeton, N.J.: Princeton University Press, 1993); King-Kok Cheung, *Articulate Silences: Hisaye Yamamoto, Maxine Hong Kingston, Joy Kogawa* (Ithaca, N.Y.: Cornell University Press, 1993); Lisa Lowe, *Immigrant Acts: On Asian American Cultural Politics* (Durham, N.C.: Duke University Press, 1996); David Lei-

wei Li, *Imagining the Nation: Asian American Literature and Cultural Consent* (Stanford, Calif.: Stanford University Press, 1998); Eileen Tabios, *Black Lightning: Poetry-in-Progress* (New York: Asian American Writers Workshop, 1998); Wendy Ho, *In Her Mother's House: The Politics of Asian American Mother-Daughter Writing* (Walnut Creek, Calif.: AltaMira, 1999); Rachel C. Lee, *The Americas of Asian American Literature: Gendered Fictions of Nation and Transnation* (Princeton, N.J.: Princeton University Press, 1999); David Palumbo-Liu, *Asian/American: Historical Crossings of a Racial Frontie* (Stanford, Calif.: Stanford University Press, 1999); Traise Yamamoto, *Masking Selves, Making Subjects: Japanese American Women, Identity, and the Body* (Berkeley: University of California Press, 1999); Patricia P. Chu, *Assimilating Asians: Gendered Strategies of Authorship in Asian America* (Durham, N.C.: Duke University Press, 2000); and Xizo-huang Yin, *Chinese American Literature since the 1850s* (Urbana: University of Illinois Press, 2000).

96. See, e.g., Victor G. and Brett de Bary Nee, *Longtime Californ': A Documentary Study of an American Chinatown* (New York: Pantheon, 1972); Peter Kwong, *Chinatown, New York: Labor and Politics, 1930–1950* (New York: Monthly Review Press, 1979); Illsoo Kim, *New Urban Immigrants: The Korean Community in New York* (Princeton, N.J.: Princeton University Press, 1981); Timothy J. Lukes and Gary Y. Okihiro, *Japanese Legacy: Farming and Community Life in California's Santa Clara Valley* (Cupertino: California History Center, 1985); Sandy Lydon, *Chinese Gold: The Chinese in the Monterey Bay Region* (Capitola, Calif.: Capitola Book, 1985); Peter Kwong, *The New Chinatown* (New York: Hill and Wang, 1987); Kay J. Anderson, *Vancouver's Chinatown: Racial Discourse in Canada, 1875–1980* (Montreal: McGill-Queen's University Press, 1991); Min Zhou, *Chinatown: The Socioeconomic Potential of an Urban Enclave* (Philadelphia: Temple University Press, 1992); Valerie J. Matsumoto, *Farming the Home Place: A Japanese American Community in California, 1919–1982* (Ithaca, N.Y.: Cornell University Press, 1993); Timothy P. Fong, *America's First Suburban Chinatown: The Remaking of Monterey Park, California* (Philadelphia: Temple University Press, 1994); Nancy Abelmann and John Lie, *Blue Dreams: Korean Americans and the Los Angeles Riots* (Cambridge: Harvard University Press, 1995); John Horton, *The Politics of Diversity: Immigration, Resistance, and Change in Monterey Park, California* (Philadelphia: Temple University Press, 1995); Pyong Gap Min, *Caught in the Middle: Korean Communities in New York and Los Angeles* (Berkeley: University of California Press, 1996); Kyeyoung Park, *The Korean American Dream: Immigrants and Small Business in New York City* (Ithaca, N.Y.: Cornell University Press, 1997); Jere Takahashi, *Nisei/Sansei: Shifting Japanese American Identities and Politics* (Philadelphia: Temple University Press, 1997); Leland T. Saito, *Race and Politics: Asian Americans, Latinos, and Whites in a Los Angeles Suburb* (Urbana: University of Illinois Press, 1998); Jan Lin, *Reconstructing Chinatown: Ethnic Enclave, Global Change* (Minneapolis: University of Minnesota Press, 1998); Edward T. Chang and Jeannette Diaz-Veizades, *Ethnic Peace in the American City: Building Community in Los Angeles and Beyond* (New York: New York University Press, 1999); Kwang Chung Kim, ed., *Koreans in the Hood: Conflict with African Americans* (Baltimore: Johns Hopkins University Press, 1999); Yong Chen, *Chinese San Francisco, 1850–1943: A Trans-Pacific Community* (Stanford, Calif.: Stanford University Press, 2000); Martin F.

Manalansan IV, ed., *Cultural Compass: Ethnographic Explorations of Asian America* (Philadelphia: Temple University Press, 2000); and David K. Yoo, *Growing Up Nisei: Race, Generation, and Culture among Japanese Americans of California, 1924–49* (Urbana: University of Illinois Press, 2000).

97. See, e.g., Roger Daniels, *Concentration Camps, U.S.A.: Japanese Americans and World War II* (New York: Holt, Rinehart and Winston, 1971); Michi Weglyn, *Years of Infamy: The Untold Story of America's Concentration Camps* (New York: William Morrow, 1976); Peter Irons, *Justice At War: The Story of the Japanese American Internment Cases* (New York: Oxford University Press, 1983); John Tateishi, *And Justice for All: An Oral History of the Japanese American Detention Camps* (New York: Random House, 1984); Masayo Umezawa Duus, *Unlikely Liberators: The Men of the 100th and 442nd*, trans. Peter Duus (Honolulu: University of Hawaii Press, 1987); Thomas James, *Exile Within: The Schooling of Japanese Americans, 1942–1945* (Cambridge: Harvard University Press, 1987); Roger Daniels, *Prisoners Without Trial: Japanese Americans in World War II* (New York: Hill and Wang, 1993); Donna K. Nagata, *Legacy of Injustice: Exploring the Cross-Generational Impact of the Japanese American Internment* (New York: Plenum Press, 1993); Sandra C. Taylor, *Jewel of the Desert: Japanese American Internment at Topaz* (Berkeley: University of California Press, 1993); Lyn Crost, *Honor by Fire: Japanese Americans at War in Europe and the Pacific* (Novato, Calif.: Presidio Press, 1994); and Yasuko I. Takezawa, *Breaking the Silence: Redress and Japanese American Ethnicity* (Ithaca, N.Y.: Cornell University Press, 1995).

98. Cf. Okihiro, *Cane Fires*, which locates the origins of the mass removal and detentions on the mainland with the anti-Japanese movement in Hawaii.

99. Ronald Takaki, *Pau Hana: Plantation Life and Labor in Hawaii, 1835–1920* (Honolulu: University of Hawaii Press, 1983); *Strangers from a Different Shore: A History of Asian Americans* (Boston: Little, Brown, 1989), 3; and *A Different Mirror: A History of Multicultural America* (Boston: Little, Brown, 1993).

100. Ethnic Studies Oral History Project, *Uchinanchu: A History of Okinawans in Hawaii* (Honolulu: University of Hawaii Press, 1981); Fred Cordova, *Filipinos: Forgotten Asian Americans* (Dubuque, Iowa: Kendall/Hunt, 1983); Joan M. Jensen, *Passage from India: Asian Indian Immigrants in North America* (New Haven: Yale University Press, 1988); Okinawa Club of America, comp., *History of Okinawans in North America*, trans. Ben Kobashigawa (Los Angeles: UCLA Asian American Studies Center, 1988); Wayne Patterson, *The Korean Frontier in America: Immigration to Hawaii, 1896–1910* (Honolulu: University of Hawaii Press, 1988); Paul R. Spickard, *Mixed Blood: Intermarriage and Ethnic Identity in Twentieth-Century America* (Madison: University of Wisconsin Press, 1989); Yen Le Espiritu, *Asian American Panethnicity: Bridging Institutions and Identities* (Philadelphia: Temple University Press, 1992); Karen Isaksen Leonard, *Making Ethnic Choices: California's Punjabi Mexican Americans* (Philadelphia: Temple University Press, 1992); Maria P. P. Root, ed., *Racially Mixed People in America* (Newbury Park, Calif.: Sage, 1992); Paul James Rutledge, *The Vietnamese Experience in America* (Bloomington: Indiana University Press, 1992); Nazli Kibria, *Family Tightrope: The Changing Lives of Vietnamese Americans* (Princeton, N.J.: Princeton University Press, 1993); Nancy D. Donnelly, *Changing Lives of Refugee Hmong Women* (Seattle: University of Washington Press, 1994); James M. Freeman,

Changing Identities: Vietnamese Americans, 1975–1995 (Boston: Allyn and Bacon, 1995); Vicente L. Rafael, ed., *Discrepant Histories: Translocal Essays on Filipino Cultures* (Philadelphia: Temple University Press, 1995); Maria P. P. Root, ed., *Filipino Americans: Transformation and Identity* (Thousand Oaks, Calif.: Sage, 1997); Shamita Das Dasgupta, ed., *A Patchwork Shawl: Chronicles of South Asian Women in America* (New Brunswick, N.J.: Rutgers University Press, 1998); Lavina Dhingra Shankar and Rajini Srikanth, eds., *A Part, Yet Apart: South Asians in Asian America* (Philadelphia: Temple University Press, 1998); Wayne Patterson, *The Ilse: First-Generation Korean Immigrants in Hawai'i, 1903–1973* (Honolulu: University of Hawai'i Press, 2000); and Vijay Prashad, *The Karma of Brown Folk* (Minneapolis: University of Minnesota Press, 2000).

101. Eileen Sunada Sarasohn, ed., *The Issei: Portrait of a Pioneer, An Oral History* (Palo Alto, Calif.: Pacific Books, 1983); Michi Kodama-Nishimoto et al., *Hanahana: An Oral History Anthology of Hawaii's Working People* (Honolulu: Ethnic Studies Oral History Project, University of Hawaii at Manoa, 1984); Joanna C. Scott, *Indochina's Refugees: Oral Histories from Laos, Cambodia and Vietnam* (Jefferson, N.C.: McFarland, 1989); James M. Freeman, *Hearts of Sorrow: Vietnamese-American Lives* (Stanford, Calif.: Stanford University Press, 1989); Mary Paik Lee, *Quiet Odyssey: A Pioneer Korean Woman in America*, ed. Sucheng Chan (Seattle: University of Washington Press, 1990); Joyce Chapman Lebra, *Women's Voices in Hawaii* (Niwot: University Press of Colorado, 1991); Joann Faung Jean Lee, *Asian American Experiences in the United States: Oral Histories of First to Fourth Generation Americans from China, the Philippines, Japan, India, the Pacific Islands, Vietnam and Cambodia* (Jefferson, N.C.: McFarland, 1991); Craig Scharlin and Lilia V. Villanueva, *Philip Vera Cruz: A Personal History of Filipino Immigrants and the Farmworkers Movement* (Los Angeles: UCLA Labor Center, Institute of Industrial Relations, 1992); Linda Tamura, *The Hood River Issei: An Oral History of Japanese Settlers in Oregon's Hood River Valley* (Urbana: University of Illinois Press, 1993); Usha Welarantna, *Beyond the Killing Fields: Voices of Nine Cambodian Survivors in America* (Stanford, Calif.: Stanford University Press, 1993); Sucheng Chan, ed., *Hmong Means Free: Life in Laos and America* (Philadelphia: Temple University Press, 1994); Steven DeBonis, *Children of the Enemy: Oral Histories of Vietnamese Amerasians and Their Mothers* (Jefferson, N.C.: McFarland, 1995); Yen Le Espiritu, *Filipino American Lives* (Philadelphia: Temple University Press, 1995); Garrett Hongo, ed., *Under Western Eyes: Personal Essays from Asian America* (New York: Anchor Books, 1995); Mary Kimoto Tomita, *Dear Miye: Letters Home from Japan, 1939–1946*, ed. Robert G. Lee (Stanford, Calif.: Stanford University Press, 1995); Elaine H. Kim and Eui-Young Yu, *East to America: Korean American Life Stories* (New York: New Press, 1996); Gordon H. Chang, ed., *Morning Glory, Evening Shadow: Yamato Ichihashi and His Internment Writings, 1942–1945* (Stanford, Calif.: Stanford University Press, 1997); Louis Fiset, *Imprisoned Apart: The World War II Correspondence of an Issei Couple* (Seattle: University of Washington Press, 1997); Lillian Faderman with Ghia Xiong, *I Begin My Life All Over: The Hmong and the American Immigrant Experience* (Boston: Beacon, 1998); Daisy Chun Rhodes, *Passages to Paradise: Early Korean Immigrant Narratives from Hawai'i* (Los Angeles: Academia Koreana, 1998); Eileen Sunada Sarasohn, *Issei Women: Echoes from Another Frontier* (Palo

Alto, Calif.: Pacific Books, 1998); Soo-Young Chin, *Doing What Had to be Done: The Life Narrative of Rosa Yum Kim* (Philadelphia: Temple University Press, 1999); Amy Ling, ed., *Yellow Light: The Flowering of Asian American Arts* (Philadelphia: Temple University Press, 1999); and Pyong Gap Min and Rose Kim, eds., *Struggle for Ethnic Identity: Narratives by Asian American Professionals* (Walnut Creek, Calif.: AltaMira, 1999).

102. University of California, *Asian Women*; Akemi Kikumura, *Through Harsh Winters: The Life of a Japanese Immigrant Woman* (Novato, Calif.: Chandler and Sharp, 1981); Evelyn Nakano Glenn, *Issei, Nisei, Warbride: Three Generations of Japanese American Women in Domestic Service* (Philadelphia: Temple University Press, 1986); Asian Women United of California, ed., *Making Waves: An Anthology of Writings By and About Asian American Women* (Boston: Beacon, 1989); Lee, *Quiet Odyssey*; Jocelyn Linnekin, *Sacred Queens and Women of Consequence: Rank, Gender, and Colonialism in the Hawaiian Islands* (Ann Arbor: University of Michigan Press, 1990); Mei T. Nakano, *Japanese American Women: Three Generations, 1890–1990* (Berkeley: Mina Press, 1990); Mari J. Matsuda, ed., *Called from Within: Early Women Lawyers of Hawai'i* (Honolulu: University of Hawaii Press, 1992); Women of the South Asian Diaspora, *Our Feet Walk the Sky*; Donnelly, *Changing Lives*; Pepi Nieva, ed., *Filipina: Hawaii's Filipino Women* (Filipino Association of University Women, 1994); Benson Tong, *Unsubmissive Women: Chinese Prostitutes in Nineteenth-Century San Francisco* (Norman: University of Oklahoma Press, 1994); Judy Yung, *Unbound Feet: A Social History of Chinese Women in San Francisco* (Berkeley: University of California Press, 1995); Dasgupta, *Patchwork Shawl*; Yen Le Espiritu, *Asian American Women and Men: Labor, Laws, and Love* (Thousand Oaks, Calif.: Sage, 1997); Shirley Hune, *Teaching Asian American Women's History* (Washington, D.C.: American Historical Association, 1997); Sonia Shah, ed., *Dragon Ladies: Asian American Feminists Breathe Fire* (Boston: South End, 1997); Elaine H. Kim et al., eds., *Making More Waves: New Writing by Asian American Women* (Boston: Beacon, 1997); Elaine H. Kim and Chungmoo Choi, eds., *Dangerous Women: Gender and Korean Nationalism* (New York: Routledge, 1998); Huping Ling, *Surviving on the Gold Mountain: A History of Chinese American Women and Their Lives* (Albany: State University of New York Press, 1998); Chin, *Doing What Had to be Done*; George Anthony Peffer, *If They Don't Bring Their Women Here: Chinese Female Immigration before Exclusion* (Urbana: University of Illinois Press, 1999); and Judy Yung, *Unbound Voices: A Documentary History of Chinese Women in San Francisco* (Berkeley: University of California Press, 1999).

103. Noel J. Kent, *Hawaii: Islands Under the Influence* (New York: Monthly Review Press, 1983); Edward D. Beechert, *Working in Hawaii: A Labor History* (Honolulu: University of Hawaii Press, 1985); Ivan Light and Edna Bonacich, *Immigrant Entrepreneurs: Koreans in Los Angeles, 1965–1982* (Berkeley: University of California Press, 1988); Renqiu Yu, *To Save China, To Save Ourselves: The Chinese Hand Laundry Alliance of New York* (Philadelphia: Temple University Press, 1992); Edna Bonacich et al., eds., *Global Production: The Apparel Industry in the Pacific Rim* (Philadelphia: Temple University Press, 1994); Chris Friday, *Organizing Asian American Labor: The Pacific Coast Canned-Salmon Industry, 1870–1942* (Philadelphia: Temple University Press, 1994); Paul Ong et al., eds., *The New Asian Immigration in Los Angeles and*

Global Restructuring (Philadelphia: Temple University Press, 1994); Rob Wilson and Arif Dirlik, eds., *Asia/Pacific as Space of Cultural Production* (Durham, N.C.: Duke University Press, 1995) John E. Reinecke, *The Filipino Piecemeal Sugar Strike of 1924–1925* (Honolulu: Social Science Research Institute, University of Hawai'i, 1996); Peter Kwong, *Forbidden Workers: Illegal Chinese Immigrants and American Labor* (New York: New Press, 1997); Ko-Lin Chin, *Smuggled Chinese: Clandestine Immigration to the United States* (Philadelphia: Temple University Press, 1999); Evelyn Hu-DeHart, ed., *Across the Pacific: Asian Americans and Globalization* (New York: Asia Society, 1999); Shirley Geok-lin Lim, Larry E. Smith, and Wimal Dissanayake, eds., *Transnational Asia Pacific: Gender, Culture, and the Public Sphere* (Urbana: University of Illinois Press, 1999); and Rob Wilson, *Reimagining the American Pacific: From South Pacific to Bamboo Ridge and Beyond* (Durham, N.C.: Duke University Press, 2000).

104. Lucie Cheng and Edna Bonacich, eds., *Labor Immigration Under Capitalism: Asian Workers in the United States Before World War II* (Berkeley: University of California Press, 1984).

105. Lucy M. Cohen, *Chinese in the Post-Civil War South: A People Without a History* (Baton Rouge: Louisiana State University Press, 1984); Alan Takeo Moriyama, *Imingaisha: Japanese Emigration Companies and Hawaii, 1894–1908* (Honolulu: University of Hawaii Press, 1985); Sucheng Chan, *This Bitter-Sweet Soil: The Chinese in California Agriculture, 1860–1910* (Berkeley: University of California Press, 1986); Richard Chalfen, *Turning Leaves: The Photograph Collections of Two Japanese American Families* (Albuquerque: University of New Mexico Press, 1991); Okihiro, *Cane Fires*; Masakazu Iwata, *Planted in Good Soil: A History of the Issei in United States Agriculture*, 2 vols. (New York: Peter Lang, 1992); Elizabeth Buck, *Paradise Remade: The Politics of Culture and History in Hawai'i* (Philadephia: Temple University Press, 1993); Barbara F. Kawakami, *Japanese Immigrant Clothing in Hawaii, 1885–1941* (Honolulu: University of Hawaii Press, 1993); Matsumoto, *Farming the Home Place*; Mitziko Sawada, *Tokyo Life, New York Dreams: Urban Japanese Visions of America, 1890–1924* (Berkeley: University of California Press, 1996).

106. Michael Omi and Howard Winant, *Racial Formation in the United States: From the 1960s to the 1980s* (New York: Routledge and Kegan Paul, 1986); Dana Y. Takagi, *The Retreat from Race: Asian-American Admissions and Racial Politics* (New Brunswick, N.J.: Rutgers University Press, 1992); Gina Marchetti, *Romance and the "Yellow Peril": Race, Sex, and Discursive Strategies in Hollywood Fiction* (Berkeley: University of California Press, 1993); Bill Ong Hing, *Making and Remaking Asian America Through Immigration Policy, 1850–1990* (Stanford, Calif.: Stanford University Press, 1993); Mari J. Matsuda et al., *Words That Wound: Critical Race Theory, Assaultive Speech, and the First Amendment* (Boulder, Colo.: Westview Press, 1993); James S. Moy, *Marginal Sights: Staging the Chinese in America* (Iowa City: University of Iowa Press, 1993); Darrell Y. Hamamoto, *Monitored Peril: Asian Americans and the Politics of TV Representation* (Minneapolis: University of Minnesota Press, 1994); Kimberlé Williams Crenshaw et al., eds., *Critical Race Theory: The Key Writings that Formed the Movement* (New York: New Press, 1995); Ian F. Haney López, *White by Law: The Legal Construction of Race* (New York: New York University Press, 1996); Lowe, *Immigrant Acts*; Mari J. Matsuda, *Where Is Your Body? And Other Essays on Race,*

Gender, and the Law (Boston: Beacon, 1996); Dorinne Kondo, *About Face: Performing Race in Fashion and Theater* (New York: Routledge, 1997); Josephine Lee, *Performing Asian America: Race and Ethnicity on the Contemporary Stage* (Philadelphia: Temple University Press, 1997); Diana Ting Liu Wu, *Asian Pacific Americans in the Workplace* (Walnut Creek, Calif.: AltaMira, 1997); Angelo N. Ancheta, *Race, Rights, and the Asian American Experience* (New Brunswick, N.J.: Rutgers University Press, 1998); Li, *Imagining the Nation*; Mia Tuan, *Forever Foreigners or Honorary Whites? The Asian Ethnic Experience Today* (New Brunswick, N.J.: Rutgers University Press, 1998); Jun Xing, *Asian America Through the Lens: History, Representations, and Identity* (Walnut Creek, Calif.: AltaMira, 1998); Alice Yang, *Why Asia? Contemporary Asian and Asian American Art* (New York: New York University Press, 1998); Alvin Eng, ed., *Tokens? The NYC Asian American Experience on Stage* (New York: Asian American Writers' Workshop, 1999); Lee, *The Americas of Asian American Literature*; Lee, *Orientals*; Amy Ling (ed.), *Yellow Light: The Flowering of Asian American Arts* (Philadelphia: Temple University Press, 1999); Palumbo-Liu, *Asian/American*; John Kuo Wei Tchen, *New York before Chinatown: Orientalism and the Shaping of American Culture, 1776–1882* (Baltimore: Johns Hopkins University Press, 1999); Eric K. Yamamoto, *Interracial Justice: Conflict and Reconciliation in Post-Civil Rights America* (New York: New York University Press, 1999); Yamamoto, *Masking Selves, Making Subjects*; Robert S. Chang, *Disoriented: Asian Americans, Law, and the Nation-State* (New York: New York University Press, 1999); and Deborah Woo, *Glass Ceilings and Asian Americans: The New Face of Workplace Barriers* (Walnut Creek, Calif.: AltaMira, 2000).

107. Stanley Sue and Nathaniel N. Wagner, eds., *Asian-Americans: Psychological Perspectives* (Palo Alto, Calif.: Science and Behavior Books, 1973); Stanley Sue and James Morishima, *The Mental Health of Asian Americans* (San Francisco: Jossey-Bass, 1982); Robert Jiobu, *Ethnicity and Assimilation: Blacks, Chinese, Filipinos, Japanese, Koreans, Mexicans, Vietnamese, and Whites* (Albany: State University of New York Press, 1988); Donna K. Nagata, *Legacy of Injustice: Exploring the Cross-Generational Impact of the Japanese American Internment* (New York: Plenum Press, 1993); Lim-Hing, *The Very Inside*; Laura Uba, *Asian Americans: Personality Patterns, Identity, and Mental Health* (New York: Guilford, 1994); Gary Y. Okihiro et al., eds., *Privileging Positions: The Sites of Asian American Studies* (Pullman: Washington State University Press, 1995); Russell Leong, ed., *Asian American Sexualities: Dimensions of the Gay and Lesbian Experience* (New York: Routledge, 1996); David L. Eng and Alice Y. Hom, eds., *Q & A: Queer in Asian America* (Philadelphia: Temple University Press, 1998).

108. Okihiro, *Reflections on Shattered Windows*; Takaki, *Strangers from a Different Shore*; Sucheng Chan, *Asian Americans: An Interpretive History* (Boston: Twayne, 1991); Karin Aguilar-San Juan, ed., *The State of Asian America: Activism and Resistance in the 1990s* (Boston: South End, 1994); Okihiro, *Margins and Mainstreams*; Hune, *Teaching Asian American Women's History*; Gary Y. Okihiro, *Teaching Asian American History* (Washington, D.C.: American Historical Association, 1997); Russell Endo et al., eds., *Current Issues in Asian and Pacific American Education* (South El Monte, Calif.: Pacific Asia Press, 1998); Timothy P. Fong, *The Contemporary Asian American Experience: Beyond the Model Minority* (Upper Saddle River, N.J.: Prentice-Hall, 1998); Lane Ryo Hirabayashi, ed., *Teaching Asian America: Diversity and the Problem*

of Community (Lanham, Md.: Rowman and Littlefield, 1998); Roshni Rustomji-Kerns, ed., *Encounters: People of Asian Descent in the Americas* (Lanham, Md.: Rowman and Littlefield, 1999); and Min Zhou and James V. Gatewood, eds., *Contemporary Asian America: A Multidisciplinary Reader* (New York: New York University Press, 2000).

109. Stanley D. Porteus, *The Porteus Maze Test and Intelligence* (Palo Alto, Calif.: Pacific Books, 1950), 107, 111.

110. J. Philippe Rushton, *Race, Evolution, and Behavior: A Life History Perspective* (New Brunswick, N.J.: Transaction, 1995).

111. Richard J. Herrnstein and Charles Murray, *The Bell Curve: Intelligence and Class Structure in American Life* (New York: Free Press, 1994).

Chapter 2

RESOURCES

This compendium of resources lists books and visual materials in Asian American studies, including history. Except for the first subsection ("Reference") and the last ("Hawai'i, Hawaiians, and Pacific Islanders"), the bibliography section of this chapter lists books arranged under the categories I define and discuss in my essay in this book on historiography: anti-Asianists, liberals, and Asian Americanists. The second section provides a selected, annotated list of visual materials available in videotape format. They are arranged under subheadings that parallel the divisions in the list of books. The third section offers a selection of current electronic resources of special relevance to Asian American studies.

1. BOOKS

Readers should note that the organization of books reflect both my readings of them and the orientations of their authors. Thus, my categories "anti-Asianists," "liberals," and "Asian Americanists" are my definitions of those terms and interpretations of the books and the authors' purposes. But authors also determine their audiences, subject matters, and approaches. Accordingly, authors position their work within single or multiple disciplines, describe and analyze one or several ethnic groups, highlight one or both genders, and so on. This list thus reveals several important aspects about the production of knowledge in the field of Asian American studies. It shows the astonishingly rapid growth in the publication of books on Asian Americans since 1970, and points to biases whereby the Chinese and Japanese, men, California, and workers are emphasized, and to absences whereby multiracials, sexuality and gender, and West Asians are neglected; much work remains to be done on class formations, religions, women, South and Southeast Asians, Hawai'i, Hawaiians, and Pacific Islanders, and regions outside California. History and the social sciences predominate. In the social sciences, there is a tilt toward sociology and away from anthropology, political science, and psychology. The relative effusion of literary works, especially fiction, has nurtured a veritable field of literary and cultural criticism.

Herein I include some works of fiction in a list consisting mostly of nonfiction (I explain this choice in my chapter "Historiography"). I stress that this resource list is selective and not comprehensive. My literature list in particular is merely a sampler of creative writing. This section of the book is, like the book as a whole, an interpretation and judgment, from my organization of the resources to the selection and placement of the books and materials in this "Resources" chapter. Some books could properly belong to several categories but appear only once in this list. All the books herein I discuss or cite in the "Historiography" chapter. Where I have not mentioned a book in that chapter and its title does not provide enough information about the book's nature, I provide a brief annotation. Except for books on Asians in Hawai'i, which I list under their respective ethnic group, I include books on Hawai'i, Hawaiians, and Pacific Islanders in a separate category distinct from my categories of anti-Asianists, liberals, and Asian Americanists. Finally, kindly note the shift in categories under the "Liberals" and "Asian Americanist" headings—from "Asian Indians" to "South Asians," and from "Vietnamese and Southeast Asians" to "Cambodians," "Hmong," and "Vietnamese."

The books are grouped as follows:

REFERENCE

Alcantara, Ruben R., et al. *The Filipinos in Hawaii: An Annotated Bibliography*. Honolulu: Social Sciences and Linguistics Institute, University of Hawaii, 1977.

"Annual Selected Bibliography," in the final number (except for 25:1, 1999) of each volume of *Amerasia Journal*, from 1977 forward.

Chan, Sucheng. "Bibliographic Essay," in *Asian Americans: An Interpretive History*. Boston: Twayne, 1991, 223–29.

Cheung, King-Kok and Stan Yogi. *Asian American Literature: An Annotated Bibliography*. New York: Modern Language Association, 1988.

Ebio, Raul, Edgar Dormitorio, Teresa Ejanda, Kay Dumlao, and R. Bong Vergara, comps. *Pilipino America at the Crossroads—100 Years of United States-Philippines Relations: A Selected, Partially Annotated Bibliography of Materials at UCLA*. Los Angeles: Asian American Studies Center, University of California, 1998.

Felsman, J. Kirk, et al. *Selected Bibliography on Indochinese Refugee Children*. Hanover, N.H.: Amerasian Project, 1985.

Friday, Chris. "Asian American Labor and Historical Interpretation." *Labor History* 35:4 (1994): 524–46.

Fujimoto, Isao, et al. *Asians in America: A Selected Annotated Bibliography*. Davis: Asian American Studies, University of California, 1971 (revised 1983).

Gardner, Arthur L. *The Koreans in Hawaii: An Annotated Bibliography*. Honolulu: Social Sciences and Linguistics Institute, University of Hawaii, 1970.

Hammond, Ruth E. and Glenn L. Hendricks. *Southeast Asian Refugee Youth: An Annotated Bibliography*. Minneapolis: Center for Urban and Regional Affairs, University of Minnesota, 1988.

Hiura, Arnold T., and Stephen H. Sumida, *Asian American Literature of Hawaii: An Annotated Bibliography*. Honolulu: Talk Story, 1979.

Hoàng, Trang, Gina Maséquesmay, and Nina Hà.*Emergence of the Vietnamese American Communities: A Bibliography of Works Including Selected Annotated Citations*. Los Angeles: Asian American Studies Center, University of California, 1996.

Hune, Shirley. *Pacific Migration to the United States: Trends and Themes in Historical and Sociological Literature*. Washington, D.C.: Smithsonian Institution, 1977.

Ichioka, Yuji, et al. *A Buried Past: An Annotated Bibliography of the Japanese American Research Project Collection*. Berkeley: University of California Press, 1974.

Ichioka, Yuji and Eiichiro Azuma, comps. *A Buried Past II: A Sequel to the Annotated Bibliography of the Japanese American Research Project Collection*. Los Angeles: Asian American Studies Center, University of California, 1999.

Kim, Hyung-chan. *Dictionary of Asian American History*. Westport, Conn.: Greenwood Press, 1986.

––––––, ed. *Asian American Studies: An Annotated Bibliography and Research Guide*. Westport, Conn.: Greenwood Press, 1989.

Kittelson, David J. *The Hawaiians: An Annotated Bibliography*. Honolulu: Social Science Research Institute, University of Hawaii, 1985.

Lai, Him Mark. *A History Reclaimed: An Annotated Bibliography of Chinese Language Materials on the Chinese of America*. Los Angeles: Asian American Studies Center, University of California, 1986.

Lee, Marjorie and Judy Soo Hoo. "Asian American Religion: A Selected Bibliography," in *New Spiritual Homes: Religion and Asian Americans*. Edited by David K. Yoo. Honolulu: University of Hawai'i Press, 1999, 281–313.

Liu, Kwang-Ching. *Americans and Chinese: A Historical Essay and a Bibliography*. Cambridge, Mass.: Harvard University Press, 1963.

Lowe, C. H. *The Chinese in Hawaii: A Bibliographic Survey*. Taipei, Taiwan: China Printing, 1972.

Marston, John. *An Annotated Bibliography of Cambodia and Cambodian Refugees*. Minneapolis: Center for Urban and Regional Affairs, University of Minnesota, 1987.

Matsuda, Mitsugu. *The Japanese in Hawaii, 1868–1967: A Bibliography of the First Hundred Years*. Honolulu: Social Science Research Institute, University of Hawaii, 1968.

––––––. *The Japanese in Hawaii: An Annotated Bibliography*. Honolulu: Social Sciences and Linguistics Institute, University of Hawaii, 1975.

Poon, Wei Chi. *Directory of Asian American Collections in the United States*. Berkeley: Asian American Studies Library, University of California, 1982.

Rubano, Judith. *Culture and Behavior in Hawaii: An Annotated Bibliography*. Honolulu: Social Science Research Institute, University of Hawaii, 1971.

Sakata, Yasuo, comp. *Fading Footsteps of the Issei: An Annotated Check List of the*

Manuscript Holdings of the Japanese American Research Project Collection. Los Angeles: Asian American Studies Center, University of California, 1992.

Singh, Jane, et al. *South Asians in North America: An Annotated and Selected Bibliography.* Berkeley: Center for South and Southeast Asians Studies, University of California, 1988.

Smith, J. Christina. *The Hmong: An Annotated Bibliography, 1983–1987.* Minneapolis: Southeast Asian Refugee Studies Project, University of Minnesota, 1988.

Spickard, Paul R. and Debbie Hippolite Wright. *Pacific Islander Americans: An Annotated Bibliography in the Social Sciences.* Laie, Hawai'i: Institute for Polynesian Studies, Brigham Young University, 1995.

Tatla, Darshan Singh. *Sikhs in North America: An Annotated Bibliography.* Westport, Conn.: Greenwood Press, 1991.

Williams, C. L. *An Annotated Bibliography on Refugee Mental Health.* Rockville, Md.: National Institute of Mental Health, 1987.

Yoshitomi, Joan, et al. *Asians in the Northwest: An Annotated Bibliography.* Seattle: Asian American Studies Program, University of Washington, 1978.

Young, Nancy Foon. *The Chinese in Hawaii: An Annotated Bibliography.* Honolulu: Social Science Research Institute, University of Hawaii, 1973.

ANTI-ASIANISTS

Abdullah, Achmed. *The Honourable Gentleman and Others.* New York: G. P. Putnam's Sons, 1919.

Adams, Brooks. *The Law of Civilization and Decay: An Essay on History.* New York: Macmillan, 1895.

Barth, Gunther. *Bitter Strength: A History of the Chinese in the United States, 1850–1870.* Cambridge, Mass.: Harvard University Press, 1964.

Bernstein, Richard and Ross H. Munro. *The Coming Conflict with China.* New York: Alfred A. Knopf, 1997.

Burke, Thomas. *Limehouse Nights.* London: Grosset & Dunlap, 1917.

Choate, Pat. *Agents of Influence.* New York: Alfred A. Knopf, 1990.

Clancy, Tom. *Debt of Honor.* New York: G. P. Putnam's Sons, 1994.

Clarke, Thurston. *Pearl Harbor Ghosts: A Journey to Hawaii Then and Now.* New York: William Morrow, 1991.

Conwell, Russell H. *Why and How: Why the Chinese Emigrate, and the Means They Adopt for the Purpose of Reaching America.* Boston: Lee and Shepard, 1871. (A focus on "the coolie" and his character.)

Crichton, Michael. *Rising Sun.* New York: Ballantine Books, 1992.

Dillon, Richard H. *The Hatchet Men: The Story of the Tong Wars in San Francisco's Chinatown.* New York: Ballantine Books, 1962. (Chinatown's good people terrorized and bullied by the tongs through extortion, assassination, and vendetta.)

Dooner, P. W. *Last Days of the Republic.* San Francisco: Alta California, 1879.

Fallows, James. *More Like Us: Putting America's Native Strengths and Traditional Values to Work to Overcome the Asian Challenge.* Boston: Houghton Mifflin, 1989.

Flowers, Montaville. *The Japanese Conquest of American Opinion*. New York: George H. Doran, 1917.

Friedman, George and Meredith Lebard. *The Coming War with Japan*. New York: St. Martin's Press, 1991.

Genthe, Arnold. *Pictures of Old Chinatown*. New York: Moffat, Yard and Company, 1909. (Stylized photographs of San Francisco's Chinatown before the 1906 earthquake, with an orientalized text by Will Irwin.)

Gong, Eng Ying and Bruce Grant. *Tong War!* New York: Nicholas L. Brown, 1930. (Sensationalist account of Chinese tongs in the United States.)

Grant, Madison. *The Passing of the Great Race Or the Racial Basis of European History*. New York: Charles Scribner's Sons, 1916.

———. *The Conquest of a Continent*. New York: Charles Scribner's Sons, 1933.

Helper, Hinton. *Dreadful California*. Indianapolis: Bobbs-Merrill, 1948.

Hernstein, Richard J. and Charles Murray.*The Bell Curve: Intelligence and Class Structure in American Life*. New York: Free Press, 1994.

Huntington, Samuel P. *The Clash of Civilizations and the Remaking of World Order*. New York: Simon & Schuster, 1996.

Hynd, Alan. *Betrayal from the East: The Inside Story of Japanese Spies in America*. New York: Stratford Press, 1943.

Irwin, Wallace. *Chinatown Ballads*. New York: Duffield, 1906. (A collection of rhymes, including "You Sabe Me1" and "'How Muchee You Pay?'")

———. *Letters of a Japanese Schoolboy*. New York: Doubleday, Page and Company, 1909.

———. *Seed of the Sun*. New York: George H. Doran, 1921.

Kinkead, Gwen. *Chinatown: A Portrait of a Closed Society*. New York: HarperCollins, 1992. (Update of the insular Chinese exemplified in author's version of New York City's Chinatown.)

Kotkin, Joel. *Tribes: How Race, Religion and Identity Determine Success in the New Global Economy*. New York: Random House, 1993.

Kyne, Peter B. *The Pride of Palomar*. New York: Cosmopolitan, 1921.

Lea, Homer. *The Valor of Ignorance*. New York: Harper & Brothers, 1909.

McClatchy, Valentine Stuart, ed. *Four Anti-Japanese Pamphlets*. New York: Arno Press, 1978.

Manson, Marsden. *The Yellow Peril in Action: A Possible Chapter in History*. San Francisco: n.p., 1907.

Marquand, John P. *Your Turn Mr. Moto*. New York: Popular Library, 1935.

Porteus, Stanley D. *The Porteus Maze Test and Intelligence*. Palo Alto, Calif.: Pacific Books, 1950.

Rohmer, Sax. *The Insidious Dr. Fu-Manchu*. New York: A. L. Burt, 1913.

Rushton, J. Philippe. *Race, Evolution, and Behavior: A Life History Perspective*. New Brunswick, N.J.: Transaction, 1995.

Steiner, Jesse Frederick. *The Japanese Invasion: A Study in the Psychology of Inter-Racial Contacts*. Chicago: A. C. McClurg, 1917.

Stoddard, Lothrop. *The Rising Tide of Color Against White World-Supremacy*. New York: Charles Scribner's Sons, 1920.

Storti, Craig. *Incident at Bitter Creek: The Story of the Rock Springs Chinese Massacre.* Ames: Iowa State University Press, 1991. (Chinese as pawns and victims in the struggle between capital and labor, and anti-Chinese sentiment as a class and not a race issue.)

van Wolferen, Karel. *The Enigma of Japanese Power.* New York: Alfred A. Knopf, 1989.

Weber, Joe. *Honorable Enemies.* New York: Jove Books, 1994.

Winchester, Simon. *Pacific Nightmare: How Japan Starts World War III, A Future History.* New York: Ivy Books, 1992.

Woltor, Robert. *A Short and Truthful History of the Taking of California and Oregon by the Chinese in the Year* A.D. 1899. San Francisco: A. L. Bancroft, 1882.

LIBERALS

General Works

Adams, Romanzo. *Interracial Marriage in Hawaii.* New York: Macmillan, 1938.

Barkan, Elliott R. *Asian and Pacific Islander Migration to the United States: A Model of New Global Patterns.* Westport, Conn.: Greenwood Press, 1992.

Coman, Katharine. *The History of Contract Labor in the Hawaiian Islands.* New York: Macmillan, 1903.

Daniels, Roger. *Asian America: Chinese and Japanese in the United States Since 1850.* Seattle: University of Washington Press, 1988.

Daniels, Roger, and Harry H. L. Kitano. *American Racism: Exploration of the Nature of Prejudice.* Englewood Cliffs, N.J.: Prentice Hall, 1970.

Fawcett, J. T., and Benjamin V. Carino. *Pacific Bridges: The New Immigration from Asia and the Pacific Islands.* Staten Island, N.Y.: Center for Migration Studies, 1986.

Kitano, Harry H. L., and Roger Daniels. *Asian Americans: Emerging Minorities.* Englewood Cliffs, N.J.: Prentice Hall, 1988.

Knoll, Tricia. *Becoming Americans: Asian Sojourners, Immigrants, and Refugees in the Western United States.* Portland, Ore.: Coast to Coast Books, 1982.

Konvitz, Milton R. *The Alien and the Asiatic in American Law.* Ithaca, N.Y.: Cornell University Press, 1946.

Mears, Eliot Grinnell. *Resident Orientals on the American Pacific Coast: Their Legal and Economic Status.* Chicago: University of Chicago Press, 1928.

Melendy, H. Brett. *Asians in America: Filipinos, Koreans, and East Indians.* Boston: G. K. Hall, 1977.

Park, Robert. *Race and Culture.* Glencoe, Ill.: Free Press, 1950.

Smith, William Carlson. *The Second Generation Oriental in America.* Honolulu: Institute of Pacific Relations, 1927.

———. *Americans in Process: A Study of Our Citizens of Oriental Ancestry.* Ann Arbor, Mich.: Edwards Brothers, 1937.

Thompson, Richard Austin. *The Yellow Peril, 1890–1924.* New York: Arno Press, 1978. (A 1957 dissertation on the racial, demographic, economic, cultural, and military peril posed by East Asians for the United States and whites.)

Asian Indians

Agarwal, Priya. *Passage from India: Post 1965 Indian Immigrants and Their Children.* Palos Verdes, Calif.: Yuvati Publications, 1991. (Generational problems among Asian Indian professionals based upon interviews.)

Bacon, Jean. *Life Lines: Community, Family, and Assimilation among Asian Indian Immigrants.* New York: Oxford University Press, 1996.

Bose, Sudhindra. *Mother America: Realities of American Life as Seen by an Indian.* Raopura, India: M. S. Bhatt, 1934.

Das, Rajani Kanta. *Hindustani Workers on the Pacific Coast.* Berlin: Walter de Gruyter, 1923.

Dasgupta, Sathi Sengupta. *On the Trail of an Uncertain Dream: Indian Immigrant Experience in America.* New York: AMS Press, 1989.

Fisher, Maxine P. *The Indians of New York City: A Study of Immigrants from India.* New Delhi: Heritage, 1980. (Focus on identity formation since 1965, especially through political participation.)

Gibson, Margaret A. *Accommodation without Assimilation: Sikh Immigrants in an American High School.* Ithaca, N.Y.: Cornell University Press, 1988.

Hawley, John Stratton, and Gurinder Singh Mann, eds. *Studying the Sikhs: Issues for North America.* Albany: State University of New York Press, 1993.

Helweg, Arthur Wesley. *An Immigrant Success Story: East Indians in America.* Philadelphia: University of Pennsylvania Press, 1990.

Jensen, Joan M. *Passage from India: Asian Indian Immigrants in North America.* New Haven: Yale University Press, 1988.

La Brack, Bruce. *The Sikhs of Northern California, 1904–1975.* New York: AMS Press, 1988.

Malik, Iftikhar Haider. *Pakistanis in Michigan: A Study of Third Culture and Acculturation.* New York: AMS Press, 1989.

Mehta, Ved Mehta. *Face to Face: An Autobiography.* Boston: Little, Brown, 1957.

Mukerji, Dhan Gopal. *Caste and Outcast.* New York: E. P. Dutton, 1923.

Saran, Parmatma. *The Asian Indian Experience in the United States.* New Delhi: Vikas, 1985. (A survey of immigration and adaptation since 1965 and a longitudinal study based upon ten in-depth interviews.)

Saund, D. S. *Congressman from India.* New York: E. P. Dutton, 1960.

Shridharani, Krishnalal. *My India, My America.* New York: Duell, Sloan and Pearce, 1941.

Chinese

Ai, Chung Kun. *My Seventy Nine Years in Hawaii.* Hong Kong: Cosmorama Pictorial, 1960.

Ai, Li Ling. *Life is for a Long Time: A Chinese Hawaiian Memoir.* New York: Hastings House, 1972.

Arkush, R. David, and Leo O. Lee, eds. *Land Without Ghosts: Chinese Impressions of America from the Mid-Nineteenth Century to the Present.* Berkeley: University of California Press, 1989. (Extracts from travel diaries, observations, and handbooks written by government officials, intellectuals, and writers.)

Biggers, Earl Derr. *The House Without a Key.* New York: Grosset and Dunlap, 1925.

Chen, Jack. *The Chinese of America: From the Beginnings to the Present.* San Francisco: Harper and Row, 1981. (A survey of Chinese American history written by a journalist.)

Condit, Ira M. *The Chinaman As We See Him and Fifty Years of Work for Him.* Chicago: Fleming H. Revell, 1900.

Coolidge, Mary Roberts. *Chinese Immigration.* New York: Henry Holt, 1909.

Dobie, Charles Caldwell. *San Francisco's Chinatown.* New York: D. Appleton-Century, 1936. (An historical account written to promote understanding and tolerance.)

Fan, Chen-Yung. *The Chinese Language School of San Francisco in Relation to Family Integration and Cultural Identity.* Nankang, Taipei: Institute of American Culture, Academia Sinica, 1981. (A study of the Chinese-language school as a means to promote family cohesion and cultural identity.)

Gibson, Otis. *The Chinese in America.* Cincinnati: Hitchcock and Walden, 1877.

Greenbie, Sydney and Marjorie Barstow Greenbie. *Gold of Ophir: The China Trade in the Making of America.* New York: Wilson-Erickson, 1937. (Significance of America's China trade in shaping its culture and its destiny as a world power.)

Hoexter, Corinne K. *From Canton to California: The Epic of Chinese Immigration.* New York: Four Winds Press, 1976. (Epic of immigration, fear and hatred, and contributions to American life with a focus on newspaper editor Ng Poon Chew.)

Hsu, Francis L. K. *The Challenge of the American Dream: The Chinese in the United States.* Belmont, Calif.: Wadsworth Publishing, 1971.

Kung, S. W. *Chinese in American Life: Some Aspects of Their History, Status, Problems, and Contributions.* Seattle: University of Washington Press, 1962.

Kuo, Helena. *I've Come a Long Way.* New York: D. Appleton-Century, 1943. (Set mainly in China, Kuo's autobiography moves to Europe and the United States.)

Kwock, Charles M. C. *A Hawaii Chinese Looks at America.* New York: Vantage Press, 1977.

Lee, Calvin. *Chinatown, U.S.A.* Garden City, N.Y.: Doubleday, 1965.

Lee, Rose Hum. *The Chinese in the United States of America.* Hong Kong: Hong Kong University Press, 1960.

——. *The Growth and Decline of Chinese Communities in the Rocky Mountain Region.* New York: Arno Press, 1978.

Leong, Gor Yun. *Chinatown Inside Out.* New York: Burrows Mussey, 1936. (A popular account of New York City's Chinatown.)

Lin, Yutang. *Chinatown Family.* New York: John Day, 1948. (Novel of the Fong family in New York City and their adventures and triumphs.)

Loewen, James W. *The Mississippi Chinese: Between Black and White.* Cambridge, Mass.: Harvard University Press, 1971.

Lowe, Pardee. *Father and Glorious Descendant.* Boston: Little, Brown, 1943.

McClain, Charles J. *In Search of Equality: The Chinese Struggle against Discrimination Nineteenth-Century America.* Berkeley: University of California Press, 1994.

McLeod, Alexander. *Pigtails and Gold Dust.* Caldwell, Idaho: Caxton Printers, 1947. (An account of the transformation of the heathen Chinese before the 1906 San Francisco earthquake to the assimilated Chinese American after the disaster.)

Martin, Mildred Crowl. *Chinatown's Angry Angel: The Story of Donaldina Cameron.* Palo Alto, Calif.: Pacific Books, 1977.

Mason, Richard. *The World of Suzie Wong.* London: Collins, 1957.

Miller, Stuart Creighton. *The Unwelcome Immigrant: The American Image of the Chinese, 1785–1882.* Berkeley: University of California Press, 1969.

Park, No-Yong. *An Oriental View of American Civilization.* Boston: Hale, Cushman and Flint, 1934.

———. *Retreat of the West: The White Man's Adventure in Eastern Asia.* Boston: Hale, Cushman and Flint, 1937. (A history of the relations between Europeans and East Asians from Atilla and the Mongols to the Sino-Japanese conflict of 1937.)

———. *Chinaman's Chance.* Boston: Meador Publishing, 1940.

Quan, Robert Seto. *Lotus Among the Magnolias: The Mississippi Chinese.* Jackson: University Press of Mississippi, 1982. (Ethnography of three generations of Chinese in the Mississippi delta and their isolation, assimilation, and dispersion.)

Riddle, Ronald. *Flying Dragons, Flowing Streams: Music in the Life of San Francisco's Chinese.* Westport, Conn.: Greenwood Press, 1983. (A social history of Chinese American music, and an explanation of its static nature.)

Salyer, Lucy E. *Laws Harsh as Tigers: Chinese Immigrants and the Shaping of Modern Immigration Law.* Chapel Hill: University of North Carolina Press, 1995.

Saxton, Alexander. *The Indispensable Enemy: Labor and the Anti-Chinese Movement in California.* Berkeley: University of California Press, 1971.

Seward, George F. *Chinese Immigration, In Its Social and Economical Aspects.* New York: Charles Scribner's Sons, 1881.

Siu, Paul C. P. *The Chinese Laundryman: A Study of Social Isolation.* New York: New York University Press, 1987.

Speer, William. *The Oldest and the Newest Empire: China and the United States.* Cincinnati: National Publishing, 1870.

Steiner, Stan. *Fusang: The Chinese Who Built America.* New York: Harper and Row, 1979. (A celebration of Chinese contributions to American life.)

Sung, Betty Lee. *Mountain of Gold: The Story of the Chinese in America.* New York: Macmillan, 1967.

Tow, J. S. *The Real Chinese in America.* New York: Academy Press, 1923. (A defense of Chinese Americans by the secretary of the consulate general in New York City.)

Weiss, Melford S. *Valley City: A Chinese Community in America.* Cambridge, Mass.: Schenkman Publishing, 1974. (An ethnography of a rural community and its social organization and changes over time.)

Wilson, Carol Green. *Chinatown Quest: The Life Adventures of Donaldina Cameron.* Stanford, Calif.: Stanford University Press, 1931.

Wong, Bernard P. *Chinatown: Economic Adaptation and Ethnic Identity of the Chinese.* New York: Holt, Rinehart and Winston, 1982. (Ethnography of New York City's Chinatown based on research conducted in the early 1970s and 1980s.)

Wong, Jade Snow. *Fifth Chinese Daughter.* New York: Harper & Row, 1950.

Wu, Tingfang. *America Through the Spectacles of an Oriental Diplomat.* New York: Frederick A. Stokes, 1914.

Yung, Wing. *My Life in China and America.* New York: Henry Holt, 1909.

Filipinos

Bulosan, Carlos. *America Is in the Heart.* New York: Harcourt, Brace, 1943.

Cressey, Paul G. *The Taxi-Dance Hall: A Sociological Study in Commercialized Recreation and City Life.* Chicago: University of Chicago Press, 1932.

Karnow, Stanley. *In Our Image: America's Empire in the Philippines.* New York: Ballantine Books, 1989.

Lasker, Bruno. *Filipino Immigration to Continental United States and to Hawaii.* Chicago: University of Chicago Press, 1931.

May, Glenn. *Social Engineering in the Philippines: The Aims, Execution and Impact of American Colonial Policy, 1900–1913.* Westport, Conn.: Greenwood Press, 1980.

Miller, Stuart Creighton. *"Benevolent Assimilation": The American Conquest of the Philippines, 1899–1903.* New Haven, Conn.: Yale University Press, 1982.

Stanley, Peter, ed. *Reappraising an Empire: New Perspectives on Philippine-American History.* Cambridge, Mass.: Harvard University Press, 1984.

Japanese

Armor, John and Peter Wright. *Manzanar.* New York: Times Books, 1988. (Commentary on the World War II expulsion and detention accompanied by Ansel Adams's photographs of the relocation center.)

Bailey, Paul. *City in the Sun: The Japanese Concentration Camp at Poston, Arizona.* Los Angeles: Westernlore Press, 1971.

Bell, Reginald. *Public School Education of Second-Generation Japanese in California.* Stanford, Calif.: Stanford University Press, 1935.

Boddy, E. Manchester. *Japanese in America.* Los Angeles: E. Manchester Boddy, 1921. (A history of relations between Japan and the United States and a description of the Japanese to counter anti-Japanese sentiment and public misunderstanding of the Japanese problem.)

Bosworth, Allan R. *America's Concentration Camps.* New York: W. W. Norton, 1967.

Broom, Leonard and John I. Kitsuse. *The Managed Casualty: The Japanese-American Family in World War II.* Berkeley: University of California Press, 1973. (Impact of the wartime camps based on ten case studies.)

Chang, Thelma. *"I Can Never Forget": Men of the 100th/442nd.* Honolulu: Sigi Productions, 1991.

Christgau, John. *"Enemies": World War II Alien Internment.* Ames: Iowa State University Press, 1985.

Chuman, Frank F. *The Bamboo People: The Law and Japanese-Americans.* Del Mar, Calif.: Publisher's Inc., 1976.

Collins, Donald E. *Native American Aliens: Disloyalty and the Renunciation of Citizenship by Japanese Americans during World War II.* Westport, Conn.: Greenwood Press, 1985.

Commission on Wartime Relocation and Internment of Civilians. *Personal Justice Denied.* Washington, D.C.: Government Printing Office, 1982.

Connor, John W. *Tradition and Change in Three Generations of Japanese Americans.*

Chicago: Nelson-Hall, 1977. (A study of acculturation across generations based on interviews.)

Conroy, Hilary. *The Japanese Frontier in Hawaii, 1868–1898*. Berkeley: University of California Press, 1953.

Conroy, Hilary and T. Scott Miyakawa. *East Across the Pacific: Historical and Sociological Studies of Japanese Immigration and Assimilation*. Santa Barbara, Calif.: Clio Press, 1972.

Consulate-General of Japan, comp. *Documental History of Law Cases Affecting Japanese Americans in the United States, 1916–1924*. 2 vols. San Francisco: Consul-General of Japan, 1925.

Crost, Lyn. *Honor by Fire: Japanese Americans at War in Europe and the Pacific*. Novato, Calif.: Presidio Press, 1994.

Daniels, Roger. *The Politics of Prejudice: The Anti-Japanese Movement in California and the Struggle for Japanese Exclusion*. New York: Atheneum, 1970.

———. *Concentration Camps, U.S.A.: Japanese Americans and World War II*. New York: Holt, Rinehart and Winston, 1971.

———. *The Decision to Relocate the Japanese Americans*. Philadelphia: J. B. Lippincott, 1975.

———. *Prisoners Without Trial: Japanese Americans in World War II*. New York: Hill and Wang, 1993.

Duus, Masayo Umezawa. *Tokyo Rose: Orphan of the Pacific*. Translated by Peter Duus. Tokyo: Kodansha International, 1979.

———. *Unlikely Liberators: The Men of the 100th and 442nd*. Translated by Peter Duus. Honolulu: University of Hawaii Press, 1987.

———. *The Japanese Conspiracy: The Oahu Sugar Strike of 1920*. Berkeley: University of California Press, 1999.

Fujita, Frank. *Foo: A Japanese-American Prisoner of the Rising Sun*. Denton: University of North Texas Press, 1993. (Memoir based on prison diaries as a POW in Java and Japan during World War II.)

Fukuda, Moritoshi. *Legal Problems of Japanese-Americans: Their History and Development in the United States*. Tokyo: Keio Tsushin, 1980.

Gardiner, C. Harvey. *Pawns in a Triangle of Hate: The Peruvian Japanese and the United States*. Seattle: University of Washington Press, 1981. (Account of the 1,800 Peruvian Japanese interned in the United States during World War II.)

Girdner, Audrie, and Anne Loftis. *The Great Betrayal: The Evacuation of the Japanese-Americans During World War II*. New York: Macmillan, 1969.

Grodzins, Morton. *Americans Betrayed: Politics and the Japanese Evacuation*. Chicago: University of Chicago Press, 1949.

Gulick, Sidney L. *The American Japanese Problem: A Study of the Racial Relations of the East and West*. New York: Charles Scribner's Sons, 1914.

Harris, Catherine Embree. *Dusty Exile: Looking Back at Japanese Relocation During World War II*. Honolulu: Mutual Publishing, 1999. (Memoir of a white schoolteacher in Poston.)

Hosokawa, Bill. *Nisei: The Quiet Americans*. New York: William Morrow, 1969.

———. *Thirty-Five Years in the Frying Pan*. New York: McGraw-Hill, 1978. (A collection of essays from the author's "From the Frying Pan" column published in the newspaper *Pacific Citizen*.)

——. *JACL: In Quest of Justice*. New York: William Morrow, 1982. (A history of the Japanese American Citizens League.)

Hunter, Louise H. *Buddhism in Hawaii: Its Impact on a Yankee Community*. Honolulu: University of Hawaii Press, 1971. (A history of Japanese Buddhism from 1865 to the 1960s.)

Ichihashi, Yamato. *Japanese in the United States: A Critical Study of the Problems of the Japanese Immigrants and Their Children*. Stanford, Calif.: Stanford University Press, 1932.

Inouye, Daniel K. *Journey to Washington*. Englewood Cliffs, N.J.: Prentice Hall, 1967.

Irons, Peter. *Justice at War: The Story of the Japanese American Internment Cases*. New York: Oxford University Press, 1983.

Irons, Peter, ed. *Justice Delayed: The Record of the Japanese American Internment Cases*. Middleton, Conn.: Wesleyan University Press, 1989.

Iwata, Masakazu. *Planted in Good Soil: A History of the Issei in United States Agriculture*. 2 vols. New York: Peter Lang, 1992. (The first volume covers California, and the second, Oregon, Washington, Colorado, Arizona, and Texas.)

Iyenaga, T., and Kenoske Sato. *Japan and the California Problem*. New York: G. P. Putnam's Sons, 1921. (The causes of anti-Japanese agitation, and a defense of the Japanese.)

James, Thomas. *Exile Within: The Schooling of Japanese Americans, 1942–1945*. Cambridge, Mass.: Harvard University Press, 1987.

Kachi, Teruko Okada. *The Treaty of 1911 and the Immigration and Alien Land Law Issue Between the United States and Japan, 1911–1913*. New York: Arno Press, 1978. (A 1957 dissertation on the international context of domestic politics.)

Kawai, Michi. *My Lantern*. n.p.: n.p., 1939. (Autobiography by the principal of Keisen Girls' School, a graduate of Bryn Mawr College and secretary of the Y.W.C.A.)

Kawakami, Kiyoshi K. *Asia at the Door: A Study of the Japanese Question in Continental United States, Hawaii and Canada*. New York: Fleming H. Revell, 1914.

——. *The Real Japanese Question*. New York: Macmillan, 1921.

Kimura, Yukiko. *Issei: Japanese Immigrants in Hawaii*. Honolulu: University of Hawaii Press, 1988. (A sociology of the first-generation, including community, work, family and social life, and World War I and II.)

Kitagawa, Daisuke. *Issei and Nisei: The Internment Years*. New York: Seabury Press, 1967. (Observations of generational conflicts by a Christian minister.)

Kitano, Harry H. L. *Japanese Americans: The Evolution of a Subculture*. Englewood Cliffs, N.J.: Prentice-Hall, 1969. (A history and sociology of assimilation in family, community, and culture.)

——. *Generations and Identity: The Japanese American*. Needham Heights, Mass.: Ginn Press, 1993. (A sociology of history, community, and identity.)

Kiyosaki, Wayne S. *A Spy in Their Midst: The World War II Struggle of a Japanese-American Hero*. Lanham, Md.: Madison Books, 1995. (Memoir of Hawai'i-born Richard Sakakida, U.S. army spy in the Philippines.)

LaViolette, Forrest E. *Americans of Japanese Ancestry: A Study of Assimilation in the American Community.* Toronto: Canadian Institute of International Affairs, 1945. (A study of family and community life and the problems of racial discrimination and assimilation.)

Leighton, Alexander H. *The Governing of Men: General Principles and Recommendations Based on Experience at a Japanese Relocation Camp.* Princeton, N.J.: Princeton University Press, 1945.

Lind, Andrew W. *Hawai'i's Japanese: An Experiment in Democracy.* Princeton, N.J.: Princeton University Press, 1946. (A sociology of Hawai'i's treatment of its Japanese during World War II as a vindication of American democracy.)

Mackey, Mike. *Heart Mountain: Life in Wyoming's Concentration Camp.* Powell, Wyo.: Western History Publications, 2000.

———, ed. *Remembering Heart Mountain: Essays on Japanese American Internment in Wyoming.* Powell, Wyo.: Western History Publications, 1998.

McWilliams, Carey. *Prejudice: Japanese-Americans: Symbol of Racial Intolerance.* Boston: Little, Brown, 1944. (California's anti-Japanese movement and the World War II relocation centers.)

Martin, Ralph G. *Boy from Nebraska: The Story of Ben Kuroki.* New York: Harper and Brothers, 1946. (Biography of a U.S. airforce gunner during World War II, winner of the Distinguished Flying Cross and propagandist for patriotism.)

Matsumoto, Toru. *Beyond Prejudice: A Story of the Church and Japanese Americans.* New York: Friendship Press, 1946. (An account of Christian churches and their ministry among Japanese Americans mainly during and after World War II by a minister of the Reformed Church in America.)

Maykovich, Minako K. *Japanese American Identity Dilemma.* Tokyo: Waseda University Press, 1972. (Focus on the *sansei*, third-generation, search for identity.)

Millis, H. A. *The Japanese Problem in the United States.* New York: Macmillan, 1915.

Miyamoto, Kazuo. *Hawaii: End of the Rainbow.* Rutland, Vermont: Charles E. Tuttle, 1964. (Historical novel of Japanese Americans from beginnings to World War II.)

Miyamoto, Shotaro Frank. *Social Solidarity Among the Japanese of Seattle.* Seattle: University of Washington, 1939.

Modell, John. *The Economics and Politics of Racial Accommodation: The Japanese of Los Angeles, 1900–1942.* Urbana: University of Illinois Press, 1977. (A history of anti-Japanese sentiment and its influences on the ethnic community, economy, and *nisei* or second-generation identity.)

Murata, Kiyoaki. *An Enemy Among Friends.* Tokyo: Kodansha International, 1991. (Memoir of a Japanese student trapped in the United States during World War II.)

Murphy, Thomas D. *Ambassadors in Arms: The Story of Hawaii's 100th Battalion.* Honolulu: University of Hawaii Press, 1954.

Myer, Dillon S. *Uprooted Americans: The Japanese Americans and the War Relocation Authority During World War II.* Tucson: University of Arizona Press, 1971. (Account by the director of the War Relocation Authority.)

Nelson, Douglas W. *Heart Mountain: The Story of an American Concentration Camp.* Madison: State Historical Society of Wisconsin, 1976.

Ogawa, Dennis M. *Jan Ken Po: The World of Hawaii's Japanese Americans.* Honolulu:

University Press of Hawaii, 1973. (Essay on the sources of Japanese American identity in the islands.)

————. *Kodomo no tame ni, For the sake of the children: The Japanese American Experience in Hawaii.* Honolulu: University Press of Hawaii, 1978. (A collection of essays from a variety of sources.)

Okimoto, Daniel I. *American in Disguise.* New York: Walker/Weatherhill, 1971. (Autobiographical account of a nisei or second-generation Japanese American and his search for identity.)

Okumura, Takie. *Seventy Years of Divine Blessings.* Honolulu: n.p., 1939. (Memoir of a Christian minister in Hawai'i, Japanese-language school proponent, and advocate for Americanization.)

Petersen, William. *Japanese Americans: Oppression and Success.* New York: Random House, 1971. (A sociology of Japanese American success rooted in history and culture by a proponent of the "model minority" hypothesis.)

Scherer, James A. B. *The Japanese Crisis.* New York: Frederick A. Stokes, 1916. (The Japanese problem and an appeal for mutual understanding.)

Shibutani, Tamotsu. *The Derelicts of Company K: A Sociological Study of Demoralization.* Berkeley: University of California Press, 1978. (Demoralization as a social process as exemplified in a Japanese American army unit during World War II.)

Smith, Bradford. *Americans from Japan.* Philadelphia: J. B. Lippincott, 1948. (A history of Japanese Americans from immigration to conflict and crisis and to redemption and triumph.)

Spicer, Edward H., Asael T. Hansen, Katherine Luomala, and Marvin K. Opler, *Impounded People: Japanese-Americans in the Relocation Centers.* Tucson: University of Arizona Press, 1969. (An account of the camps by anthropologists employed as community analysts by the War Relocation Authority.)

Strong, Edward K. *The Second Generation Japanese Problem.* Stanford, Calif.: Stanford University Press, 1934.

Suzuki, Lester E. *Ministry in the Assembly and Relocation Centers of World War II.* Berkeley, Calif.: Yardbird Publishing, 1979. (Account by a Methodist minister.)

Takabuki, Matsuo. *An Unlikely Revolutionary: Matsuo Takabuki and the Making of Modern Hawai'i.* Honolulu: University of Hawai'i Press, 1998. (Memoir of a *nisei*, or second-generation, businessman, politician, and participant in the changes initiated by the Democratic Party in the islands.)

Tamura, Eileen H. *Americanization, Acculturation, and Ethnic Identity: The Nisei Generation in Hawaii.* Urbana: University of Illinois Press, 1994. (A study of the form of the Americanization movement in Hawai'i after World War I, and Japanese American adaptation and acculturation.)

Tanaka, Chester. *Go For Broke: A Pictorial History of the Japanese American 100th Infantry Battalion and the 442d Regimental Combat Team.* Richmond, Calif.: Go For Broke, 1982.

Taylor, Sandra C. *Advocate of Understanding: Sidney Gulick and the Search for Peace with Japan.* Kent, Ohio: Kent State University Press, 1984.

————. *Jewel of the Desert: Japanese American Internment at Topaz.* Berkeley: University of California Press, 1993.

tenBroek, Jacobus, Edward N. Barnhart, and Floyd W. Matson. *Prejudice, War, and the Constitution*. Berkeley: University of California Press, 1954.

Thomas, Dorothy Swaine. *The Salvage*. Berkeley: University of California Press, 1952.

Thomas, Dorothy Swaine, and Richard S. Nishimoto. *The Spoilage*. Berkeley: University of California Press, 1946.

Van Sant, John E. *Pacific Pioneers: Japanese Journeys to America and Hawaii, 1850–80*. Urbana: University of Illinois Press, 2000. (A history of early Japanese travelers along with biographical sketches of those Japanese and their American benefactors.)

Van Valkenburg, Carol Bulger. *An Alien Place: The Fort Missoula, Montana, Detention Camp, 1941–1944*. Missoula, Mont.: Pictorial Histories Publishing, 1995.

Wax, Rosalie H. *Doing Fieldwork: Warnings and Advice*. Chicago: University of Chicago Press, 1971.

Weglyn, Michi. *Years of Infamy: The Untold Story of America's Concentration Camps*. New York: William Morrow, 1976.

Wilson, Robert A., and Bill Hosokawa. *East to America: A History of the Japanese in the United States*. New York: William Morrow, 1980. (A project of the Japanese American Citizens League for a comprehensive, scholarly history.)

Yanagisako, Sylvia Junko. *Transforming the Past: Tradition and Kinship Among Japanese Americans*. Stanford, Calif.: Stanford University Press, 1985. (Ethnography of kinship and its symbolic meanings and transformation across generations.)

Yoshida, Jim. *The Two Worlds of Jim Yoshida*. New York: William Morrow, 1972. (Autobiography of a *nisei* or second-generation Japanese American who lost his U.S. citizenship during World War II and regained it after the Korean War.)

Yoshitsu, Masao. *My Moments in the Twentieth Century: An Immigrant's Story*. New York: Vantage Press, 1987. (A "schoolboy," graduate of Stanford University, internee at Gila River, and aerospace mathematician at Cape Canaveral.)

Koreans

Charr, Easurk Emsen Charr. *The Golden Mountain*. Boston: Forum, 1961.

Choy, Bong-young. *Koreans in America*. Chicago: Nelson-Hall, 1979.

Kang, Younghill. *The Grass Roof*. New York: Charles Scribner's Sons, 1931.

———. *The Happy Grove*. New York: Charles Scribner's Sons, 1933.

———. *East Goes West*. New York: Charles Scribner's Sons, 1937.

Kim, Hyung-chan, ed. *The Korean Diaspora: Historical and Sociological Studies of Korean Immigration and Assimilation in North America*. Santa Barbara, Calif.: ABC-Clio, 1977.

Yim, Louise. *My Forty Year Fight for Korea*. New York: A. A. Wyn, 1951.

Vietnamese and Southeast Asians

Caplan, Nathan, John K. Whitmore, and Marcella H. Choy. *The Boat People and Achievement in America: A Study of Family Life, Hard Work, and Cultural Values*. Ann Arbor: University of Michigan Press, 1989.

Caplan, Nathan, Marcella H. Choy, and John K. Whitmore. *Children of the Boat*

People: A Study of Educational Success. Ann Arbor: University of Michigan Press, 1991.

Fadiman, Anne. *The Spirit Catches You and You Fall Down: A Hmong Child, Her American Doctors, and the Collision of Two Cultures*. New York: Farrar, Straus and Giroux, 1997.

Haines, David W. *Refugees as Immigrants: Cambodians, Laotians, and Vietnamese in America*. Totowa, N.J.: Rowman and Littlefield, 1989.

Kelly, Gail Paradise. *From Vietnam to America: A Chronicle of the Vietnamese Immigration to the United States*. Boulder, Colo.: Westview Press, 1977.

Montero, Darrel. *Vietnamese Americans: Patterns of Resettlement and Socioeconomic Adaptation in the United States*. Boulder, Colo.: Westview Press, 1979.

Sheehy, Gail. *Spirit of Survival*. New York: William Morrow, 1986. (Author's account of Cambodian refugee Phat Mohm.)

Strand, Paul and Woodrow Jones, Jr. *Indochinese Refugees in America: Problems of Adaptation and Assimilation*. Durham, N.C.: Duke University Press, 1985.

Treuba, Henry T., Lila Jacobs, and Elizabeth Kirton. *Cultural Conflict and Adaptation: The Case of Hmong Children in American Society*. New York: Falmer Press, 1990.

Wain, Barry. *The Refused: The Agony of the Indochinese Refugees*. New York: Simon and Schuster, 1981.

Zhou, Min, and Carl L. Bankston, III. *Growing Up American: How Vietnamese Children Adapt to Life in the United States*. New York: Russell Sage Foundation, 1998.

ASIAN AMERICANISTS

General Works

Aguilar-San Juan, Karin, ed. *The State of Asian America: Activism and Resistance in the 1990s*. Boston: South End Press, 1994.

Chan, Sucheng. *Asian Americans: An Interpretive History*. Boston: Twayne, 1991.

Chang, Edward T., and Jeannette Diaz-Veizades, *Ethnic Peace in the American City: Building Community in Los Angeles and Beyond*. New York: New York University Press, 1999.

Espiritu, Yen Le. *Asian American Panethnicity: Bridging Institutions and Identities*. Philadelphia: Temple University Press, 1992.

Fong, Timothy P. *The Contemporary Asian American Experience: Beyond the Model Minority*. Upper Saddle River, N.J.: Prentice-Hall, 1998.

Fong, Timothy P., and Larry H. Shinagawa, eds. *Asian Americans: Experiences and Perspectives*. Upper Saddle River, N.J.: Prentice-Hall, 2000.

Gee, Emma, ed. *Counterpoint: Perspectives on Asian America*. Los Angeles: Asian American Studies Center, University of California, 1976.

Horton, John. *The Politics of Diversity: Immigration, Resistance, and Change in Monterey Park, California*. Philadelphia: Temple University Press, 1995.

Hune, Shirley, et al., eds. *Asian Americans: Comparative and Global Perspectives*. Pullman: Washington State University Press, 1991.

Kodama-Nishimoto, Michi, et al. *Hanahana: An Oral History Anthology of Hawaii's Working People.* Honolulu: Ethnic Studies Oral History Project, University of Hawaii at Manoa, 1984.

Lee, Joann Faung Jean. *Asian American Experiences in the United States: Oral Histories of First to Fourth Generation Americans from China, the Philippines, Japan, India, the Pacific Islands, Vietnam and Cambodia.* Jefferson, N.C.: McFarland, 1991.

Lyman, Stanford M. *The Asian in the West.* Reno: Western Studies Center, University of Nevada System, 1970.

Manalansan, Martin F. IV, ed. *Cultural Compass: Ethnographic Explorations of Asian America.* Philadelphia: Temple University Press, 2000.

Min, Pyong Gap, and Rose Kim, eds. *Struggle for Ethnic Identity: Narratives by Asian American Professionals.* Walnut Creek, Calif.: AltaMira, 1999.

Mokuau, Noreen, ed. *A Handbook of Social Services for Asians and Pacific Islanders.* New York: Greenwood Press, 1991.

Ng, Franklin, ed. *The Asian American Encyclopedia.* New York: M. Cavendish, 1995.

———, ed. *Adaptation, Acculturation, and Transnational Ties Among Asian Americans.* New York: Garland, 1998.

———, ed. *Asian American Family Life and Community.* New York: Garland, 1998.

———, ed. *Asian American Interethnic Relations and Politics.* New York: Garland, 1998.

———, ed. *Asian American Issues Relating to Labor, Economics, and Socioeconomic Status.* New York: Garland, 1998.

———, ed. *Asians in America: The Peoples of East, Southeast, and South Asia in American Life and Culture.* New York: Garland, 1998.

———, ed. *The History and Immigration of Asian Americans.* New York: Garland, 1998.

Ng, Franklin, et al., eds. *New Visions in Asian American Studies: Diversity, Community, Power.* Pullman: Washington State University Press, 1994.

Nomura, Gail M., et al., eds. *Frontiers of Asian American Studies: Writing, Research, and Commentary.* Pullman: Washington State University Press, 1989.

Okihiro, Gary Y. *Margins and Mainstreams: Asians in American History and Culture.* Seattle: University of Washington Press, 1994.

Okihiro, Gary Y., et al., eds. *Reflections on Shattered Windows: Promises and Prospects for Asian American Studies.* Pullman: Washington State University Press, 1988.

———. *Privileging Positions: The Sites of Asian American Studies.* Pullman: Washington State University Press, 1995.

Rustomji-Kerns, Roshni, ed. *Encounters: People of Asian Descent in the Americas.* Lanham, Md.: Rowman and Littlefield, 1999.

Saito, Leland T. *Race and Politics: Asian Americans, Latinos, and Whites in a Los Angeles Suburb.* Urbana: University of Illinois Press, 1998.

Scott, Joanna C. *Indochina's Refugees: Oral Histories from Laos, Cambodia and Vietnam.* Jefferson, N.C.: McFarland, 1989.

Tachiki, Amy, et al., eds. *Roots: An Asian American Reader.* Los Angeles: Asian American Studies Center, University of California, 1971.

Takaki, Ronald. *Pau Hana: Plantation Life and Labor in Hawaii, 1835–1920.* Honolulu: University of Hawaii Press, 1983.

————. *Strangers from a Different Shore: A History of Asian Americans*. Boston: Little, Brown, 1989.

————. *A Different Mirror: A History of Multicultural America*. Boston: Little, Brown, 1993.

Wei, William. *The Asian American Movement*. Philadelphia: Temple University Press, 1993. (An account of the social movement of the late 1960s around identity, culture, and activism.)

Woo, Deborah. *Glass Ceilings and Asian Americans: The New Face of Workplace Barriers*. Walnut Creek, Calif.: AltaMira, 2000.

Wu, Diana Ting Liu. *Asian Pacific Americans in the Workplace*. Walnut Creek, Calif.: AltaMira, 1997.

Wu, Jean Yu-Wen Shen, and Min Song, eds. *Asian American Studies: A Reader*. New Brunswick, N.J.: Rutgers University Press, 2000.

Zhou, Min, and James V. Gatewood, eds. *Contemporary Asian America: A Multidisciplinary Reader*. New York: New York University Press, 2000.

Zia, Helen. *Asian American Dreams: The Emergence of an American People*. New York: Farrar, Straus and Giroux, 2000. (Semi-autobiographical survey of contemporary Asian America, especially community formations and social activism.)

Cambodians

Smith-Hefner, Nancy. *Khmer American: Identity and Moral Education in a Diasporic Community*. Berkeley: University of California Press, 1999.

Welarantna, Usha. *Beyond the Killing Fields: Voices of Nine Cambodian Survivors in America*. Stanford, Calif.: Stanford University Press, 1993.

Chinese

Anderson, Kay J. *Vancouver's Chinatown: Racial Discourse in Canada, 1875–1980*. Montreal: McGill-Queen's University Press, 1991.

Chan, Sucheng. *This Bitter-Sweet Soil: The Chinese in California Agriculture, 1860–1910*. Berkeley: University of California Press, 1986.

Chan, Sucheng, ed. *Entry Denied: Exclusion and the Chinese Community in America, 1882–1943*. Philadelphia: Temple University Press, 1991. (A collection of essays on the exclusion laws and their influences on individuals and communities.)

Char, Tin-Yuke. *The Bamboo Path: Life and Writings of a Chinese in Hawaii*. Honolulu: Hawaii Chinese History Center, 1977.

————, ed. *The Sandalwood Mountains: Readings and Stories of the Early Chinese in Hawaii*. Honolulu: University Press of Hawaii, 1975.

Chen, Hsiang-Shui. *Chinatown No More: Taiwan Immigrants in Contemporary New York*. Ithaca, N.Y.: Cornell University Press, 1992. (Social and cultural life of Taiwan immigrants in diverse, multi-ethnic neighborhoods of New York City.)

Chen, Yong. *Chinese San Francisco, 1850–1943: A Trans-Pacific Community*. Stanford, Calif.: Stanford University Press, 2000.

Chinn, Thomas W. *Bridging the Pacific: San Francisco Chinatown and Its People*. San

Francisco: Chinese Historical Society of America, 1989. (Accounts of Chinatown's institutions, but mainly biographies of individuals.)

Chinn, Thomas W., ed. *A History of the Chinese in California: A Syllabus*. San Francisco: Chinese Historical Society of America, 1969.

Cohen, Lucy M. *Chinese in the Post-Civil War South: A People Without a History*. Baton Rouge: Louisiana State University Press, 1984.

Dye, Bob. *Merchant Prince of the Sandalwood Mountains: Afong and the Chinese in Hawai'i*. Honolulu: University of Hawai'i Press, 1997.

Fong, Timothy P. *America's First Suburban Chinatown: The Remaking of Monterey Park, California*. Philadelphia: Temple University Press, 1994.

Gillenkirk, Jeff, and James Motlow. *Bitter Melon: Stories from the Last Rural Chinese Town in America*. Seattle: University of Washington Press, 1987. (Photographs of Locke, California, and oral histories of some of its residents.)

Glick, Clarence E. *Sojourners and Settlers: Chinese Migrants in Hawaii*. Honolulu: Hawaii Chinese History Center, 1980.

Hildebrand, Lorraine Barker. *Straw Hats, Sandals and Steel: The Chinese in Washington State*. Tacoma: Washington State Historical Society, 1977. (From a series of ethnic histories commissioned by the Washington State American Revolution Bicentennial Commission.)

Hom, Gloria Sun, ed. *Chinese Argonauts: An Anthology of the Chinese Contributions to the Historical Development of Santa Clara County*. Los Altos Hills, Calif.: Foothill Community College, 1971.

Larson, Louise Leung. *Sweet Bamboo: A Saga of a Chinese American Family*. Los Angeles: Chinese Historical Society of Southern California, 1989.

Leung, Peter C. Y. *One Day, One Dollar: Locke, California and the Chinese Farming Experience in the Sacramento Delta*. El Cerrito, Calif.: Chinese/Chinese American History Project, 1984.

Lin, Jan. *Reconstructing Chinatown: Ethnic Enclave, Global Change*. Minneapolis: University of Minnesota Press, 1998.

Loo, Chalsa M. *Chinatown: Most Time, Hard Time*. New York: Praeger, 1991. (A collection of essays on the well-being of San Francisco's Chinatown community.)

Low, Victor. *The Unimpressible Race: A Century of Educational Struggle by the Chinese in San Francisco*. San Francisco: East/West Publishing, 1982. (The fight for educational equity was a struggle for social equality both for Chinese America and America as a whole.)

Lum, Arlene, ed. *Sailing for the Sun: The Chinese in Hawaii, 1789–1989*. Honolulu: Center for Chinese Studies, University of Hawaii, 1988.

Lydon, Sandy. *Chinese Gold: The Chinese in the Monterey Bay Region*. Capitola, Calif.: Capitola Book, 1985.

Lyman, Stanford M. *Chinese Americans*. New York: Random House, 1974. (Historical sociology of Chinese Americans, including community organizations, racism, class formation, and social problems.)

Ma, L. Eve Armentrout. *Revolutionaries, Monarchists, and Chinatowns: Chinese Politics in the Americas and the 1911 Revolution*. Honolulu: University of Hawaii Press, 1990. (Relationship of Chinese in North America and Hawai'i to the Chinese revolution of 1911, and its place within Chinese American communities and Asian American politics.)

Minnick, Sylvia Sun. *Samfow: The San Joaquin Chinese Legacy*. Fresno, Calif.: Panorama West Publishing, 1988. (A history of the Chinese in California's Central Valley.)

Nee, Victor G. and Brett de Bary. *Longtime Californ': A Documentary Study of an American Chinatown*. New York: Pantheon, 1972.

Ng, Franklin. *The Taiwanese Americans*. Westport, Conn.: Greenwood Press, 1998.

Schwendinger, Robert J. *Ocean of Bitter Dreams: Maritime Relations Between China and the United States, 1850–1915*. Tucson, Ariz.: Westernlore Press, 1988. (U.S. involvement in the coolie trade and transportation of migrants and their impacts on anti-Chinese attitudes and violence in the United States.)

Tsai, Shih-shan Henry. *China and the Overseas Chinese in the United States, 1868–1911*. Fayetteville: University of Arkansas Press, 1983.

———. *The Chinese Experience in America*. Bloomington: Indiana University Press, 1986. (A general survey of Chinese American history from the mid-nineteenth century to the 1980s.)

Wegars, Priscilla, ed. *Hidden Heritage: Historical Archaeology of the Overseas Chinese*. Amityville, N.Y.: Baywood Publishing, 1993. (Collection of essays on rural and urban contexts, work and leisure, and method and theory centered mainly on the U.S. West.)

Wong, K. Scott, and Sucheng Chan, eds. *Claiming America: Constructing Chinese American Identities During the Exclusion Era*. Philadelphia: Temple University Press, 1998.

Wu, Cheng-Tsu, ed. *"Chink!" A Documentary History of Anti-Chinese Prejudice in America*. New York: World, 1972. (A collection of laws, testimonies, reports, speeches, and essays documenting anti-Chinese racism.)

Wyman, Nona Mock. *Chopstick Childhood: In a Town of Silver Spoons*. Walnut Creek, Calif.: MQ Press, 1997. (Memoir of the Ming Quong Home Orphanage for Chinese girls in Los Gatos, California, established in 1915.)

Zhou, Min. *Chinatown: The Socioeconomic Potential of an Urban Enclave*. Philadelphia: Temple University Press, 1992.

Class Formation

Beechert, Edward D. *Working in Hawaii: A Labor History*. Honolulu: University of Hawaii Press, 1985.

Bonacich, Edna and John Modell. *The Economic Basis of Ethnic Solidarity: Small Business in the Japanese American Community*. Berkeley: University of California Press, 1980.

Bonacich, Edna, et al., eds. *Global Production: The Apparel Industry in the Pacific Rim*. Philadelphia: Temple University Press, 1994.

Cheng, Lucie, and Edna Bonacich, eds. *Labor Immigration Under Capitalism: Asian Workers in the United States Before World War II*. Berkeley: University of California Press, 1984.

Chin, Ko-Lin. *Smuggled Chinese: Clandestine Immigration to the United States.* Philadelphia: Temple University Press, 1999.

Friday, Chris. *Organizing Asian American Labor: The Pacific Coast Canned-Salmon Industry, 1870–1942.* Philadelphia: Temple University Press, 1994.

Kent, Noel J. *Hawaii: Islands Under the Influence.* New York: Monthly Review Press, 1983.

Kwong, Peter. *Chinatown, New York: Labor and Politics, 1930–1950.* New York: Monthly Review Press, 1979.

———. *The New Chinatown.* New York: Hill and Wang, 1987.

———. *Forbidden Workers: Illegal Chinese Immigrants and American Labor.* New York: New Press, 1997.

Light, Ivan, and Edna Bonacich. *Immigrant Entrepreneurs: Koreans in Los Angeles, 1965–1982.* Berkeley: University of California Press, 1988.

Ong, Paul, et al., eds. *The New Asian Immigration in Los Angeles and Global Restructuring.* Philadelphia: Temple University Press, 1994.

Reinecke, John E. *The Filipino Piecemeal Sugar Strike of 1924–1925.* Honolulu: Social Science Research Institute, University of Hawai'i, 1996.

Yoneda, Karl G. *Ganbatte: Sixty-Year Struggle of a Kibei Worker.* Los Angeles: Asian American Studies Center, University of California, 1983. (Memoir and commentary on the Communist Party and U.S. labor history.)

Yu, Renqiu. *To Save China, To Save Ourselves: The Chinese Hand Laundry Alliance of New York.* Philadelphia: Temple University Press, 1992.

Critical Race Theory and Legal Studies

Ancheta, Angelo N. *Race, Rights, and the Asian American Experience.* New Brunswick, N.J.: Rutgers University Press, 1998.

Chang, Robert S. *Disoriented: Asian Americans, Law, and the Nation-State.* New York: New York University Press, 1999.

Crenshaw, Kimberlé Williams, et al., eds. *Critical Race Theory: The Key Writings that Formed the Movement.* New York: New Press, 1995.

Haney López, Ian F. *White by Law: The Legal Construction of Race.* New York: New York University Press, 1996.

Hing, Bill Ong. *Making and Remaking Asian America Through Immigration Policy, 1850–1990.* Stanford, Calif.: Stanford University Press, 1993.

Matsuda, Mari J. *Where Is Your Body? And Other Essays on Race, Gender, and the Law.* Boston: Beacon Press, 1996.

Matsuda, Mari J., et al. *Words That Wound: Critical Race Theory, Assaultive Speech, and the First Amendment.* Boulder, Colo.: Westview Press, 1993.

Omi, Michael, and Howard Winant. *Racial Formation in the United States: From the 1960s to the 1980s.* New York: Routledge and Kegan Paul, 1986.

San Juan, E., Jr. *Racial Formations/Critical Transformations: Articulations of Power in Ethnic and Racial Studies in the United States.* Atlantic Highlands, N.J.: Humanities Press, 1992.

Takagi, Dana Y. *The Retreat from Race: Asian-American Admissions and Racial Politics.* New Brunswick, N.J.: Rutgers University Press, 1992.

Yamamoto, Eric K. *Interracial Justice: Conflict and Reconciliation in Post-Civil Rights America.* New York: New York University Press, 1999.

Cultural Studies and Cultural Criticism

Brown, Michael D. *Views from Asian California, 1920–1965: An Illustrated History.* San Francisco: Michael Brown, 1992.

Buck, Elizabeth. *Paradise Remade: The Politics of Culture and History in Hawai'i.* Philadephia: Temple University Press, 1993.

Choy, Philip P., Lorraine Dong, and Marlon K. Hom. *The Coming Man: 19th Century American Perceptions of the Chinese.* Seattle: University of Washington Press, 1994. (Illustrations and political cartoons in popular publications organized around community life, Sino-American relations, and domestic politics.)

Desmond, Jane C. *Staging Tourism: Bodies on Display from Waikiki to Sea World.* Chicago: University of Chicago Press, 1999.

Eaton, Allen H. *Beauty Behind Barbed Wire: The Arts of the Japanese in Our War Relocation Camps.* New York: Harper and Brothers, 1952.

Eng, Alvin, ed. *Tokens? The NYC Asian American Experience on Stage.* New York: Asian American Writers' Workshop, 1999.

Gesensway, Deborah, and Mindy Roseman. *Beyond Words: Images from America's Concentration Camps.* Ithaca, N.Y.: Cornell University Press, 1987.

Hamamoto, Darrell Y. *Monitored Peril: Asian Americans and the Politics of TV Representation.* Minneapolis: University of Minnesota Press, 1994.

Hamamoto, Darrell Y., and Sandra Liu, eds. *Countervisions: Asian American Film Criticism.* Philadelphia: Temple University Press, 2000.

Higa, Karin M. *The View from Within: Japanese American Art from the Internment Camps, 1942–1945.* Los Angeles: Japanese American National Museum, 1992.

Hill, Kimi Kodani, ed. *Topaz Moon: Chiura Obata's Art of the Internment.* Berkeley, Calif.: Heyday Books, 2000.

Kondo, Dorinne. *About Face: Performing Race in Fashion and Theater.* New York: Routledge, 1997.

Lee, Josephine. *Performing Asian America: Race and Ethnicity on the Contemporary Stage.* Philadelphia: Temple University Press, 1997.

Lee, Robert G. *Orientals: Asians in Popular Culture.* Philadelphia: Temple University Press, 1999.

Leong, Russell, ed. *Moving the Image: Independent Asian Pacific American Media Arts.* Los Angeles: Asian American Studies Center, University of California, 1991.

Li, David Leiwei. *Imagining the Nation: Asian American Literature and Cultural Consent.* Stanford, Calif.: Stanford University Press, 1998.

Ling, Amy, ed. *Yellow Light: The Flowering of Asian American Arts.* Philadelphia: Temple University Press, 1999.

Lowe, Lisa. *Immigrant Acts: On Asian American Cultural Politics.* Durham, N.C.: Duke University Press, 1996.

Machida, Margo, et al. *Asia/America: Identities in Contemporary Asian American Art.* New York: Asia Society Galleries and New Press, 1994.

Marchetti, Gina. *Romance and the "Yellow Peril": Race, Sex, and Discursive Strategies in Hollywood Fiction.* Berkeley: University of California Press, 1993.

Moy, James S. *Marginal Sights: Staging the Chinese in America.* Iowa City: University of Iowa Press, 1993.

Okubo, Mine. *Citizen 13660.* New York: Columbia University Press, 1946. (Drawings and commentary of Tanforan assembly center and Topaz concentration camp.)

Palumbo-Liu, David. *Asian/American: Historical Crossings of a Racial Frontier.* Stanford, Calif.: Stanford University Press, 1999.

Tchen, John Kuo Wei. *New York before Chinatown: Orientalism and the Shaping of American Culture, 1776–1882.* Baltimore: Johns Hopkins University Press, 1999.

Tsutakawa, Mayumi, ed. *They Painted from Their Hearts: Pioneer Asian American Artists.* Seattle: Wing Luke Asian Museum, 1994.

Tsutakawa, Mayumi, and Alan Chong Lau, eds. *Turning Shadows Into Light: Art and Culture of the Northwest's Early Asian/Pacific Community.* Seattle: Young Pine Press, 1982.

Xing, Jun. *Asian America Through the Lens: History, Representations, and Identity.* Walnut Creek, Calif.: AltaMira, 1998.

Yang, Alice. *Why Asia? Contemporary Asian and Asian American Art.* New York: New York University Press, 1998.

Education

Endo, Russell, et al., eds. *Current Issues in Asian and Pacific American Education.* South El Monte, Calif.: Pacific Asia Press, 1998.

Hirabayashi, Lane Ryo, ed. *Teaching Asian America: Diversity and the Problem of Community.* Lanham, Md.: Rowman and Littlefield, 1998.

Nakanishi, Don T., and Marsha Hirano-Nakanishi, eds. *The Education of Asian and Pacific Americans: Historical Perspectives and Prescriptions for the Future.* Phoenix: Oryx Press, 1983.

Okihiro, Gary Y. *Teaching Asian American History.* Washington, D.C.: American Historical Association, 1997.

Park, Clara C., and Marilyn Mei-Ying Chi, eds. *Asian American Education: Prospects and Challenges.* Granby, Mass.: Bergin and Garvey, 1999.

Filipinos

Anderson, Robert N. *Filipinos in Rural Hawaii.* Honolulu: University of Hawaii Press, 1984.

Bonus, Rick. *Locating Filipino Americans: Ethnicity and the Cultural Politics of Space.* Philadelphia: Temple University Press, 2000.

Cayaban, Ines V. *A Goodly Heritage.* Hong Kong: Gulliver Books, 1981. (Memoir of a nurse and cultural worker in Hawai'i.)

Chen, Anita Beltran. *From Sunbelt to Snowbelt: Filipinos in Canada.* Calgary: Canadian Ethnic Studies Association, University of Calgary, 1998.

Cordova, Fred. *Filipinos: Forgotten Asian Americans.* Dubuque, Iowa: Kendall/Hunt, 1983.

de la Cruz, Enrique B., and Pearlie Rose Baluyut, eds. *Confrontations Crossings and Convergence: Photographs of the Philippines and the United States, 1989–1998*. Los Angeles: Asian American Studies Center, University of California, 1998.

DeWitt, Howard A. *Anti-Filipino Movements in California: A History, Bibliography and Study Guide*. San Francisco: R and E Research Associates, 1976.

Dionisio, Juan C., Stu Glauberman, and Carl H. Zimmerman, eds. *From Mabuhay to Aloha: The Filipinos in Hawaii*. Honolulu: Filipino Association of University Women, 1991.

Dorita, Mary. *Filipino Immigration to Hawaii*. San Francisco: R and E Research Associates, 1975.

Espina, Marina E. *Jacinto E. Esmele: Profile of a Successful Filipino in the United States of America*. New Orleans: A. F. Laborde and Sons, 1980.

———. *Filipinos in Louisiana*. New Orleans: A. F. Laborde and Sons, 1988.

Espiritu, Yen Le. *Filipino American Lives*. Philadelphia: Temple University Press, 1995.

Filipino Oral History Projecct. *Voices: A Filipino American Oral History*. Stockton, Calif.: Filipino Oral History Project, 1984.

Morantte, P. C. *Remembering Carlos Bulosan (His Heart Affair with America)*. Quezon City: New Day Publishers, 1984.

Okamura, Jonathan Y. *Imagining the Filipino American Diaspora: Transnational Relations, Identities, and Communities*. New York: Garland, 1998.

Pido, Antonio J. A. *The Pilipinos in America: Macro/Micro Dimensions of Immigration and Integration*. New York: Center for Migration Studies, 1986.

Quinsaat, Jesse, ed. *Letters in Exile: An Introductory Reader on the History of Pilipinos in America*. Los Angeles: Asian American Studies Center, University of California, 1976.

Rafael, Vicente L. *White Love and Other Events in Filipino History*. Durham, N.C.: Duke University Press, 2000.

Rafael, Vicente L., ed. *Discrepant Histories: Translocal Essays on Filipino Cultures*. Philadelphia: Temple University Press, 1995.

Root, Maria P. P., ed. *Filipino Americans: Transformation and Identity*. Thousand Oaks, Calif.: Sage, 1997.

Rodis, Rodel E. *Telltale Signs: Filipinos in America*. n.p.: INA Development, 1991.

San Juan, E., Jr. *Allegories of Resistance: The Philippines at the Threshold of the Twenty-First Century*. Quezon City: University of the Philippines Press, 1994.

———. *The Philippine Temptation: Dialectics of Philippines-U.S. Literary Relations*. Philadelphia: Temple University Press, 1996.

———. *From Exile to Diaspora: Versions of the Filipino Experience in the United States*. Boulder, Colo.: Westview Press, 1998.

———. *After Postcolonialism: Remapping Philippines–United States Confrontations*. Lanham, Md.: Rowman and Littlefield, 2000.

San Juan, E., Jr., ed. *On Becoming Filipino: Selected Writings of Carlos Bulosan*. Philadelphia: Temple University Press, 1995.

Scharlin, Craig, and Lilia V. Villanueva. *Philip Vera Cruz: A Personal History of Filipino Immigrants and the Farmworkers Movement*. Los Angeles: Labor Center, Institute of Industrial Relations, University of California, 1992.

Teodoro, Luis V., Jr., ed. *Out of This Struggle: The Filipinos in Hawaii.* Honolulu: University Press of Hawaii, 1981.

Vallangca, Caridad Concepcion. *The Second Wave: Pinay & Pinoy (1945–1960).* San Francisco: Strawberry Hill Press, 1987.

Vallangca, Roberto V. *Pinoy: The First Wave (1898–1941).* San Francisco: Strawberry Hill Press, 1977.

Vergara, Benito M., Jr. *Displaying Filipinos: Photography and Colonialism in Early 20th Century Philippines.* Quezon City: University of the Philippines Press, 1995.

Hmong

Chang, Sucheng, ed. *Hmong Means Free: Life in Laos and America.* Philadelphia: Temple University Press, 1994.

Donnelly, Nancy D. *Changing Lives of Refugee Hmong Women.* Seattle: University of Washington Press, 1994.

Faderman, Lillian with Ghia Xiong. *I Begin My Life All Over: The Hmong and the American Immigrant Experience.* Boston: Beacon Press, 1998.

Identity and Psychology

Jiobu, Robert. *Ethnicity and Assimilation: Blacks, Chinese, Filipinos, Japanese, Koreans, Mexicans, Vietnamese, and Whites.* Albany: State University of New York Press, 1988.

Nagata, Donna K. *Legacy of Injustice: Exploring the Cross-Generational Impact of the Japanese American Internment.* New York: Plenum Press, 1993.

Sue, Stanley and James Morishima. *The Mental Health of Asian Americans.* San Francisco: Jossey-Bass, 1982.

Sue, Stanley, and Nathaniel N. Wagner, eds. *Asian-Americans: Psychological Perspectives.* Palo Alto, Calif.: Science and Behavior Books, 1973.

Tuan, Mia. *Forever Foreigners or Honorary Whites? The Asian Ethnic Experience Today.* New Brunswick, N.J.: Rutgers University Press, 1998.

Uba, Laura. *Asian Americans: Personality Patterns, Identity, and Mental Health.* New York: Guilford Press, 1994.

Japanese

Beechert, Alice M., and Edward D. Beechert, eds. *From Kona to Yenan: The Political Memoir of Koji Ariyoshi.* Honolulu: University of Hawai'i Press, 2000.

Chalfen, Richard. *Turning Leaves: The Photograph Collections of Two Japanese American Families.* Albuquerque: University of New Mexico Press, 1991.

Chang, Gordon H., ed. *Morning Glory, Evening Shadow: Yamato Ichihashi and His Internment Writings, 1942–1945.* Stanford, Calif.: Stanford University Press, 1997.

Drinnon, Richard. *Keeper of Concentration Camps: Dillon S. Myer and American Racism.* Berkeley: University of California Press, 1987. (History of the head of the War Relocation Authority and Bureau of Indian Affairs and the nature of U.S. racism.)

Embrey, Sue Kunitomi, Arthur A. Hansen, and Betty Kulberg Mitson. *Manzanar Martyr: An Interview with Harry Y. Ueno*. Fullerton: Oral History Program, California State University, 1986. (Account of a principal in the Manzanar riot of 1942.)

Ethnic Studies Oral History Project. *Uchinanchu: A History of Okinawans in Hawaii*. Honolulu: University of Hawaii Press, 1981.

Fiset, Louis. *Imprisoned Apart: The World War II Correspondence of an Issei Couple*. Seattle: University of Washington Press, 1997.

Fugita, Stephen S., and David J. O'Brien. *Japanese American Ethnicity: The Persistence of Community*. Seattle: University of Washington Press, 1991. (A sociology of ethnic retention amidst structural assimilation based on a two-generation survey.)

Fukuda, Yoshiaki. *My Six Years of Internment: An Issei's Struggle for Justice*. Translated by the Konko Church of San Francisco and the Research, Information Center of the Konko Churches of North America. San Francisco: Konko Church of San Francisco, 1990.

Gorfinkel, Claire, ed. *The Evacuation Diary of Hatsuye Egami*. Pasadena, Calif.: Intentional Productions, 1995.

Hansen, Arthur A., ed. *Japanese American World War II Evacuation Oral History Project*. 6 vols. Munich, Germany: K. G. Saur, 1991–94.

Hata, Donald Teruo, Jr. *"Undesirables": Early Immigrants and the Anti-Japanese Movement in San Francisco, 1892–1893*. New York: Arno Press, 1978. (Dissertation on Japanese sailors, entertainers, students, gamblers, prostitutes, and laborers and the anti-Japanese movement.)

Hazama, Dorothy Ochiai, and Jane Okamoto Komeiji. *Okage Sama De: The Japanese of Hawai'i, 1885–1985*. Honolulu: Bess Press, 1986. (A centennial popular history by two *nisei*, or second-generation, teachers.)

Heuterman, Thomas H. *The Burning Horse: Japanese-American Experience in the Yakima Valley, 1920–1942*. Cheney: Eastern Washington University Press, 1995. (Study of anti-Japanese sentiment and its nuances based on documents, newspapers, and oral interviews.)

Higa, Thomas Taro. *Memoirs of a Certain Nisei, 1916–1985*. Translated by Mitsugu Sakihara. Kaneohe, Hawai'i: Higa Publications, 1988. (Born in Hawai'i, studied in Japan, a U.S. soldier during World War II, and a leader among Okinawans in the islands.)

Higashide, Seiichi. *Adios to Tears: The Memoirs of a Japanese-Peruvian Internee in U.S. Concentration Camps*. Honolulu: E&E Kudo, 1993.

Hirabayashi, Lane Ryo. *The Politics of Fieldwork: Research in an American Concentration Camp*. Tucson: University of Arizona Press, 1999. (The ethics and politics of fieldwork exemplified in the work of anthropologist Tamie Tsuchiyama at Poston.)

Hirano, Kiyo. *Enemy Alien*. San Francisco: JAM Publications, 1983. (A woman's memoir of World War II, including life in Amache concentration camp and labor in Brigham, Utah.)

Hohri, William Minoru. *Repairing America: An Account of the Movement for Japanese-American Redress*. Pullman: Washington State University Press, 1988.

Ichioka, Yuji. *The Issei: The World of the First Generation Japanese Immigrants, 1885–1924*. New York: Free Press, 1988.

Ichioka, Yuji, ed. *Views from Within: The Japanese American Evacuation and Resettlement Study*. Los Angeles: Asian American Studies Center, University of California, 1989.

Ige, Tom. *Boy from Kahaluu: An Autobiography*. Honolulu: Kin Cho Jin Kai, 1989. (Born in Hawai'i, World War II veteran, and an economist.)

Ito, Kazuo. *Issei: A History of Japanese Immigrants in North America*. Translated by Shinichiro Nakamura and Jean S. Gerard. Seattle: Japanese Community Service, 1973.

Kawakami, Barbara F. *Japanese Immigrant Clothing in Hawaii, 1885–1941*. Honolulu: University of Hawaii Press, 1993.

Kessler, Lauren. *Stubborn Twig: Three Generations in the Life of a Japanese American Family*. New York: Plume, 1993. (A social history of the Yasui family of Oregon.)

Kikumura, Akemi. *Promises Kept: The Life of an Issei Man*. Novato, Calif.: Chandler and Sharp, 1991. (Follow-up and companion book to author's biography of her mother, *Through Harsh Winters*.)

Knaefler, Tomi Kaizawa. *Our House Divided: Seven Japanese American Families in World War II*. Honolulu: University of Hawaii Press, 1991.

Kotani, Roland. *The Japanese in Hawaii: A Century of Struggle*. Honolulu: Hawaii Hochi, 1985.

Levine, Ellen. *A Fence Away from Freedom: Japanese Americans and World War II*. New York: G. P. Putnam's Sons, 1995. (A collection of reminiscences and commentary.)

Lukes, Timothy J., and Gary Y. Okihiro. *Japanese Legacy: Farming and Community Life in California's Santa Clara Valley*. Cupertino: California History Center, 1985.

Maki, Mitchell T., Harry H. L. Kitano, and S. Megan Berthold. *Achieving the Impossible Dream: How Japanese Americans Obtained Redress*. Urbana: University of Illinois Press, 1999.

Matsumoto, Valerie J. *Farming the Home Place: A Japanese American Community in California, 1919–1982*. Ithaca, N.Y.: Cornell University Press, 1993.

Moriyama, Alan Takeo. *Imingaisha: Japanese Emigration Companies and Hawaii, 1894–1908*. Honolulu: University of Hawaii Press, 1985.

Nagara. Susumu. *Japanese Pidgin English in Hawaii: A Bilingual Description*. Honolulu: University Press of Hawaii, 1972.

Nakamura, Hiroshi. *Treadmill: A Documentary Novel*. Oakville, Ont., Canada: Mosaic Press, 1996. (Written while in the concentration camps for Japanese American readers.)

Nakane, Kazuko. *Nothing Left in My Hands: An Early Japanese American Community in California's Pajaro Valley*. Seattle: Young Pine Press, 1985. (An agricultural history based on printed and oral sources.)

Nishimoto, Richard S. *Inside an American Concentration Camp: Japanese American Resistance at Poston, Arizona*. Edited by Lane Ryo Hirabayashi. Tucson: University of Arizona Press, 1995.

Noda, Kesa. *Yamato Colony: 1906–1960*. Livingston, Calif.: Livingston-Merced Japanese American Citizens League, 1981.

O'Brien, David J., and Stephen S. Fugita. *The Japanese American Experience*. Bloomington: Indiana University Press, 1991. (A survey historical sociology.)

Oda, James. *Heroic Struggles of Japanese Americans: Partisan Fighters from America's Concentration Camps*. North Hollywood, Calif.: James Oda, 1980. (Memoir and commentary by a labor organizer and U.S. veteran of World War II.)

Odo, Franklin, and Kazuko Sinoto. *A Pictorial History of the Japanese in Hawai'i, 1885–1924*. Honolulu: Bishop Museum Press, 1985.

Okahata, James H., ed. *A History of Japanese in Hawaii*. Honolulu: United Japanese Society of Hawaii, 1971.

Okihiro, Gary Y. *Cane Fires: The Anti-Japanese Movement in Hawaii, 1865–1945*. Philadelphia: Temple University Press, 1991.

———. *Storied Lives: Japanese American Students and World War II*. Seattle: University of Washington Press, 1999.

Okihiro, Gary Y., and Joan Myers. *Whispered Silences: Japanese Americans and World War II*. Seattle: University of Washington Press, 1996.

Okinawa Club of America, comp. *History of Okinawans in North America*. Translated by Ben Kobashigawa. Los Angeles: Asian American Studies Center, University of California, 1988.

Sarasohn, Eileen Sunada, ed. *The Issei: Portrait of a Pioneer, An Oral History*. Palo Alto, Calif.: Pacific Books, 1983.

Sawada, Mitziko. *Tokyo Life, New York Dreams: Urban Japanese Visions of America, 1890–1924*. Berkeley: University of California Press, 1996.

Spickard, Paul R. *Japanese Americans: The Formation and Transformation of an Ethnic Group*. New York: Twayne, 1996. (A survey history.)

Takahashi, Jere. *Nisei/Sansei: Shifting Japanese American Identities and Politics*. Philadelphia: Temple University Press, 1997.

Takezawa, Yasuko I. *Breaking the Silence: Redress and Japanese American Ethnicity*. Ithaca, N.Y.: Cornell University Press, 1995.

Tamura, Linda. *The Hood River Issei: An Oral History of Japanese Settlers in Oregon's Hood River Valley*. Urbana: University of Illinois Press, 1993.

Tateishi, John. *And Justice for All: An Oral History of the Japanese American Detention Camps*. New York: Random House, 1984.

Tomita, Mary Kimoto. *Dear Miye: Letters Home from Japan, 1939–1946*. Edited by Robert G. Lee. Stanford, Calif.: Stanford University Press, 1995. (Life in Japan during World War II as revealed in a Japanese American woman's letters to her friends in the United States.)

Uchida, Yoshiko. *Desert Exile: The Uprooting of a Japanese-American Family*. Seattle: University of Washington Press, 1982. (A woman writer's memoir of Tanforan assembly center and Topaz concentration camp during World War II.)

Uyeda, Clifford I. *Suspended: Growing Up Asian in America*. San Francisco: National Japanese American Historical Society, 2000. (Autobiography of a *nisei*, or second-generation, community leader and activist.)

Wakukawa, Ernest K. *A History of the Japanese People in Hawaii*. Honolulu: Toyo Shoin, 1938.

Walls, Thomas K. *The Japanese Texans*. San Antonio: Institute of Texan Cultures, University of Texas, 1987. (A history from the 1890s to the 1990s based on written and oral sources.)

Whelchel, Toshio. *From Pearl Harbor to Saigon: Japanese American Soldiers and the*

Vietnam War. London: Verso, 1999. (A commentary and collection of eleven oral histories.)

Yoo, David K. *Growing Up Nisei: Race, Generation, and Culture among Japanese Americans of California, 1924–49*. Urbana: University of Illinois Press, 2000.

Koreans

Abelmann, Nancy and John Lie. *Blue Dreams: Korean Americans and the Los Angeles Riots*. Cambridge, Mass.: Harvard University Press, 1995.

Barringer, Herbert R., and Sung-Nam Cho. *Koreans in the United States: A Fact Book*. Honolulu: Center for Korean Studies, University of Hawaii, 1989.

Hurh, Won Moo. *The Korean Americans*. Westport, Conn.: Greenwood Press, 1998.

Hurh, Won Moo, Hei Chu Kim, and Kwang Chung Kim. *Assimilation Patterns of Immigrants in the United States: A Case Study of Korean Immigrants in the Chicago Area*. Washington, D.C.: University Press of America, 1978.

Hurh, Won Moo, and Kwang Chung Kim. *Korean Immigrants in America: A Structural Analysis of Ethnic Confinement and Adhesive Adaptation*. Madison, N.J.: Fairleigh Dickinson University Press, 1984.

Hyun, Peter. *Man Sei! The Making of a Korean American*. Honolulu: University of Hawaii Press, 1986.

———. *In the New World: The Making of a Korean American*. Honolulu: University of Hawai'i Press, 1991. (Autobiography and sequel to *Man Sei!*)

Kang, K. Connie. *Home Was the Land of the Morning Calm: A Saga of a Korean-American Family*. Reading, Mass.: Addison-Wesley, 1995.

Kim, Claire Jean. *Bitter Fruit: The Politics of the Black-Korean Conflict in New York City*. New Haven, Conn.: Yale University Press, 2000.

Kim, Elaine H., and Eui-Young Yu. *East to America: Korean American Life Stories*. New York: New Press, 1996.

Kim, Illsoo. *New Urban Immigrants: The Korean Community in New York*. Princeton, N.J.: Princeton University Press, 1981.

Kim, Kwang Chung, ed. *Koreans in the Hood: Conflict with African Americans*. Baltimore: Johns Hopkins University Press, 1999.

Kim, Warren Y. *Koreans in America*. Seoul, Korea: Po Chin Chai, 1971. (A survey history, especially of community organizations and nationalism, from beginnings to 1948.)

Min, Pyong Gap. *Ethnic Business Enterprise: Korean Small Business in Atlanta*. New York: Center for Migration Studies, 1988.

———. *Caught in the Middle: Korean Communities in New York and Los Angeles*. Berkeley: University of California Press, 1996.

Pai, Margaret K. *The Dreams of Two Yi-min*. Honolulu: University of Hawaii Press, 1989. (Biography of author's parents, Do In Kwon and Hee Kyung Lee, in Hawai'i.)

Park, Kyeyoung. *The Korean American Dream: Immigrants and Small Business in New York City*. Ithaca, N.Y.: Cornell University Press, 1997.

Patterson, Wayne. *The Korean Frontier in America: Immigration to Hawaii, 1896–1910*. Honolulu: University of Hawaii Press, 1988.

———. *The Ilse: First-Generation Korean Immigrants in Hawai'i, 1903–1973*. Honolulu: University of Hawai'i Press, 2000.

Rhee, Helen Choi. *The Korean-American Experience: A Detailed Analysis of How Well Korean-Americans Adjust to Life in the United States*. New York: Vantage Press, 1995.

Rhodes, Daisy Chun. *Passages to Paradise: Early Korean Immigrant Narratives from Hawai'i*. Los Angeles: Academia Koreana, 1998.

Yoon, In-Jin. *On My Own: Korean Businesses and Race Relations in America*. Chicago: University of Chicago Press, 1997.

Yu, Eui-Young, et al., eds. *Koreans in Los Angeles: Prospects and Promises*. Los Angeles: Center for Korean-American and Korean Studies, California State University, 1982.

Literature and Literary Criticism

Alexander, Meena. *The Shock of Arrival: Reflections on Postcolonial Experience*. Boston: South End Press, 1996.

Baker, Houston A., Jr., ed. *Three American Literatures: Essays in Chicano, Native American, and Asian-American Literature for Teachers of American Literature*. New York: Modern Language Association of America, 1982.

Bloom, Harold, ed. *Asian-American Women Writers*. Philadelphia: Chelsea House Publishers, 1997.

Bruchac, Joseph, ed. *Breaking Silence, An Anthology of Contemporary Asian American Poets*. Greenfield Center, N.Y.: Greenfield Review Press, 1983.

Bulosan, Carlos. *The Cry and the Dedication*. Edited by E. San Juan, Jr. Philadelphia: Temple University Press, 1995.

Cha, Theresa Hak Kyung. *Dictee*. New York: Tanam Press, 1982.

Chang, Juliana, ed. *Quiet Fire: A Historical Anthology of Asian American Poetry, 1892–1970*. New York: Asian American Writers' Workshop, 1996.

Cheung, King-Kok, ed. *An Interethnic Companion to Asian American Literature*. New York: Cambridge University Press, 1997.

Chin, Frank. *The Chickencoop Chinaman and The Year of the Dragon: Two Plays*. Seattle: University of Washington Press, 1981.

Chin, Frank, et al., eds. *Aiiieeeee! An Anthology of Asian-American Writers*. Garden City, N.Y.: Anchor Press, 1974.

Chock, Eric, et al., eds. *Talk Story: An Anthology of Hawaii's Local Writers*. n.p.: Petronium Press, 1978.

Far, Sui Sin. *Mrs. Spring Fragrance and Other Writings*. Edited by Amy Ling and Annette White-Parks. Urbana: University of Illinois Press, 1995.

Francia, Luis H., and Eric Gamalinda, eds. *Flippin': Filipinos on America*. New York: Asian American Writers' Workshop, 1996.

Hagedorn, Jessica. *Dogeaters*. New York: Pantheon Books, 1990.

Hagedorn, Jessica, ed. *Charlie Chan Is Dead: An Anthology of Contemporary Asian American Fiction*. New York: Penguin Books, 1993.

Hom, Marlon K. *Songs of Gold Mountain: Cantonese Rhymes from San Francisco Chinatown*. Berkeley: University of California Press, 1987. (Selection of 220 folk-songs published in 1911 and 1915, and their contexts and revelations of Chinese American life.)

Hongo, Garrett, ed. *The Open Boat: Poems from Asian America.* New York: Doubleday, 1993.

———. *Under Western Eyes: Personal Essays from Asian America.* New York: Anchor Books, 1995.

Hwang, David Henry. *M. Butterfly.* New York: Plume, 1986,

Kim, Elaine H. *Asian American Literature: An Introduction to the Writings and Their Social Contexts.* Philadelphia: Temple University Press, 1982.

Kingston, Maxine Hong. *Woman Warrior: Memoirs of a Girlhood Among Ghosts.* New York: Random House, 1975.

Lai, Him Mark, Genny Lim, and Judy Yung. *Island: Poetry and History of Chinese Immigrants on Angel Island, 1910–1940.* Seattle: University of Washington Press, 1980. (A selection of poems carved on the interior walls of the barracks at Angel Island immigration station in San Francisco Bay.)

Lahiri, Jhumpa. *Interpreter of Maladies.* Boston: Houghton Mifflin, 1999.

Lee, Rachel C. *The Americas of Asian American Literature: Gendered Fictions of Nation and Transnation.* Princeton, N.J.: Princeton University Press, 1999.

Lew, Walter K., ed. *Premonitions: The Kaya Anthology of New Asian North American Poetry.* New York: Kaya, 1995.

Lim, Shirley Geok-lin, and Amy Ling, eds. *Reading the Literatures of Asian America.* Philadelphia: Temple University Press, 1992.

Mori, Toshio. *Yokohama California.* Caldwell, Idaho: Caxton Printers, 1949.

Mukherjee, Bharati. *Jasmine.* New York: Grove Weidenfeld, 1989.

Murayama, Milton. *All I Asking for Is My Body.* San Francisco: Supa Press, 1959.

Nakano, Jiro, and Kay Nakano, eds. *Poets Behind Barbed Wire.* Honolulu: Bamboo Ridge Press, 1983. (Poems by Keiho Soga, Taisanboku Mori, Sojin Takei, and Muin Ozaki from Hawai'i written during World War II.)

Nelson, Emmanuel S. *Bharati Mukherjee: Critical Perspectives.* New York: Garland, 1993.

———, ed. *Reworlding: The Literature of the Indian Diaspora.* New York: Greenwood Press, 1992.

———, ed. *Asian American Novelists: A Bio-bibliographical Critical Notebook.* Westport, Conn.: Greenwood Press, 2000.

Okada, John. *No-No Boy.* Seattle: University of Washington Press, 1976.

Realuyo, Bino A., ed. *The Nuyor Asian Anthology: Asian American Writings About New York City.* New York: Asian American Writers' Workshop, 1999.

Ruoff, A. LaVonne Brown, and Jerry W. Ward, eds. *Redefining American Literary History.* New York: Modern Language Association of America, 1990.

Rustomji-Kerns, Roshni, ed. *Living in America: Poetry and Fiction by South Asian American Writers.* Boulder, Colo.: Westview Press, 1995.

Sakamoto, Edward. *Hawaii No Ka Oi: The Kamiya Family Trilogy.* Honolulu: University of Hawai'i Press, 1995. (Plays of Japanese Americans in Hawai'i.)

Santos, Bienvenido N. *Scent of Apples: A Collection of Stories.* Seattle: University of Washington Press, 1955.

274 HISTORIOGRAPHY AND RESOURCES

Singh, Amritjit, and Peter Schmidt, eds. *Postcolonial Theory and the United States: Race, Ethnicity, and Literature*. Jackson: University Press of Mississippi, 2000.

Sumida, Stephen H. *And the View from the Shore: Literary Traditions of Hawai'i*. Seattle: University of Washington Press, 1991.

Tabios, Eileen. *Black Lightning: Poetry-in-Progress*. New York: Asian American Writers Workshop, 1998.

White-Parks, Annette. *Sui Sin Far/Edith Maude Eaton: A Literary Biography*. Urbana: University of Illinois Press, 1995.

Wong, Sau-ling Cynthia. *Reading Asian American Literature: From Necessity to Extravagance*. Princeton, N.J.: Princeton University Press, 1993.

Yamamoto, Hisaye. *Seventeen Syllables and Other Stories*. Latham, N.Y.: Kitchen Table: Women of Color Press, 1988.

Yamauchi, Wakako. *Songs My Mother Taught Me: Stories, Plays, and a Memoir*. New York: Feminist Press, 1994.

Yin, Xiao-huang. *Chinese American Literature since the 1850s*. Urbana: University of Illinois Press, 2000.

Multiracials

DeBonis, Steven. *Children of the Enemy: Oral Histories of Vietnamese Amerasians and Their Mothers*. Jefferson, N.C.: McFarland, 1995.

Hara, Marie, and Nora Okja Keller, eds. *Intersecting Circles: The Voices of Hapa Women in Poetry and Prose*. Honolulu: University of Hawai'i Press, 2000.

Root, Maria P. P., ed. *Racially Mixed People in America*. Newbury Park, Calif.: Sage, 1992.

Spickard, Paul R. *Mixed Blood: Intermarriage and Ethnic Identity in Twentieth-Century America*. Madison: University of Wisconsin Press, 1989.

Religion

Britsch, R. Lanier. *Moramona, the Mormons in Hawaii*. Laie, Hawai'i: Institute for Polynesian Studies, 1989.

Centennial Publication Committee. *A Grateful Past, A Promising Future: Namu Amida Butsu, 100 Centennial Commemoration, 1889–1989*. Honolulu: Honpa Hongwanji Mission of Hawaii, 1989.

Coward, Howard, John R. Hinnells, and Raymond Brady Williams, eds. *The South Asian Religious Diaspora in Britain, Canada, and the United States*. Albany: State University of New York Press, 2000.

Farber, Don. *Taking Refuge in L.A.: Life in a Vietnamese Buddhist Temple*. New York: Aperture Foundation, 1987.

Fein, Helen. *Congregational Sponsors of Indochinese Refugees in the United States, 1979–1981*. Cranbury, N.J.: Fairleigh Dickinson University Press, 1987.

Fenton, John Y. *Transplanting Religious Traditions: Asian Indians in America*. New York: Praeger, 1988.

Haddad, Yvonne Yazbeck, and Jane Idleman Smith. *Mission to America: Five Islamic Sectarian Communities in North America*. Gainesville: University Press of Florida, 1993.

Hasegawa, Atsuko, and Nancy S. Shiraki, eds. *Hoshu: A Pictorial History of Jodo Shinshu Women in Hawaii*. Honolulu: Hawaii Federation of Honpa Hongwanji Buddhist Women's Associations, 1989.

Hayashi, Brian Masaru. *"For the Sake of Our Japanese Brethren": Assimilation, Nationalism, and Protestantism Among the Japanese of Los Angeles, 1895–1942*. Stanford, Calif.: Stanford University Press, 1995.

Kashima, Tetsuden. *Buddhism in America: The Social Organization of an Ethnic Religious Institution*. Westport, Conn.: Greenwood Press, 1977.

Khalidi, Omar, ed. *Indian Muslims in North America*. Watertown, Mass.: South Asia Press, 1991.

Kikuchi, Shigeo. *Memoirs of a Buddhist Woman Missionary in Hawaii*. Honolulu: Buddhist Center Press, 1991.

Kim, Ai Ra. *Women Struggling for a New Life*. Albany: State University of New York Press, 1996.

Kim, Jung Ha. *Bridge-Makers and Cross-Bearers: Korean-American Women and the Church*. Atlanta: Scholars Press, 1997.

Kuramoto, Mary Ishii. *Dendo: One Hundred Years of Japanese Christians in Hawaii and the Nuuanu Congregational Church*. Honolulu: Nuuanu Congregational Church, 1986.

Kyung, Chung Hyun. *Struggle to Be the Sun Again: Introducing Asian Women's Theology*. Maryknoll, N.Y.: Orbis Books, 1990.

Lundell, In-Gyeong Kim. *Bridging the Gaps: Contextualization Among Korean Nazarene Churches in America*. New York: P. Lang, 1995.

McLellan, Janet. *Many Petals of the Lotus: Five Asian Buddhist Communities in Toronto*. Toronto: University of Toronto Press, 1999.

Mark, Diane Mei Lin. *Seasons of Light: The History of Chinese Christian Churches in Hawaii*. Honolulu: Chinese Christian Association of Hawai'i, 1989.

Matsuoka, Fumitaka. *Out of Silence: Emerging Themes in Asian American Churches*. Cleveland: United Church Press, 1995.

Minatoya, Lydia. *Talking to the High Monks in the Snow: An Asian American Odyssey*. New York: HarperCollins, 1992.

Nash, Jesse W. *Vietnamese Catholicism*. Harvey, Louisiana: Art Review Press, 1992.

Ng, David. *People on the Way: Asian North Americans Discovering Christ, Culture, and Community*. Valley Forge, Penn.: Judson Press, 1996.

Palinkas, L. A. *Rhetoric and Religious Experience: The Discourse of Immigrant Chinese Churches*. Fairfax, Va.: George Mason University Press, 1989.

Park, Andrew Sung. *Racial Conflict and Healing: An Asian-American Theological Perspective*. Maryknoll, N.Y.: Orbis Books, 1996.

Stokes, John F. G. *Heiau of the Island of Hawaii*. Honolulu: Bishop Museum Press, 1991.

Williams, Raymond Brady. *Religions of Immigrants from India and Pakistan: New Threads in the American Tapestry*. New York: Cambridge University Press, 1988.

———. *Christian Pluralism in the United States: The Indian Immigrant Experience.* New York: Cambridge University Press, 1996.

Yep, Jeannette, Peter Cha, Susan Cho Van Rieson, Greg Jao, and Paul Tokunaga. *Following Jesus Without Dishonoring Your Parents.* Downers Grow, Ill.: InterVarsity Press, 1998.

Yoo, David K., ed. *New Spiritual Homes: Religion and Asian Americans.* Honolulu: University of Hawai'i Press, 1999.

Sexuality and Gender

Eng, David L., and Alice Y. Hom, eds. *Q & A: Queer in Asian America.* Philadelphia: Temple University Press, 1998.

Espiritu, Yen Le. *Asian American Women and Men: Labor, Laws, and Love.* Thousand Oaks, Calif.: Sage, 1997.

Leong, Russell, ed. *Asian American Sexualities: Dimensions of the Gay and Lesbian Experience.* New York: Routledge, 1996.

Lim-Hing, Sharon, ed. *The Very Inside: An Anthology of Writing by Asian and Pacific Islander Lesbian and Bisexual Women.* Toronto,: Sister Vision Press, 1994.

Kudaka, Geraldine, ed. *On a Bed of Rice: An Asian American Erotic Feast.* New York: Doubleday, 1995.

Nakayama, Thomas K., ed. *Asian Pacific American Genders and Sexualities.* Tempe: Arizona State University Press, 1999.

Ratti, Rakesh, ed. *A Lotus of Another Color: An Unfolding of the South Asian Gay and Lesbian Experience.* Boston: Alyson Publications, 1993.

Robertson, Carol E. "The *Mahu* of Hawaii." *Feminist Studies* (1989): 313–26.

South Asians

Abraham, Margaret. *Speaking the Unspeakable: Marital Violence Among South Asian Immigrants in the United States.* New Brunswick, N.J.: Rutgers University Press, 2000.

Alexander, Meena. *Fault Lines: A Memoir.* New York: Feminist Press, 1993.

Bahri, Deepika, and Mary Vasudeva, eds. *Between the Lines: South Asians and Postcoloniality.* Philadelphia: Temple University Press, 1996.

Brown, Emily Clara. *Har Dayal: Hindu Revolutionary and Rationalist.* Tucson: University of Arizona Press, 1975.

Jain, Usha R. *The Gujaratis of San Francisco.* New York: AMS Press, 1989.

Josh, Sohan Singh. *My Meetings With Bhagat Singh and On Other Early Revolutionaries.* New Delhi: Communist Party of India, 1976.

———. *Hindustan Gadar Party: A Short History.* 2 vols. New Delhi: People's Publishing House, 1977–78.

Leonard, Karen Isaksen. *The South Asian Americans.* Westport, Conn.: Greenwood Press, 1997.

Leonard, Karen Isaksen. *Making Ethnic Choices: California's Punjabi Mexican Americans.* Philadelphia: Temple University Press, 1992.

Maira, Sunaina, and Rajini Srikanth, eds. *Contours of the Heart: South Asians Map North America.* New York: Asian American Writers' Workshop, 1996.

Mathur, L. P. *Indian Revolutionary Movement in the United States of America.* New Delhi: S. Chand, 1970. (History of the Ghadar party, its formation, organization, and activities in North America and Indian, and the U.S. government's attitude toward it.)

Prashad, Vijay. *The Karma of Brown Folk.* Minneapolis: University of Minnesota Press, 2000.

Puri, Harish K. *Ghadar Movement: Ideology, Organisation & Strategy.* Amritsar: Guru Nanak Dev University Press, 1983.

Shankar, Lavina Dhingra, and Rajini Srikanth, eds. *A Part, Yet Apart: South Asians in Asian America.* Philadelphia: Temple University Press, 1998.

Tatla, Darshan Singh. *The Sikh Diaspora: The Search for Statehood.* Seattle: University of Washington Press, 1999.

Transnationalism

Hu-DeHart, Evelyn, ed. *Across the Pacific: Asian Americans and Globalization.* New York: Asia Society, 1999.

Lal, Brij V., Doug Munro, and Edward D. Beechert, eds. *Plantation Workers: Resistance and Accommodation.* Honolulu: University of Hawaii Press, 1993.

Lim, Shirley Geok-lin, Larry E. Smith, and Wimal Dissanayake, eds. *Transnational Asia Pacific: Gender, Culture, and the Public Sphere.* Urbana: University of Illinois Press, 1999.

Muthanna, I. M. *People of India in North America: United States, Canada, W. Indies & Fiji: Immigration History of East-Indians Up to 1960.* Bangalore: Gangarams Book Distributors, 1982.

Wilson, Rob. *Reimagining the American Pacific: From South Pacific to Bamboo Ridge and Beyond.* Durham, N.C.: Duke University Press, 2000.

Wilson, Rob, and Arif Dirlik, eds. *Asia/Pacific as Space of Cultural Production.* Durham, N.C.: Duke University Press, 1995.

Vietnamese

Freeman, James M. *Hearts of Sorrow: Vietnamese-American Lives.* Stanford, Calif.: Stanford University Press, 1989.

——. *Changing Identities: Vietnamese Americans, 1975–1995.* Boston: Allyn and Bacon, 1995.

Huynh, Jade Ngoc Quang. *South Wind Changing.* St. Paul, Minn.: Greywolf Press, 1994. (A memoir.)

Kibria, Nazli. *Family Tightrope: The Changing Lives of Vietnamese Americans.* Princeton, N.J.: Princeton University Press, 1993.

Rutledge, Paul James. *The Role of Religion in Ethnic Self-Identity: A Vietnamese Community.* Lanham, Md.: University Press of America, 1985.

——. *The Vietnamese Experience in America.* Bloomington: Indiana University Press, 1992.

Tran, Barbara, et al., eds. *Watermark: Vietnamese American Poetry & Prose*. New York: Asian American Writers' Workshop, 1998.

Women

Asian Women. Berkeley: University of California, 1971.

Asian Women United of California, ed. *Making Waves: An Anthology of Writings By and About Asian American Women*. Boston: Beacon Press, 1989.

Chang, Grace. *Disposable Domestics: Immigrant Women Workers in the Global Economy*. Cambridge, Mass.: South End Press, 2000.

Cheung, King-Kok. *Articulate Silences: Hisaye Yamamoto, Maxine Hong Kingston, Joy Kogawa*. Ithaca, N.Y.: Cornell University Press, 1993.

Chin, Soo-Young. *Doing What Had to be Done: The Life Narrative of Rosa Yum Kim*. Philadelphia: Temple University Press, 1999.

Chow, Rey. *Women and Chinese Modernity: Reading Between West and East*. Minneapolis: University of Minnesota Press, 1991.

Chu, Patricia P. *Assimilating Asians: Gendered Strategies of Authorship in Asian America*. Durham, N.C.: Duke University Press, 2000.

Dasgupta, Shamita Das, ed. *A Patchwork Shawl: Chronicles of South Asian Women in America*. New Brunswick, N.J.: Rutgers University Press, 1998.

Editorial Committee, *Linking Our Lives: Chinese American Women of Los Angeles*. Los Angeles: Chinese Historical Society of Southern California, 1984.

Glenn, Evelyn Nakano. *Issei, Nisei, Warbride: Three Generations of Japanese American Women in Domestic Service*. Philadelphia: Temple University Press, 1986.

Ho, Wendy. *In Her Mother's House: The Politics of Asian American Mother-Daughter Writing*. Walnut Creek, Calif.: AltaMira, 1999.

Houston, Velina Hasu, ed. *The Politics of Life: Four Plays by Asian American Women*. Philadelphia: Temple University Press, 1993.

Hune, Shirley. *Teaching Asian American Women's History*. Washington, D.C.: American Historical Association, 1997.

John, Mary E. *Discrepant Dislocations: Feminism, Theory, and Postcolonial Histories*. Berkeley: University of California Press, 1996.

Kikumura, Akemi. *Through Harsh Winters: The Life of a Japanese Immigrant Woman*. Novato, Calif.: Chandler and Sharp, 1981.

Kim, Elaine H., et al, eds. *Making More Waves: New Writing by Asian American Women*. Boston: Beacon Press, 1997.

Kim, Elaine H., and Chungmoo Choi, eds. *Dangerous Women: Gender and Korean Nationalism*. New York: Routledge, 1998.

Kono, Juliet S., and Cathy Song, eds. *Sister Stew: Fiction and Poetry by Women*. Honolulu: Bamboo Ridge Press, 1991.

Lebra, Joyce Chapman. *Women's Voices in Hawaii*. Niwot: University Press of Colorado, 1991.

Lee, Mary Paik. *Quiet Odyssey: A Pioneer Korean Woman in America*. Edited by Sucheng Chan. Seattle: University of Washington Press, 1990.

Lim, Shirley Geok-lin, and Mayumi Tsutakawa, eds. *The Forbidden Stitch: An Asian American Women's Anthology*. Corvallis, Ore.: Calyx Books, 1989.

Ling, Amy. *Between Worlds: Women Writers of Chinese Ancestry*. New York: Pergamon Press, 1990.

Ling, Huping. *Surviving on the Gold Mountain: A History of Chinese American Women and Their Lives*. Albany: State University of New York Press, 1998.

Linnekin, Jocelyn. *Sacred Queens and Women of Consequence: Rank, Gender, and Colonialism in the Hawaiian Islands*. Ann Arbor: University of Michigan Press, 1990.

Mabanglo, Elynia S. *Invitation of the Imperialist/Anyaya ng Imperialista*. Quezon City: University of the Philippines Press, 1998.

Matsuda, Mari J., ed. *Called from Within: Early Women Lawyers of Hawai'i*. Honolulu: University of Hawaii Press, 1992.

Moraga, Cherríe and Gloria Anzaldúa, eds. *This Bridge Called My Back: Writings by Radical Women of Color*. New York: Kitchen Table Women of Color Press, 1983.

Nakano, Mei T. *Japanese American Women: Three Generations, 1890–1990*. Berkeley: Mina Press, 1990.

Ng, Franklin, ed. *Asian American Women and Gender*. New York: Garland, 1998.

Nieva, Pepi, ed. Filipina: *Hawaii's Filipino Women*. n.p.: Filipino Association of University Women, 1994.

Nunes, Shiho S., and Sara Nunes-Atabaki. *The Shishu Ladies of Hilo: Japanese Embroidery in Hawai'i*. Honolulu: University of Hawai'i Press, 1999.

Peffer, George Anthony. *If They Don't Bring Their Women Here: Chinese Female Immigration Before Exclusion*. Urbana: University of Illinois Press, 1999.

Sarasohn, Eileen Sunada. *Issei Women: Echoes from Another Frontier*. Palo Alto, Calif.: Pacific Books, 1998.

Shah, Nita. *The Ethnic Strife: A Study of Asian Indian Women in the United States*. New York: Pinkerton and Thomas, 1993.

Shah, Sonia, ed. *Dragon Ladies: Asian American Feminists Breathe Fire*. Boston: South End Press, 1997.

Tong, Benson. *Unsubmissive Women: Chinese Prostitutes in Nineteenth-Century San Francisco*. Norman: University of Oklahoma Press, 1994.

Tsuchida, John Nobuya. *Reflections: Memoirs of Japanese American Women in Minnesota*. Covina, Calif.: Pacific Asia Press, 1994.

Uno, Roberta, ed. *Unbroken Thread: An Anthology of Plays by Asian American Women*. Amherst: University of Massachusetts Press, 1993.

Women of South Asian Descent Collective, eds. *Our Feet Walk the Sky: Women of the South Asian Diaspora*. San Francisco: Aunt Lute Books, 1993.

Yamamoto, Traise. *Masking Selves, Making Subjects: Japanese American Women, Identity, and the Body*. Berkeley: University of California Press, 1999.

Yamazaki, Tomoko. *The Story of Yamada Waka: From Prostitute to Feminist Pioneer*. Translated by Wakako Hironaka and Ann Kostant. Tokyo: Kodansha International, 1985. (Biography of a leading Japanese feminist of the early twentieth century who was forced into prostitution in Seattle.)

Yung, Judy. *Chinese Women of America: A Pictorial History*. Seattle: University of

Washington Press, 1986. (The diversity of Chinese American women from 1834 to 1985 in photographs and texts, including census data.)

———. *Unbound Feet: A Social History of Chinese Women in San Francisco.* Berkeley: University of California Press, 1995.

———. *Unbound Voices: A Documentary History of Chinese Women in San Francisco.* Berkeley: University of California Press, 1999.

HAWAI'I, HAWAIIANS, AND PACIFIC ISLANDERS

Abbott, Isabella A. *Lā'au Hawai'i: Traditional Hawaiian Uses of Plants.* Honolulu: Bishop Museum Press, 1992.

Adler, Jacob. *Claus Spreckels: The Sugar King in Hawaii.* Honolulu: University Press of Hawaii, 1966.

Ahlberg, Dennis, and Michael J. Levin. *The North-east Passage: A Study of Pacific Islander Migration to American Samoa and the United States.* Canberra: National Centre for Development Studies, Australian National University, 1990.

Allen, Gwenfread. *Hawaii's War Years.* Honolulu: University of Hawaii Press, 1950.

Allen, Helena G. *The Betrayal of Liliuokalani: Last Queen of Hawaii, 1838–1917.* Glendale, Calif.: Arthur H. Clark, 1982.

———. *Sanford Ballard Dole: Hawaii's Only President, 1844–1926.* Glendale, Calif.: Arthur H. Clark, 1988.

Andrade, Ernest, Jr. *Unconquerable Rebel: Robert W. Wilcox and Hawaiian Politics, 1880–1903.* Niwot: University Press of Colorado, 1996.

Anthony, J. Garner. *Hawaii Under Army Rule.* Stanford, Calif.: Stanford University Press, 1955.

Bailey, Beth, and David Farber. *The First Strange Place: The Alchemy of Race and Sex in World War II Hawaii.* New York: Free Press, 1992.

Baker, Paul T., Joel M. Hanna, and Thelma S. Baker, eds. *The Changing Samoans: Behavior and Health in Transition.* New York: Oxford University Press, 1986.

Beaglehole, Ernest. *Some Modern Hawaiians.* Honolulu: Research Publications, 1937.

Beckwith, Martha. *Hawaiian Mythology.* Honolulu: University Press of Hawaii, 1970.

———, ed. *The Kumulipo: A Hawaiian Creation Chant.* Honolulu, University Press of Hawaii, 1972.

Beechert, Edward D. *Working in Hawaii: A Labor History.* Honolulu: University of Hawaii Press, 1985.

———. *Honolulu: Crossroads of the Pacific.* Columbia: University of South Carolina Press, 1991.

———. *Aupuni I Lā'au: A History of Hawai'i's Carpenters Union Local 745.* Honolulu: College of Continuing Education and Community Service, University of Hawai'i, 1993.

Bell, Roger. *Last Among Equals: Hawaiian Statehood and American Politics.* Honolulu: University of Hawaii Press, 1984.

Bingham, Hiram. *A Residence of Twenty-One Years in the Sandwich Islands.* New York: Praeger, 1969.

Boggs, Stephen T. *Speaking, Relating, and Learning: A Study of Hawaiian Children at Home and at School.* Norwood, N.J.: Ablex, 1985.

Burrows, Edwin Grant. *Hawaiian Americans: An Account of the Mingling of Japanese, Chinese, Polynesian, and American Cultures.* New Haven: Yale University Press, 1947.

Bushnell, O. A. *The Gifts of Civilization: Germs and Genocide in Hawai'i.* Honolulu: University of Hawaii Press, 1993.

Carr, Elizabeth Ball. *Da Kine Talk: From Pidgin to Standard English in Hawaii.* Honolulu: University Press of Hawaii, 1972.

Chinen, Jon J. *The Great Mahele: Hawaii's Land Division of 1848.* Honolulu: University Press of Hawaii, 1958.

Coffman, Tom. *Catch a Wave: A Case Study of Hawaii's New Politics.* Honolulu: University Press of Hawaii, 1973.

———. *Nation Within: The Story of America's Annexation of the Nation of Hawai'i.* Kāne'ohe, Hawai'i: Epicenter, 1998.

Cooper, George, and Gavan Daws. *Land and Power in Hawaii: The Democratic Years.* Honolulu: Benchmark Books, 1985.

Cox, J. Halley. *Hawaiian Sculpture.* Honolulu: University of Hawaii Press, 1988.

Creighton, Thomas. *The Lands of Hawaii: Their Use and Misuse.* Honolulu: University Press of Hawaii, 1978.

Daws, Gavan. *Shoal of Time: A History of the Hawaiian Islands.* Honolulu: University Press of Hawaii, 1968.

———. *Holy Man: Father Damien of Molokai.* Honolulu: University of Hawaii Press, 1984.

Dening, Greg. *The Death of William Gooch: A History's Anthropology.* Honolulu: University of Hawai'i Press, 1995.

Dole, Sanford B. *Memoirs of the Hawaiian Revolution.* Honolulu: Advertiser Publishing, 1936.

Dougherty, Michael. *To Steal a Kingdom: Probing Hawaiian History.* Waimanalo, Hawai'i: Island Style Press, 1992.

Dudley, Michael Kioni, and Keoni Kealoha Agard. *A Call for Hawaiian Sovereignty.* Honolulu: Nā Kāne O Ka Malo Press, 1990.

Ellis, William. *Journal of William Ellis.* Honolulu: Advertiser Publishing, 1963.

Farrell, Bryan H. *Hawaii, the Legend That Sells.* Honolulu: University Press of Hawaii, 1982.

Forbes, David W. *Encounters with Paradise: Views of Hawaii and Its People, 1778–1941.* Honolulu: Honolulu Academy of Arts, 1992.

Fuchs, Lawrence H. *Hawaii Pono: A Social History.* New York: Harcourt, Brace and World, 1961.

Gallimore, Ronald, Joan Whitehorn Boggs, and Cathie Jordan. *Culture, Behavior and Education: A Study of Hawaiian-Americans.* Beverly Hills, Calif.: Sage, 1974.

Gallimore, Ronald, and Alan Howard. *Studies in a Hawaiian Community: Na Makamaka o Nanakuli.* Honolulu: Department of Anthropology, Bernice Pauahi Bishop Museum, 1968.

Grimshaw, Patricia. *Paths of Duty: American Missionary Wives in Nineteenth-Century Hawaii.* Honolulu: University of Hawaii Press, 1989.

Hammatt, Charles H. *Ships, Furs, and Sandalwood: A Yankee Trader in Hawai'i, 1823–*

1825. Edited by Sandra Wagner-Wright. Honolulu: University of Hawai'i Press, 2000.

Handy, E. S. Craighill, and Elizabeth Green Handy. *Native Planters in Old Hawaii: Their Life, Lore, and Environment*. Honolulu: Bishop Museum Press, 1972.

Handy, E. S. Craighill, and Mary Kawena Pukui. *The Polynesian Family System in Ka-'U, Hawai'i*. Wellington, New Zealand: Polynesia Society, 1958.

He Alo Ā He Alo, Face To Face: Hawaiian Voices on Sovereignty. Honolulu: American Friends Service Committee, 1993.

Hitch, Thomas Kemper. *Islands in Transition: The Past, Present, and Future of Hawaii's Economy*. Honolulu: First Hawaiian Bank, 1992.

Holmes, T. Michael. *The Specter of Communism in Hawaii*. Honolulu: University of Hawaii Press, 1994.

Holt, John Dominis. *On Being Hawaiian*. Honolulu: Star-Bulletin, 1964.

Hooper, Paul F. *Elusive Destiny: The Internationalist Movement in Modern Hawaii*. Honolulu: University Press of Hawaii, 1980.

Howard, Alan. *Ain't No Big Thing: Coping Strategies in a Hawaiian American Community*. Honolulu: University Press of Hawaii, 1974.

Hughes, Judith Dean Gething. *Women and Children First: The Life and Times of Elsie Wilcox of Kaua'i*. Honolulu: University of Hawai'i Press, 1996.

Ii, John Papa. *Fragments of Hawaiian History*. Translated by Mary Kawena Pukui. Honolulu: Bishop Museum Press, 1959.

Janes, Craig Robert. *Migration, Social Change, and Health: A Samoan Community in Urban California*. Stanford, Calif.: Stanford University Press, 1990.

Joesting, Edward. *Hawaii: An Uncommon History*. New York: W. W. Norton, 1972.

Judd, Bernice. *Voyages to Hawaii Before 1860*. Honolulu: University Press of Hawaii, 1974.

Judd, Walter F. *Hawai'i Joins the World*. Honolulu: Mutual Publishing, 1998.

Kamakau, Samuel Manaiakalani. *Ka Po'e Kahiko: The People of Old*. Translated by Mary Kawena Pukui. Honolulu: Bishop Museum Press, 1964.

———. *The Works of the People of Old: Na Hana a ka Po'e Kahiko*. Translated by Mary Kawena Pukui. Honolulu: Bishop Museum Press, 1976.

Kanahele, George Hu'eu Sanford. *Ku Kanaka—Stand Tall: A Search for Hawaiian Values*. Honolulu: University of Hawaii Press, 1986.

Kent, Harold Winfield. *Dr. Hyde and Mr. Stevenson*. Tokyo: Charles E. Tuttle, 1973.

Kent, Noel J. *Hawaii: Islands Under the Influence*. New York: Monthly Review Press, 1983.

Kirch, Patrick V. *Feathered Gods and Fishhooks: An Introduction to Hawaiian Archaeology and Prehistory*. Honolulu: University of Hawai'i Press, 1997.

Kirch, Patrick V., and Marshall Sahlins. *Anahulu: The Anthropology of History in the Kingdom of Hawaii*. 2 vols. Chicago: University of Chicago Press, 1992.

Kodama-Nishimoto, Michi, Warren S. Nishimoto, and Cynthia A. Oshiro, eds. *Hanahana: An Oral History Anthology of Hawaii's Working People*. Honolulu: Ethnic Studies Oral History Project, University of Hawaii, 1984.

Koppel, Tom. *Kanaka: The Untold Story of Hawaiian Pioneers in British Columbia and the Pacific Northwest*. Vancouver: Whitecap Books, 1995.

Korn, Alfons L. *The Victorian Visitors*. Honolulu: University of Hawaii Press, 1958.

Krauss, Beatrice H. *Plants in Hawaiian Culture*. Honolulu: University of Hawaii Press, 1993.

Kuykendall, Ralph S. *The Hawaiian Kingdom*. Vol. 1, *Foundation and Transformation, 1778–1854*. Honolulu: University Press of Hawaii, 1938.

———. *The Hawaiian Kingdom*. Vol. 2, *Twenty Critical Years, 1854–1874*. Honolulu: University of Hawaii Press, 1953.

———. *The Hawaiian Kingdom*. Vol. 3, *The Kalakaua Dynasty, 1874–1893*. Honolulu: University of Hawaii Press, 1967.

Kuykendall, Ralph S., and A. Grove Day. *Hawaii: A History, from Polynesian Kingdom to American Statehood*. Englewood Cliffs, N.J.: Prentice-Hall, 1948.

Liliuokalani. *Hawaii's Story by Hawaii's Queen*. Rutland, Vermont: Charles E. Tuttle, 1964.

Lind, Andrew W. *Hawaii's People*. Honolulu: University Press of Hawaii, 1967.

———. *Hawaii: The Last of the Magic Isles*. London: Oxford University Press, 1969.

Linnekin, Jocelyn. *Children of the Land: Exchange and Status in a Hawaiian Community*. New Brunswick, N.J.: Rutgers University Press, 1985.

McDermott, John F., Jr., Wen-Shing Tseng, and Thomas W. Maretzki, eds. *People and Cultures of Hawaii: A Psychocultural Profile*. Honolulu: University Press of Hawaii 1974.

MacKenzie, Melody K. *Native Hawaiian Rights Handbook*. Honolulu: Office of Hawaiian Affairs, 1991.

Malo, David. *Hawaiian Antiquities*. Translated by Nathaniel B. Emerson. Honolulu: Bishop Museum Press, 1951.

Mast, Robert H., and Anne B. Mast. *Autobiography of Protest in Hawai'i*. Honolulu: University of Hawai'i Press, 1996.

Moriarty, Linda Paik. *Ni'ihau Shell Leis*. Honolulu: University of Hawaii Press, 1986.

Nordhoff, Charles. *Northern California, Oregon, and the Sandwich Islands*. Berkeley, Calif.: Ten Speed Press, 1974.

Nordyke, Eleanor C. *The Peopling of Hawaii*. Honolulu: East-West Center, 1977.

Obeyesekere, Gananath. *The Apotheosis of Captain Cook: European Mythmaking in the Pacific*. Princeton, N.J.: Princeton University Press, 1992.

Osborne, Thomas J. *"Empire Can Wait": American Opposition to Hawaiian Annexation, 1893–1898*. Kent, Ohio: Kent State University Press, 1981.

Parker, Linda S. *Native American Estate: The Struggle over Indian and Hawaiian Lands*. Honolulu: University of Hawaii Press, 1989.

Porteus, Elizabeth Dole. *Let's Go Exploring: The Life of Stanley D. Porteus, Hawaii's Pioneer Psychologist*. Honolulu: Ku Pa'a, 1991.

Porteus, Stanley D. *And Blow Not the Trumpet: A Prelude to Peril*. Palo Alto, Calif.: Pacific Books, 1947.

———. *A Century of Social Thinking in Hawaii*. Palo Alto, Calif.: Pacific Books, 1962.

Puette, William J. *The Hilo Massacre: Hawaii's Bloody Monday, August 1st, 1938*. Honolulu: College of Continuing Education and Community Service, University of Hawaii, 1988.

Pukui, Mary Kawena, ed. *'Ōlelo No'eau: Hawaiian Proverbs and Poetical Sayings.* Honolulu: Bishop Museum Press, 1983.

Pukui, Mary Kawena, Samuel H. Elbert, and Esther T. Mookini. *Place Names of Hawaii.* Honolulu: University of Hawaii Press, 1974.

Reinecke, John E. *Language and Dialect in Hawaii: A Sociolinguistic History to 1935.* Edited by Stanley M. Tsuzaki. Honolulu: University of Hawaii Press, 1969.

———. *A Man Must Stand Up: The Autobiography of a Gentle Activist.* Edited by Alice M. Beechert and Edward D. Beechert. Honolulu: Biographical Research Center, University of Hawaii, 1993.

———. *The Filipino Piecemeal Sugar Strike of 1924–1925.* Honolulu: Social Science Research Institute, University of Hawai'i, 1996.

Ritchie, Jane, and James Ritchie. *Growing Up in Polynesia.* Sydney, Australia: George Allen and Unwin, 1979.

Russ, William A., Jr. *The Hawaiian Revolution (1893–94).* Selinsgrove, Penn.: Susquehanna University Press, 1959.

———. *The Hawaiian Republic (1894–98).* Selinsgrove, Penn.: Susquehanna University Press, 1961.

Sahlins, Marshall. *Historical Metaphors and Mythical Realities: Structure in the Early History of the Sandwich Islands Kingdom.* Ann Arbor: University of Michigan Press, 1981.

———. *Islands of History.* Chicago: University of Chicago Press, 1985.

———. *How "Natives" Think: About Captain Cook, For Example.* Chicago: University of Chicago Press, 1995.

Schmitt, Robert C. *Demographic Statistics of Hawaii, 1778–1965.* Honolulu: University Press of Hawaii, 1968.

Shook, E. Victoria. *Ho'oponopono: Contemporary Uses of a Hawaiian Problem-Solving Process.* Honolulu: University of Hawaii Press, 1985.

Small, Cathy A. *Voyages: From Tongan Villages to American Suburbs.* Ithaca, N.Y.: Cornell University Press, 1997.

Stannard, David E. *Before the Horror: The Population of Hawai'i on the Eve of Western Contact.* Honolulu: Social Science Research Institute, University of Hawaii, 1989.

Stern, Bernard W. *Rutledge Unionism: Labor Relations in the Honolulu Transit Industry.* Honolulu: Center for Labor Education and Research, University of Hawaii, 1986.

Stevenson, Robert Louis. *Travels in Hawaii.* Edited by A. Grove Day. Honolulu: University of Hawaii Press, 1973.

Sutter, Frederic Koehler. *The Samoans: A Global Family.* Honolulu: University of Hawaii Press, 1989.

Takaki, Ronald. *Pau Hana: Plantation Life and Labor in Hawaii, 1835–1920.* Honolulu: University of Hawaii Press, 1983.

Tate, Merze. *The United States and the Hawaiian Kingdom: A Political History.* New Haven: Yale University Press, 1965.

———. *Hawaii: Reciprocity or Annexation.* East Lansing: Michigan State University Press, 1968.

Thurston, Lorrin A. *Memoirs of the Hawaiian Revolution*. Honolulu: Advertiser Publishing, 1936.

Trask, Haunani Kay. *From a Native Daughter: Colonialism and Sovereignty in Hawai'i*. Monroe, Maine: Common Courage Press, 1993.

Varigny, Charles De. *Fourteen Years in the Sandwich Islands, 1855–1868*. Translated by Alfons L. Korn. Honolulu: University Press of Hawaii, 1981.

Watts, Margit Misangyi. *High Tea at Halekulani: Feminist Theory and American Clubwomen*. Brooklyn, N.Y.: Carlson Publishing, 1993.

Whittaker, Elvi. *The Mainland Haole: The White Experience in Hawaii*. New York: Columbia University Press, 1986.

Zalburg, Sanford. *A Spark Is Struck! Jack Hall and the ILWU in Hawaii*. Honolulu: University Press of Hawaii, 1979.

2. VISUAL MATERIALS

ACKNOWLEDGMENT

I acknowledge the research assistance of Elda Tsou in compiling this section.

For a critical discussion of many of the movies cited under the categories of anti-Asianists and liberals, see Eugene Franklin Wong, *On Visual Media Racism: Asians in the American Motion Pictures* (New York: Arno Press, 1978), and Gina Marchetti, *Romance and the "Yellow Peril": Race, Sex, and Discursive Strategies in Hollywood Fiction* (Berkeley: University of California Press, 1993). See Jun Xing, *Asian America Through the Lens: History, Representations, and Identity* (Walnut Creek, California: AltaMira, 1998), for an analysis of many of the works by Asian Americanists and for a selected list of films and videos and their distributors. For television representations, see Darrell Y. Hamamoto, *Monitored Peril: Asian Americans and the Politics of TV Representation* (Minneapolis: University of Minnesota Press, 1994).

ANTI-ASIANISTS

The Cheat (1915)
Director: Cecil B. DeMille
Starring: Sessue Hayakawa
Sessue Hayakawa is Hishuru Tori, a wealthy art dealer who lends money to a Long Island socialite in exchange for sex. When she tries to call off the deal, he brands her with his curio iron and she shoots him. Her husband assumes the blame. At the trial, charges against the husband are dismissed, but the courtroom crowd nearly lynches Tori when her brand is revealed.

Madame Butterfly (1915)
Starring: Mary Pickford

Based on John Luther Long's novel rather than Puccini's opera, the film features Pickford as Cho Cho San, who falls in love with Pinkerton, an American Navy officer. The affair ends tragically when she commits suicide and gives up their child to be raised by Pinkerton's American wife.

The Sable Lorcha (1915)
Supervised by: D. W. Griffith

Based on the novel by Horace Hazeltine, the film features as its protagonist a retired businessman drugged and imprisoned by a Chinese castaway who has mistaken him for his evil twin brother. The evil twin made his money by smuggling illegal aliens on a Chinese junk (called a "sable lorcha"). Eventually, the twin brother is punished and the police rescue the businessman.

The War of the Tongs (1917)

Written by a Chinese writer and led by a cast of Imperial Chinese players, the film was lauded by the press for its accurate portrayal of the exotic world of the Chinese tong. Wong Wing loves Suey Lee, but her father's landlord, a tong leader, wants her for himself. When the tong leader's offer of marriage is refused, Wong Wing is given permission to wed Suey if he provides a $900 dowry. He tries to win the money at the tong lord's gambling house but is cheated of his life savings. His accusations of trickery precipitate a tong war in which he disposes of his rival and wins the hand of Suey.

Broken Blossoms (1919)
Director: D. W. Griffith

Set in London and based on the short story "The Chink and the Child" by Thomas Burke in his *Limehouse Nights* (1917), the film features Richard Barthelmess in the role of the protagonist, a young Chinese aristocrat whose tender love toward a young, abused white girl (Lillian Gish) causes him to sacrifice himself to protect her.

Li Ting Lang (1920)
Starring: Sessue Hayakawa

Li Ting Lang is a popular college student until he falls in love with a white socialite, Marion. After their engagement is announced, Marion is ostracized. Realizing this, Li breaks off their engagement. Soon after, he receives instructions to return to China, where he becomes a great military leader. Years later, while visiting the East on her honeymoon, Marion encounters Li again. He saves her life only to bid her goodbye.

Pagan Love (1920)
Director: Hugo Ballin
   A young Chinese exchange student falls in love with a blind Jewish-Irish girl who returns his affections. However, after she undergoes an operation to restore her sight, she flees from him in fear. He returns to China and commits suicide, and the girl marries the surgeon who had operated on her.

The Mysterious Dr. Fu Manchu (1929)
Starring: Warner Oland
   The first of a three-picture series from Paramount, the film recounts the events that caused a mandarin of scientific bent to go insane after a British officer named Petrie kills his family during the Boxer Rebellion. He plots revenge on the British colonists using "diabolical cunning" and "fiendish methods." The film is based on the book of this title by Sax Rohmer.

Shanghai Express (1932)
Starring: Marlene Dietrich, Anna May Wong, and Warner Oland
   Dietrich is Shanghai Lily, the "notorious white flower of China," who is reunited with an old flame on the Shanghai Express. When a Eurasian warlord ambushes the train, Lily offers herself to him to save her former lover.

The Bitter Tea of General Yen (1932)
Director: Frank Capra
   A romance between a Chinese warlord and an American missionary (played by Barbara Stanwyck) in Shanghai ends in tragedy when the general commits suicide.

Klondike Annie (1936)
Starring: Mae West
   In San Francisco's Chinatown of the 1890s, Mae West is the kept woman of a Chinese gambler. When he becomes jealous and threatens her, she is forced to kill him in self-defense. She leaves for Alaska's gold rush and escapes arrest by impersonating a nun. After a failed attempt on her life by the gambler's avengers, she decides to return to face charges.

Think Fast Mr. Moto (1937)
Starring: Peter Lorre and Lotus Long
   Based on the short story "That Girl and Mr. Moto" by John P. Marquand, this is the first episode of an eight-part series by Twentieth Century Fox. Mr. Moto, a mysterious adventurer, explorer, and soldier of fortune, solves the case involving an international ring of smugglers.

Dangerous to Know (1938)
Starring: Anna May Wong

Anna May Wong is Madame Lan Ying, the mistress of a notorious gangster. When he tries to blackmail a socialite into marrying him, Lan Ying warns him that proper society is out of his reach, and plays a record of "Thanks for the Memory" as a farewell. She commits suicide and he is arrested for her murder.

Lady of the Tropics (1939)
Starring: Hedy Lamarr

Hedy Lamarr plays a Eurasian seductress in Vietnam. She seduces the husband of an American couple and then commits suicide to expiate her sins.

Little Tokyo, U.S.A. (1942)

A prologue voice-over asserts that for more than a decade Japanese mass espionage had been carried out in a complacent America. In the movie, Japanese spies from the Black Dragon Society in Tokyo use a Japanese American business as a front for espionage. With the help of Maris, a radio commentator, a police detective exposes the spy ring, and the gang is rounded up. Soon after, the Japanese American internment leaves Little Tokyo a ghost town, and on her radio show Maris concludes that, in the interest of national security, the loyal Japanese Americans must suffer along with the disloyal.

The Lady from Shanghai (1948)
Director: Orson Welles

Based on the novel *If I Die Before I Wake* by Raymond Sherwood King, this movie features Rita Hayworth as Elsa Bannister, a femme fatale with a shady past in Shanghai. Orson Welles is an Irish merchant sailor who falls in love with her. After she arranges for him to be hired by her lawyer husband, he is drawn into an elaborate plot of deception and murder.

China Gate (1957)
Starring: Angie Dickinson

Angie Dickinson is Lia, a notorious femme fatale who is French-Chinese with connections to a Viet Minh commander. French legionnaires recruit her to bomb a Viet Minh munitions depot. She sacrifices herself in the final explosion.

The World of Suzie Wong (1960)
Starring: William Holden and Nancy Kwan

Based on the book of this title by Richard Mason, the movie features as its protagonist a young American artist in Hong Kong. He befriends a prostitute who becomes his muse. They become lovers but because she is a financial burden he cannot afford her. However, they are reconciled when he tries to rescue her baby from a flood.

Year of the Dragon (1985)
Starring: Mickey Rourke, John Lone, and Ariane
Mickey Rourke is an uncorrupted lawman assigned to clean up the vice in Chinatown. His adversary is a young gangster, played by John Lone, and he has an affair with a Chinese American TV news reporter.

Rising Sun (1993)
Starring: Sean Connery and Wesley Snipes
Based on the novel by Michael Crichton, the movie revolves around a Los Angeles detective and a retired Special Services officer. They uncover a Japanese plot to dominate the United States through politics and trade.

LIBERALS

The House Without a Key (1926)
Starring: George Kuwa
Charlie Chan first appeared on the screen in the Pathé serial, adapted from Earl Derr Biggers's novels. In this installment, *The House Without a Key*, based on Biggers's book of the same title, Chan, a Honolulu police detective, and his eldest son search for the murderer of a man from a respected Boston family.

Mr. Wong, Detective (1938)
Starring: Boris Karloff
Based on characters created by Hugh Wiley in the "James Lee Wong" short stories, this is the first of Monogram's six-part Mr. Wong series. Famous detective James Lee Wong (Karloff) solves a mystery involving a string of murders caused by a mysterious sphere containing poison gas.

Little Mister Jim (1947)
Based on the novel *Army Brat* by Tommy Wadelton, this movie features as its protagonist a Chinese house servant, Sui Jen, who must raise the young son of a recently widowed U.S. military captain. The bereaved father loses himself in drink until Sui Jen, by dressing the child in Chinese garb, shocks the father into realizing that he has neglected his son. Soon after, Sui Jen is revealed to be a famous Chinese general who has to return to China to fight the Japanese.

The Big Hangover (1950)
Starring: Elizabeth Taylor
 A young law student does the right thing when he helps to defend a Chinese couple unfairly evicted from their apartment.

Japanese War Bride (1952)
Starring: Shirley Yamaguchi and Don Taylor
 A young American lieutenant falls in love with a Japanese nurse during the Korean War. They marry and settle down in Salinas, California, but prejudice and vicious rumors make it difficult for the wife to find acceptance. Shiro Hasagawa and his family, second-generation Japanese Americans newly returned from the concentration camps, befriend her, but soon after the birth of her son she is once again confronted by malicious rumors. Devastated, she leaves town. Her husband pursues her after persuading Shiro that he genuinely loves her.

Love Is a Many-Splendored Thing (1955)
Starring: Jennifer Jones and William Holden
 Based on the novel of this title by Han Suyin, Jennifer Jones is a young Eurasian physician in Hong Kong who meets and falls in love with an American journalist played by William Holden. Their affair ruins her career; he dies on assignment in Korea.

Sayonara (1957)
Starring: Marlon Brando and Red Buttons
 Based on the novel by James A. Michener, this movie shows how a love affair between an American pilot and the star of a Japanese musical company during the Korean War transforms the pilot from a virulent bigot to a supporter of interracial romance. The object of his affection gives up her career for love.

Walk Like a Dragon (1960)
Starring: Jack Lord, Nobu McCarthy, and James Shigeta
 Set in the American West, *Walk Like a Dragon* features as its protagonist Kim, a Chinese girl sold into prostitution. She is saved by Linc Barlett (Jack Lord) and taken to the mining town of Jericho. Cheng (James Shigeta), a young Chinese man who speaks perfect English, accompanies them. Linc feels the Chinese are inferior and Cheng resents that his countrymen have to grovel before the whites. The antagonism between the two men grows when they discover that they both desire Kim. Once in Jericho, Linc intervenes when Cheng is framed for murder. When he is released, Cheng, determined to win Kim, challenges Linc to a gunfight. Kim steps between them and chooses Cheng, who orders her to cut off his queue.

Bridge to the Sun (1961)
Starring: Carroll Baker and James Shigeta
   A Japanese diplomat meets and marries a naïve Southern belle. They move to Japan during World War II, but after the birth of their child their marriage grows increasingly strained under the clash of cultures.

My Geisha (1962)
Starring: Shirley MacLaine
   MacLaine plays a popular Hollywood actress who tricks her husband, a director who is about to film Madame Butterfly, into thinking she is a geisha. She is so successful that her husband is attracted to her geisha alter ego.

ASIAN AMERICANISTS

General Works

Ancestors in the Americas: Coolies, Sailors, Settlers (2000)
Director/Producer: Loni Ding
   Sweeping history of Filipino, Chinese, and Asian Indian migrations to the Americas, and the effects that European imperialism in Asia had on those movements of peoples.
   64 minutes; documentary

Chinese

Carved In Silence (1988)
Director: Filicia Lowe
   Story of Angel Island in San Francisco Bay, where immigration officials held potential immigrants after the Chinese Exclusion Act of 1882 and after the San Francisco earthquake and fire of 1906. Features scenes recreated in the actual barracks and interviews with detainees.
   45 minutes; docudrama

Chan Is Missing (1981)
Director: Wayne Wang
   Wayne Wang's debut feature, a comedy in the guise of a detective story about a middle-aged Chinese American cabbie and his wisecracking young nephew's search for their elusive friend, Chan.
   1 hour, 20 minutes

Dim Sum: A Little Bit of Heart (1980)
Director: Wayne Wang
    A mother-daughter story, focusing on the generation gap between those two women (played by Kim Chew and Laureen Chew) and, from the daughter's perspective, the pull between taking care of her mother and having a life of her own.
    1 hour, 28 minutes

Fists of Fury (1971)
    In his first starring role, martial artist Bruce Lee vows never to fight again despite his abusive boss. But when company thugs kidnap his cousin, Lee fights to save her. A classic of the martial arts genre.
    Approximately 1 hour, 39 minutes

Han Chee (Sweet Potato) (1998)
Director: Jean Cheng
    A Taiwanese American's reflection on Taiwanese history and identity, and a meditation on colonialism, culture, memory, and nation.
    30 minutes; documentary

The Joy Luck Club (1993)
Director: Wayne Wang
    Film version of the novel by Amy Tan, interweaving the life histories of four seemingly ordinary mah-jongg club members and their daughters.
    2 hours, 19 minutes

Mississippi Triangle (1984)
Director: Christine Choy, Worth Long, and Allan Siegel
    An examination of Chinese Americans in the Mississippi delta, and the questions of race and community, are presented through the story of Arlee Hen, an elderly African Chinese woman.
    1 hour, 50 minutes; documentary

Who Killed Vincent Chin? (1987)
Producer/Director: Christine Choy and Renee Tajima
    Documentary of the 1982 killing of Vincent Chin, a young Chinese American, by two Detroit automobile workers. The film attempts to unravel the complex web of fact and emotion surrounding Chin's murder and the subsequent trial of his assailants.
    1 hour, 22 minutes; documentary

Cultural Studies and Cultural Criticism

The Bhangra Wrap (1994)
Director: Nandini Sikand
A documentary of South Asian youth culture, *The Bhangra Wrap* fuses hip-hop, rap, and Bhangra music. Based mainly in New York and Toronto, Bhangra House is propagated through alternative radio, party DJs, and hip-hop clubs where South Asian American youth have carved out their own sense of style, identity, and voice.
20 minutes; documentary

The Colour of Britain (1994)
Director: Pratibha Parmar
A look at the works of Asian artists at the forefront of redefining British culture. Interviews with sculptor Anish Kapoor, choreographer Shobana Jeyasingh, and theatre director Jatinder Verma.
58 minutes; documentary

Forbidden City, U.S.A. (1989)
Director: Arthur Dong
An account of the Chinese American nightclub Forbidden City and of the lives of men and women who defied stereotypes and familial opposition to sing and dance for mainly white audiences during the 1930s and 1940s.
56 minutes; documentary

Jazz Is My Native Language: A Portrait of Toshiko Akiyoshi (1983)
Director/Producer: Renee Cho
Story of Toshiko Akiyoshi—wife, mother, and artist—and her ascent in the American jazz world. Akiyoshi played with John Coltrane, Miles Davis, and Duke Ellington and later created the Akiyoshi/Tabackin Big Band.
58 minutes; documentary

Filipinos

A Dollar a Day, Ten Cents a Dance (1984)
Director: Geoffrey Dunn and Mark Schwartz
The life and labor of Filipino farm workers in California.
29 minutes; documentary

The Fall of the I-Hotel (1993, revised)
Director/Producer: Curtis Choy

The forcible eviction in 1977 of the International Hotel's tenants, mainly Filipino Americans, brought to a head a decade of battle for housing in San Francisco. Many of its elderly surviving residents still seek affordable housing after demolition of the I-Hotel, located in the heart of what was once a vibrant Manilatown.

58 minutes; documentary

The Great Pinoy Boxing Era (1994)
Director: Corky Pasquil and Agrafino Edralin

Filipino men came to the United States not only as farm laborers; some, during the 1920s and 1930s, were prize-winning boxers. This film reveals the contributions that Filipino American boxers made to the sport.

30 minutes; documentary

In No One's Shadow: Filipinos in America (1988)
Director: Naomi De Castro

A survey of Filipino American history from the first years of the twentieth century to the 1980s, focusing on the contributions of Filipinos in agriculture, the arts, and politics.

28 minutes; documentary

Japanese

Color of Honor: The Japanese American Soldier in World War II (1988)
Director/Producer: Loni Ding

Focuses on Japanese American soldiers of the Military Intelligence Service who served as translators and interrogators in the Pacific theater during World War II.

1 hour, 30 minutes; documentary

Days of Waiting (1988)
Director: Steven Okazaki

Story of a white American woman whose husband was a Japanese American internee during World War II. Oscar winner in 1991.

18 minutes; documentary

Nisei Soldier: Standard Bearer for an Exiled People (1984)
Director/Producer: Loni Ding

Documentary of Japanese American soldiers of the 442nd Regimental Combat Team during World War II.

29 minutes; documentary

Rabbit in the Moon (1999)
Producers: Emiko Omori and Chizuko Omori
    Documentary and memoir of the lingering effects of the World War II internment of Japanese Americans, and the story of two sisters and their search for the memory of their mother. Racism prompted dislocation and fractures within the Japanese American community, especially around the questions of the loyalty questionnaire and military draft.
    1 hour, 25 minutes; documentary

Unfinished Business: The Japanese American Internment Cases (1986)
Producer/Director: Steven Okazaki
    Story of three Japanese Americans, Fred Korematsu, Gordon Hirabayashi, and Minoru Yasui, who refused evacuation and internment during World War II. The film follows the efforts of those men and their attorneys to reopen their cases some forty years later in order to overturn their original convictions.
    58 minutes; documentary

Quiet Passages: The Japanese American War Bride Experience (1991)
Director: Tim DePaepe
    During the Occupation, thousands of Japanese women married American servicemen. The determination and perseverance of many of these couples during the early 1950s helped end the longstanding restrictions on Japanese immigration into the United States. Through interviews with their children and photos and footage, this film follows the journey of several Japanese American war brides to the Midwest.
    26 minutes; documentary

Koreans

Another America (1996)
Director/Producer: Michael Cho
    An exploration of Korean and African American conflict in the inner city as exemplified by the 1992 Los Angeles riots and Michael Cho's family history. In Los Angeles and Detroit, Cho's hometown, stories reveal that dreams have fallen short and racism and violence continue unchecked.
    56 minutes; documentary

First Person Plural (1999)
Director/Editor: Deann Borshay Liem

1966, at the age of nine, Deann Borshay came to the United States from Korea as one of thousands of children adopted by white Americans after the Korean War. In this personal documentary, Borshay Liem asks questions about how we define self, family, culture, and race, and stresses the importance of individual and collective histories.

56 minutes; documentary

Sa-I-Gu: From Korean Women's Perspectives (1993)
Director: Dai Sil Kim-Gibson and Christine Choy
"Sa-I-Gu," literally "April 29," documents the 1992 Los Angeles riots from the voices of Korean American women shopkeepers. Moreover, the film explores gender and race relations, and racism in the United States.

36 minutes; documentary

Searching for Go-Hyang (1998)
Director: Tammy Tolle
Korean adoptees, their lives in the United States, and their search for and reunion with their birth parents in Korea.

32 minutes; documentary

Silence Broken: Korean Comfort Women (1999)
Director/Producer: Dai Sil Kim-Gibson
A documentary of Korean women who were forced into sexual servitude by the Japanese Imperial Army during World War II. The film includes archival footage, dramatized images, and the testimony of former "comfort women" who demand justice for the "crimes against humanity" committed against them, and combines this with the contravening interviews of Japanese soldiers and contemporary scholars who deny the existence of "comfort women."

57 minutes; documentary

Multiracials

Afterbirth (1982)
Director/Producer: Jason Hwang
An examination of the unpredictable relationship between inner identity and external pressures to be "Asian" and/or "American." Including footage of an "African Chinese" and a "Caucasian Chinese," the film portrays cultural and national identity as non-absolute concepts and categories.

34 minutes; documentary

Banana Split (1990)

Director/Producer: Kip Fulbeck

A personal exploration of biracial (Chinese and white) identity, peer pressure, interethnic dating, and media stereotypes. Movie stills, family photos, and newspaper clippings add to the monologue in a diary format.

37 minutes; documentary

Mixed Feelings (1998)

Director/Producer: Mikko Jokela

Through interviews with five students and teachers at the University of California, Berkeley, this film examines the shifting identities of persons of mixed ethnicity as they recount personal anecdotes and humorous experiences. It tackles the difficult issue of racial reconciliation while celebrating difference and diversity.

45 minutes; documentary

None of the Above (1993)

Director: Erika Surat Andersen

Focuses on the lives of three multiracials, and the complexities of establishing race through the ambiguities of biracial and multiracial identities.

23 minutes; documentary

Sexuality and Gender

Chinese Characters (1986)

Director: Richard Fung

Through depictions of an eroticized Asian male image that is commonly absent in the mainstream discourse, this film critiques the racism of gay male pornography.

21 minutes; documentary

Fated to Be Queer (1992)

Director: Pablo Bautista

Focus on the lives of four Filipino American gay men in San Francisco.

25 minutes; documentary

Khush (1991)

Director: Pratibha Parmar

Explores a global queer identity through interviews with Asian lesbian, gay, and bisexual groups in Europe and North America, including Shakti of Britain, Trikon of the United States, and Khush of Canada.

24 minutes; documentary

The Love Thang Trilogy (1994)
Director: Mari Keiko Gonzales
  Three vignettes of different aspects of Asian and Pacific lesbian issues.
  12 minutes; documentary

Toc Storee (1992)
Director: Ming-Yuen S. Ma
  Asian gay sexuality, subjectivity, myth, language, and desire.
  22 minutes; documentary

South Asians

Bhaji on the Beach (1994)
Director: Gurinder Chadha
  A collection of stories about women who travel from their homes in London, England, to seek respite on a day trip to the resort town of Blackpool. Their lives reveal conflicts, contradictions, and choices made over behavior, love, sex, and family obligations.
  1 hour, 40 minutes

I'm British, But . . . (1990)
Director: Gurinder Chadha
  A celebration of British Bhangra and Bangla music reveals the complexities of a British identity through portraits of a Pakistani sheep farmer in Scotland, a Bangladeshi women in Belfast, and an Asian Indian girl in Glasgow.
  30 minutes; documentary

Mississippi Masala (1991)
Director: Mira Nair
  An Asian Indian and African American romance that opens with the eviction of South Asians from Uganda in 1972 and moves to Greenwood, Mississippi, where the main story unfolds. Mina (Sarita Choudhury) and Demetrius (Denzel Washington) fall in love, and their romance sets off a chain reaction of racial intolerance by both South Asians and African Americans.
  1 hour, 57 minutes

The New Puritans: The Sikhs of Yuba City (1985)
Directors/Producers: Ritu Sarin and Tenzing Sonam
  Forced from their farms in the Punjab, the first Sikh migrants came to Cali-

fornia in the early twentieth century. Here, they created a rural life that mirrored that of their native India, but also faced cultural and generational conflicts.

27 minutes; documentary

Roots in the Sand (1998)
Directors/Producers: Jayasri Majumdar Hart

Sikh, Moslem, and Hindu migrants settled in the American West. One of those pioneers, Purn Singh, arrived in Southern California from the Punjab during the early 1900s. In the Imperial Valley, he farmed amid racism, miscegenation laws, and mob violence. Based on archival materials and personal interviews, this film shows that survival required physical stamina and an indomitable spirit.

57 minutes; documentary

Sari Red (1988)
Director: Pratibha Parmar

An examination of racial violence in Britain, *Sari Red* was produced in memory of Kalbinder Kaur Hayre, a South Asian woman murdered by three white men in a racially motivated attack in 1985.

12 minutes; documentary

Vietnamese and Southeast Asians

a.k.a. Don Bonus (1995)
Directors/Producers: Sokly Ny and Spencer Nakasako

A self-portrait of a young Cambodian immigrant growing up in America. In 1979, Sokly Ny and his family escaped from the Khmer Rouge. They eventually reached San Francisco, where eighteen-year-old Sokly "Don Bonus" Ny struggles in school and with life in general.

55 minutes; documentary

Anatomy of a Springroll (1993)
Directors/Producers: Paul Kwan and Arnold Iger

The childhood memories Paul Kwan, a Vietnamese American, here revolve around cooking, eating, and sharing the celebrated spring roll. Food preparation is a family affair, and food connects individuals to culture and history.

56 minutes; documentary

Between Two Worlds: The Hmong Shaman in America (1985)
Producers: Taggart Siegel and Dwight Conquergood
   Story of the importance of folk religion for the Hmong in Chicago.
   30 minutes; documentary

Blue Collar and Buddha (1988)
Director: Taggart Siegel
   A Laotian community in Rockford, Illinois, survives terrorist bombings and
drive-by shootings of its Buddhist temple. This film shows Asian resistance to
anti-Asian violence, and provides insights into racial scapegoating during difficult economic times.
   57 minutes; documentary

Bui Doi: Life Like Dust (1994)
Producers: Ahrin Mishan and Nick Rothenberg
   For many young Vietnamese, living in the United States is "life like dust."
This film portrays life through the eyes of Ricky Phan, a former gang leader in
Southern California and a prison inmate serving an eleven-year sentence for
armed robbery. Violence involves both flight from a war-ravaged nation and
survival in an alien culture.
   28 minutes; documentary

From Hollywood to Vietnam (1993)
Director: Tiana (Thi Thanh Nga)
   A documentary of the filmmaker's journey from the United States to postwar Vietnam.
   1 hour, 16 minutes; documentary

Monterey's Boat People (1982)
Producers/Directors: Spencer Nakasako and Vincent DiGirolamo
   This film examines the tension between the established Italian and recently
arrived Vietnamese fishermen in California's Monterey Bay peninsula. It documents anti-Asian sentiment and the conflicts in an industry that is fighting for
survival.
   29 minutes; documentary

Women

Art to Art: Expressions of Asian American Women (1993)
Producer: Valerie Soe

Filmmakers, painters, and sculptors collaborate on a project devoted to identity and aesthetics. The artists featured are Pacita Abad, Hung Liu, Yong Soon Min, and Barbara Takanaga. The filmmakers are Christine Chang, Christine Choy, Karen Kavery, and Chuleenan Svetvilas.

30 minutes; documentary

Knowing Her Place (1990)
Director: Indu Krishnan

Follows the life of Vasundara Varadhan, an Asian Indian reared in the United States and sent to India at the age of sixteen to enter an arranged marriage. Varadhan returns to the United States as a wife and the mother of two sons.

40 minutes; documentary

Mitsuye and Nellie: Asian American Poets (1981)
Director: Allie Light

Film biography of Asian American women poets Mitsuye Yamada and Nellie Wong.

58 minutes; documentary

Picture Bride (1994)
Director: Kayo Hatta

The love story of Riyo (Youki Kudoh), a seventeen-year-old picture bride, and Matsuji (Akira Takayama), her sugar plantation worker husband, set in Hawai'i. Also, the film depicts the bonds among women, the search for family, and the desire to belong.

1 hour, 35 minutes

Picturing Oriental Girls: A (Re)Educational Videotape (1992)
Director: Valerie Soe

Clips from Hollywood films and television programs, and a voice-over critique of those media images of Asian women.

15 minutes; documentary

Sewing Woman (1982)
Producer/Director: Arthur Dong

The story of one woman's journey from an arranged marriage in China to life as a garment factory worker in the United States for more than thirty years. The filmmaker's mother, Zem Ping, narrates, and her reflections reveal the inner strength that helped her overcome restrictive U.S. immigration policies, family separation, and the hard life of a first-generation immigrant.

14 minutes; documentary

Slaying the Dragon (1988)
Producer/Director: Deborah Gee

Using clips from film classics and contemporary works, this video reveals the historical and political forces that influenced the depictions of Asians and, in particular, Asian women on the screen.

60 minutes; documentary

Voices of Challenge: Hmong Women in Transition (1996)
Director: Candace Lee Egan
Producer: Katsuyo Howard

In candid discussions, several women share their experiences and insights into the realities faced by Southeast Asian refugees and their children. The challenges these women face as they break from Hmong patriarchal family structure, enter U.S. schools, and find careers reveal the complexity of situations (and decisions) created by societal and personal expectations.

39 minutes; documentary

Yuri Kochiyama: Passion for Justice (1993)
Directors/Producers: Rea Tajiri and Pat Saunders

For more than forty years, political activist Yuri Kochiyama has worked for nuclear disarmament, Japanese American redress and reparations, and the political-prisoners' rights movement. A supporter of black liberation and a follower and friend of Malcolm X, Kochiyama was at his side when he was assassinated.

57 minutes; documentary

HAWAI'I, HAWAIIANS, AND PACIFIC ISLANDERS

Act of War: The Overthrow of the Hawaiian Nation (1993)
Directors/Producers: Puhipau and Joan Lander

Focuses on the events surrounding the overthrow of the Hawaiian monarchy in 1893, from the point of view of native Hawaiians. Through archival photos, government documents and films, political cartoons, and dramatic reenactments, this film explores colonialism and conquest as perpetrated by white missionaries and capitalists.

60 minutes; documentary

Hawaii's Last Queen (1997)
Producer: Vivian Ducat

Story of Lili'uokalani and the takeover of Hawai'i's government by white residents with complicity from the American minister to the kingdom and, later, from the U.S. Congress and president.

60 minutes; documentary

Nation Within (1998)
Producer: Tom Coffman
 Focuses on the period between the overthrow of the Hawaiian monarchy and U.S. annexation, especially on native Hawaiians and Theodore Roosevelt's interest in Hawai'i.
 1 hour, 26 minutes; documentary

Omai Fa'atasi: Samoa Mo Samoa (1974)
Director: Takashi Fujii
 The dilemmas and challenges faced by Samoan Americans as exemplified in Omai Fa'atasi, a Southern California community organization.
 30 minutes; documentary

Then There Were None (1996)
Director/Producer: Elizabeth Kapu'uwailani Lindsey
 Focuses on the destruction and demise of indigenous Hawaiians, especially in terms of population.
 26 minutes; documentary

Troubled Paradise (1991)
Director/Producer: Steven Okazaki
 Features four stories of native Hawaiians, and celebrates the richness of Hawaiian culture and the social and political problems facing Hawaiians.
 58 minutes; documentary

3. ELECTRONIC RESOURCES

I would like to thank Kevin Kawamoto for suggesting most of the sites on this list, and Franklin Odo for his kind help.

There are hundreds of thousands of Asian American sites on the Internet. Those selected for this list offer a mere sampling of Web resources pertinent to Asian American studies.

GENERAL

http:/libraries.mit.edu/humanities/ethnicstudies/asamsites.html
 Asian American sites from the MIT libraries, including links to MIT's Asian American Resources, Asian American theater review, New York's Asian American Writers' Workshop, National Association of Asian American Professionals,

queer Asian Pacific American resources, and Sawnet (South Asian Women's Net).

www.ai.mit.edu/people/irie/aar/
Asian American Resources created by Robert Irie at MIT, including information on Asian American student organizations in universities and colleges, Asian American community organizations, and media connections (including art, theater, bands and music, film, and magazines).

www.public.iastate.edu/svega/asian_am.htm
Resources assembled by Susan A. Vega García "for academic research and information purposes." Of special interest are Asian American Cybernauts (begun in 1995, one of the first collections of Asian American internet resources on community and culture by Wataru Ebihara), Asian American Resources (an extensive collection of Asian American Web resources developed by Robert Irie at MIT), Asian American Studies Resources (a list of Asian American studies programs, libraries, periodicals, and queer resources), Hmong Net (a collection of information on the Hmong), Little Saigon Net (Vietnamese community and media), and Asian American journals and magazines (including A. *Magazine*, *Asian American Policy Review*, *AsianWeek*, *Filipinas Magazine*, *Journal of Asian American Studies*, *Little India*, *Yisei Magazine*, and *Yolk*).

ACADEMIC INSTITUTIONS

http://www.aasp.cornell.edu/
Cornell University's Asian American Studies Program, its courses and resources, and also the Web site of the Association for Asian American Studies, the national professional organization in the field. The Association sponsors an annual conference and publishes a quarterly newsletter and, with Johns Hopkins University Press, the *Journal of Asian American Studies*.

http://www.uidaho.edu/ls/aacc/
The site of the Asian American Comparative Collection at the University of Idaho maintained by Priscilla Wegars. The Collection holds the most complete record of Asian American archaeological excavations in the western United States, artifacts, and bibliographical materials.

http://www.sscnet.ucla.edu/aasc.html
UCLA's Asian American Studies Center, its courses, publications, opportunities and activities, library, and bibliographies and resources.

http://www.library.ucsb.edu/subj/asian-am.html

Asian American studies InfoSurf from the University of California, Santa Barbara, containing: the California Ethnic Multicultural Archives; archival collections and museums (Chinese American Museum of Los Angeles; Chinese Historical Society of American, Filipino American National Museum; Korean American Historical Society; Southeast Asian Archive at University of California, Irvine; and the Wing Luke Museum of Seattle); Asian American studies centers and programs; Asian American professional organizations; and bibliographies and library resources.

COMMUNITY ORGANIZATIONS

http://vconline.org.htm

Visual Communications in Los Angeles and its production facilities, photographic and film archive, and sales.

http://www.aarising.com/aalink/

An Asian Pacific American entertainment guide in music, theater, art, fashion, and food.

http://www.aaww.org/

Asian American Writers' Workshop in New York City, a resource for writers, readers, and publishers. The Workshop acts as a clearinghouse for events, publishes books and a journal and literary magazine, sells books, and offers fellowships to authors.

http://www.asianamericanbooks.com/

Asian American Curriculum Project in California and its list of books and educational materials, including K-12 and college and university texts.

http://www.cetel.org/about.html

The Center for Educational Telecommunications, devoted to educational television and multimedia programs, was founded by Loni Ding in 1983. Its site includes links to Asian American history Web sites, K-12 curricular resources, media organizations, Asian American studies programs and museums, journals and magazines, and sites relevant to Asian Indians, Chinese, Japanese, Filipinos, Koreans, Pacific Islanders, and Southeast Asians.

http://www.janm.org/main.htm

Site of the Japanese American National Museum in Los Angeles, including its Hirasaki National Resource Center and its archives, projects, and books.

http://www.naatanet.org.html

National Asian American Telecommunications Association site, including its rental and sales list of videos and films, calendar and forums, and opportunities at NAATA.

http://www.si.edu/resource/faq/nmah/asianam.htm

Smithsonian Institution's site for Asian Pacific American history and culture with links to the Institution's Asian Pacific American Studies Program, and Smithsonian exhibits and resources.

http://www.wingluke.org

Site of the Wing Luke Asian Museum in Seattle, including its calendar, exhibitions, and collections.

www.moca-nyc.org./information_about_moca.html

Site for the Museum of Chinese in the Americas in New York City, its research library and archive and its educational programs.

INDEX

Cornell University, xv
Cornwallis, Lord, 16
Costello, John, 107
Counterpoint: Perspectives on Asian America, xv
courts. *See* legal system
credit-ticket system, 69–70
Cressey, Paul G., 211–212
Crichton, Michael, 201, 225
Cuba, 18
curfews, 23, 158

da Gama, Vasco, 6
Daily Alta California (newspaper), 81
Daniels, Roger, 103, 118, 165, 169–170, 218
Danish, 64
d'Aquino, Iva Toguri (Tokyo Rose), 25, 30, 189
Das, Rajani Kanta, 209–210
death lists, 168
de Balboa, Vasco, 6
deductive history, 195
de Gama, Vasco, 36–37
Delano grape strike, 28
Democrats. *See* politics
detention, 25–26. *See also* concentration camps
De Witt, John, 102–103, 108, 125; Executive Order 9066 and, 114–115; exoneration of, 115–118; final recommendation of, 113; martial law and, 123–124; Roosevelt and, 118–120
Diaz-Veizades, Jeannette, 137
Diem, Ngo Dinh, 26
Different Mirror: A History of Multicultural America, A (Takaki), 223–224
disease, 12; Chinese and, 85, 92; population and, 47, 53–54
Disoriented: Asian Americans, Law, and the Nation-State (Chang), 161–162
Dixon, George, 45, 48–49
Documental History of Law Cases Affecting Japanese in the United States, 1916–1924, 157
Doing Fieldwork (Wax), 216

Dooner, Pierton W., 195–196, 225
Dunn, James, 8
Dutch East India Company, 6, 178

East Goes West: The Making of an Oriental Yankee (Kang), 211
economics: Chinese and, 88–90, 202; concentration camps and, 167; Japan and, 201–202; liberals and, 216–217; Pacific Rim, 133–134. *See also* labor; trade
education, 13, 35, 87; Chinese Educational Mission, 205; Japanese schoolteachers, 113, 122–123; Koreans and, 38; legal system and, 157; segregation and, 104
effeminism, 4
Emerson, Ralph Waldo, 96
Emory, Kenneth P., 54
Empress of China (ship), 7–8, 17, 178
Endeavour (ship), 59–60
Engelman, Rose C., 102, 115
English East India Company, 37
Enlightenment, 57, 63
Espiritu, Yen Le, 145
Ethnic Peace in the American City: Building Community in Los Angeles and Beyond (Chang and Diaz-Veizades), 137
eugenics, 196–197
Europeans: bonded labor and, 36; colonialism of, 36–37; Cook and, 59–63; disease and, 56; Hawaiians and, 56–66; immigration and, 160; imperialism and, 72–74; Khan and, 5; orientalism and, xiv; Pearson on, 195; Speer on, 204; trade and, 6–7; warfare and, 8–9
Exclusion Act, 20, 37–38, 180; concentration camps and, 104–105, 110; Coolidge on, 205–206; gender and, 141, 152; Gyory on, 95–98; legal system and, 157; migration policy and, 70, 75–76, 78, 82–83, 86–87; renewal of, 182; repeal of, 186
Executive Order 13125, 190